OPPORTUNITIES FOR STUDENT WRITING IN THIS BOOK

RESPONDING TO WRITING

Working collaboratively or on their own, students reflect on writing models, including their own, to see how this writing exemplifies the concepts and strategies introduced in the chapter.

JOURNAL WRITING

Opportunities for writers to reflect on their reading, writing, and the information presented within a chapter.

CRITICAL THINKING IN CONNECTING TEXTS

This collaborative brainstorming activity challenges students to synthesize information, making connections and drawing parallels from a chapter's student and professional writings. See pp. 32, 58, 79, 110, 139, 169, 203, 234, 270, 309, 346, 376.

OPTIONS FOR WRITING

Writing prompts offer numerous thoughtfully designed, relevant, and exciting assignments. See pp. 22, 51, 73, 104, 131, 157, 192, 221, 245, 256, 284, 285, 296, 321, 322, 332, 333, 368.

For more writing resources, be sure to see the Longman English Pages Website at http://longman.awl.com/englishpages

Keys to Successful Writing

....

Keys to Successful Writing

Unlocking the Writer Within

MARILYN ANDERSON

El Camino College

 LONGMAN

An imprint of Addison Wesley Longman, Inc.

New York • Reading, Massachusetts • Menlo Park, California • Harlow, England
Don Mills, Ontario • Sydney • Mexico City • Madrid • Amsterdam

Acquisitions Editor: Steven Rigolosi
Development Editors: Sharon Balbos and Meg Botteon
Marketing Manager: Ann Stypuloski
Supplements Editor: Donna Campion
Project Coordination and Text Design: York Production Services
Cover Design Manager: Nancy Danahy
Cover Designer: Kay Petronio
Full Service Production Manager: Richard Ausburn
Senior Print Buyer: Hugh Crawford
Electronic Page Makeup: York Production Services
Printer and Binder: R.R. Donnelley and Sons Company
Cover Printer: The Lehigh Press, Inc.

For permission to use copyrighted material, grateful acknowledgment is made to the copyright holders on pp. 478–479, which are hereby made part of this copyright page. The photograph on page 1 © Jean-Claude LeJeune/Stock Boston. Those on pages 205 and 377 © Hugh Rogers/Monkmeyer. The photograph on page 413 © 1997 Ilene Perlman/Stock Boston.

Library of Congress Cataloging-in-Publication Data

Anderson, Marilyn, 1946-
    Keys to successful writing: unlocking the writing within/Marilyn Anderson.
        p.   cm.
    Includes index.
    ISBN 0-321-01576-2
    1. English language—Rhetoric.   2. Report writing.   I. Title.
PE1408.A586   1998
808′.042—dc21   98–30750
                                                                                    CIP

Please visit our website at *http://longman.awl.com/englishpages*

ISBN 0-321-01576-2

2345678910—DOC—0100999

True ease in writing comes from art, not chance,
As those move easiest who have learned to dance.

—ALEXANDER POPE,
from *An Essay on Criticism*

This book is dedicated with my gratitude and love to those who have taught me to dance: El Camino College students, colleagues, and dean; editors at Longman; dear friends; and family—Guy, Alisa, Michael, Emily, and Austin, the dancing partner who continues to sweep me off my feet.

Brief Contents

Adapted from *Process and Practice: A Guide for Developing Writers,* Fourth Edition, by Philip Eggers.

Contents

(Note: For a full list of reading selections included, by subject, see Thematic Contents, page xxvii.)

PART ONE
Exploring the Realm of College Reading and Writing   1

CHAPTER 1   Reading, Thinking, and Writing for College   3

(Note: Photographs of student authors accompany the titles of their essays.)

Student
Essay
(Photo Not
Available)

PART TWO
Exploring Development Options:
Choosing Patterns to Fit Purpose   205

CHAPTER 8   Writing About Events: Narration   207

CHAPTER 9   Observing the World: Description and Definition   235

CHAPTER 11   Showing Relationships: Comparison/Contrast and Division/Classification   310

CHAPTER 12 Taking a Stand: Argument 348

PART THREE
Exploring Other Options:
A Writer's Toolkit   377

UNIT 4 Application Letters 401

UNIT 5 Résumés 406

PART FOUR
Editing Essays: A Concise Handbook 413

Adapted from *Process and Practice: A Guide for Developing Writers,*
Fourth Edition, by Philip Eggers.

Thematic Contents

(Note: Some selections appear under more than one heading.)

College Community

Work Community

Civic Community

Sports/Entertainment/Leisure Community

Writer's Community

Family Community

Global Community

Media Community

Preface for Instructors

After observing the students who entered my classroom, after experiencing frustration with texts that fail to address adequately these students' needs, and after discovering that many of my colleagues face similar challenges, I decided to write a text that would meet these complex needs. This new textbook, I decided, would:

- entice students to participate in the community of college readers and writers;

- familiarize students with the writing process, offering them plenty of practice in the skills and strategies necessary to build competency and confidence;

- empower students to communicate clearly in written and electronic modes, both on the job and in their civic and personal lives.

Keys to Successful Writing, I believe, will help meet all these diverse needs while using a friendly and assuring tone. In *Keys,* I address students not as individuals lacking in certain skills but as writers about to embark on an odyssey of self-discovery. *Keys* also provides flexibility and support to the instructor: lots of good student models and professional readings on a variety of thought-provoking topics, computer activities adaptable to the ever-changing technology on campus, and a rubric—the five *Keys*—allowing relevant and clear evaluation of student writings.

For the past several years, I have worked with many talented students, editors, colleagues, and reviewers in the creation of *Keys to Successful Writing: Unlocking the Writer Within.* Together, we have created a fresh new approach for developmental writers in the paragraph-to-essay level course, an approach that considers students' needs as well as the strengths. *Keys* unlocks the composing process for developmental students by offering practical, class-tested solutions to their problems. It also makes clear the connection between classroom assignments and workplace writing.

FEATURES

I wanted to write a text that was practical and pedagogically sound, yet innovative. I hope that instructors and students will appreciate the traditional organization of *Keys* and the support it lends to the following dynamic features:

A strong process-plus-skills orientation, in a 3-in-1 format

Keys describes the recursive process of essay writing, offering a smoothly integrated series of fill-in exercises that reinforce skills and encourage students to practice new skills and strategies as well as to reflect upon what they are reading. The 3-in-1 format offers writing instruction, a wide range of readings, and a concise handbook, all in one package.

An appreciation of the real-world goals of student writers

Today's students face many challenges and opportunities in their course work, their career planning, and their personal lives. *Keys* is deeply concerned with making the work of the writing classroom relevant to all that today's students do. Each chapter includes photographs and profiles of students who share their essays, journals, and goals to help make the link.

Toolkit of practical applications

Part Three of the text offers specific strategies for special writing situations, from timed classroom writing to resumes. The toolkit furthers this emphasis by giving students confidence in timed writing situations that they will encounter both in college and in their careers, and it also allows students to grasp the importance of on-the-spot writing skills in the real-world situations that they will continue to encounter. Because increasing numbers of college students work for at least a portion of their college careers, this toolkit includes strategies and guidelines for writing employment letters and resumes.

A distinctive "5 Keys" heuristic to ease learning and retention

The text offers a system for teaching writing (and becoming a writer) that is easily grasped through repetition and reinforcement. The following five KEYS are defined and consistently applied to the formal elements of the writing process:

PURPOSE: The writer's primary goal in writing.

FOCUS: The writer's choice of subject and the main point the writer makes about the subject.

MATERIAL: The writer's content, including details, facts, and supporting evidence.

STRUCTURE: The writer's organization or arrangement of material to support the main point clearly and completely.

STYLE: The writer's sentence structure, sentence variety, word choice, and placement of words within sentences to present a unique piece of writing.

This class-tested set of principles helps students become better readers as well as develop their writing skills. Reviewers and instructors who have class-tested the text have responded enthusiastically to the structure and consistent application of the KEYS throughout the text, noting that the five KEYS lead to greater student writing success and ease in essay evaluation. Students affirm that the KEYS are easy to grasp and applicable to a variety of college and real-world writing situations. Whenever the five KEYS are listed in the text, they appear in all capital letters, again to ease learning through repetition and reinforcement.

A unique emphasis on using computers

"Using the Computer" activities in each chapter show students how the computer can enhance their writing process, help them do research, and find a job. These activities are specially screened, boxed features highlighted with a special icon. *Keys* offers computer activities that go beyond enhanced typing—I encourage students to join online communities, to research areas of personal and professional interest, to report back to the class on their findings, and ultimately to use the vast resources of the Web to achieve their goals. All activities use straightforward, nontechnical language, and many are designed to be fun as well as practical. In addition, the same invitation to visit the Longman English Pages Web site appears at the end of each chapter, highlighting Longman's commitment to providing opportunities for *all* students to work online.

A wide variety of engaging writing assignments

The writing opportunities in *Keys* are geared to student sensibilities, using interesting contemporary content as the prompting for journal writing, collaboration, critical reading, and analysis. Within each chapter, numerous and varied assignments can be used to complete in-class writing and more complex or reflective prompts that could lead to longer essays. There are three kinds of assignments within each chapter, highlighted with a special "pen" icon for easy reference:

Options for Writing: Innovative, thoughtful, and absorbing prompts for writing compositions. These paragraph and multi-paragraph essay choices build on the chapter's discussion of an aspect of the writing process or a specific pattern of development. Choices that are especially appropriate for paragraph-length responses are marked with a "¶" symbol.

Some writing options for each chapter ask students to respond to one of the student models or professional readings as a point of reference, some challenge students to consult an outside source or conduct an interview, and others suggest personal experience and/or the experiences of others in the class as material. All prompts have been classroom-tested. Many are collaborative.

Journal Writing: These prompts include advice on working with a journal as well as exercises for journal writing. Reflective and suggestive, these prompts are casual enough to allow for a wide range of student response, yet close enough to chapter content to be useful as the starting point for essay drafts.

Responding to Writing: Students learn to become critical readers as they reflect upon and write in response to a wide range of texts, from the work of other students to the essays of professional writers. Many prompts can be used for either individual or collaborative work. In the "Responding" section of each chapter, students see the KEYS at work in the writings of others, and then they are asked to apply the strategies and principles in these models to their own drafts in progress or to the drafts of their peers.

Solid, provocative, and varied readings

Keys features student and professional models of writing on issues both contemporary and of enduring interest, ranging from pets, roommates, and car repair to career planning, AIDS awareness, and social justice. The wide range of selections includes full-length pieces and excerpts, from a variety of genres that includes essays, interviews, journalism, even poetry. Classic writers as well as new voices are represented, as well as a rich diversity of perspectives and experiences. A thematic table of contents (see pp. xxv–xxvii) allows students and instructors to find readings that explore similar themes.

Opportunities for critical thinking and collaboration

Critical thinking and reading are given extensive attention throughout *Keys.* Chapter 1, "Reading, Thinking, and Writing for College," affirms the reading/writing connection that continues to be emphasized throughout the text. Students are introduced to six strategies for active reading—strategies such as previewing and annotating texts, for example, that will be stressed consistently throughout the text in examining readings, student models, or peer drafts.

Critical Thinking in Connecting Texts activities at the end of each chapter challenge students to synthesize reading from student and professional models. In this collaborative brainstorming activity, students are asked to make connections in themes, points of view, and subjects presented within each chapter and occasionally between different chapters. Critical thinking and collaborative activities are the goals here.

Collaborative work and peer editing also appear frequently in the writing options section as well as in several "Responding to Writing" sections with the inclusion of peer editing strategies and helpful peer editing worksheets.

ORGANIZATION

Recognizing the diversity of departmental and individual approaches to developmental writing, the structure of *Keys* allows for a variety of classroom, lab, and writing conference uses. Instructors can easily adapt chapters and chapter sections to course schedules, instructional emphases, and programs that vary from ten to eighteen weeks in length. In addition, instructors will appreciate the quick assessment of student in-text response and general comprehension the book offers.

- Part One focuses on the reading-writing connection, the parts of the essay, and the stages of the composing process.

- Part Two builds on this knowledge by introducing specific patterns of essay development and encouraging writers to explore these patterns in their reading and writing.

- Part Three is a toolkit of models and strategies for future academic and professional writing: portfolio preparation, timed in-class writing, introductory research, and resumes and cover letters.

- Part Four, the handbook, begins with an overview of basic grammar and usage and then focuses on helping students to pinpoint and solve habitual errors in grammar, usage, sentence boundaries, punctuation, mechanics, and format. Practice items throughout help students reinforce their skills.

Keys is easy to use and teach from. A **predictable organizational structure** increases familiarity from chapter to chapter. Each chapter's opening "Preview" concisely presents the strategies and content to be covered in the chapter. Following the "Characteristics" and "Guidelines" sections, each chapter's "Strategies" section applies the five KEYS to the particular structure or process under discussion. Chapters are activity-driven, making the book easy to use in the classroom, lab, or writing center. The student models early in each chapter provide a starting-off point to teach the writing process and build toward the writing assignments. A format that allows each chapter and section to stand alone enhances flexibility, and the great variety of reading and exercise options in each chapter provide instructors with multiple choices about how to adapt the text to their particular classroom needs. A glossary (pp. 469–477) further assists students and instructors in locating specific content and concepts for classroom discussion and individual study. Most important, this is a text that has been written *for* the student, in language that is refreshingly accessible, honest, engaging, and clear. *Keys* takes a friendly approach toward writing and academic work, emphasizing explanation and reassurance over prescriptive formulas.

DESIGN

A friendly, clear design establishes consistency within and among chapters of *Keys*, helping students and teachers locate specific content from chapter to chapter and reinforcing through visual cues important new concepts and skills.

Features and exercises that appear in each chapter are highlighted with special icons for easy reference:

Indicates writing opportunities within each chapter, including "Journal Writing," "Options for Writing," and "Responding to Writing" assignments.

"Key Questions" follow all student models, helping students read critically and recognize writing strategies. The icon also denotes the "Strategies for Writers" boxes, which remind students of how to put the KEYS to use in their own writing.

Helps you and your students locate "Using the Computer" activities and additional writing resources on our Website.

Shows you where to find "Reading and Additional Activities," which provide still more opportunities for your students to practice their reading skills and discover ways in which writers put the KEYS to use.

SUPPLEMENTS

Many high-quality supplements are available to students and instructors using *Keys* in the classroom.

The Longman Teaching and Learning Package

Instructor's Manual. The Instructor's Manual provides numerous suggestions for using *Keys*, including how to structure and organize the course and how to approach each section of the text. To order the Instructor's Manual, use ISBN 0-321-04755-9.

A series of other skills-based supplements are available for both instructors and students. All these supplements are either free or available at greatly reduced prices.

For Additional Reading and Reference

The Dictionary Deal. Two dictionaries can be shrinkwrapped with any Longman Basic Skills title at a nominal fee. *The New American Webster Handy College Dictionary* (0-451-18166-2) is a paperback reference text with more than 100,000 entries. *Merriam Webster's Collegiate Dictionary,* tenth edition (0-87779-709-9), is a hardback reference with a citation file of more than 14.5 million examples of English words drawn from actual use.

Penguin Quality Paperback Titles. A series of Penguin paperbacks is available at a significant discount when shrinkwrapped with any Longman Basic Skills title. Some available titles are Toni Morrison's *Beloved* (0-452-26446-4), Julia Alvarez's *How the Garcia Girls Lost Their Accents* (0-452-26806-0), Mark Twain's *Huckleberry Finn* (0-451-52650-3), and plays by Shakespeare, Miller, and Albee. For more information, please contact your Addison Wesley Longman sales consultant.

80 Readings (Second Edition). This inexpensive volume contains 80 brief readings (1–3 pages each) on a variety of themes: writers on writing, nature, women and men, customs and habits, politics, rights and obligations, and coming of age. Also included is an alternate rhetorical table of contents. 0-321-01648-3.

100 Things to Write About. This 100-page book contains 100 individual assignments for writing on a variety of topics and in a wide range of formats, from expressive to analytical. Ask your Addison Wesley Longman sales representative for a sample copy. 0-673-98239-4.

Electronic and Online Offerings

The Longman English Pages Website. Both students and instructors can visit our free content-rich Website for additional reading selections and writing exercises. From the Longman English pages, visitors can conduct a simulated Web search, learn how to write a resume and cover letter, or try their hand at poetry writing. Stop by and visit us at ⟨**http://longman.awl.com/englishpages**⟩.

The Basic Skills Newsletter. Twice a month during the spring and fall, instructors who have subscribed receive a free copy of the Longman Basic Skills Newsletter in their e-mailbox. Written by experienced classroom instructors, the newsletter offers teaching tips, classroom activities, book reviews, and more. To subscribe, visit the Longman Basic Skills Website at ⟨**http://longman.awl.com/basicskills**⟩, or send an e-mail to **BasicSkills@awl.com.**

Longman Grammar Software. For computerized practice and tutorial, download Longman's free grammar software from our Website. Organized by topic, the Longman Grammar Package is the ideal complement to any basic writing text. Find the software at ⟨**http://longman.awl.com/basicskills/grammar**⟩.

The Writer's Workshop. The Writer's Workshop "pops up" over any commercial word processing program to provide writing prompts for students as they compose their papers. An online handbook provides instant reference. Available for a nominal fee shrinkwrapped with any text. IBM: 0-321-04756-7; Mac: 0-321-04757-5.

For Instructors

Competency Profile Test Bank (Second Edition). This series of 60 objective tests covers ten general areas of English competency, including fragments, comma splices and run-ons, pronouns, commas, and capitalization. Each test is available in remedial, standard, and advanced versions. Available as reproducible sheets or in computerized versions. Free to instructors. Paper version: 0-321-02224-6. Computerized IBM: 0-321-02633-0. Computerized Mac: 0-321-02632-2.

Diagnostic and Editing Tests (Second Edition). This collection of diagnostic tests helps instructors assess students' competence in standard written English for purpose of placement or to gauge progress. Available as reproducible sheets or in computerized versions, and free to instructors. Paper: 0-321-02222-X. Computerized IBM: 0-321-02629-2. Computerized Mac: 0-321-02628-4.

ESL Worksheets (Second Edition). These reproducible worksheets provide ESL students with extra practice in areas they find the most troublesome. A diagnostic test and post-test are provided, along with answer keys and suggested topics for writing. Free to adopters. 0-321-01955-5.

80 Practices. A collection of reproducible, ten-item exercises that provide additional practices for specific grammatical usage problems, such as comma splices, capitalization, and pronouns. Includes an answer key, and free to adopters. 0-673-53422-7.

CLAST Test Package (Fourth Edition). These two 40-item objective tests evaluate students' readiness for the CLAST exams. Strategies for teaching CLAST preparedness are included. Free with any Longman English title. Reproducible sheets: 0-321-01950-4. Computerized IBM version: 0-321-01982-2. Computerized Mac version: 0-321-01983-0.

TASP Test Package (Third Edition). These 12 practice pre-tests and post-tests assess the same reading and writing skills covered in the TASP examination. Free with any Longman English title. Reproducible sheets: 0-321-01959-8. Computerized IBM version: 0-321-01985-7. Computerized Mac version: 0-321-01984-9.

Teaching Online: Internet Research, Conversation, and Composition (Second Edition). Ideal for instructors who have never surfed the Net, this easy-to-follow guide offers basic definitions, numerous examples, and step-by-step information about finding and using Internet sources. Free to adopters. 0-321-01957-1.

Reading Critically: Texts, Charts, and Graphs. For instructors who would like to emphasize critical thinking in their courses, this brief book (65 pages) provides additional critical thinking material to supplement coverage in the text. Free to instructors. 0-673-97365-4.

Teaching Writing to the Non-Native Speaker. This booklet examines the issues that arise when non-native speakers enter the developmental classroom. Free to instructors, it includes profiles of international and permanent ESL students, factors influencing second-language acquisition, and tips on managing a multicultural classroom. 0-673-97452-9.

For Students

Researching Online (Second Edition). A perfect companion for a new age, this indispensable new supplement helps students navigate the Internet. Adapted from Teaching Online, the instructor's Internet guide, Researching Online speaks directly to students, giving them detailed step-by-step instructions for performing electronic searches. Perfect-bound, **free** when bundled with any Longman Basic Skills text: 0-321-02714-0. Spiral-bound also available at nominal price: 0-321-05117-3.

Using WordPerfect in Composition and Using Microsoft Word in Composition. These two brief guides assume no prior knowledge of WordPerfect or Word. Each guide begins with word processing basics and gradually leads into more sophisticated functions. Shrinkwrapped free with any Longman Basic Skills text. WordPerfect: 0-673-52448-5. Word: 0-673-52449-3.

Learning Together. This brief guide to the fundamentals of collaborative learning teaches students how to work effectively in groups, how to revise with peer response, and how to co-author a paper or report. Shrinkwrapped free with any Longman Basic Skills text. 0-673-46848-8.

A Guide for Peer Response (Second Edition). This guide offers students forms for peer critiques, including general guidelines and specific forms for different stages in the writing process. Also appropriate for freshman-level course. Free to adopters. 0-321-01948-2.

ACKNOWLEDGMENTS

Keys to Successful Writing: Unlocking the Writer Within would not exist without the talent and work of a large number of dedicated people. Although I'll never be able to thank them adequately, I want to acknowledge their invaluable contribution to the creation of this text.

Heartfelt thanks to all the reviewers of this book: Kelly Belanger, Youngstown State University; Bob Brannan, Johnson County Community College; Kathleen Britton, Florence-Darlington Technical College; Alice Cleveland, College of Marin; Sally Crisp, University of Arkansas; Norma Cruz-Gonzales, San Antonio College; Scott Douglass, Chattanooga State Technical Community College; Eileen Eliot, Broward Community College; Doug Fossek, Santa

Barbara City College; Joe Fulton, Dalton College; Clifford Gardiner, Augusta College; Timothy Giles, Georgia Southern University; Rima Gulshan, University of Maryland; Mary Hart, Laramie County Community College; Christine Hubbard, Tarrant County Junior College Southeast Campus; Judy Hubbard, De Anza Community College; Lee Brewer Jones, DeKalb College; Laurie Knox, Kennesaw State College; Patricia J. McAlexander, University of Georgia; Michael McKay, Community College of Denver; Patricia Malinowski, Finger Lakes Community College; Marilyn Martin, Quinsigamond Community College; Elizabeth Meehan, San Diego City College; Tim Miank, Lansing Community College; Elizabeth Ott, El Camino College; Sylvia Pack, Weber State University; Richard Rawnsley, College of the Desert; Julie Segedy, Chabot College; Karen Standridge, Pike's Peak Community College; David Steinhart, Community College of Allegheny County; Dreama Stringer, Marshall Community College; Elaine Sundberg, Sonoma State University; Bill Sweet, Lane Community College; Carolyn Varvel, Red Rocks Community College; Martha Vertreace, Kennedy-King College; Michael Warren, Maple Woods Community College; Richard W. White, Edison Community College; Sam Zahran, Fayetteville Technical Community College.

In addition, I am indebted to Karen Standridge not only for her review, but for her enthusiasm and her helpful comments, suggestions, and kind sharing of her own strategies and assignments in the "Using the Computer" sections of this text.

I am forever grateful for the privilege of working with and learning from such wonderful students. Some are still on my campus and they drop by to say "hello." Some are now studying in other colleges and universities, while still others are out in the workforce pursuing careers in various fields. These student writers had the faith in me and in this project to share their writing, their photographs, and their informal comments on writing, college, career, and personal goals. I thank them and wish them success in all their future endeavors: Erika Staggers, Matt Cirillo, Cindy Sharp, Douglas Cwiak, Joel Lopez, Elias Kary, Deanna McAmis, Corona Reynolds, Margarita Figueroa, Jeremy Smith, Leah Ford, Mitchell Wexler, Brian Morton, Nicoll Grijalva, Keith Seigman, Desirea Espinoza, Grethel Peralta, Peter Huang, In Sung Song, Shelly Grieve, Letictia Elder, Laura Rezende, Greg McMillan, Carlos De Jesus, Tommy Honjo, Cenovio Maeda, Candi German, Lucy Mardirossian, Cinthya Martinez, Robert Amerson, Monifa Winston, Patty Crippen, Carmen Tull, Edwin Ksiezopolski, Dawn Beverly, Ginell Cabanilla, Anthony Diaz, Tori Ueda, Courtney Risdon, Brenda Grant, Bryant Burns, Charles Kim, Jinnie Delacruz, Swarupa Reddy, Yen Glassman, Chuks Ofoegbu, Brian Villapudua, Russell Fullerton, Rebecca Obidi.

Special thanks go to two other contributors who were not college students, but were kind enough to grant permission to let me use their writing anyway: Mindy Balgrosky, a generous and thoughtful friend, and my son Mike Anderson, a high school senior who looks forward to his first year of college this fall.

My foremost note of gratitude goes to Wendy Wright, longtime friend, office mate, running partner, and frequent contributor to conferences, workshops, and college teaching publications. Wendy designed the splendid diagram for the composing process that appears in Chapter 2. In addition, she spent many hours of her time on book-related activities. I greatly admire her abilities, and I am forever grateful for her input.

Elizabeth Ott, another office mate, bravely volunteered to use the manuscript in her classroom and offered excellent feedback in the form of a daily journal. Her carefully composed written response gave me and the editors at Longman the opportunity to compare her students' responses to writing assignments, chapter content, and strategies, so that I was not limited to my own classroom experience with the manuscript.

Adrienne Sharp, Steve Montgomery, and Jeff McMahon, editors of *Our Voices,* an El Camino College publication for developmental writers, deserve my hearty thanks because they afforded me yet another excellent source for student essays. Each year this group of instructors continues to take on the worthy task of choosing developmental student writing for publication in this magazine.

My gratitude also goes to Alice Grigsby, El Camino College reference librarian, who put on her super-sleuth hat and tracked down several sources for me even though I fear the job took her a lot longer than she ever admitted.

I want to thank the tutors I worked with in many English A classes while the book was being tested in manuscript form. These people—talented teachers and writers—worked for several semesters with a very bulky manuscript and never complained. They went through trial-and-error with me to discover what worked and what didn't in the classroom and in the writing conference scenario. Then after class, they were willing victims, letting me mercilessly pick their brains to discover if they had held any shred of information back. They deserve a round of applause: Susan Mrazek, Beth Shibata, Martin Addleman, and Mark Sundeen.

A special note of gratitude goes to Barbara Budrovich, Writing Center Coordinator, for lending me textbooks on several occasions, for having such wonderful support staff, and for the terrific resource and back-up support the Writing Center offers to developmental among other students on our campus.

Thanks go also to the Special Resource Center and to the Learning Resource Center. Over the years, the SRC has referred many talented writers to my classes and other students and I have grown tremendously from the opportunity to work with SRC students and their interpreters, signers, note-takers, and other assistants. Thanks to testing, counseling, and available resources through the SRC, many students have been able to succeed in developmental writing and in their other college courses.

I want to give my supreme gratitude to Dean Tom Lew, who over the years has continued to inspire me with his calm intelligence, his dedication, and his love of the humanities.

I would also like to thank Jean Smeltzer in the Computer-Assisted-Instruction Center for her patience and understanding in response to the many questions from me and from my students. Jean continues to be calm, cool, and collected when the rest of us panic at the thought of a computer freeze-up, lost file, or virus-infected disk.

The final thank-you's for my El Camino colleagues go to Melinda Barth and Susan Bachmann, who "got me into this" in the first place. Although at many moments of crisis and fatigue during the process of writing, re-writing, and yet again re-writing this text I would have expressed anything but gratitude, I can now offer my sincere appreciation to you both for giving my name to Longman: thanks to you, I have learned so much more about the composing process—that same process that I had been teaching for so many years but had not really encountered head-on until I embarked on the writing of this text.

I don't really know if many textbook authors establish such a solid E-mail relationship with their editors, but everyone I worked with at Longman put up with my many e-mail queries and comments. This correspondence began with Ellen Schatz, Acquisitions Editor at Longman at the time work on this text commenced. Ellen's sense of humor and the firm, reassuring advice of Patricia Rossi, former Editor-in-Chief at Longman, helped keep me on task. Midway through the completion of the manuscript, I was fortunate enough to work with Steven Rigolosi, Acquisitions Editor for Basic Skills and someone who was always there to listen to my concerns and offer sound advice and encouraging words.

However, the "miracle duo" who deserve to be singled out for unreserved praise are Meg Botteon, Development Editor, and Sharon Balbos, Development Editor. I will never be able to thank these two gifted people enough. Meg Botteon worked with me tirelessly on tightening and clarifying chapters; her editorial comments and suggestions were invariably clear and correct. In addition, she proved to be a priceless resource for computer use; with her technical expertise, Meg overhauled the "Using the Computer" sections to add Web and online activities that correlate beautifully with each chapter's content.

Sharon Balbos is the person I had the extreme privilege of getting to know the best during the course of this project. Her sincere enthusiasm tempered with honesty and intelligence steered the text from inception to completion. Without Sharon's guiding hand in troubleshooting, editing, brainstorming, and in several instances, personal counseling, I would never have been able to complete the manuscript. I am forever grateful for the patience and thoughtfulness Sharon displayed in our many lengthy phone calls, e-mails, memos, and letters and for her insightful comments in numerous edits. I had what I'm sure many textbook writers envy: someone who shared my vision and wanted to see it unfold clearly. I thank her for unlocking the writer within me.

Marilyn Anderson
El Camino College

Preface for Students

PERSONAL INVENTORY

If you were to answer truthfully, what would you say in response to the following set of questions:

1. Do you believe good writers are born, not made? _____

2. Do you enjoy personal writing? _____

3. Do you worry about your ability to succeed in a college writing class? _____

4. How long has it been since you've been in a classroom situation? _____

5. Was your last classroom writing experience positive, negative, or a little of both? (Explain briefly.)

   _____

   _____

6. What are two specific things you'd like to learn from this course?

   _____

   _____

HOW THIS TEXT CAN HELP YOU

No matter how you have answered these questions—regardless of your concerns, hopes, expectations, or fears upon beginning this course—rest assured that you can use *Keys to Successful Writing: Unlocking the Writer Within* to improve your skills and confidence. Just as metal keys are instruments for unlocking and opening doors, the "keys" presented in this text will offer you access into the realm of effective college, workplace, and everyday writing.

Please consider this preface your personal invitation to embark on an exciting journey of self-discovery through reading, writing and thinking.

You may have less than completely pleasant memories of past classes involving writing, or you may worry that you've been "away" from classrooms or from writing assigments too long to succeed in college. Although you might not feel confident about your writing now at the beginning of your course, your careful reading and interaction with this book, its clear explanations, and its engaging writing options will enable you to succeed in this writing course.

As you watch your writing abilities increase, you will undoubtedly find that, even though you may already enjoy writing in some circumstances, you will take even more pleasure from being able to write clearly and effectively in many writing situations. As you progress in your reading and application of *Keys*, you'll be gratified that the skills you've learned through study of this text will lead directly to your increased success in other college courses and on the job. Regardless of your college major or future career plans, clear writing is crucial. You'll be able to transfer the guidelines and rules from *Keys* to almost all writing situations because although every writing circumstance is unique, almost all real-world writing situations ask you to read actively, think critically, and write clearly. Your understanding of the five KEYS and your knowledge of how the composing process really works will enable you to do just that.

HOW TO FIND INFORMATION QUICKLY

Familiarizing yourself now with the information-access features of this text will help you later when you want to find a particular subject, reading, or term quickly. Check off each feature after you've found it in this text and become acquainted with its contents.

Index (pp. 480–486) ☐

The index is a complete alphabetical listing of topics, reading titles, and authors found in *Keys to Successful Writing*. The index tells you on what page you will find information about a particular topic, or where you will find a particular reading. For example, if your teacher asks you to read the Amitai Etzioni essay for your homework, you can look up "Etzioni" in the index to find the page number of that essay. If you are trying to start an essay, looking up "prewriting" will guide you to those places in the book that describe strategies and give examples of successful prewriting. Although the glossary (see above) will provide you with definitions of important terms, the index will help you find places in the book where that term is explained and often supported with a practice exercise.

Use the index to find the answers to these two questions:

On what pages do you find versions of the essay "Dishonesty"? _____

_____

On how many pages will you find help with creating a thesis statement?

_____

Brief Table of Contents (p. ix) ☐

The brief table of contents gives you a sense of the overall structure of *Keys to Successful Writing*. It gives the titles and page numbers of each main part and each chapter of the book. If you're looking for a particular chapter or general subject, the brief table of contents is the quickest way to find that information. Refer to the brief table of contents. On which page will you find the chapter that will help you learn to begin and conclude an essay? _____

Contents (pp. xi–xxvi) ☐

The table of contents offers a listing of every heading and essay, and most activities within each chapter, arranged in order of appearance and listing title and author. You will find the complete table of contents especially helpful when you are looking up a homework assignment or when you want to review a particular skill.

Refer to the complete table of contents. On which page will you find information to help you write formal and informal outlines? _____

Glossary (pp. 469–477) ☐

The glossary includes in alphabetical order all of the important, **boldfaced** terms used in the text, along with a concise definition of each term. You can use the glossary for quick review and handy referencing of important information. To see how this information appears, examine the following glossary sample of the first three entries:

abstract subject A subject possessing no physical properties but still existing as an idea, concept, or principle.

academic research Exploration of sources completed formally and according to an accepted format for a collegiate audience. Such research requires the acknowledgment of sources.

active reading Reading in which the reader remains engaged with the text, constantly questioning and responding to the material.

Now turn to p. 469 and write the next term you find in the following space:

_____

Icons ☐

You will notice "icons," or small images, at certain points in each chapter. These icons help you find the same kind of material in each chapter. We use four icons in *Keys to Successful Writing.*

 The most important icon—as you might have already guessed—is a set of keys. Every time you see these keys in the text, it means that another aspect of the five KEYS is being discussed.

 This icon marks "Options for Writing," "Journal Writing," and "Responding to Writing" activities. Your instructor might ask you to write in response to these activities, and you can gain additional experience by responding on your own to those activities that interest you.

 This icon indicates computer-related activities and explanations in each chapter. Every time you see the "mouse," you'll know that you can find more information about using the computer to enhance your writing. The icon appears with each "Using the Computer" activity and to remind you to visit *The English Pages* Web site, which includes many useful and interesting resources to help you with your writing.

 This icon points out "Readings and Additional Activities," which your instructor might assign to you or which we hope you'll enjoy reading and thinking about on your own.

List of Special Elements and Activities on Inside Front and Back Covers ☐

The inside front and back covers can help you find information and activities on specific topics. The inside front cover lists the subjects and page numbers of the "Strategies" boxes and the "Using the Computer" activities. You'll also find a list of the "Five Keys" here. The facing page lists all the opportunities for writing in *Keys to Successful Writing: Unlocking the Writer Within,* along with their page numbers. These lists, organized by chapter, will help you swiftly locate exercises and strategies for practice and review.

The inside back cover includes a list of editing symbols. Your instructor may use many of these symbols in responding to your writing, and you will want to use them in peer review activities. The last two pages of text list the titles, authors, and quick page references for student and professional readings.

Referring to the list of charts and activities, on what page will you find a checklist to help you write in-class essays? _____

On what page will you find a computer exercise about seeking job information using the Internet? _____

Editing Symbols on Inside Back Cover ☐

You can refer to this list when your completed assignment has been commented on and returned to you by your instructor, modifying the list if your instructor uses different or additional symbols.

These editing symbols will also help you find specific, helpful information in the handbook. For example, the symbol "SF" ("sentence fragment") on the list of editing symbols is also an easy-to-find tab in the handbook that directs you to a definition of sentence fragments and advice on how to correct them (see p. 424). Turn to the back inside cover and find the correction symbol for comma splices. In the following space, write the correction symbol and the page where you would find a definition of this sentence error.

_____

Ask your instructor if she or he uses any additional or different correction symbols. If so, modify the list on the inside back cover.

Tabbed Handbook with User's Guide (pp. 413–468) ☐

Part Four of *Keys* has many useful features to help you find information quickly and efficiently. The color bars that you see when the book is closed show you where to turn for the handbook. In addition, the Handbook Guide provides many helpful hints to finding the answers to your writing questions.

Keeping the tabbed handbook by your computer, desk, or wherever you write will allow you quick access during all stages of your composing process. After you've had one or more written assignments returned by your instructor with comments, the handbook will help you zero in on your weak areas, obtain a quick description of the problem, and complete appropriate practice exercises so that you can solve the problem.

HOW TO WORK WITH *KEYS TO SUCCESSFUL WRITING*

If you are ready, you can begin your journey by reading some basic navigation instructions for this user-friendly text. Your instructor may assign all or part of a chapter, or perhaps more than one chapter at a time. When you are assigned a section of the book, you will want to read and also complete the activities in the assigned section so you'll be assured that you understand fully the content of the section. That way you can apply the concepts and strategies to your own writing and to your evaluation of writings in the text and those of your fellow students. Some activities will instruct you to write in your book, and for others you can use your own paper or a computer. Some may be completed in class working alone or with a small group or partner; others will be assigned for out-of-class completion.

Every chapter in this text is designed to help you succeed as a writer. It's helpful to know that each chapter follows the same basic format. You'll notice that special sections are highlighted for you. Here is an overview of those helpful sections.

Preview

By reading this brief, bulleted section at the beginning of every chapter, you'll get a "preview of coming attractions." You'll have a specific idea of the information that will be covered within the chapter. Later, when you've finished a chapter, the preview is useful as a quick self-check of your comprehension of the material.

Here is the preview for Chapter 2:

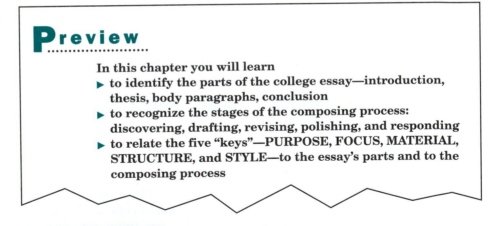

Preview

In this chapter you will learn
- ▶ **to identify the parts of the college essay—introduction, thesis, body paragraphs, conclusion**
- ▶ **to recognize the stages of the composing process: discovering, drafting, revising, polishing, and responding**
- ▶ **to relate the five "keys"—PURPOSE, FOCUS, MATERIAL, STRUCTURE, and STYLE—to the essay's parts and to the composing process**

Characteristics

This brief section focuses on a specific aspect of the writing process or on a method of essay development and will always include an example of the concept being discussed. For example, in Chapter 3, "Discovering Through Prewriting," you'll learn how *not* to stare at a blank computer screen or blank piece of paper;

you'll become familiar with strategies that other writers use to generate ideas. Then, when your instructor gives you your next writing assignment, you'll be able to draw upon a variety of prewriting techniques. In Chapter 8, "Writing about Events: Narration," you'll see how telling about an event can influence your reader to see your side of a particular issue. When you are asked to use narration in an essay, you'll be able to organize your essay to fit your purpose. In Part Three, you'll be presented with the characteristics of effective resumes and employment letters. When you're in need of a new job or thinking of switching jobs, you can refer to this section of the book and know specifically how to create your own "employment package."

Model with Key Questions

Here you'll read an essay written by a student author. These won't always be "perfect" final drafts; in some chapters, you'll see essays-in-progress, instructor and peer editor comments on those essays, and descriptions of real-life writing obstacles that students have faced. You'll see photos of the authors and read brief profiles centering on personal goals and particular writing challenges for each student writer. After you have read the student essay, answering the five "key questions" will help you relate the student model to the particular writing assignment you're preparing for in the chapter. Below is a sample student model from Chapter 4.

DISHONESTY
Margarita Figueroa

Margarita Figueroa decided in the first weeks of her writing class that learning to write clearly would be crucial to her future profession, nursing. Throughout the semester, she worked hard not only on getting first drafts on paper but also on revising and polishing them. Margarita confides that right now she has little free time, but when she does have a few hours, she enjoys reading mysteries.

1   I was reading an essay written by Marya Mannes called "The Thin Grey Line." It was a very interesting article, separating honesty from dishonesty. It made me really think about if people are dishonest or honest. I feel that dishonesty is more characteristic of our society than honesty.

2   Well, first there is the fake car accident that results in getting money out of auto insurance companies. For instance, I had friends that would get together and collaborate with one another and would report to the insurance company about an

Guidelines

In this section, you'll get step-by-step directions *and hands-on experience* to help you complete a writing assignment. Most steps are also accompanied by activities or exercises that you will be completing alone or with a partner. The guidelines have been designed to move you smoothly from a brief introduction by example in the short "characteristics" section to practice exercises that apply directly to the chapter's upcoming writing assignments. To see how the guidelines can help you break down a writing assignment into a series of steps, examine the list of guidelines for Cause/Effect covered in the second part of Chapter 10. For each of these guidelines, an activity will help you develop your skill in the particular step.

Strategies

Once you've read and completed the activities in the "Guidelines" section of a chapter, this boxed section can serve you well as a summary and memory aid. Then, once you have chosen or have been given a writing assignment, you'll be able to consult this checklist and write a successful draft because you can quickly be sure that you haven't left out any steps.

STRATEGIES FOR BODY PARAGRAPHS

1. **PURPOSE** Know what you want to accomplish in each of your body paragraphs as well as the broader purpose of each paragraph in relation to your entire essay. When revising, check to see that each body paragraph has achieved its individual purpose and also works with the other body paragraphs to support the essay's thesis.

2. **FOCUS** Use a topic sentence (or an implied topic sentence) to focus on a main point and connect all details in each body paragraph. Make sure your topic sentence names the main point and has a controlling idea. In your support material for each body paragraph, omit or revise any information that does not clearly relate to the topic sentence, or rephrase the topic sentence so that it relates to the support material you have presented.

3. **MATERIAL** Check your draft to see that each body paragraph has clearly stated, reliable, adequate support for the topic sentence. Revise any vague or underdeveloped paragraphs.

4. **STRUCTURE** Use an organizational plan for each body paragraph that seems to work best for your material—chronological, spatial, or logical order. Create a new paragraph when you move on to a new main point. Insert cue words to signal a change in direction or level of detail, both within each body paragraph and from one body paragraph to the next.

5. **STYLE** Reread, respond, and revise all body paragraphs so that they use the most precise words possible. Make sure you repeat important words and use parallel sentence structures.

Journal Writing

Your instructor may assign certain numbered activities in this section, or you may discover that even though not assigned, journal writing can help you gather and organize material for an essay. From reading logs to personal entries, the many activities offered—several in every chapter—are all practical and will give you a written record of your thoughts. As an example, in Chapter 9, you will be able to examine both description and definition as techniques that you can use to develop ideas in your writing. In support of the chapter's main topics, one journal activity, "sensory isolation," challenges you to use your senses in getting ideas on paper, and another journal activity allows you to free-associate to come up with some strategies for definition. While you're having fun with these unique exercises, you'll also be generating material that you can use in an essay focused on the strategies discussed in the chapter.

Using the Computer

You may be using this section on your own, on a campus or home computer, or your class may attend a computer lab as a group. And rest easy; no activity in the computer section requires that you be a computer expert. Each computer section connects in activities with the topics discussed within the chapter. And once you've discovered the many benefits of computer use, you may find that you are developing computer activities of your own. For instance, have you ever accessed the wealth of information available online to help you make a decision about your travel plans, your next car, or your career training? Are you familiar with all the ways a word processing program can help you write more easily and effectively? This section shows you how to get more out of your computer. To give you an idea of how this computer section works, here is an activity from Part Three.

USING THE COMPUTER: DISCOVERING A CAREER

1. See if your word-processing program offers *templates,* or *model documents* for resumes, memos, letters and other businees documents. A template provides all the basic structure and formatting for a document, freeing you to fill in the blanks with relevant information. You might find this especially useful for producing a resume. Choose a template. Following the guidelines and strategies for resumes presented in this chapter, create your own resume or update an earlier version of it.

2. Whether you are just beginning to plan your career or are contemplating a midlife career shift, there is a wealth of resources available to you on the World Wide Web. The following two sites are particularly comprehensive:

   • *Monster Board* ⟨http://www.monsterboard.com⟩ may have a scary name, but it includes profiles of thousands of companies, information on career fairs, job search assistance, and advice on career planning. Use this resource to find out if a particular company is hiring, or who you should contact at that company if you want to send a resume and cover letter. Be sure to look up that company's profile before you draft your cover letter and resume. You may find particular information and details that will make your cover letter more interesting and specific.

   • *About Work* ⟨http://www.aboutwork.com⟩ also includes company profiles and employment opportunities, as well as chat groups on specific work-related issues and articles on workplace concerns. A special section, *StudentCenter,* is designed for college students beginning their

continued

Options for Writing

These detailed writing assignments offer you the exciting and practical challenge of putting the information in a chapter into practice. The options for writing have been created and classroom-tested to be fresh alternatives to the "My Summer Vacation" variety of topics you may have been asked to write on in past classes. Your instructor may ask you to choose one from the list, or you may be assigned a specific assignment. However, you should know that all the options develop the writing skills you will continue to use in other college courses and in your future career. You may even discover that once you have a valid and specific purpose, your writing "lifts off" as it has never done before. One student who called himself a reluctant writer found that he felt so strongly about the issue he was arguing against in an essay that he submitted his writing for publication in the college newspaper. Like this student, you will share the excitement of seeing your writing influence the thinking of others as you exchange drafts with peers and receive comments on your writing from your instructor.

To examine the connection this textbook makes between the options for writing and the real world, in Chapter 10 you may be asked to use process writing to explain how something works. You will notice, in looking at the assignments on pages 297–298, that all these options connect with real-world writing situations that you will continue to encounter.

Do not be surprised if you become so interested in your subject that you're actually motivated to engage in additional research—in fact, this text encourages just that! In several chapters, computer activities featuring websites that relate to writing options help you gather more information. In other chapters, you're encouraged to participate in online or in-person interviews, to consult a specialized dictionary, encyclopedia, or other reference, or to seek out campus experts, for example.

Responding to Writing

This section will challenge you to apply what you've learned in the chapter to specific writing situations: here you'll read and respond to student and professional writers. You'll comment on one student's freewriting and try to figure out how she could organize it into a first draft; you'll take a look at student-generated body paragraphs to discover their strengths and weaknesses; you'll read students' introductory and concluding paragraphs and see if you can identify the strategies they use to begin and end their essays; you'll pick up valuable strategies for becoming an effective peer editor; you'll learn how to keep your own progress log; you'll go on a scavenger hunt to see if you can identify ways that writers develop contrast and divide or classify subjects.

Additional Readings

These end-of-chapter readings demonstrate the particular aspect of writing discussed within the chapter. For example, in Chapter 12, "Taking a Stand," there are two additional readings: the provocative and controversial essay "Offering Euthanasia Can Be an Act of Love" by Derek Humphry, the same man who has been praised and damned for writing *Final Exit,* a book which tells the reader how to end a life, and the well-known poem "Do Not Go Gentle into That Good Night" by Dylan Thomas, a pro-life argument if there ever was one. Your instructor may assign one or more readings from the chapter, or you may wish to read them on your own. Although these readings introduce you to the kinds of texts and authors you'll find in your college courses, *Keys* also incorporates readings that you will want to discuss with your family and friends. Each reading is accompanied by a brief set of questions that will develop your active reading skills by asking you about the content of the selection, and another brief set of questions about the writer's strategy. Answering this second set of questions for as many of the readings as you can will really strengthen your own writing because you will make connections between a writer's strategy and the reaction of the audience.

Critical Thinking in Connecting Texts

In this section, you'll be paired up with a partner or you may be asked to engage in brainstorming with a small group in the classroom. These critical thinking activities at the ends of chapters will help you to get to know your fellow students, their values, past experiences, and reactions to issues and topics. In addition, these activities will prepare you for the world of work, where often you'll be collaborating with at least one other person to problem-solve or to present a proposal. You'll share the excitement that comes from making connections between reading selections, exploring similarities in themes, points of view, subjects, or strategies presented by two or more writers within a chapter. Your group may even decide to share its findings with other class members, poll the class, or initiate additional research.

OTHER HELPFUL INFORMATION

Part Three of this text, **A Writer's Toolkit,** includes specific guidelines for assembling and keeping a portfolio, writing an in-class timed essay, engaging in introductory research, and writing job application letters and résumés.

    The Longman English Pages Website. Both students and instructors can visit our free content-rich Website for additional reading selections and writing exercises. From the Longman English pages, visitors can conduct a simulated Web search, learn how to write a resume and cover letter, or try their hand at poetry writing. Stop by and visit us at ⟨http://longman.awl.com/englishpages⟩.

Although it's unlikely that you'll get to every section of every chapter as a class, whatever additional reading, writing, and thinking you can do will certainly help you in your journey as a college writer.

The **Handbook,** specifically designed to help you polish your writing and minimize problems with grammar, spelling, usage, and punctuation, is located in Part Four. Your instructor may assign specific sections of the handbook to your class or you may be asked to complete sections on your own that correspond to your particular problem areas in writing. You can find information about specific problem areas by using the tabs and correction symbols.

In the following space, note any question you have about the location or content of any part of this text:

_____

_____

At the end of your course, return to the Personal Inventory on page xliii. Review your original answers. If there are additional comments you would like to make about your writing experience and what you have learned in this course and from the text, please respond in the following space:

_____

_____

Throughout this text, you may have noticed that every chapter has opened with a short passage about some aspect of writing. Now it's your turn. In twenty five words or less, what would you like to say about any aspect of writing?

_____

_____

Keys to Successful Writing

. . . .

PART ONE

Exploring the Realm of College Reading and Writing

Reading, Thinking, and Writing for College

Like writers, readers plan by determining their purposes for reading a text, assessing what they know about the topic, focusing their goals and topics, and questioning themselves.

—*Robert Tierney and P. David Pearson, "Toward a Composing Model of Reading"*

Preview

In this chapter you will learn
- why we read
- what is meant by a writer's audience
- how to recognize the five "keys"—PURPOSE, FOCUS, MATERIAL, STRUCTURE, and STYLE
- how to use the five keys in active reading, critical thinking, and effective writing
- how to keep a reading log
- the advantages of computer use for college reading and writing

THE READING/WRITING CONNECTION

The news is out—national studies as well as countless experiences in classrooms prove beyond all doubt that active readers are better writers. When you read well and often, you absorb new ideas, information, and vocabulary. In addition, you think about these ideas, questioning and challenging them with ideas and information of your own. Thanks to active reading, you end up with a wealth of material for writing.

Still, many college students lack confidence in their reading and writing. Even professional writers like Jane Smiley confide the following: "I am not a good reader. I am slow and not very determined. I never make myself read a book to the end if I get bored in the middle." Clues to our attitudes about reading and writing may be related to *why* we read and how.

Why We Read

Think back to what you have read most eagerly and easily—chances are that your interest in the material motivated you to continue reading. And since no two people have identical interests, this motivation varies tremendously. One student reports that she reads her friend's letters because they "make me feel good about myself"; another student confides that he finished an entire article at a grocery checkout stand because "this mega rap star and I come from similar backgrounds and faced the same obstacles as young inner-city African-American males." Your purpose in reading may be one or more of the following:

- **To be emotionally moved**
  A student asserts, "I enjoy reading mysteries because they make my imagination run wild. I imagine myself putting on a long black coat and hat and turning into a sly detective."

- **To be informed**
  Another student reports, "I like to read *Time* and *Popular Mechanics* because these magazines have short articles informing me of science innovations."

- **To be persuaded**
  According to this student, "Reading *Chicken Soup for the Soul* persuades me that I can do anything I put my mind to."

Practice 1.1 Take a moment to think about what you have read in the past weeks. Don't exclude any type of printed material. In the space provided, write the last printed work you remember reading, and then try to explain in a few words why you were motivated to continue reading.

_____

_____

◆ ◆ ◆

CHARACTERISTICS OF SUCCESSFUL
COLLEGE WRITERS AND READERS

While you probably enjoy reading about subjects of personal interest, you may not feel the same about your college textbooks. They may be more demanding, and as a result, you may not be as willing, eager, or alert an audience. For one thing, the sheer size of many college texts, sometimes several hundred pages, may be intimidating. In addition, college texts often require greater concentration and effort on your part because of the complex material, technical terms, unfamiliar words, and concepts they contain. You may be motivated not by personal interest but by a different motive instead: the text is required reading. If, however, you examine the habits of successful college writers, you can identify three strategies they use in making the reading/writing connection: (1) they read actively, (2) they think critically, and (3) they employ helpful keys in both reading and writing.

To see how a writer uses these three strategies, read the following essay.

Let's Tell the Story of All America's Cultures

Ji-Yeon Mary Yufill

1   I grew up hearing, seeing and almost believing that America was white—albeit with a little black tinge here and there—and that white was best.

2   The white people were everywhere in my 1970s Chicago childhood: Founding Fathers, Lewis and Clark, Lincoln, Daniel Boone, Carnegie, presidents, explorers and industrialists galore. The only black people were slaves. The only Indians were scalpers.

3   I never heard one word about how Benjamin Franklin was so impressed by the Iroquois federation of nations that he adapted that model into our system of state and federal government. Or that the Indian tribes were systematically betrayed and massacred by a greedy young nation that stole their land and called it the United States.

4   I never heard one word about how Asian immigrants were among the first to turn California's desert into fields of plenty. Or about Chinese immigrant Ah Bing, who bred the cherry now on sale in groceries across the nation. Or that plantation owners in Hawaii imported labor from China, Japan, Korea and the Philippines to work the sugar cane fields. I never learned that Asian immigrants were the only immigrants denied U.S. citizenship, even though they served honorably in World War I. All the immigrants in my textbook were white.

5 I never learned about Frederick Douglass, the runaway slave who became a leading abolitionist and statesman, or about black scholar W. E. B. Du Bois. I never learned that black people rose up in arms against slavery. Nat Turner wasn't one of the heroes in my childhood history class.

6 I never learned that the American Southwest and California were already settled by Mexicans when they were annexed after the Mexican-American War. I never learned that Mexico once had a problem keeping land-hungry white men on the U.S. side of the border.

7 So when other children called me a slant-eyed chink and told me to go back where I came from, I was ready to believe that I wasn't really an American because I wasn't white.

8 America's bittersweet legacy of struggling and failing and getting another step closer to democratic ideals of liberty and equality and justice for all wasn't for the likes of me, an immigrant child from Korea. The history books said so.

9 Well, the history books were wrong.

10 Educators around the country are finally realizing what I realized as a teenager in the library, looking up the history I wasn't getting in school. America is a multicultural nation, composed of many people with varying histories and varying traditions who have little in common except their humanity, a belief in democracy and a desire for freedom.

11 America changed them, but they changed America too.

12 A committee of scholars and teachers gathered by the New York State Department of Education recognizes this in their recent report, "One Nation, Many Peoples: A Declaration of Cultural Interdependence."

13 They recommend that public schools provide a "multicultural education, anchored to the shared principles of a liberal democracy."

14 What that means, according to the report, is recognizing that America was shaped and continues to be shaped by people of diverse backgrounds. It calls for students to be taught that history is an ongoing process of discovery and interpretation of the past, and that there is more than one way of viewing the world.

15 Thus, the westward migration of white Americans is not just a heroic settling of an untamed wild, but also the conquest of indigenous peoples. Immigrants were not just white, but Asian as well. Blacks were not merely passive slaves freed by northern whites, but active fighters for their own liberation.

16 In particular, according to the report, the curriculum should help children "to assess critically the reasons for the inconsistencies between the ideals of the U.S. and social real-

ities. It should provide information and intellectual tools that can permit them to contribute to bringing reality closer to the ideals."

17   In other words, show children the good with the bad, and give them the skills to help improve their country. What could be more patriotic?

18   Several dissenting members of the New York committee publicly worry that America will splinter into ethnic fragments if this multicultural curriculum is adopted. They argue that the committee's report puts the focus on ethnicity at the expense of national unity.

19   But downplaying ethnicity will not bolster national unity. The history of America is the story of how and why people from all over the world came to the United States, and how in struggling to make a better life for themselves, they changed each other, they changed the country, and they all came to call themselves Americans.

20   *E pluribus unum.* Out of many, one.

21   This is why I, with my Korean background, and my childhood tormentors, with their lost-in-the-mist-of-time European backgrounds, are all Americans.

22   It is the unique beauty of this country. It is high time we let all our children gaze upon it.

Notice that Yufill connects her reading to her writing by using the following strategies:

- **Active reading**
  Paragraphs 1 though 6 reveal that in reading her textbooks, Yufill remained alert and involved with her subjects, for she offers specific examples, including Lincoln, Lewis and Clark, Benjamin Franklin, and Carnegie. Yufill began to question certain statements that she read: "the only black people were slaves," "the only Indians were scalpers," and "all the immigrants . . . were white."

- **Critical thinking**
  Yufill analyzed what she had read in her history books. After a time of acceptance, as a teenager she evaluated her reading and its source, and she concluded that "the history books were wrong." This evaluative step in her critical thinking led Yufill to read further, to look up "the history I wasn't getting in school." Later in her essay, in paragraphs 12 through 18, Yufill demonstrates her critical thinking skills again: After reading the New York State Department of Education report, Yufill analyzed, summarized, and evaluated it for herself and, later, for her reading audience.

- **Tools to connect reading and writing**
  Only after engaging in active reading and critical thinking did Yufill begin to think of writing an essay. When she did write, she used a set of tools or "keys" to help her evaluate and develop her own writing.

You can first identify and then employ guidelines for active reading, critical thinking, and effective writing.

GUIDELINES FOR ACTIVE READING

When you engage in **active reading,** you are constantly questioning and responding to what you're reading. To be an active reader, you need to ask yourself periodically how you feel or think about what you're reading. "Aha," you say. "But how do I remain connected to material which might not interest me? What if I'm confused from the beginning about what's on the page?" The following are six strategies for active reading.

STRATEGIES FOR ACTIVE READING

1. Preview the reading.

2. Use a dictionary and contextual definitions.

3. Annotate your text.

4. Summarize what you have read.

5. Respond in a journal.

6. Use critical thinking to evaluate what you have read.

Preview the Reading

To **preview** a reading, look at the chapter titles and section headings printed in larger lettering or in bold type. These will give you a good idea of all the topics to be discussed in the chapter. (You will notice that this book contains a "Preview" section at the beginning of every chapter.) Then for a reading assigned within a chapter, examine any background information on the author, look closely at the title, and then flip the pages quickly to the end to get an idea of the length and complexity of the reading. Previewing the entire reading by skimming it quickly will give you a better idea of how challenging your reading assignment will be. For example, if you see that the article has long paragraphs, statistics, or charts, you might schedule more time for your reading. If, on the other hand, your previewing reveals that the article has short paragraphs and few technical terms, you can plan to spend less time and perhaps less effort on active reading.

In addition to giving you an edge on your reading assignment, previewing may help you discover important clues about a writer's subject and **point of view,** or attitude, regarding the subject. These clues will help you in active reading, giving you added insight into whether a particular writer is qualified to address the issue or if the writer has a bias on the subject.

Practice 1.2 To test this for yourself, take a look at the following background information and titles and see if you can figure out what the author's point of view toward the subject might be. The first example has been done for you.

<u>**Point of View About Subject**</u>

"Sex, Lies, and Advertising" *advertising is deceitful*

"The Woes of a Waitress"

Author is an environmentalist and
the subject is our national parklands

"Crime Is the Basic Problem, Not Guns"

(For additional information on point of view, see p. 215 in Chapter 8 and p. 282 in Chapter 10.)

◆ ◆ ◆

Use Dictionary Definitions and Contextual Definitions

To increase your understanding of the material you are reading, keep a good college-level dictionary close at hand and use it to look up words that you don't know. You'll be amazed at your increasing retention of information and also at your growing vocabulary.

If you don't have a dictionary handy or you don't have time to look up all unknown words, try to determine the meaning of a word from the **context** of the passage. A contextual definition is one that is reached by looking at the words and sentences both before and after the unfamiliar word.

Practice 1.3 Return to the essay "Let's Tell the Story of All America's Cultures" (pp. 5–7). Find the words *tinge* in paragraph 1 and *galore* in paragraph 2. See if you can come up with a contextual definition for both words.

tinge _____

galore _____

◆ ◆ ◆

Annotate

When you **annotate,** you mark up or highlight the reading, and you take notes in the margins of your text. You can annotate in a number of ways: you can ask questions, underline important points, insert definitions, or indicate with notes your agreement or disagreement with the author. Here is a student's annotated copy of a college text used in a physics course.

When scientists are trying to understand a particular set of phenomena they often make use of a **model**. A model, in the scientist's sense, is a kind of analogy or mental image of the phenomena in terms of something we are familiar with. One example is the wave model of light. We cannot see waves of light as we can water waves; but it is valuable to think of light as if it were made up of waves because experiments indicate that light behaves in many respects as water waves do.

like from everyday life?

having peaks? how?

phenomena= event that can be described

analogy= similarity

Giancoli, Douglas C. From Physics: Principles W/Applications 4/E *by Giancoli ©1995. Reprinted by permission of Prentice-Hall, Inc. Upper Saddle River, NJ.*

Practice 1.4 To work on this skill, try annotating the following paragraphs, which come immediately after the sample (above) you just read.

The purpose of a model is to give us a mental or visual picture—something to hold onto—when we cannot see what actually is happening. Models often give us a deeper understanding: the analogy to a known system (for instance, water waves in the above example) can suggest new experiments to perform and can provide ideas about what other related phenomena might occur.

No model is ever perfect, and scientists are constantly trying to refine their models or to think up new ones when the old ones do not seem adequate. The atomic model of matter has gone through many refinements. At one time or another, atoms were imagined to be tiny spheres with hooks on them (to explain chemical bonding), or tiny billiard balls continually bouncing against each other. More recently, "the planetary model" of the atom visualized the atom as a nucleus with electrons revolving around it, just as the planets revolve about the Sun. Yet this model too is oversimplified and fails crucial tests.

◆ ◆ ◆

Summarize

Summarizing what you read is another way to read actively. A **summary** is a statement of the main points or the most important ideas of the text. When you write a summary, you are using your own words to create a much more condensed version of the original. Here's an illustration: before you arrive on campus each day, you complete any number of chores and activities; if you were asked to recount these in detail, you might write from one to several pages. However, you could summarize, by omitting all details and grouping information into two or three broad categories to give your reader the general idea: "Today, I dressed, ate breakfast, gathered my supplies together, and left for school." Notice that the example omits information on the kind of cereal eaten for breakfast and the exact content of "supplies."

Summaries are good tests of whether you are understanding what you are reading; if you cannot easily write a summary, you need to go back, reread more carefully, and possibly engage in more annotating. To examine summary writing more closely, look back at the first paragraph from the physics text (p. 10). As you read the following summary of this paragraph, notice that the summary is written in the writer's own words, using no passages from the original text, it is substantially more condensed than the original, and it omits details, presenting instead only the most important ideas.

Models help scientists to understand events
because models compare scientific events
to happenings we do understand already.

Practice 1.5 Review the second and third paragraphs from the same physics text (in Practice 1.4, beginning on p. 10) and write your summary.

_____

_____

_____

◆ ◆ ◆

Respond in a Journal

Responding to your reading in a journal, or **journal writing,** is an excellent way to form a personal connection to what you have read. This active reading strategy will help you focus your thoughts and can furnish you with lots of information for future writing assignments. In fact, journal writing is so important that every chapter in this book contains a section on journals. To get started, track down a notebook to suit your personal tastes (unless your instructor specifies a certain type of notebook). Consider what you write in your journal as your personal and very informal record of your ideas about and reactions to what you have read. You may also want to use your journal to complain about, to question, or to ponder anything you read. No matter what format for journal writing your instructor may ask you to follow, keeping a journal can help you generate ideas for the writing assignments in this text.

To illustrate, take a look at a journal entry from a student who was asked by her instructor to respond in her journal to an essay about a young mother trying to attend college for the first time:

> I liked what she had to say about the problems she had. It reminded me of what I am going through. I'm learning to juggle my time between my sons and school. My eight-year-old thinks he is getting away with things. So I have to take time out to help him with his school work. My three-year-old isn't hiding his feelings, and since he is still a little boy, he needs his own time and attention from me. Like the author, I may not think there is enough time in a day, but there is, and it can be done.
>
> —Erika Staggers, student

Practice 1.6 To get your journal started, write for five minutes about one obstacle or difficulty you have encountered while attending college.

◆ ◆ ◆

Think Critically

You engage in **critical thinking** when you carefully probe or inspect what you read. The word *critical* used with *thinking* doesn't refer to negative thinking or finding fault with something, as when someone is *critical* of the way you look or act. Instead, critical thinking refers to thinking beyond what is obvious—to reading "between the lines." You probably do this kind of thinking every day. For example, suppose you have just finished interviewing for a job and the interviewer gestures to the exit door with the words, "We'll be getting back to you, but I want you to know that the competition for this job is tremendous." You read between the lines that your chances of getting that job are probably less than if the interviewer personally escorts you to the door with these slightly different words: "We'll be getting back to you, but I want to tell you how impressed I am with your resume." If you think about it, every time you hear someone speak, you're taking in not only the words but also the speaker's tone and body language. As a college student, you need to transfer these critical thinking skills to your reading of college textbooks. And because you can't see the writer when you read, you need to examine closely every new thought, phrase, and word on the page. To be a critical thinker, follow these steps:

1. **Analyze a reading by breaking it down into smaller parts.**
   To illustrate, if you're asked to read a ten-page article for psychology class, try to break it up in logical sections or idea chunks. Then take each chunk and consider it separately.

2. **Summarize the main point—the most important idea—of the reading.**
   Now that you've had a chance to practice summarizing, continue to ask yourself after every reading, "How would I state the main point in one sentence?"

3. **Evaluate the reading based on your analysis.**
   When you evaluate, ask yourself, "How do I feel about what I've read? Do I agree or disagree?" Think of the last movie you saw or book you read. Did you like it? Did you ask yourself "why" or "why not"? Did you share your reaction with a friend? Were you surprised to find that your friend's reaction was different?

In order to think critically about what you are reading, you need to go beyond understanding the main points and summarizing. You need to read between the lines so that you can then decide if you agree or disagree with what you have read.

To get a better idea of the critical thinking process, take a third look at the paragraphs from the physics text (pp. 10–11). You previously analyzed the writer's content by examining each paragraph separately. You completed the second step in critical thinking when you summarized the writing. Now after rereading the text excerpts and the student summary, ask yourself, "What does the writer want the reader to think?" Take the last critical thinking step by asking yourself, "Do I agree with the paragraphs? Why or why not?"

Practice 1.7 Write a brief evaluation of the paragraphs from the physics text.

_____

_____

_____

◆ ◆ ◆

If you continue to work on the steps involved in active reading and critical thinking, you'll be rewarded with a better understanding and more of a sense of control rather than being confused by what you read. Finally, mastering the process of critical thinking will allow you to participate thoughtfully in writings, discussions, and public forums in your college, career, and community life.

GUIDELINES FOR CONNECTING READING AND WRITING

So far in this chapter, the focus has been on reading, thinking, and the **private writing** you engage in to be an active reader. Private writing includes annotating, summarizing, and responding in a journal; it is not meant to be shared with a reading audience and is for your own use only, unless your instructor asks to see it. But your success as a writer in college and in your career will depend on your ability to compose **public writing**—the college essays, memos, reports, business letters, and other kinds of writing meant to be read by a specific audience.

To help you connect your reading and thinking about the writings of others with the public writing you'll be doing, this text offers you a set of principles called _keys_—the tools you can use to examine and evaluate what you read, and later what you write. Much as a carpenter uses hammer, saw, and nails to build a sturdy house, you will be using the following five keys to build your confidence and ability as a college reader, critical thinker, and writer: PURPOSE, FOCUS, MATERIAL, STRUCTURE, and STYLE. For now the keys will be introduced and defined briefly, but in future chapters you'll be examining them in greater detail. In the same way you check your pockets or purse to make sure you have your house keys or car keys, get in the habit of mentally reviewing the five keys whenever you read the writings of others or engage in public writing.

Purpose

Your reading **audience** is comprised of those who respond to your words on paper or on a computer screen in much the same way that an audience sits in a darkened movie theater or concert hall and responds to the performance.

Purpose refers to a writer's primary goal in writing for a particular audience of readers. As a writer, you will want to do one of the following:

- Express

- Inform

- Persuade

Although a writer often has more than one purpose, only one stands out as primary or most important for any piece of writing.

If you're writing a letter to complain about faulty merchandise you've purchased, you're certainly expressing yourself (and your irritation, perhaps!); you're informing your audience (in this case the company that sold you the product); but above all, you want to persuade this audience to offer you a refund.

Practice 1.8 Reread Ji Yeon Mary Yufill's essay beginning on page 5. Identify the writer's primary purpose in the following space.

_____

_____

◆ ◆ ◆

Focus

Focus refers to a writer's choice of a subject and the main point being made about that subject. Let's take that same complaint letter. Your subject is a household appliance you recently bought, and the main point you are making to your reader is that the appliance did not perform as you expected.

Practice 1.9 Review Yufill's essay again, this time searching the writing for its subject and main point. In the following space, write Yufill's focus in your own words.

_____

_____

◆ ◆ ◆

Material

Material refers to the content of a piece of writing and may include details, facts, and supporting evidence. A writer's material can be drawn from a variety of sources: personal experience, observation, imagination, interviews, outside readings, or research. For instance, in your letter of complaint, you should mention every detail and fact that will persuade your reader: the date you bought the appliance, the nature of your conversation with the salesperson, how many times you've used the merchandise, and any other information that will convince the reader that you should get a refund.

Practice 1.10 Scan Yufill's essay, this time writing down three or more examples of the material that this writer employs.

_____

_____

_____

◆ ◆ ◆

Structure

The **structure** of a text is the writer's arrangement of the material to support the main point clearly and completely. For instance, when you sit down to put all your evidence about your kitchen appliance in your letter, you will decide which details to put first, second, third, and so forth. At some point you'll come up with a logical way of ordering all information clearly so that the reader is never confused.

Practice 1.11 Return to Yufill's essay, this time focusing on the writer's "ordering" of material. Make a brief list of this order in the following space.

_____

_____

_____

◆ ◆ ◆

Style

The **style** involves three separate parts:

- First, style refers to the way a writer puts words together to form sentences and then groups of sentences to form longer passages. Your style communicates your own unique signature. For example, once you've sketched out the information you want to include in your letter and you have an idea of the organization you want to use, you need to think about those specific words and phrases that would be most effective in getting your point across.

- Second, style refers to the "correctness" of a piece of writing. To illustrate, before you mail your complaint letter, you'll want to **proofread,** or check to see that you've used complete sentences as well as grammatically correct constructions, punctuation, and spelling. For help with proofreading for correctness, consult your handbook section of this text (pp. 413–468).

- Third, style involves conforming to **format,** or the proper appearance of a piece of a finished writing. For instance, in the case of your letter, you should check for appropriate letter margins, tabs, and spacing.

Practice 1.12   Reread Yufill's essay, focusing this time on her sentence structure and variety and her word choice. In the following space, write one or two memorable phrases or sentences and try to explain briefly why you chose them.

_____

_____

◆ ◆ ◆

To observe how all five "keys" come together to connect writer with reader, examine the following complaint letter—a letter written about a frustrating experience with faulty merchandise. Like many college students faced with writing assignments, you might say to yourself, "I know what I want to say. I just have trouble making my reader understand." However, if you were to use the five keys to unlock a method for getting these ideas on paper and communicating them clearly to your intended audience, the following letter might result.

MODEL WITH KEY QUESTIONS

When Matt Cirillo and Cindy Sharp purchased a coffeemaker that proved defective, they called the store. The customer service representative asked them to write a complaint letter.

A LETTER OF COMPLAINT
Matt Cirillo and Cindy Sharp

Matt Cirillo and Cindy Sharp are roommates who wanted to voice their disappointment with a product they had recently purchased. They found that getting their ideas on paper was easier than they had thought it would be and that collaborating on their writing was fun. Matt has plans to become a computer animator, and Cindy hopes to become a teacher for the deaf.

January 29, 1998

Dear Customer Service Representative:

1 We believe we are valued customers of yours. Both of us have purchased items from your department store in the past. We want to tell you about some faulty merchandise we recently bought from you in the hope that you will grant us a refund of our money or a cash credit.

2 Two weeks ago, January 15, we purchased from Rick, a salesperson on your staff, a Wilson coffeemaker, Model XJ. When we told Rick that we were searching for a fairly inexpensive yet dependable coffeemaker, he suggested several possible brands and models, describing the features of each. We decided on the Wilson coffeemaker even though it was a little more expensive—we really liked the automatic timer feature since this would allow us to "program" our coffee the night before for a particular time early the next morning. We paid with a credit card and happily took our new kitchen appliance home.

3 We were quite excited to test out our new coffeemaker, so that same evening we set the automatic timer, carefully following the instructions on the manual. Unfortunately, this feature did not work. When we came into the kitchen early the following morning, there was no fresh brewed coffee but instead an empty glass coffeepot. Not giving up, we made the coffee without the automatic timer, and the machine worked well.

4 Since that first day, we have each reread the manual several times, checking to make sure we were following directions. The results have been the same: we have never been able to get the automatic timer feature to work for us. Although the coffeemaker works fine otherwise, we had looked forward to this feature and had been willing to spend more to get it. Because the automatic timer does not seem to work with this particular machine, we'd rather have a cheaper model.

5 We would appreciate it if you would consider our request for a refund or credit. To expedite this process, we're enclosing in this letter the credit card receipt and our home and work phone numbers.

Sincerely,

Matt Cirillo
Cindy Sharp

Now take a look at the following set of "key" questions to go with the letter you've just read. These are similar to questions you'll encounter throughout this text after each student writing sample. The key questions challenge you

to analyze and evaluate what you've read by examining the five keys—
PURPOSE, FOCUS, MATERIAL, STRUCTURE, and STYLE—to decide
whether the writers have effectively communicated with their audience. In the
course of your close examination of all student and professional readings in
this text, use the keys to discover what strategies writers use for particular
situations. In the process of reading the writing of others, you'll discover what
does and doesn't work for writers. Then when you turn to your own writing assignments, you'll have practice and confidence in using the keys as your tools
for successful writing.

 ## KEY QUESTIONS

1. **PURPOSE** Where in the letter do the writers state the primary goal or aim

   of the writing? _____

   _____

2. **FOCUS** Can you state in your own words what subject and what main point

   about that subject the writers are making? _____

   _____

3. **MATERIAL** What kinds of information or detail do the writers offer?

   _____

   _____

4. **STRUCTURE** Can you explain how the letter is organized?

   _____

   _____

5. **STYLE** Write down any words or phrases that stand out as especially effec-

   tive in getting across the writers' primary goal. _____

   _____

   _____

As you work through the reading and writing assignments in this text, remember that every writer presented here faced a blank page at one time. These writers had to decide on their primary purpose, how to focus on a subject and stay focused, what details, facts, and other material to use, how to organize this material effectively, and finally, which specific language and format would get their point and purpose across most successfully. Also remember the reading/writing connection—as a college student embarking on many semesters of challenging classes, the more essays you read, analyze, discuss, and think about using the keys, the better equipped you'll be as a thinker and writer.

JOURNAL WRITING: THE READING LOG

Journal writing, one of the tips for active reading mentioned earlier, allows you to reflect and respond by writing about what you've read. Often "for your eyes only" unless your instructor tells you otherwise, journal writing frees you from worrying about your writing as a finished product.

While a journal may take many forms, creating a **reading log** will help you pinpoint meaningful passages from a reading and then question and evaluate these passages. Students who consistently keep reading logs in their journals find that they have more detailed information to share and a better understanding of the material when they are asked to complete a written assignment. In addition, these students learn more and perform at a higher level academically because their reading logs lead them to greater understanding of their textbooks and classroom lectures and activities.

1. To set up your reading log, simply make two columns by drawing a line down the middle of your paper. (If you prefer to use the computer, click on "Help" in your word-processing program or refer to your program manual and follow the instructions for "columns.") In the left column, you will be recording brief **direct quotes,** passages from the text copied word for word that you want to explore further, along with their page numbers. In the right column write your reaction to the specific quote on the left column. Include here summaries, feelings, connections, evaluations, opinions, and especially, questions—any comments in your own words that help you to "re-see" part or all of the reading. To see how a reading log might look, examine a portion of the student log shown here for a college textbook excerpt entitled "American Health, Then and Now" (pp. 26–30).

    Read this excerpt and respond to it in your reading log. If you prefer, choose a reading from one of your own college textbooks for your first reading log entry.

Text	Reaction
1. "Your habits matter." (30)	1. What habits do I have that could be harmful to my health?
2. "Introduction of wonder drugs" (27)	2. Ask instructor if the wonder drugs are those listed on figure 1 - insulin, sulfa, penicillin, anti - TB - or if there are others.
3. "For several years, life expectancy rates no longer improved" (27)	3. This is surprising-why not, especially with open-heart surgery, etc.?!
4. "Less fat in the diet, more exercise, and reduction in tobacco use" (27)	4. Wonder which one has the greatest impact on decline in death rates-I would guess less fat, but not sure.

2. In another journal entry, explore where, how, and when you like to read and write. Do you have a special place or scheduled time? A particular comfortable chair for reading or a favorite pen or paper for writing? Writer Louise Erdrich reports that she used to write with her free hand while holding a child in her other arm. Another writer, Truman Capote, confided that he was a "completely horizontal author," who must be lying down in order to think and write. How about you?

USING THE COMPUTER FOR COLLEGE READING AND WRITING

1. Just about every word-processing program includes a built-in *help* feature—the online user's manual. Find and click on the word "help" or a "?" on your screen (or, if you're working in a computer lab, ask a technician to help you). Like an owner's manual, you will find an "index" that will help you locate information and step-by-step instructions on specific features, as well as demonstrations and examples. This textbook will offer you suggestions on using a word-processing program to enhance your writing; the words to look up in an online help feature's index will appear in *italics*. Getting familiar with your word processor's "help" feature now will make it easier to use those suggestions later.

continued

USING THE COMPUTER FOR COLLEGE READING AND WRITING   *continued*

....

2. You may have access to a computer at home and already know the many ways computers can help you in reading and writing. However, if you don't have your own computer, you can take advantage of computers on your campus. Most often this is a free service. Find out the location of your campus computer labs (rooms where students can work on computers and receive help with computing questions) as well as their operating hours, when tutors and other technical support staff are available to help you, and what you need to bring. Then drop by and get some "hands-on" experience in the form of a word-processing tutorial from the lab staff, or practice with a self-guided tutorial included with most popular word-processing programs. Record your findings in the following space:

Lab location _____

Hours _____

Phone for campus computer information _____

OPTIONS FOR WRITING

Many of the following writing assignments ask you to reflect on your reading habits and write about them. As with all of the Options for Writing in this text, you may be directed by your instructor to respond to a particular one, or you may be able to choose the option that most appeals to you. When you have made your decision, take a moment to read the interview with Annie Dillard (p. 24) to explore the way one writer gathers her material and sets about preparing to write. Notice that for Dillard, the process of writing involves active reading and critical thinking. Her writing does not happen all at once but rather is broken down into separate steps. To help you get started, the Options for Writing will always include a few brief tips, but don't forget that your instructor and your fellow students can be excellent sources for additional help.

1. Write a personal reading history. Some people love to read while others avoid it. How about you? You may belong to a family or culture that emphasizes oral storytelling rather than the printed text. Maybe you remember being read to as a child, or listening to stories, poems, or songs on cassette. Per-

haps you now read to your own children. List on paper as many different examples of your activities relating to reading, writing, and language as you can remember. Include reading materials in your home and work environment, in both your native and nonnative languages. One student reports, "I found out that although I dislike reading, I read every day on the job because as a doorman at a club, I have to check people's IDs." Also take notes on your attitude and that of other family members toward reading and writing. When you feel you have enough material on paper, try to arrange this information to introduce yourself and your reading history to another student or to your instructor. Use specific book and story titles that you remember.

2. Write about a particular experience with reading. Many of us can remember when reading a particular novel, magazine article, or letter from a friend or loved one became so consuming that we almost forgot time and place—we were totally engrossed in what we were reading. A student confides, "My girlfriend's letters gave me the heart to finish boot camp." Think back to such a time and then take notes, getting down as much detail as you can remember about the event. Where were you sitting? Was anyone else in the room during this time? What was the reading material that so involved you? Do you remember the color of the book cover or the pages themselves? If it was a letter, what did the stationery look like? When you feel that you have enough detail to communicate this clearly to your reader, arrange the details in a clear order.

3. In "Let's Tell the Story of All America's Cultures" (p. 5), Yufill mentions certain leaders she read about and others she learned about through her own research: Lewis and Clark, Abraham Lincoln, Daniel Boone, Andrew Carnegie, Benjamin Frankin, Ah Bing, Frederick Douglass, W.E.B. Du Bois, and Nat Turner. Look up any one of these leaders in an encyclopedia in your college or local library. Read about your subject using active reading strategies and then write a summary of what you read.

4. Read "American Health, Then and Now" (p. 26). Imagining that your audience is a group of classmates in a health class, write a summary of this reading to share with your class.

¶ 5. Write about your personal reading plan. Now that you are a college student, you may notice that your textbooks are full of fairly complicated information. This type of reading requires greater concentration and critical thinking on your part. Complete the first journal activity on p. 20. Take notes about how college has affected your reading—get as much information on paper as you can. Ask yourself how your textbooks differ from books that you're used to reading, what information you're expected to retain from what you've read, what schedule you've made for yourself to make sure you have time to read, how you handle distractions, which tips for active reading you currently follow and which you intend to try. When you feel you have enough information to explain your plan for successful college reading, organize this information in a logical pattern.

✏ RESPONDING TO WRITING

Becoming an active reader involves responding to what you are reading. Throughout this course, you will be reacting to your own writing, writings of other students, and the work of professional writers. For some practice in responding, read the following interview and then respond to it by using the Guidelines for Active Reading (p. 8). Test the validity of Annie Dillard's comments by trying her strategy for yourself. In this interview Dillard, a writing teacher and author of numerous books and essays, talks with Elizabeth Cowan, a college English instructor. (The names of both interview participants have been abbreviated.)

EC: How did the book [*Pilgrim at Tinker Creek*] come about?

AD: I read a lot. After I got out of college, I settled down to educate myself. I read books and read books. Then I started keeping notes on my reading, because like any normal human being I can't remember what I read. So I started taking notes on my reading in little spiral notebooks.

EC: What exactly would you put in those notebooks from the books?

AD: Well, I would put interesting facts. I would put down quotations I liked. And I would also put my own observations down in writing. . . .

EC: So, this reading was the first stage of your writing *Pilgrim at Tinker Creek*?

AD: . . . What I was doing was gathering facts; when you gather enough facts, you will start to have ideas about those facts. When you have material, you will automatically shape. The facts in this case were just like the potter's clay. They were material. You can't do art without material. It turns out that when you have a lot of material, you just automatically sort of organize it. . . . I copied all the information from the journals which I thought would be pertinent—which was just about everything. . . . I copied all these on four-by-six index cards. . . .

EC: What did you do with these cards?

AD: Then I put them into piles—which anyone can do. You know, if you think about writing a book, you think it is overwhelming. But actually you break it down into tiny tasks that any moron could do. A pile of index cards divides itself into categories. . . .

EC: And then . . .

AD: The question was how in the hell to write about it! I went back to the good nature books that I had read. And I analyzed them. I wrote outlines of whole books—outlines of chapters—so that I could see their structure. And I copied down their transitional sentences or their main sentences or their closing sentences or their lead sentences. I especially paid attention to how these writers made transitions between paragraphs and scenes. . . .

EC: And after analyzing these books?

AD: Then I put all these index cards into a filing cabinet, arranged by chapter, and started writing. . . . And, of course, I would immediately get carried away. The chapter would just develop itself. In fact, the stuff on the index cards actually occupied only about a quarter of the material of the chapter. But the cards anchored, gave me something to start with, a direction to go in. I had an outline. . . . And almost instantly [I would] depart from the outline. "Oh, shoot, I have departed from the outline once again!". . . . You are always going back and forth between the outline and the writing, bringing them closer together, or just throwing out the outline and making a new one.

Now that you have read this interview, in which Dillard clearly connects her reading with her writing activities, answer the following questions, reviewing this chapter's main points if necessary.

1. Name one fact you learned about Dillard from the background information you previewed. _____

_____

2. Look up the meaning of the word *pertinent* in a dictionary. Write the meaning in your own words. _____

_____

3. Write a contextual definition of *transitional*. _____

_____

4. Annotate the interview.

5. Summarize Dillard's most important ideas in no more than three sentences._____

_____

_____

6. Respond in your journal.

7. To evaluate Dillard's strategies, test them by choosing an Option for Writing for this chapter. Do the following as you work through the writing assignment:

- Take some notes in your journal to "gather facts," as Dillard recommends, to serve as your material for the writing assignment.

- Organize this material by sorting similar ideas and points and putting these together. Refer to this sorted list as you are writing your first version of the assignment.

- Examine your writing in light of the five keys (p. 14) and implement any changes you feel will improve what you've written.

 **READING AND ADDITIONAL ACTIVITIES**

The following reading is taken from a current health textbook, *Healthy for Life,* written by Bryan Williams and Sharon Knight. As you read the selection, try to use the strategies for active reading and critical thinking discussed throughout this chapter.

American Health, Then and Now

Bryan Williams and Sharon Knight

1 During the past century, life expectancy has risen because of improvements in public health, drugs and medical technology, and better lifestyle. Still, a great many Americans are in ill health, and many suffer premature deaths—young people principally from injuries and violence, adults from cancer and heart disease—most of which are preventable by lifestyle changes. The lesson is: your habits matter.

2 More than a century ago, people were pretty much obliged to look after their own health, because the "health authorities" themselves were not much more knowledgeable. Then came the revolutions that have led to modern medicine.

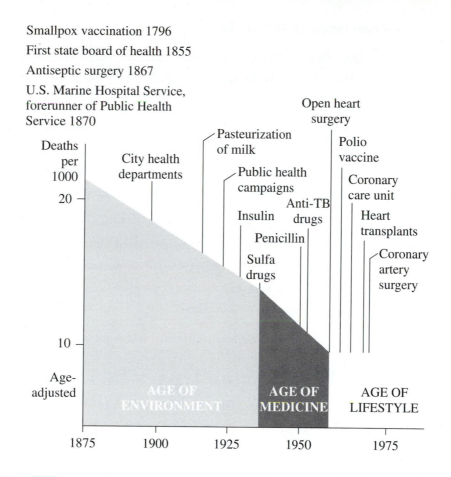

Smallpox vaccination 1796

First state board of health 1855

Antiseptic surgery 1867

U.S. Marine Hospital Service, forerunner of Public Health Service 1870

Figure 1

One hundred years of health advancement

Physician Donald Vickery describes three stages of health advancement in the United States that took place in the 100 years between 1885 and 1985:

- In stage 1, the *Age of Environment* (approximately 1875–1935), 70% of the decline in the death rate occurred *before* the introduction of wonder drugs and organ transplants—the result of improvements in the environment and public health policy.
- In stage 2, the *Age of Medicine* (approximately 1935–1955), there was further progress resulting from antibiotics and other drugs.
- In stage 3, the *Age of Lifestyle* (approximately 1955–present), for several years life-expectancy rates no longer improved, despite the introduction of many high-tech innovations such as open-heart surgery. Then, in the early 1970s, death rates began to decline again as the effects of lifestyle programs took hold, with their emphasis on less fat in the diet, more exercise, and reduction in tobacco use.

From Public Health to Lifestyle

3   Over the past 100 years or so, death rates have declined through three stages, according to Donald M. Vickery (see Figure 1, p. 27.).

* *Age of Environment—Improved public health:* From about 1885 until the 1930s, public health policies and improvements in the environment dramatically lowered death rates, especially those for infant mortality. During this period, city health departments were established, city water supplies were cleaned up, milk became pasteurized, and public health campaigns were introduced.

* *Age of Medicine—Improved drugs and technology:* In the 1930s, sulfa drugs, penicillin, and other antibiotics were introduced, further accelerating the drop in death rates. However, in the early 1950s, life-expectancy rates stopped increasing, even though many high-tech innovations—open-heart surgery, polio vaccine, and so on—continued to be introduced.

* *Age of Lifestyle—Better living habits:* It was not until the 1970s that life-expectancy rates began to increase again. This coincided with attempts to deal with what are called **lifestyle disorders**—ill health brought about by individuals' behavior patterns, such as those involving eating, safety, and drug use.

4   Today we are still living in the Age of Lifestyle. Unfortunately, people find lifestyle a lot less fascinating than medical wizardry. "We're so in love with the chrome and glitter of high-tech medicine," says medical-ethics consultant Bruce Hilton, "we forget to ask how the patient got this way. . . . How many people remember that Barney Clark, the first artificial-heart patient, whose bravery we all admired, had been a lifelong chain smoker?"

Is *Everyone* Sick?

5   Where have these ages of health advancement brought us today? A researcher on the staff of former U.S. surgeon general C. Everett Koop added up the numbers of Americans suffering from various diseases. He found, according to Koop, "that the total exceeded by a good measure *the entire population of the United States*" (our emphasis added). More remarkable, this total was for physical ailments only. It did not include the estimated 30 million with mental illnesses and psychiatric disorders, Koop says.

6   It should not be surprising, therefore, that the research assistant concluded that pretty "near everyone in this country is sick!" Some researchers might object that many of the people measured had multiple disorders that were counted singly. Even so, the great majority of Americans, says Koop, "are victims of chronic, crippling, or incapacitating diseases ranging from alcoholism to Alzheimer's. Sexually transmitted diseases alone have infected 40 million." (**Chronic** means of long duration or recurring, as opposed to an **acute** disorder, which is of short duration.)

7   However one may argue about numbers, the news from the health front is not good. For instance, Koop was also part of a commission of physicians and educators looking into what schools and communities might do to improve adolescent health. The panel concluded that the United States is raising a generation of adolescents plagued by pregnancies, illegal drug use, suicide, and violence. Although you might not consider pregnancies, drunkenness, arrests, and homicides parts of the usual definition of ill health, they are indicative of frightening trends—signs of massive declines in the quality of American life.

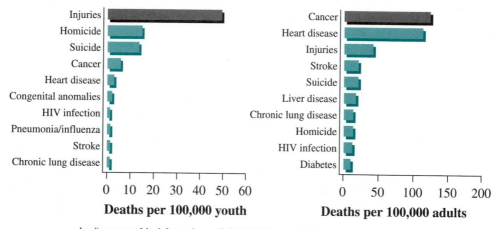

Leading causes of death for youth ages 15–24 (in 1987)   Leading causes of death for adults ages 25–64 (in 1987)

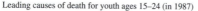

Figure 2

Leading causes of death for youth and adults

The Importance of Prevention

8   It should be clear by now that a lot of ill health is *preventable.* Consider the age group you are in, which most likely is either ages 15–24 (adolescents and young adults) or ages 25–64 (adults).

- *Adolescents and young adults:* There are two categories of preventable health problems found among people between the ages of 15 and 24.

  The first category consists of *injuries and violence* that kill and disable them while they are still young.

  The second category consists of *emerging lifestyles,* such as those having to do with diet, physical activity, use of alcohol and other drugs, safety, tobacco use, and sexual behavior. These are important because they affect one's health many years later.

- *Adults:* Many of the principle areas of ill health for people between the ages of 25 and 64 are also preventable, in whole or in part through changes in lifestyle, such as tobacco and alcohol use, diet, exercise, and safety.

  For adults in this age group, the leading causes of death are cancer and heart disease. Cancer is actually not one but many diseases, the significant ones being lung cancer, cancers of the colon and rectum, breast cancer, cervical cancer, and cancer of the mouth and throat. Other leading causes of death are heart disease and stroke (blood clot in the brain), and injuries, as from car crashes. (Refer back to Figure 2, p. 29.)

Health and Personal Responsibility

9   No doubt you know of someone who avoided all the standard advice for a healthy life and lived to a ripe old age. Or, conversely, you know someone who ate and did all the right things and still developed a severe illness. We need, then, to point out a fundamental fact: health-promoting habits *are not guarantees.* As health writer Jane Brody points out, "they do not offer 100% protection, like a vaccine against a disease. Good habits merely weight the odds in one's favor."

10   Physician Gary Williams, director of medical sciences at the American Health Foundation, a health research organization, has ranked the value of various recommendations in preventing particular illnesses, based on thousands of studies. Although his analysis is not all-inclusive, it does show that lifestyle matters do make a difference.

11   The lesson is clear: *Your habits matter.* The lifestyle choices you make today could have a tremendous influence on the quality of your life, both now and later.

QUESTIONS ON CONTENT

1. Which of the three stages of health advancement in the United States are we living in now? _____

    _____

2. What health problems plague adolescents in the United States according to a commission of physicians and educators? _____

    _____

    _____

3. What are the leading causes of death for people between the ages of 25 and 64? _____

    _____

4. Find and underline the definitions given in the text for *chronic* and *acute*. Think of an example for each kind of disorder. _____

    _____

    _____

QUESTIONS ON STRATEGY

1. Describe the technique the writers use to get your attention in the first paragraph._____

    _____

2. Figure 1 is accompanied by a boxed explanation. Does this information help you to understand the figure? How? _____

    _____

3. Why do you think the writers omit any boxed explanation for Figure 2?

_____

4. What strategy have the writers used to break down the information into

separate sections? _____

_____

5. Skim the entire reading, looking for direct quotes from individuals. How

many different quotes do you find? _____ Why do you think the

writers have included these comments?_____

_____

CRITICAL THINKING IN CONNECTING TEXTS

You've seen how reading shaped the perceptions and the writing of student Ji Yeon Mary Yufill in her essay on p. 5. Yufill began to question and evaluate her early textbooks and she discovered misrepresentation and omission of certain truths. Annie Dillard reports in her interview (p. 24) that she "settled down to educate myself" by engaging in active reading.

With a partner or in a small group, work together to draw up a list of misconceptions, false statements, or questionable comments that you or others in your group have read. Consider your past reading in newspapers, magazines, books, posters, advertisements, and other printed material as well as electronic material. If time permits, share your findings with the rest of the class. Take notes and keep them; they might serve as material for a future essay.

**For more writing resources, be sure to see the
Longman English Pages Website at
http://longman.awl.com/englishpages**

Defining the Essay and the Composing Process

Essay: A short literary composition dealing with its subject . . . and, usually, expressive of the author's outlook and personality.

—*Webster's* New World Dictionary

Preview

In this chapter you will learn
► to identify the parts of the college essay—introduction, thesis, body paragraphs, conclusion
► to recognize the stages of the composing process: discovering, drafting, revising, polishing, and responding
► to relate the five "keys"—PURPOSE, FOCUS, MATERIAL, STRUCTURE, and STYLE—to the essay's parts and to the composing process

How do the types of writing mentioned in Chapter 1—annotating, note-taking, summarizing, and journal writing—differ from a type of writing found in a college essay? The types of writings discussed in Chapter 1 are private responses designed not for communication with other readers but as activities to help you with active reading. The essay, in contrast, is designed as a public writing, one meant to be shared with an audience of readers. If you think about it, you're already experienced in public writing. Every time you write a note or memo, register a complaint, dash off an E-mail, or send out an invitation, you write for an audience. Just as each of these public writings has specific characteristics, so has the essay.

CHARACTERISTICS OF THE ESSAY

An **essay** is made up of a number of paragraphs that develop and support a single idea, impression, or point. Although the term *essay* may be used to refer in general to writing that explores a topic or presents factual information, in the context of most college writing, *essay* refers to a composition that is carefully structured and contains particular parts that work together to communicate the writer's main ideas. Because readers want to see material in manageable portions, writers use **paragraphs,** or several sentences that together develop one thought. The essay can be divided into parts based on the function of its paragraphs.

To observe an essay and its parts, take a look at the following essay by the late Arthur Ashe, keeping in mind that no two essays are exactly alike. Ashe, an American tennis champion, became famous as the first African-American male to win both Wimbledon and the U.S. Open tournaments.

A Black Athlete Looks at Education

Arthur Ashe

THESIS — 1

INTRODUCTION

Since my sophomore year at UCLA, I have become convinced that we blacks spend too much time on the playing fields and too little time in the libraries. Consider these facts: for the major professional sports of hockey, football, basketball, baseball, golf, tennis, and boxing, there are roughly only 3170 major league positions available (attributing 200 positions to golf, 200 to tennis and 100 to boxing). And the annual turnover is small.

BODY PARAGRAPHS

2

There must be some way to assure that those who try but don't make it to pro sports won't wind up on street corners or in unemployment lines. Unfortunately, our most widely recognized role models are athletes or entertainers—"runnin'," and "jumpin'" and singin'" and dancin'."

3

Our greatest heroes of the century have been athletes—Jack Johnson, Joe Louis, Muhammad Ali. Racial and economic discrimination forced us to channel our energies into athletics and entertainment. These were the ways out of the ghetto, the ways to get that Cadillac, those regular shoes, that cashmere sport coat.

4   Somehow, parents must instill a desire for learning alongside the desire to be Walt Frazier. Why not start by sending black professional athletes into high schools to explain the facts of life?

5   I have often addressed high school audiences and my message is always the same: "For every hour you spend on the athletic field, spend two in the library. Even if you make it as a pro athlete, your career will be over by the time you are 35. You will need that diploma."

BODY PARAGRAPHS Continued

6   Have these pro athletes explain what happens if you break a leg, get a sore arm, have one bad year or don't make the cut for five or six tournaments. Explain to them the star system, wherein for every star earning millions there are six or seven others making $15,000 or $20,000 or $30,000. Invite a bench-warmer or a guy who didn't make it. Ask him if he sleeps every night. Ask him whether he was graduated. Ask him what he would do if he became disabled tomorrow. Ask him where his old high school athletic buddies are.

7   We have been on the same roads—sports and entertainment—too long. We need to pull over, fill up at the library and speed away to Congress and the Supreme Court, the unions and the business world.

CONCLUSION

8   I'll never forget how proud my grandmother was when I graduated from UCLA. Never mind the Davis Cup. Never mind the Wimbledon title. To this day, she still doesn't know what those names mean. What mattered to her was that of her more than thirty children and grandchildren, I was the first to be graduated from college, and a famous college at that. Somehow, that made up for all those floors she scrubbed all those years.

Notice that Ashe's essay contains the following parts:

- **Thesis**
  This statement, usually one sentence, is often found within the essay's first paragraph and contains the main point, idea, or opinion the writer wants to convey about a subject along with his or her attitude toward the subject.

  Ashe jumps right into his thesis with his first sentence. The main idea of his essay is that "we blacks spend too much time on the playing fields and too little time in the libraries."

- **Introduction**
  This beginning part of the essay approaches the subject and captures the interest of the audience.

  When Ashe states, "I have become convinced . . ." in paragraph 1 of his essay, he is presenting a signal to his readers about his purpose: to convince his audience of his main point.

- **Body paragraphs**
  These paragraphs form the middle of the essay and develop the writer's thesis through the use of details, examples, and evidence from a variety of sources.

  Ashe's body paragraphs include information he recalls from his past as athlete, student, and later pro tennis player and guest speaker. In addition, his body paragraphs contain details and facts that he has researched. Every piece of information in Ashe's body paragraphs relates clearly to his thesis.

- **Conclusion**
  At the end of the essay, this closing paragraph (or sometimes paragraphs) serves to emphasize the author's thesis, offer closure, and tie the contents of the essay together.

In a moving and persuasive closing, Ashe emphasizes his thesis and his overall purpose by telling the audience about his own background. The information he shares in the conclusion serves as evidence that his college degree mattered more to him and to his grandmother than a much-sought-after tennis championship. Ashe's final image of his grandmother scrubbing floors is a powerful one with which to conclude the essay.

Even though essays can vary tremendously in length and content, they will always share the following parts: introduction, thesis, body paragraphs, and conclusion. Now that you are familiar with the basic essay format, read the following student model and see if you can identify the parts of a college essay.

MODEL WITH KEY QUESTIONS

Douglas Cwiak wrote the following essay for his college English class; a few months later, he submitted the essay to a local newspaper. "Matilda" was subsequently published in the October 31, 1996, issue of *The Beach Reporter,* a California newspaper with a readership of approximately 61,000 people.

MATILDA
Douglas W. Cwiak

In a conference with his instructor on the first day of his writing class, Douglas Cwiak revealed his fear of writing and of failing in the class. Doug confided that after being diagnosed as dyslexic, he had given up on school for several years. At the end of the semester, he shared his new outlook on the composing process this way: "I have fallen in love with writing and I write every day now." Doug has been accepted in UCLA's film school and hopes to work in the film industry as a writer or cinematographer.

1   Many people have owned a dog at sometime in their lives. I have owned many: Labradors, Irish setters and a German shepherd. All my dogs have been what I consider normal. At least, that was until Matilda entered my life. Matilda is a one-year-old female pug. What sets her apart from other dogs are her unconventional personality traits. She is simply not a normal dog.

2   Her dining habits go far beyond anything that I have seen. A meal begins with Matilda standing in the corner of the room like a child who has just been punished. Then as her food bowl is placed in its proper place, she begins a ritual dance. It commences with one or two steps toward the bowl. Then comes a pause. What follows can only be described as pure chaos: a mad dash to the bedroom followed by two perfectly executed laps around the dining room table. Finally she performs a slide across the kitchen floor that would make any baseball player envious, right up to her bowl. She then calmly eats her meal.

3   For Matilda, playing is not just for fun. It is the reason for her existence. A simple game of tug of war becomes an epic battle of wits. She with one end of the rope in her mouth and I with the other end in my hand, both maneuver to gain the advantage. Her tactics range from violently shaking her head back and forth, attempting to tear the rope from my hands to a simple whimper for sympathy. Then when she has won the battle, she ceremoniously parades through the house with the rope dangling from her mouth and head held high. Needless to say, she has never lost a game of tug of war.

4   After the food has been served and the battles won, sleep is Matilda's last activity of the day. She struggles to keep her eyes open as she patiently waits for me to shuffle off to bed. As she makes the brief journey to the bedroom, she stops to retrieve her most treasured toy—a yellow and purple stuffed dinosaur. Once in bed she performs a fifteen-minute search for the most comfortable spot. This spot is always in the same place, under the covers with her head just peering out. As she slips into a deep trance-like sleep, something happens that can only be appreciated through

personal experience. From this little dog comes an earth-shattering snore. This snore, which sometimes awakens neighbors, is continuous throughout the night.

5   Most dogs lead their lives quietly performing their daily tasks and always wishing for more. Matilda, on the other hand, lives her life with an excitement and quest that few dogs, let alone humans, could ever hope to achieve. For her, simple mundane tasks become wild new adventures while bedtime becomes a nap under a star-filled sky. What seems to me like strange and unusual behavior is really an extreme love of life and I believe, in the end, a much more natural behavior than my own.

 ## Key Questions

1. **PURPOSE** What is the writer's purpose in this essay (to express, inform, or persuade)?_____

   _____

2. **FOCUS** What main point is the writer making about his dog? Annotate the essay by finding and labeling Cwiak's thesis. Copy Cwiak's thesis here:

   _____

   _____

3. **MATERIAL** Where does the writer get his material? _____

   _____

4. **STRUCTURE** How has the writer ordered or arranged the material?

   _____

5. **STYLE** What makes this animal essay different from other essays about pets? Why does Cwiak end with the words, "a much more natural behavior than my own"? _____

   _____

GUIDELINES FOR WRITING THE ESSAY

By taking a second look at each of the parts of the essay and applying the five keys—PURPOSE, FOCUS, MATERIAL, STRUCTURE, and STYLE—introduced in Chapter 1, you can begin to establish some useful guidelines for writing essays.

Purpose

Use your essay's introduction to make your purpose in writing clear—to inform, express, or persuade. The introduction is in one sense a promise you are making to your reader. Think of your introduction as a pledge to discuss a particular topic from your own point of view. For example, Arthur Ashe's point of view in his essay (p. 34) is evident in the straightforward attitude he takes in the first three words of his second sentence: "Consider these facts." Then in the second paragraph, Ashe keeps his audience and purpose firmly in mind—he begins with a problem his audience is already familiar with: unemployment lines.

In your introduction, you can also briefly preview what is to come later in the essay, but first you need to grab your reader's attention. Think for a few minutes about how you begin reading a magazine or newspaper. What attracts your attention to an article and makes you keep reading? What qualities sometimes cause you to flip the page or to put aside the article? Chances are, like many readers, you look to the opening sentences or paragraphs. The introductory paragraph of your essay is your reader's first impression of your writing and your point of view. Readers of an essay often decide in the first paragraph whether they want to read further.

Practice 2.1 Think about an article, book, essay, poem, note from a friend, or any other type of writing that you have read recently. In the following space, note what it is that you remember reading and then describe the writer's purpose.

_____

_____

◆ ◆ ◆

Focus

In writing your thesis, focus on the main point you wish to make in the essay. Remember that this thesis is the seed from which your entire essay will grow as you give detailed support and elaboration in your body paragraphs. This focus usually begins near the end of the introductory paragraph (the first paragraph, in many cases). Notice that Douglas Cwiak places the thesis in his essay (p. 37) near the end of the first paragraph but Arthur Ashe places his thesis in the first sentence, (p. 34). Wherever you decide to place your thesis, check to make sure you have a clear main point. To get helpful feedback, you might try comparing your thesis with others as a class or in groups, rephrasing and refocusing as necessary.

In your essay's conclusion, you'll want to relate your comments clearly to your thesis; try to reinforce or emphasize the thesis in your concluding remarks. Notice that both Ashe and Cwiak connect their final comments with their original purpose and thesis. Ashe concludes by contrasting the insignificance of the Davis Cup and Wimbledon when compared with a college degree, thus restating his idea that athletes need to spend more time studying and less time worrying about their sport. Cwiak concludes by stating that "what seems to me like strange and unusual behavior is really an extreme love of life." The writer hearkens back to his thesis that Matilda is "not a normal dog" to conclude that she really possesses a "much more natural behavior than my own."

Practice 2.2 For practice in identifying an essay's thesis, read "Ambition" by Perri Klass (p. 54). Remember that although a writer's thesis is often found in the first or second paragraph, it can come anywhere in the essay. When you've found Klass's thesis, write it in the following space.

_____

_____

◆ ◆ ◆

Material

In developing body paragraphs, make sure you have enough material to convince the reader of your main point. You should evaluate all material to make sure that it is effective in supporting your main point. For example, Ashe has chosen specific examples as the material for paragraph 3. Many of us are familiar with at least some of these famous athletes, and the images of a "Cadillac" and a "cashmere sport coat" further support Ashe's main point. In paragraph 5, Ashe's material effectively establishes his authority on the subject: he has had personal experiences in these high schools, speaking before these students. To evaluate material for effectiveness, check each detail, example, or piece of evidence in your body paragraphs to make certain this material will convince the reader of your thesis. To be effective, your material must be sufficient and clearly related to your thesis. Your essay, like Ashe's and Cwiak's, should state your opinion or point of view in the thesis and then use the material in the body paragraphs to explain why you feel this way.

Practice 2.3 To gain more experience spotting material that is used to develop a thesis reread either Ashe's or Cwiak's essay, underlining all pieces of information you find. Look for any content—facts, examples, statistics, illustrations, comments from experts—that helps develop the writer's thesis.

◆ ◆ ◆

Structure

As you arrange the material for your body paragraphs, determine the most effective structure for communicating your main point. Experiment with different ways of arranging your details. Arthur Ashe's first or second draft of this final published essay probably ordered paragraphs and ideas differently. In the final version of his essay, you can see that Ashe has chosen a particular structure. For example, in his first two body paragraphs, he mentions first the unemployed, failed athletes. Then in the following body paragraphs, he mentions the athletes who became heroes. What if Ashe had reversed this order? The impact on his audience would not have been the same. Try out different arrangements for your body paragraphs to learn what structure works best for your essay.

Practice 2.4 Reread Douglas Cwiak's essay (p. 37), thinking about the order of the material. In the following space, list the writer's main points in the order that they appear.

1. _____

2. _____

3. _____

◆ ◆ ◆

Style

Examine your entire essay for considerations of style. For you as well as other student writers like Cwiak and professional writers like Ashe, checking for style involves three separate components:

- First, you'll want to look at the *way* you've written the essay rather than *what* you've written in it. To do this, examine your choice of specific words, phrases, and sentences, including how the sentences work together in a paragraph. Ask yourself what it is about your writing style, just like your speaking or clothing style, that makes it distinctive—that establishes your own signature or flair. For instance, Arthur Ashe's writing style is effective in making his point in paragraph 2 of his essay. The phrase "on street corners" works because it creates a powerful image for the reader. A distinctive style is at work again in paragraph 6, where Ashe uses repetition effectively to drive home a point. Ashe chooses to begin four sentences with the same two words—"Ask him . . ."—showing how a simple phrase can be used to reinforce a point. In paragraph 7, Ashe chooses images related to roads with the phrases "fill up at the library" and "speed away to Congress"—to make a point about career paths.

- Second, examine the grammar, spelling, punctuation, and word usage in your essay. This process includes **proofreading**—reading over every sentence and making corrections before presenting the essay to its intended audience.

- Finally make sure that your essay conforms to the accepted **manuscript format,** the layout of the essay with title, margins, and page numbers specified by your instructor.

These finishing touches will give you confidence that your essay presents your main point effectively and clearly, and that it presents you as a thoughtful and careful writer.

Practice 2.5 Reread Douglas Cwiak's essay (pp. 37–38), this time looking only at the writing style. Note in particular Cwiak's choice of words and phrases: in paragraph 2, he refers to Matilda's "dining habits," her "perfectly executed laps," and her "slide . . . that would make any baseball player envious." In paragraph 3, Cwiak uses the term "epic battle," and in paragraph 5 he refers to Matilda's "quest." In the space below, explain how you think these words work to communicate Cwiak's main point about Matilda to his audience.

_____

_____

◆ ◆ ◆

How can you create your own effective college essay? Just as Arthur Ashe could not have learned to play championship tennis without many hours logged on the courts, essays as good as Ashe's or Cwiak's are not usually the result of sudden, last-minute inspiration. Nor are they the products of a single effort. No doubt both Ashe and Cwiak wrote multiple drafts before arriving at the polished drafts you just read. They also shared their drafts with an editor, and perhaps with friends, for suggestions and ideas.

Just as there is no magical formula for athletic skill or musical ability, there is no secret trick to creating a memorable essay. However, many successful writers who began by struggling with writer's block have found that they can relax and enjoy writing if they accept it as a process with several stages.

AN OVERVIEW OF THE COMPOSING PROCESS

The **composing process** involves stages in taking an idea from its beginning to its final presentation, in writing, to a reading audience. The four broad stages in this process are *discovering, drafting, revising,* and *polishing,* in addition to a recurring stage, *responding.* Each stage will be discussed briefly in this section and then in greater detail in later chapters.

Writers and researchers agree that these are the stages most writers work through. The diagram shown below presents the stages of the composing process in visual terms. Notice that the diagram emphasizes writing as being **recursive**—having certain stages and activities that can be returned to or repeated. In other words, as you move forward in the composing process, you can also look back.

You can see from the diagram "The Composing Process" that writing does not necessarily proceed in neat, straightforward, or predictable steps. During the course of a writing assignment, for example, you may collect and sort your initial ideas, draft a section of the paper, return to an earlier stage to gather additional material, revise a part of the draft, and adjust your organization before moving on.

When you view writing in this flexible way, you need not feel trapped by the anxiety that sometimes comes when you face the blank screen or page: you don't have to worry if the words that finally come aren't "just right" the first time. By experimenting with and practicing the various stages of the composing process, you will come to realize that beginnings are just that—beginnings—which you can alter, improve, and refine.

The Composing Process
Devised by Wendy Wright, El Camino College

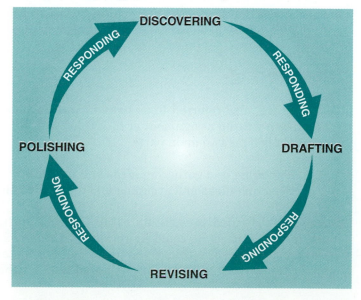

Keep in mind that these stages represent a model only. No two writers will follow exactly the same routines in working; the way you began your last writing project may not be the way you proceed with the next. Nor will you always perform the same activities in a particular order.

Practice 2.6   Close your eyes and visualize in your "mind's eye" the last time you took pen to paper or clicked on the computer to write. Try to remember what it was that you were attempting to write and how you began and then continued the process right through to a final draft. Write as many details as you can remember about that process.

_____

_____

_____

If you have a chance to share your responses with other class members, you'll quickly discover the unique nature of each writer's process.

◆ ◆ ◆

Knowing the *kinds* of activities that occur during the composing process and having a ready supply of techniques and strategies for dealing with them will help you to feel more in control when you write. You will be able to progress confidently through the many writing opportunities you will encounter.

To observe what writers do during each of the four stages of the composing process and as they respond to their writing, consider the following stages of composing. Douglas Cwiak experienced each of them in creating his essay (p. 37).

Discovering

Discovering, also referred to as **prewriting,** includes everything you do in relation to a writing assignment or task that leads to your first draft. The discovering stage has two main parts:

1. Exploring and gathering ideas and information
2. Selecting ideas and grouping and organizing the material

Once Cwiak decided to write an essay focusing on his pet, he gathered as much information as he could by recalling Matilda's habits. Sometimes, too, discovering can involve things you "don't do." For instance, you might refrain from writing a draft until you have allowed time for thought. In Cwiak's case, his period of reflection allowed him to realize that he needed to extend his discovery tactics to include observation. He decided to watch his dog and take notes on her activities.

Giving yourself time to reflect—to consider, explore, inquire, and analyze your ideas—is important to the discovering stage. The organizing that occurs as you group ideas and begin to think of ordering them can move you confidently toward the first draft.

Drafting

Drafting refers to "getting your thoughts on paper" in the form of sequenced sentences, paragraphs, and sections. A **draft** is a rough sketch or early version of an essay; a **working draft** is a draft-in-progress. This second term also hints at what drafting involves: work! When you draft, you take all the ideas and information you've gathered in discovering and then choose those you want to use in your first draft. Next, you attempt to put these ideas in some logical order to develop the main point you want to make in your essay. Focusing on a main point and then sorting and arranging material are your goals when you draft. Drafting can be an exciting stage once you feel that you are beginning to communicate with your reader, making your thoughts and ideas available through the pages of a written text. For Cwiak, drafting began after he gathered information and reflected. He had learned from a prior hastily composed and poorly received essay not to wait until the night before the assignment was due.

Keep in mind that drafting involves shaping, shifting, and rethinking your writing. It is rarely a neat or easy process. Cwiak experienced this reality when a student in his class who read his first draft for "Matilda" reported that she was confused by his organization. Cwiak found the feedback of his peer editor helpful rather than threatening. Since he had drafted on a computer, Cwiak returned to the keyboard to begin revising.

Revising

Revising—which means "looking back" or "seeing again"—is the third stage of the composing process. In this stage, you are not so much concerned with correcting your draft sentence by sentence as with reflecting on it and re-seeing it. This involves reexamining the effectiveness of the whole paper in terms of the ideas presented and the ordering of those ideas.

After a conference with his instructor, Cwiak reflected on his essay. During the conference, he defended his ordering of the paragraphs, which took Matilda from playtime to bedtime to mealtime, but later he felt that to avoid reader confusion, he should use a chronological order to take Matilda from the beginning to the end of her typical day. When you are revising, think in terms of adding, deleting, and rearranging ideas if necessary. These steps in revising should not be rushed through; be sure to allow yourself sufficient time to think about your revisions.

Polishing

Polishing, the fourth stage of the composing process, involves refining language for effect, proofreading for correctness, and checking manuscript format. In the polishing stage, examine your writing for effective and precise words, sentences that have variety—that do not begin and end the same way—and fresh, specific images that activate the senses. During polishing, you can take the time to find that "just-right" word, to create the unexpected phrase or sentence, and to add the details that will bring your subject vividly to life.

When Douglas Cwiak was notified that "Matilda" was going to be published by a local newspaper, he began the process of reviewing his essay. He noticed that there were vague word choices as well as errors in sentence structure that his instructor had circled in her evaluation of his essay. In paragraph 2, he replaced the word *strangeness* with *chaos;* in paragraph three, he substituted the word *maneuver* for *try.* He wanted to stress the contrast between Matilda and most dogs, so he added the phrase "on the other hand" in paragraph 5. Finally he corrected a sentence that was actually an incomplete thought: he had originally written, in paragraph 4, "Always in the same place, under the covers with her head just peering out."

Polishing is best addressed after you have made larger adjustments to content and organization in the drafting and revising stages. The handbook section of this text (Part Four, pp. 413–468) will help you in proofreading for correctness.

Responding

Responding is a crucial part of the entire composing process. As you can see in "The Composing Process" diagram on page 43, responding involves reacting to and interacting with what you've written during and after *each* stage of the process. Responding can also be a shared activity, as you consider the questions, comments, or suggestions from peer readers, a collaborator, or an instructor. In order to respond thoughtfully and make the necessary adjustments, set aside the time to reflect on and review your writing. Ask yourself if you have achieved your goals and met the expectations of your original assignment and of your audience.

The following three steps for responding to an essay will help you take more control of your writing:

1. Recognize strengths as well as troublesome areas in your writing.
2. Identify needed improvements by testing your writing against the five "keys"—PURPOSE, FOCUS, MATERIAL, STRUCTURE, and STYLE.
3. Make the appropriate changes to improve your writing.

Responding can have a range of results. You might discover your real concerns beneath the surface of a first draft, launch a search for new material, or mark places in the margin where you stumble over sentences as you reread.

Practice 2.7 Identify the appropriate stage in the composing process, for each of the following statements. Review the stages (pp. 43–46) if necessary.

Example: You receive your assignment and you begin to gather material.

Discovering
_____

1. You have gathered sufficient material, you have a thesis or main point to focus on, and you have an idea of how to structure the material, so you begin writing your first version of the essay.

_____

2. Your essay is almost ready, and the deadline is approaching, but there are a few words and sentences that are not as effective as you would like them to be. You have not yet proofread your essay for spelling errors and typos.

_____

3. After sharing a draft of your essay with your peers, you're now reflecting on their comments before attacking the essay once more.

_____

4. You've written a couple of drafts of your essay, but after responding to reader feedback, you decide the structure needs adjusting and your focus in the thesis needs to be sharper.

_____

The five keys and your composing process are closely related. If you think about it, the composing process involves putting purpose, focus, material, structure, and style "into action" as you write. While you work through any of the Options for Writing in this chapter (pp. 51–52), refer to the following strategies to see how you can use the keys during the stages of your composing process.

STRATEGIES FOR WRITERS

1. **PURPOSE** During the discovering stage, determine if your purpose in writing the essay is to express, to inform, or to persuade your audience. Identify the specific audience you want to address in your essay. In revising, check to see that you have an introduction that engages your audience and advances your purpose. Check to ensure that your conclusion offers closure and connects the essay with your purpose.

2. **FOCUS** Early in the composing process, try to form a "working" thesis that you may revise and refine as you continue to focus your essay. In gathering information and in drafting, make certain that each piece of information relates clearly to your working thesis.

3. **MATERIAL** During the discovering stage, gather as much information as you can from a variety of sources, if possible.

4. **STRUCTURE** In preparation for drafting, try to arrange your material in a logical sequence. Decide, at least for now, which material you will include first, second, third, and so forth. As you draft and revise, question this order, get feedback on your draft, and experiment with the order to come up with the best organization for your particular essay.

5. **STYLE** In polishing, make sure that you're using the most effective words and that you're varying your sentences to keep your audience interested in your subject. Proofread your essay to eliminate any distracting errors or typos. Check your manuscript to be sure that it conforms to your instructor's directions for format.

JOURNAL WRITING: EXAMINING YOUR COMPOSING PROCESS

As you learned in Chapter 1, journal writing is a valuable way to reflect on your reading. But your journal is also a useful place to reflect on your writing. Perhaps your instructor requires that you submit your journal at various intervals throughout the semester. Or maybe your journal is for your eyes only. In either case, you should feel comfortable using a journal as an outlet for expressing your thoughts—both good and bad—about writing. After answering the questions below for the first two activities in your journal, you will have a better idea of how the stages of the composing process have worked for you in the past and how you might use them in the future to become a more relaxed and efficient writer. The second journal activity, focusing on the writers featured in this chapter, will provide useful ideas and material for an essay.

1. Think about your own composing process. How do you usually go about a writing assignment, business or personal letter, or workplace report? In a journal entry, describe your composing process. Answering some of the following questions will help you to recall various aspects of how you write:

    • How much time do you spend thinking before beginning to write?

    • What activities help you to generate ideas? Do you make notes, discuss your ideas with others, or read?

    • How and when do you organize your material?

    • How do you get started on a draft?

    • How long does it take you to produce a page? A first draft?

    • How many drafts do you usually work through?

    • How do you decide what changes to make or what needs work?

2. Answer the following questions in another short journal writing to consider some ways in which you could become a better, more efficient writer:

    • What are your strengths as a writer?

    • Which aspects of writing do you enjoy or find easy?

    • What are the difficult parts of writing for you?

    • At what stage or stages in the process do you meet obstacles or have trouble continuing?

3. In a journal entry, write your ideas about and reactions to any of the four essays in this chapter: "A Black Athlete Looks at Education" (p. 34), "Matilda" (p. 37), "What I Have Lived For" (p. 52), or "Ambition" (p. 54).

    • What did you like about the essay?

    • What questions or comments would you address to this writer?

- What connections can you make to your own personal experiences and attitudes?

- If writing about "Matilda," you might ask yourself if there are any "Matildas" in your life. That is, do you have some special person, animal, object, or place which has not only impressed you as unique but may have led you to reconsider some of your own attitudes and behaviors?

- If writing about "A Black Athlete Looks at Education," think about the last time you were in a library. Why were you there and how long did you stay? Do you agree with Ashe that libraries are important to college students? Why?

- If writing about "What I Have Lived For," think about the author's statement that love "relieves loneliness." Do you agree with the author's vision of love? If not, how is your vision of love different?

- If writing about "Ambition," think about the writer's claim that ambition is a positive trait. Explain why you agree or disagree with the writer. Have you known people who were too ambitious?

USING THE COMPUTER: OPENING A PLANNING FILE

1. As you become more comfortable with using a computer for writing, you'll discover that it's especially helpful in the early stages of planning and drafting an essay. On page 43 writing is described as a "recursive" process, meaning that you continue to have new ideas and revisit old ones as you write. To help you in the discovery stage of your essay writing, try creating a **planning file,** in which you record and save your plans for a particular essay. You can create this file either on disc or on your hard drive. After you have created and named your file, type the following planning questions, leaving enough space to insert your answers. You can answer each question later when you begin prewriting.

   a. Who is my audience?

   b. What is my purpose in writing to them? (To express, inform, or persuade?)

   c. What main point am I trying to make about my subject?

   d. Where should I look for material to support my main point?

e. What specific example or piece of evidence would help me prove my main point?

Because this is a planning file, you might want to continue adding ideas to it as you draft your essay. But try not to delete any text from this planning file—even the ideas you think you won't use. (*Hint:* If you want to move text directly from your planning file into your essay draft, use the *copy* function instead of *cut*.)

2. A *split screen* or *windows* option lets you keep two different files open on the screen at the same time. You can move back and forth between the files, cut text from one file and paste it in the other, or compare different drafts of the same essay. For example, open your prewriting file on one side of the screen and the planning file on the other side. That way, you can refer to your prewriting as you answer the planning file questions. (*Hint:* You might want to practice opening and closing split screens using "junk" files—files of text that you don't need to save, or into which you've typed text straight from your book.)

OPTIONS FOR WRITING

For this assignment, you will be integrating the five keys—PURPOSE, FOCUS, MATERIAL, STRUCTURE, and STYLE—into your composing process. Whatever option you choose, try to gather as much material as you can in your discovery stage, and then work on focusing and structuring the material in the drafting stage.

¶ **1.** Bertrand Russell's essay "What I Have Lived For" (p. 52) develops "three passions" for which the writer has lived: love, knowledge, and pity. In a paragraph, discuss one passion for which you live.

¶ **2.** In "Ambition" (p. 54), Perri Klass mentions three ambitions in her concluding paragraph: "to write as well as I can, . . . to have a family . . . and to be a good pediatrician." Reread the essay to understand exactly what Klass means by the term *ambition,* and then write a paragraph of your own supporting one of the following theses:

- In my life, I want to accomplish three things. (You can also mention obstacles to be overcome.)
- Ambitious people are obnoxious and ruthless.
- Having lofty ambitions allows us to dream, plan, and overcome obstacles.
- Having lofty ambitions often leads to disappointment.

3. In "Matilda," Douglas Cwiak gives readers a close look at his dog. Write an essay about a subject you are familiar with: a person, animal, or a specific place. Gather as much material as you can from memory, observation, or photos.

4. In "What I Have Lived For," Bertrand Russell mentions the objects of pity in his life: "children in famine, victims tortured by their oppressors, helpless old people a hated burden to their sons." Find a newspaper or magazine article that discusses an object of pity in our current world. After reading the article, write an essay explaining the situation and possibly offering some solutions.

5. Both Ashe in "A Black Athlete Looks at Education" and Klass in "Ambition" mention role models in their essays. If you have had an important role model or mentor figure in the form of a relative, teacher, coworker, or friend, explain the nature of your relationship and describe the impact this person has had on your ambitions and achievements.

6. In their separate essays, both Ashe and Klass grapple with the concept of *delayed gratification*. Examine the meaning of this term by looking in a psychology textbook or interviewing other students. In an essay, explain what the term means to you personally by giving examples from your own college and work experience and the experience of others you know.

RESPONDING TO WRITING: ANNOTATION

Practice in recognizing the five "keys"—PURPOSE, FOCUS, MATERIAL, STRUCTURE, and STYLE—and how they function in essays will allow you to become more confident in responding to your own essays and those of others. In the following short essay, Bertrand Russell—a British philosopher, mathematician, and political activist who worked for individual freedoms—shares the three overriding passions of his life. As you read, notice how clearly the essay exhibits the characteristics and guidelines presented in this chapter.

What I Have Lived For

Bertrand Russell

1   Three passions, simple but overwhelmingly strong, have governed my life: the longing for love, the search for knowledge, and unbearable pity for the suffering of mankind. These passions, like great winds, have blown me hither and thither, in a wayward course, over a deep ocean of anguish, reaching to the very verge of despair.

2   I have sought love, first, because it brings ecstasy—ecstasy so great that I would often have sacrificed all the rest of life for a few hours of this joy. I have sought it, next, because it relieves loneliness—that terrible loneliness in which one shivering consciousness looks over the rim of the world into the cold unfathomable lifeless abyss. I have sought it, finally, because in the union of love I have seen, in a mystic miniature, the prefiguring vision of the heaven that saints and poets have imagined. This is what I sought, and though it might seem too good for human life, this is what—at last—I have found.

3   With equal passion I have sought knowledge. I have wished to understand the hearts of men. I have wished to know why the stars shine. And I have tried to apprehend the Pythagorean power by which number holds sway above the flux. A little of this, but not much, I have achieved.

4   Love and knowledge, so far as they were possible, led upward toward the heavens. But always pity brought me back to earth. Echoes of cries of pain reverberate in my heart. Children in famine, victims tortured by oppressors, helpless old people a hated burden to their sons, and the whole world of loneliness, poverty, and pain make a mockery of what human life should be. I long to alleviate the evil, but I cannot, and I too suffer.

5   This has been my life. I have found it worth living, and would gladly live it again if the chance were offered me.

Now reread the essay, annotating it (as explained in Chapter 1), making notes in your text. Follow the instructions below for annotating, but feel free to include additional comments of your own.

1. Label the introduction, the body paragraphs, and the conclusion.

2. Underline and label the thesis in this essay. Remember that to be effective, a thesis statement should focus an essay by making a point about the topic.

3. Each of the body paragraphs also has a particular focus. Underline and label the words or sentences that state the focus of each body paragraph.

4. Each paragraph supports the thesis with material—reasons, details, and examples. A paragraph is well developed when it contains enough material to support the main idea and allow the reader to "see" and understand an author's subject. Note several instances of specific details or examples that name and show the writer's material rather than simply tell about it.

5. The writer has structured his material very clearly. Note any words or groups of words that help you follow his structure easily.

6. An author's style includes effective use of language, the author's word choice, the length and variety of sentences, and the author's voice that we can "hear" as we read. Choose a few specific words, groups of words, or sentences that make this essay effective or memorable for you. Label these for later discussion.

7. Return to the title of the essay and examine the title once more. Decide whether Russell's primary purpose is to express, inform, or persuade. Write the purpose next to the title.

Now that you are familiar with annotating an essay, use this technique to examine your own writing as soon as you have a first draft. If you find this practice helpful, repeat the process with later drafts.

READING AND ADDITIONAL ACTIVITIES

In the following essay Perri Klass discusses *ambition*—what it has meant through the ages, what it meant to her as a college student, and what it means to her today as a mother, professional writer, and pediatrician. Klass was born in Trinidad but came to the United States at an early age. Her mother and father as well as her sisters and brothers are all published authors. Klass acknowledges that ambition and expectations played a large role in her upbringing. As you read, see if you can find the writer's thesis and the other parts of the essay discussed earlier in this chapter.

Ambition

Perri Klass

1   In college, my friend Beth was very ambitious, not only for herself but for her friends. She was interested in foreign relations, in travel, in going to law school. . . . I was a biology major, which was a problem: Beth's best friend from childhood was also studying biology, and Beth had already decided *she* would win the Nobel Prize. This was resolved by my interest in writing fiction. I would win *that* Nobel, while her other friend would win for science.

2   It was a joke; we were all smart-ass college freshmen, pretending the world was ours for the asking. But it was not entirely a joke. We were *smart* college freshmen, and why should we limit our ambitions?

3   I've always liked ambitious people, and many of my closest friends have had grandiose dreams. I like such people, not because I am desperate to be buddies with a fu-

ture secretary of state but because I find ambitious people entertaining, interesting to talk to, fun to watch. And, of course, I like such people because I am ambitious myself, and I would rather not feel apologetic about it.

4   Ambition has gotten bad press. Back in the seventeenth century, Spinoza thought ambition and lust were "nothing but species of madness, although they are not enumerated among diseases." Especially in women, ambition has often been seen as a profoundly dislikable quality; the word "ambitious" linked to a "career woman" suggested that she was ruthless, hard as nails, clawing her way to success on top of bleeding bodies of her friends.

5   Then, in the late Seventies and the Eighties, ambition became desirable, as books with titles like *How to Stomp Your Way to Success* became bestsellers. It was still a nasty sort of attribute, but nasty attributes were good because they helped you look out for number one.

6   But what I mean by ambition is dreaming big dreams, putting no limits on your expectations and your hopes. I don't really like very specific, attainable ambitions, the kind you learn to set in the career-strategy course taught by the author of *How to Stomp Your Way to Success.* I like big ambitions that suggest that the world could open up at any time, with work and luck and determination. The next book could hit it big. The next research project could lead to something fantastic. The next bright idea could change history.

7   Of course, eventually you have to stop being a freshman in college. You limit your ambitions and become more realistic, wiser about your potential, your abilities, the number of things your life can hold. Sometimes you get close to something you wanted to do, only to find it looks better from far away. Back when I was a freshman, to tell the truth, I wanted to be Jane Goodall, go into the jungle to study monkeys and learn things no one had ever dreamed of. This ambition was based on an interest in biology and several *National Geographic* television specials; it turned out that wasn't enough of a basis for a life. There were a number of other early ambitions that didn't pan out either. I was not fated to live a wild, adventurous life, to travel alone to all the most exotic parts of the world, to leave behind a string of broken hearts. Oh well, you have to grow up, at least a little.

8   One of the worst things ambition can do is tell you you're a failure. The world is full of measuring tapes, books and articles to tell you where you should be at your age, after so-and-so many years of doing what you do. . . .

9   The world is full of disappointed people. Some of them probably never had much ambition to start with; they sat back and waited for something good and feel cheated because it never happened. Some of them had very set, specific ambitions and, for one reason or another, never got what they wanted. Others got what they wanted but found it wasn't ex-

actly what they'd expected it to be. Disappointed ambition provides fodder for both drama and melodrama: aspiring athletes (who coulda been contenders), aspiring dancers (all they ever needed was the music and the mirror).

10   The world is also full of people so ambitious, so consumed by drive and overdrive that nothing they pass on the way to success has any value at all. Life becomes one long exercise in delayed gratification; everything you do, you're doing only because it will one day get you where you want to be. Medical training is an excellent example of delayed gratification. You spend years in medical school doing things with no obvious relationship to your future as a doctor, and then you spend years in residency, living life on a miserable schedule, staying up all night and slogging through the day, telling yourself that one day all this will be over. . . .

11   As you grow up, your ambitions may come into conflict. Most prominently nowadays, we have to hear about Women Torn Between Family and Career, about women who make it to the top only to realize they left their ovaries behind. Part of growing up, of course, is realizing that there is only so much room in one life, whether you are male or female. You can do one thing wholeheartedly and single-mindedly and give up some other things. Or you can be greedy and grab for something new without wanting to give up what you already have. This leads to a chaotic and crowded life in which you are always late, always overdue, always behind, but rarely bored. Even so, you have to come to terms with limitations; you cannot crowd your life with occupations and then expect to do each one as well as you might if it were all you had to do. I realize this when I race out of the hospital, offending a senior doctor who had offered to explain something to me, only to arrive late at the daycare center, annoying the people who have been taking care of my daughter.

12   People consumed by ambition, living with ambition, get to be a little humorless, a little one-sided. On the other hand, people who completely abrogate their ambition aren't all fun and games either. I've met a certain number of women whose ambitions are no longer for themselves at all; their lives are now dedicated to their offspring. I hope my children grow up to be nice people, smart people, people who use good grammar; and I hope they grow up to find things they love to do, and do well. But my ambitions are for *me.*

13   Of course, I try to be mature about it all. I don't assign my friends Nobel Prizes or top government posts. I don't pretend that there is room in my life for any and every kind of ambition I can imagine. Instead, I say piously that all I want are three things: I want to write as well as I can, I want to have a family and I want to be a good pediatrician. And then, of course, a voice inside whispers . . . to write a bestseller, to have ten children, to do stunning medical research.

Fame and fortune, it whispers, fame and fortune. Even though I'm not a college freshman anymore, I'm glad to find that little voice still there, whispering sweet nothings in my ear.

QUESTIONS ON CONTENT

1. Although Klass explores the merits of ambition, she also sets limits, hint-
ing that too much ambition is not good. Find the paragraph in which she
discusses the negative effects of ambition and write one negative consequence you found. _____

_____

2. Search the body paragraphs of the essay and name two sources for the author's material._____

_____

3. Explain what Klass means in her concluding paragraph when she mentions a little voice "whispering sweet nothings in my ear." _____

_____

_____

QUESTIONS ON STRATEGY

1. Note any details in the first paragraph that might draw you as a reader
into the essay and make you want to read further._____

_____

_____

2. In your estimation, does the material presented in body paragraphs offer
effective support for Klass's views? Explain. _____

_____

_____

3. Throughout the essay, the author moves from an examination of the negative aspects of ambition to an indication of its benefits. Find an example of this pattern. Why is this an effective strategy? _____

_____

_____

4. Find several specific examples of ambition that help to illustrate the author's general ideas for you by "showing" as well as "telling."

_____

_____

5. How does the author emphasize her main point in the conclusion?

_____

_____

CRITICAL THINKING IN CONNECTING TEXTS

Although the authors of the four essays in this chapter differ in their choice of subject matter—Ashe focuses on education, Cwiak describes a pet, Russell talks of passions, and Klass writes about ambition—they all touch on the issue of *values,* those qualities we consider important in our lives. Get together with a partner or group and take another look at each of these essays. See if you can come up with a phrase or sentence for each author that sums up what he or she seems to value most. Now examine your response to see if the four writers share any values. At this point, you might want to brainstorm with your group, taking notes about the values that each of you holds dear. Are they the same as the shared values of the authors? Keep your notes; you might use them as material for an essay on the subject of values.

**For more writing resources, be sure to see the
Longman English Pages Website at
http://longman.awl.com/englishpages**

Discovering Through Prewriting

> Writing is easy; all you do is sit staring at a blank sheet of paper until the drops of blood form on your forehead.
>
> —*Gene Fowler, journalist, scriptwriter, biographer*

Preview

In this chapter you will learn
- how to gather material in prewriting
- how to identify and use prewriting strategies: freewriting, brainstorming, listing, questioning, clustering, branching
- how to respond to prewriting using the "keys"

CHARACTERISTICS OF PREWRITING

Have you had the unpleasant experience Fowler mentions of staring endlessly at a blank sheet of paper? Once you've received a writing assignment, do you agonize over how to begin? Or do the words sometimes seem to flow effortlessly onto the page or the computer screen? Some writers have no trouble finding those first words to put on paper, but for many others, actually getting started can be the most challenging aspect of writing. As you read about and test out several strategies for prewriting in this chapter, remember that no two writing situations are exactly alike. Oftentimes a strategy that works well for one essay may not be the one you want to use for the next. Experimenting and practicing will allow you to feel comfortable with different prewriting strategies. You'll learn which techniques work best for you in a given writing situation.

MODEL WITH KEY QUESTIONS

Joel Lopez was asked to write an essay about a meaningful insight that he had gained from his work experience. Lopez began with the prewriting list below. When he felt he had enough information on the list, he went back, reconsidered his assignment, and came up with a second prewriting list. He then drafted, revised, and polished his essay—three stages we'll cover in greater detail later in this text.

LET'S ALL LAUGH
Joel Lopez

Joel Lopez has no trouble getting material for his essays because while attending college, he works part-time as a doorman at a famous comedy club. Joel wanted to write about the jokes some of these performers told, but rather than include the names of well-known comedians, he decided to use pseudonyms for reasons of privacy. Although Joel has enjoyed working with entertainers, his future career plans focus on computer programming.

List 1
What I do —check I.D.'s of people at door
get to know all types of customers
some get huffy, some are nice
older couples tend to be nice
drunks are a pain in the ...
boss is a nice guy
comedians work really hard
they're on the line —make it or bomb
Kevin Jones —jokes about personal experiences
Bobby Hinton I don't respect —ethnic material
Rych Schneider uses personal life —wife jokes
learned a lot of jokes on different subjects
learned to respect comics, some more than others
they work hard, take chances in different ways

List 2
What job taught me about performers and material
They use religion, events, stereotypes, relationships.
religion: guy who used "Olympics of religion" and "baddest god"
events: Kevin Jones' ski trip
Stereotyping: Bobby Hinton and bashing
            Cindy Dziminski's polish jokes
relationships: Rych Schneider —wife's birthday gift

1   I believe I am one of very few people who can go to work knowing I'm going to laugh; in fact, if I didn't laugh, my workplace would soon be out of business. I work at the prestigious Comedy and Magic Club, and during the nine
months I've been employed at the club as a doorman, I have learned that
every talented comedian has his or her type of material that is spawned from
a specific brand of humor. While each comedian gathers material from subjects the audience can relate to, some of the most popular subjects for
comedic material are religion, life experiences, relationships, and ethnic
stereotyping.

2   There are so many religions to choose from that a comic could use religion
as the subject for an entire routine if he or she wanted to. Most comics who decide to bring up a certain faith choose the most commonly occurring ones in the
area in which they're performing. Because my club is located in greater Los Angeles, many different religions are usually represented in an audience. I remember one comedian who decided to go for broke: he said he thought it would help
people decide which church to attend if we staged a kind of "Olympics of religion"—this way we could pit the various gods against each other and decide
which god was really the strongest. We could hold this contest in the coliseum
and offer trophies for the god that gets all 10s—the meanest, toughest, "baddest" god of all.

3   Another subject useful to comedians is personal life experiences. I find these
jokes very funny, and they tend to draw a larger audience because the crowd has
either shared the same experience or can imagine what the experience would be
like. One comedian talked about a water skiing trip he took that ended with "water boogers"—he had a huge strand from his nose to his shoulder! He then
warned the crowd to watch out when they are out there in the ocean—these nose
excretions look a lot like jellyfish.

4   Another topic that works for comics centers on relationships between the sexes. A particular comedian began by saying that men have always been baffled by women and women find it hard to know what makes men tick. The comedian continued that he heard his wife whining and complaining about how their bathroom scale never worked and was not accurate when she got on it. When shopping for her birthday present, he decided she'd love a new scale. He couldn't understand her fury with him when she opened his thoughtful gift.

5   Thus far, the topics are fairly safe, in the sense that the comedians have a lesser chance of insulting or alienating the audience, but there are comedians who take a greater risk and dabble with ethnic material. The chance for error goes up dramatically when this sensitive issue is used for comedic material— even though the comic may get a laugh, the ones I respect are those that handle ethnic material without offending any particular group. One comedian I like did this well: she is Polish herself, and she stated that she was sick of the stereotypical "dumb Polak" jokes; she continued that maybe it took three "Polaks" to change a light bulb because the three were Joseph Conrad, worried over one of his literary masterpieces, Frederic Chopin, preoccupied with his latest musical composition, and Nicolaus Copernicus, distracted by his scientific discoveries.

6   I have tremendous respect for the comedians who perform at my club. Working in this place has taught me not just to laugh with the audience at a comedian's funny routine, but also to appreciate all the hard work, creativity, trial-and-error, and sweat that go into getting comic material together in the first place. I can't imagine having a funnier job, and I hope the crowds never stop laughing.

KEY QUESTIONS

1. **PURPOSE** Identify the writer's audience—who would want to read this essay and what might be the extent of the reader's knowledge on the subject?

_____

_____

2. **FOCUS** State the writer's thesis in your own words.

_____

_____

3. **MATERIAL** In which body paragraph does the writer give the audience the clearest sense of the comedian's subject matter? Which is the weakest body paragraph in this respect? Be sure to state your reasons for your answers.

_____

_____

4. **STRUCTURE** How is the information organized—in other words, how does Lopez break down the information into sections of material and establish a sequence for his essay? _____

_____

5. **STYLE** What sentence or phrase leaves you with the most vivid impression of the writer's subject? Write it down in the following space.

_____

_____

GUIDELINES FOR PREWRITING

As you remember from the discussion of the composing process in Chapter 2, discovering through **prewriting** is the first of four stages. In this stage, you explore and gather ideas and information, reflect on the material you have gathered, and then begin to select and group this material into a workable structure for an essay, just as Lopez does in his prewriting list. Prewriting is not a "finished writing"; it is a way to get ideas on paper. Before you can decide which prewriting strategy for gathering material you'd like to try, you need to consider why and for whom you're writing the essay.

Consider Your Audience

Your essay assignment might describe a specific audience you should write for. Even if a specific audience is not part of the assignment, it will help you focus your essay if you consider the audience that you would like to address and your purpose in addressing them. Of course, you can choose to write for your classmates and your instructor—people like you who are a part of the college community but represent a variety of different backgrounds, interests, and general knowledge. Addressing the following questions about your intended audience will help you develop appropriate material for your essay:

Audience Assessment Questions

- What group of readers would be most interested in your proposed subject?

- What might this group want to learn about your subject?

- What might they already know about your subject?

- How can you help this particular audience understand your information? Are there terms you need to define? Background information you should mention? Misconceptions you should clear up?

When Joel Lopez had completed his first prewriting list, it included several insights he had gained on the job. In reading this list, Lopez reconsidered his assignment. He decided that his intended audience would be his college classmates. This led him to revise his original list to focus on the different kinds of material that comedians develop. This was the subject for which he felt his audience might have the most interest.

Practice 3.1 For practice in considering audience, turn to the Options for Writing (p. 104) and answer these audience questions for the first writing option.

◆ ◆ ◆

Allow Prewriting Free Rein

The goal of any prewriting strategy is to try to get down as much information as you can without stopping to evaluate it. This is not the time for censorship; later you can decide what information to keep and what to scrap. In the discovering stage of your writing, have fun, be playful, experiment with ideas, and develop unexpected connections.

Freewriting

One strategy for prewriting is **freewriting**—when you freewrite, you write nonstop on a subject for a fixed length of time, perhaps fifteen minutes. While you're freewriting, don't stop to correct spelling, punctuation, or inappropriate words. Just try to get on paper or computer the things that pop into your mind when you think of the subject. Include the mental connections and leaps in thought you make to any other aspects of the subject.

To illustrate, examine this freewriting by student writer and mother April Buell.

Over and over again hearing everybody say you won't amount to anything —teen mom and having to raise my child on my own I had to prove that they were wrong. Put downs and staying up late, diapers and schoolbooks and no support still with 2 yrs of high school left. Then got a job at U.S. Customs, became independent if felt so good not to have to ask my parents for money. I learned to be prompt, made 8 dollars an hr. Graduated with a 4 point GPA and now am a full-time college student —I have to do this for me and for my son, incl. washing clothes, cleaning house, studying without enough sleep, taking him to the doctor and trying to juggle classes and work, on and on, it never ends, I deserve recognition for all that I have achieved in spite of negative comments —my goals are still set high I won't quit.

Practice 3.2   Choose an option for writing from this chapter (pp. 104–105) that interests you. Write on the subject for fifteen minutes without stopping.

◆ ◆ ◆

Brainstorming

Another strategy for prewriting is **brainstorming,** a group prewriting activity in which participants call out ideas and comments on a subject while one person records them. Brainstorming generates lots of material because two or more heads are often better than one for coming up with information.

Here are the results from three students who brainstormed about drug legalization:

Pros	Cons
Quality Control	Effects on certain foreign economies?
Eliminate motive for smuggling	Many trained staff members needed
Monitoring users	Additional cost to taxpayers for staff
Regulate dosage	Still those who want more illegally??
Supervise activities of users?	Condoning a bad activity
Driving?	Hospitals for observation?
Drug testing?	Cheating by staff members?
Reduction in drug-related deaths (sellers, go-betweens, etc.)	Cost to taxpayers for the drugs themselves

Practice 3.3   With a partner or small group, organize a brainstorming session. Choose a subject, appoint a recorder for your group, and start collecting information on your subject.

◆ ◆ ◆

Listing

Listing is yet another prewriting technique that can be used to generate ideas for essays. You simply make a random list, perhaps similar to a shopping or "to do" list, including everything you can think of related to your subject. Later you can examine your list and find large groups of ideas in which to divide the material.

Return to the lists used by Joel Lopez (p. 60) to gather material for his essay. After a brief review, you'll see that in his second list, Lopez found four large groups of ideas into which to divide his material: the four types of subjects comedians address in their performances.

Practice 3.4   Choose another Option for Writing from this chapter and draw up a list of information on your subject. For your first list, don't worry about grouping your information. Just keep your pen moving and get down as much information as you can.

◆ ◆ ◆

Questioning

Reporters have an effective way of gathering information on a story—they ask, then answer, a set of standard questions about their subject: *who?, what?, when?, where?, how?,* and *why?* You can use these **journalists' questions** as a prewriting technique, eliminating any of the questions that don't seem to apply to your subject. If your subject is a person, for example, you might ask yourself the following questions:

> *Who* am I writing about?
>
> *What* is my relationship with this person? What is it that makes this person unique? What do I want to say about this person to my reading audience?
>
> *When* did we meet? When did particular aspects of the person that are unique appear?
>
> *Where* did the person exhibit the qualities I find unique?
>
> *How* can I communicate this person's special quality to readers?
>
> *Why* am I writing about this person? Why do I find him or her special?

Practice 3.5   Choose a subject to write about for Writing Option 3 (p. 104), and then answer the six journalists' questions on a separate sheet of paper.

◆ ◆ ◆

Clustering

Clustering is a prewriting technique for randomly discovering information in a purely visual format. For some writers, clustering is less threatening than trying to fill up a blank page from top to bottom. To create a clustering diagram, write your subject in the middle of a blank page and then circle it. You then draw lines to connect that subject to more specific details or examples related to your subject. You can keep adding clusters to whatever ideas seem to lead you to more details. Note that your clusters can be in the form of single words, phrases, or questions. The diagram below illustrates Elias Kary's clustering on the subject of reading.

—*Elias Kary, student*

Practice 3.6   Choose a Writing Option (p. 104 you haven't worked with and complete the clustering diagram provided. You can add more clusters if necessary.

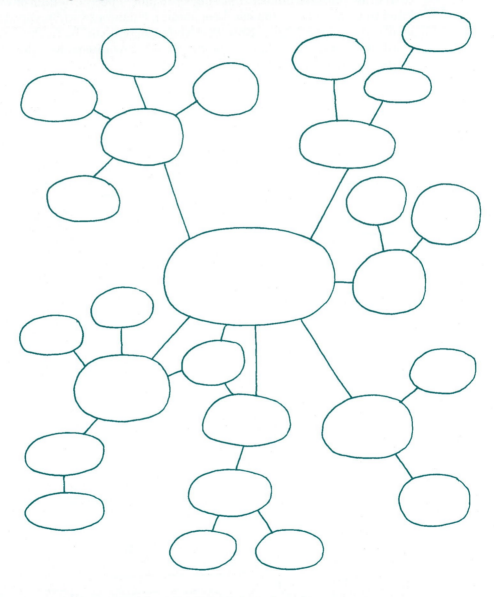

❖ ❖ ❖

Branching
Branching is a prewriting technique utilizing a diagram in the shape of a "tree," with a main trunk representing the subject and three or four smaller areas or separate branches representing major ideas or information chunks.

The writer then fills in each major branch with details and specifics. The diagram shown here illustrates how one student used branching not only to gather information but also to begin to organize it.

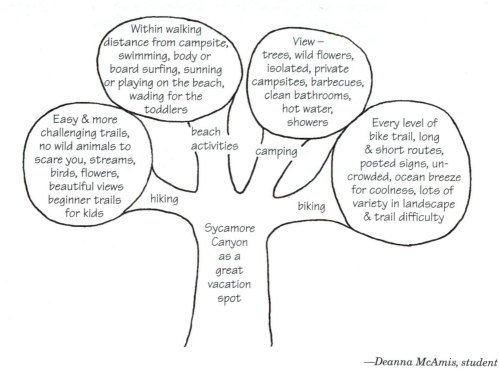

—*Deanna McAmis, student*

Practice 3.7   To see how branching helps organize material, create a branching diagram for the clustering you created in Practice 3.6.

◆ ◆ ◆

STRATEGIES FOR PREWRITING

1. **PURPOSE** When you have a subject for your essay, ask yourself why you want to write about it. Think of any information you might want to collect to ease the readers' understanding of the subject.

2. **FOCUS** Once you have completed one prewriting activity, examine your information carefully to discover which pieces of information you want to concentrate on. If helpful, repeat the same prewriting activity or use a different one to gather more information on your more focused subject.

continued

3. **MATERIAL** Experiment with different prewriting strategies to discover which one allows you to collect the most information for a particular assignment. Write down every idea that comes to you without censoring. In prewriting, too much material is better than not enough material.

4. **STRUCTURE** Once you've gathered all the prewriting information you can, reread what you have written, identify large groups of ideas in which to divide the material, and then delete any information that does not relate clearly to these groups.

5. **STYLE** Reread your prewriting or get a peer or instructor to respond by indicating effective details and clear examples as well as confusing or vague information.

JOURNAL WRITING: DISCOVERY ENTRY

The Journal Writing in Chapter 1 introduced you to the reading log, a reading and writing strategy that you can now use to respond to a poem. Although the poem, on the surface, is about digging, as its title indicates, it's also about the discovery stage of the composing process—specifically, "digging" to develop material for essays, poems, or other forms of writing. Read the poem silently to yourself and then out loud. Respond in your reading log by following the instructions on p. 20. In the left column, try to include phrases from the poem that relate to gathering and developing material for writing.

Digging

Seamus Heaney

1   Between my finger and my thumb
The squat pen rests; snug as a gun.
Under my window, a clean rasping sound
When the spade sinks into gravelly ground:
My father, digging. I look down

6   Till his straining rump among the flowerbeds
Bends low, comes up twenty years away

Stooping in rhythm through potato drills

Where he was digging.

10   The coarse boot nestled on the lug, the shaft

Against the inside knee was levered firmly.

He rooted out tall tops, buried the bright edge deep

To scatter new potatoes that we picked

Loving their cool hardness in our hands.

15   By God, the old man could handle a spade.

Just like his old man.

17   My grandfather cut more turf in a day

Than any other man on Toner's bog.

Once I carried him milk in a bottle

Corked sloppily with paper. He straightened up

To drink it, then fell to right away.

22   Nicking and slicing neatly, heaving sods

Over his shoulder, going down and down

For the good turf. Digging.

25   The cold smell of potato mould, the squelch and slap

Of soggy peat, the curt cuts of an edge

Through the living roots awaken in my head.

But I've no spade to follow men like them.

29   Between my finger and my thumb

The squat pen rests.

I'll dig with it.

Remember to use the left column for passages from the poem and the right column for your responses. Here's how one student began his reading log for this poem:

"Squat pen."	Why squat?
"Like a gun."	Snug. The gun is comfortable in some way.

Using the Computer: Organizing Prewriting

1. Many of the prewriting strategies described in this chapter can be enhanced by using a word-processing program. For example, a *columns* or *table* feature can make it easier to cluster similar ideas, helping you to see patterns in your thoughts that might lead to an essay after you have brainstormed on paper.

   This is what Elias Kary's clustering (p. 67) might look like if it were sorted using columns:

Feelings about books	Feelings about reading	Feelings about family reading
Liked books on political figures Science fiction books	Was a slow reader Stuttered over words Disliked reading out loud Got sweaty	English was second language in my house Older brother helped me read

   Find a cluster or another kind of prewriting you've generated. Use your word-processing program's columns or tables feature to organize your prewriting into similar ideas. Be sure to *name* and *save* this work.

2. Find out if your college offers you a free E-mail account and access to the World Wide Web. Get yourself signed up for both services, and be sure to take any tutorials the computer lab offers on how to use these services. You may already need to keep track of a variety of E-mail addresses:

   Campus E-mail address _____

   Writing instructor's E-mail address _____

   Friend's E-mail address _____

   E-mail address of student in my writing class _____

   Learn to *attach* files to your E-mail messages. For example, try "attaching" a word-processing document, like an essay draft, and sending it to another student in your writing class. Ask for suggestions or comments on that draft. Your instructor might also allow papers and assignments to be submitted via E-mail; be sure to ask.

OPTIONS FOR WRITING

You're now familiar with the characteristics of the college essay (discussed in Chapter 2) and the many promising ways of discovering material for essays through the prewriting discussed in this chapter. Choose one of the options listed below. Keeping your audience and purpose in mind, gather information using one or more prewriting strategies. After you have worked through the discovering stage of the composing process, give yourself time and distance, and possibly get some feedback from your instructor or peers. You can then evaluate your prewriting, making adjustments before proceeding to the next stage in your composing process. Write an essay developing your subject with an introduction, thesis, body paragraphs, and conclusion.

1. Discuss one or more major problems with your college or university. This could be something connected to facilities—classrooms, parking, cafeteria food or service, for example. Or the problem could have to do with class size, attendance policies, or course requirements. You may want to interview faculty members, administrators, other college personnel, or your classmates. Detail the problem as you see it and then try to put forth one or more solutions.

2. Write an essay about something you've learned on the job. Share your newfound knowledge and how you came to it.

3. In "Let's All Laugh" (p. 61) Joel Lopez asserts that "relationships between the sexes" make effective material for comedians. Search newsstands or your college or local library for an article dealing with gender differences. You might also track down some information by interviewing class members, friends, and relatives. You might want to read the student essay "Men Are Makita, Women Are Marigolds" (p. 313). Write an essay exploring your views on gender differences.

4. After reading "Digging" (p. 70) and completing the journal writing activity with this poem, develop some of the ideas, details, or themes you've discovered in your reading journal.

5. Write about an area of your life in which you would like to achieve recognition. Student April Buell writes in her freewriting assignment (p. 64) that she would like recognition as a single mother, worker, and struggling college student. Have you accomplished something for which you feel you should be recognized?

RESPONDING TO WRITING: DISCOVERING KEYS FOR PREWRITING

For this activity, read the following student's freewriting and then answer the key questions that follow. You can then offer peer suggestions to help the student writer evaluate the success of her prewriting.

Prejudiced —what most people think they're not. Ha! Most people think they're so open-minded and accepting and different from their parents and ancestors in that respect but what about what happens to them when they come face to face with an HIV victim? These same people who think they're so free of prejudice are afraid they'll catch the deadly virus just by touching him, so they avoid him and shun him for no reason other than prejudice. And the obese teenage girl who is made fun of and sits alone eating in the school cafeteria because her peers are too cool to sit by her or even say hi to her, what is she if not another victim of PREJUDICE! What has she done to deserve this hurt of being ignored or shunned except if we believe being overweight is a sin, but people are still so smug saying oh no, I'm not prejudiced. Let's see, oh, I can think of lots of examples it just makes me mad all this hypocrisy, oh yeah, how about the factory worker whose boss drives an expensive car to work and wears an Armani suit and then gets the hate look from the worker just because the man is rich and the factory worker is poor, it's not the fault of the rich man, again what did he DO to deserve this prejudice? Nothing, not a thing. And what about the prostitute who has to make her living that way because she had a rotten childhood and doesn't have another skill and she really wants to turn her life around but she can't find a decent place to live or get a normal date because the minute people find out she's a prostitute they don't want a person like this as a neighbor or even a friend, they just shun her meanwhile saying to themselves that they are open-minded and have no prejudices.

—*Corona Reynolds, student*

KEY QUESTIONS

1. **PURPOSE** If the writer were to decide to develop this freewriting into an essay, state what purpose she might have in writing on this subject.

_____

In a phrase or sentence, identify the audience that would be most interested in the subject. _____

_____

What might this group of readers already know about the subject?

_____

_____

2. **FOCUS** What is the word or phrase that forms the focal point of Reynolds's freewriting? _____

_____

Based on this freewriting, write a possible working thesis Reynolds might consider. _____

_____

3. **MATERIAL** Do you think the writer has enough material here for an essay, or should she continue to gather more material with this or another form of prewriting? (Support your answer with specific statements referring to Reynolds's prewriting.) _____

_____

4. **STRUCTURE** Could you suggest a way Reynolds might want to break up her information into smaller sections developing similar ideas?

_____

5. **STYLE** Jot down one phrase that was powerful for you, and then explain why you reacted to it strongly. _____

_____

READING AND ADDITIONAL ACTIVITIES

Natalie Goldberg is a writer and teacher. She reports that she has written a book on writing because even though there is no "logical A-to-B-to-C way to become a good writer," the discovery and consistent practice of different techniques and methods will help writers build confidence and skill. In this excerpt from her book *Writing Down the Bones,* Goldberg focuses on some techniques to help writers get started in generating material. Toward the end of the selection, the author offers a large list of writing ideas. As you read this list, annotate with a check or other mark those numbered topics that you might like to try by using one or more specific strategies for prewriting discussed in this chapter.

A List of Topics for Writing Practice

Natalie Goldberg

1   Sometimes we sit down to write and can't think of anything to write about. The blank page can be intimidating, and it does get boring to write over and over again for ten minutes of practice, "I can't think of what to say. I can't think of what to say." It is a good idea to have a page in your notebook where you jot down, as they come to you, ideas of topics to write about. . . .

2   Making a list is good. It makes you start noticing material for writing in your daily life, and your writing comes out of a relationship with your life and its texture. In this way, the composting process is beginning. Your body is starting to digest and turn over your material, so even when you are not actually at the desk physically writing, there are parts of you raking, fertilizing, taking in the sun's heat, and making ready for the deep green plants of writing to grow.

3   If you give your mind too much time to contemplate a beginning when you sit down to write, your monkey mind might meander over many topics and never quite get to putting a word on the page. So the list also helps to activate your writing quickly and cut through resistance. Naturally, once you begin writing you might be surprised where your mind takes the topic. That's good. You are not trying to control your writing. You are stepping out of the way. Keep your hand moving.

4   But until you get your own list, here are some writing ideas:

1. Tell about the quality of light coming in through your window. Jump in and write. Don't worry if it is night and your curtains are closed or you would rather write about the light up north—just write. Go for ten minutes, fifteen, a half hour.

2. Begin with "I remember." Write lots of small memories. If you fall into one large memory, write that. Just keep going. Don't be concerned if the memory happened five seconds ago or five years ago. Everything that isn't this moment is memory coming alive again as you write. If you get stuck, just repeat the phrase "I remember" again and keep going.

3. Take something you feel strongly about, whether it is positive or negative, and write about it as though you love it. Go as far as you can, writing as though you love it, then flip over and write about the same thing as though you hate it. Then write about it perfectly neutral.

4. Choose a color—for instance, pink—and take a fifteen-minute walk. On your walk notice wherever there is pink. Come back to your notebook and write for fifteen minutes.

5. Write in different places—for example, in a laundromat, and pick up on the rhythm of the washing machines. Write at bus stops, in cafés. Write what is going on around you.

6. Give me your morning. Breakfast, waking up, walking to the bus stop. Be as specific as possible. Slow down in your mind and go over the details of the morning.

7. Visualize a place that you really love, be there, see the details. Now write about it. It could be a corner of your bedroom, an old tree you sat under one whole summer, a table at McDonald's in your neighborhood, a place by a river. What colors are there, sounds, smells? When someone else reads it, she should know what it is like to be there. She should feel how you love it, not by your saying you love it, but by your handling of the details.

8. Write about "leaving." Approach it any way you want. Write about your divorce, leaving the house this morning or a friend dying.

9. What is your first memory?

10. Who are the people you have loved?

11. Write about the streets of your city.

12. Describe a grandparent.

13. Write about:

> swimming
>
> the stars
>
> the most frightened you've ever been
>
> green places
>
> how you learned about sex
>
> your first sexual experience
>
> the closest you ever felt to God or nature
>
> reading and books that have changed your life
>
> physical endurance
>
> a teacher you had

Don't be abstract. Write the real stuff. Be honest and detailed.

QUESTIONS ON CONTENT

1. What is the "composting process" Goldberg refers to in paragraph 2?

_____

_____

2. Why do you think Goldberg suggests as a writing idea choosing a color and then taking a walk to notice that color? What is to be gained from this activity from a writer's point of view?_____

_____

3. What does Goldberg mean after number 13, "Don't be *abstract*"? Look up the word and then write your own definition. _____

_____

QUESTIONS ON STRATEGY

1. Why do you think Goldberg begins with specific examples? _____

_____

2. Find at least two places in her list of writing ideas where Goldberg uses specific images of sight, smell, sound, or touch in order to convey the importance of these specific details in writing to her audience.

_____

_____

3. Who would you say Goldberg's specific audience is, and how carefully does she consider them? Find evidence of audience consideration and the writer's purpose in the excerpt. _____

_____

_____

CRITICAL THINKING IN CONNECTING TEXTS

In this chapter you've heard from three writers who, although having chosen various subjects, share a common theme: the search for and discovery of material. Joel Lopez discusses the challenge that comedians face in the development of material for their acts; Seamus Heaney contrasts his father's laborious digging for potatoes with his own efforts to discover ideas for his poems; Natalie Goldberg advises writers to work steadily at generating topics for writing. In their discussion of the discovery of material, each of these writers uses a **metaphor**—a direct comparison of one thing with another. Lopez speaks of comedians "spawning" their material, using a term that links discovery with the birth process. Heaney focuses on "digging," and compares a spade, used to bring up the precious bounty of potatoes, and a pen, employed by the poet to bring about a response in his readers. Goldberg uses two metaphors. One is in her title—for her "the bones" are the essence of the experience, the details and images that a writer uses

continued

CRITICAL THINKING IN CONNECTING TEXTS *continued*

to enable readers to connect with the writing. Goldberg also develops images related to composting: "raking, fertilizing, taking in the sun's heat, and making ready for the deep green plants of writing to grow." Using these writers' metaphors as examples, work with a partner or small group and come up with your own metaphor for the discovery stage of the writing process. It may help to think of some totally unrelated but physical activity, just as Heaney does with his father's digging in the earth. Once you have an effective and powerful metaphor, see if you can develop it with details—for instance, if digging for potatoes symbolizes searching for details and images in poetry writing, then the spade and pen are both tools; furthermore, just as the potatoes are found only in the "good turf" far down, so also the best material comes from the most intense and deepest thought. Share your metaphor with the rest of the class if time permits. If you would like more information on the use of metaphors in writing, see "Responding to Writing: Comparisons" in Chapter 9 (p. 260).

**For more writing resources, be sure to see the
Longman English Pages Website at
http://longman.awl.com/englishpages**

Finding a Thesis and Drafting

> The first essential is to choose a subject which is clear and precise in your mind and which interests you personally. . . . The next thing is to devise a form for your essay.
>
> —*Gilbert Highet, writer and educator*
>
> My first draft usually has only a few elements worth keeping. I have to find out what those are and build from them and throw out what doesn't work, or what simply is not alive.
>
> —*Susan Sontag, playwright, novelist, and critic*

 Preview

In this chapter you will learn
- ▶ how to identify and create the parts of an effective thesis: subject, controlling idea, specific language, appropriate tone
- ▶ how to use an outline to focus and organize your draft
- ▶ how to draft an essay with the "keys" in mind
- ▶ how to participate in peer editing

Now that you are familiar with prewriting strategies, you're ready to narrow your subject and organize and shape the essay. Although each writer's composing process is unique, the narrowing, organizing, and shaping of an essay often take place in the drafting stage of the process. As you focus on a particular aspect of your subject, you will want to develop an effective thesis. An effective thesis is the foundation of your entire essay. Your essay will develop as you give detailed support to your thesis in your body paragraphs. Do you remember playing with blocks or Legos as a child? You needed to create your base first, and that base had to be sound or the blocks you stacked would come tumbling down. In a similar way, your thesis forms the foundation or spine of your entire essay.

CHARACTERISTICS OF A THESIS STATEMENT

You'll recall that a thesis, one of the parts of the essay introduced in Chapter 2, contains the main point, idea, or opinion the writer wants to convey about a subject. It also enables the reader to identify what a writer is going to focus on, usually before the end of the first paragraph of the essay. An effective thesis has four characteristics:

- It states the subject of the essay clearly.

- It includes a controlling idea about the subject.

- It uses specific language rather than vague words.

- It establishes a tone that is appropriate for the subject and the intended audience.

If any one of these four qualities is missing, the thesis will not provide the needed focus and the essay will not have a strong foundation. In addition, the thesis *may* include a plan of development.

To see how these characteristics work together to strengthen the foundation of your essay, read the following sample thesis:

Living in a large city has become increasingly challenging due to higher costs of housing, more crowded roads and freeways, and increasing crime rates.

—Greg Smith, student

If you want to find Smith's **subject,** ask yourself, "What is he writing about?" Now write Smith's subject in the following space.

_____

If you want to find the **controlling idea,** or the writer's opinion about the subject, ask yourself, "What is Smith's feeling about his subject? Write Smith's controlling idea in a few words.

_____

To identify **specific language,** ask yourself, "Which word or group of words in this thesis paints the strongest 'word picture' by using precise words?" Jot down the word or group of words that paints a word picture for Smith's audience.

_____

When you're analyzing the thesis for **tone,** look for hints about the writer's attitude and whether or not this attitude is appropriate for the subject and audience. In identifying Smith's tone, you could ask, "Does he seem rational in his approach to the subject, or does he appear to rant and rave offensively? Is he humorous or more serious?" In a few words, describe the tone of Smith's thesis.

_____

You'll notice that Smith includes a **plan of development**—a group of words that breaks his subject into separate parts. While a plan of development is not a characteristic of all thesis statements, sometimes it is helpful as a kind of road map for the writer, and later, the reader. In his drafting, Smith decided to focus his discussion of the challenges of big city living on three specific problems. Review Smith's thesis and write down his plan of development in the following space:

_____

Practice 4.1 For practice in recognizing the characteristics of a thesis, read the following thesis statements and then identify the characteristics you find in each. You may want to refer back to the sample thesis and accompanying questions.

1. Love is an illness, and it has its own set of obsessive thoughts.

—Richard Selzer, from "Love Sick"

Subject _____

Controlling idea _____

Example of specific language _____

Tone _____

Plan of development? _____

2. The life support systems of this almost impossibly beautiful planet are being violated and degraded, causing often irreparable damage, yet only a small proportion of humans have focused on this crisis.

—Charlene Spretnak, from _Reweaving the World: The Emergence of Ecofeminism_

Subject _____

Controlling idea _____

Example of specific language _____

Tone _____

Plan of development? _____

3. The Arab-Israeli conflict and the oil crisis of the 1970s have exacerbated an atmosphere of hostility toward Arabs who have chosen to make their home in the U.S.

—Mustafa Nabil, from "The Arab's Image"

Subject _____

Controlling idea _____

Example of specific language _____

Tone _____

Plan of development? _____

4. The most important day I remember in all my life is the one on which my teacher, Anne Mansfield Sullivan, came to me. I am filled with wonder when I consider the immeasurable contrast between the two lives which it connects.

—Helen Keller, from "The Day Language Came into My Life"

Subject _____

Controlling idea _____

Example of specific language _____

Tone _____

Plan of development? _____

5. I had cybersex the other night, and, boy, am I sorry.

—Sandra Tsing Loh, from "Cybersex Gal"

Subject _____

Controlling idea _____

Example of specific language _____

Tone _____

Plan of development? _____

◆ ◆ ◆

Did you notice a lot of variety in these thesis statements? While each author makes unique choices, each of these thesis statements has a clear and interesting subject, a controlling idea, specific language, and a tone appropriate for the intended audience. When you are trying to create an effective thesis for your own essay, how can you be sure that your thesis also contains these characteristics? Using the following guidelines and considering the five "keys" will help. Also, remember that you should experiment with and then periodically evaluate your thesis statement as you develop your entire essay. This trial-and-error process will help you discover if you have omitted any of the four characteristics of an effective thesis. You can then make the necessary changes and adjustments.

GUIDELINES FOR WRITING THESIS STATEMENTS

Consider Audience in Selecting a Subject

Once you have chosen or have been assigned a particular writing option, you'll want to consider subjects that will be interesting and suitable. While a gifted writer may be able to write a fascinating essay on almost any subject, it's a good idea to avoid subjects about which readers are either experts or completely uninterested. For instance, if you are asked to write about friends and friendships, you might bore an audience with a thesis such as this:

> In my life I have had three different types of friends—the best friend, the good friend, and the acquaintance.

While this thesis has a helpful plan of development, most readers are already familiar with these categories of friends—you wouldn't really be sharing any new information. Instead, if you want to explore the subject of friends, and if the assignment permits personal experience as material, you might consider a thesis like this:

> I have a distinct relationship and I take on a different persona with each of the following: my friends at work, my friends at college, and my longtime friends from childhood.

In your selection process, avoid a subject that is so broad you can only discuss it in general terms without offering your audience in-depth information or insight. It is much wiser to focus on a particular aspect of a broader subject that interests you rather than trying to cover, say, the causes of the Persian Gulf War or the impact of environmental pollution. If one of these topics excites you, you could choose to explore the effects of a particular battle in the Persian Gulf or the fight to save pelicans that have been affected by a recent oil spill.

Practice 4.2

For practice in identifying appropriate and interesting subjects for a thesis, examine the following sentences. If you think the sentence is suitable for a thesis, explain why you think so. If not, revise the sentence to create an effective thesis for an essay.

1. Colors are interesting. _____

_____

2. Many couples choose to adopt children. _____

_____

3. Belief in God varies throughout the world. _____

_____

4. The Supreme Court justices are appointed for life. _____

_____

5. Although compact discs cost more than cassette tapes, the sound quality is

better with the discs. _____

_____

◆ ◆ ◆

Check for a Controlling Idea

A quick way to determine the quality of your thesis is the "so what?" test. If your thesis statement might prompt a reader to respond, "So what?" you know you need do some reworking of the thesis, possibly to clarify your controlling idea. Look at the following thesis statement:

Parks are places where a lot of people gather every weekend.

This thesis is too general for specific development; it states the information but has no focus on the writer's opinion. It does not pass the "so what?" test. Perhaps this was the writer's first thesis in prewriting or even early drafting. However, after more consideration, the writer might come up with the following revised version of a working thesis:

Parks in my neighborhood have become a place where people of all ages enjoy individual pursuits and interact with one another.

Notice that the subject, parks, has been narrowed, and that the writer now has an evident controlling idea, that these parks have become a positive force in the neighborhood. The reader can now determine the writer's opinion about the subject.

Practice 4.3   You can test your ability to narrow a subject by including a controlling idea for the following subjects. Once you've added a controlling idea, try to create a working thesis for each subject. Remember that a working thesis is not "written in stone," but is one that you feel you can work with as you write and revise the essay. The first thesis has been done for you.

<u>Subject</u>	<u>Controlling Idea</u>	<u>Working Thesis</u>
1. Pro sports stars	Outrageous salaries	The outrageous salaries of many pro sports stars lead to unrealistic expectations on the part of hopeful teen athletes.
2. Part-time jobs	_____	_____
3. Single-parent families	_____	_____
4. Violence	_____	_____
5. Television	_____	_____

◆ ◆ ◆

Avoid an Announcement

While you want to be as specific as possible, some writers make the mistake of "announcing" their thesis. They refer to their process and distract the reader from the subject by writing phrases such as "In this essay, I will attempt to show," or "I believe that this statement is true," or "This essay will now describe. . . ." You want to avoid the announcement approach.

Practice 4.4   In the following thesis statements identify those that are announcements and then on a separate sheet of paper rewrite them so that they refer to the subject, not the process.

1. I'm going to discuss the pros and cons of body piercing.

2. The Internet offers us an opportunity to research a subject in the privacy and comfort of our homes.

3. I will argue that freshman composition should not be a required course.

4. I will describe my sister for you so that you can see how different we are.

5. My sister and I, although twins, couldn't look more alike or be more different in our tastes, interests, and friends.

◆ ◆ ◆

Use Specific Language

If you've ever talked with someone who says "kinda" or "sorta" or "all that stuff," you'll grasp the importance of using specific language in a thesis. While specific word choice is desirable throughout your essay, it is perhaps most essential to your thesis. After all, the thesis is often in your introductory paragraph—the one that tells the reader what the entire essay will focus on. If your word choices are vague, confusing, dull, or misleading, your thesis statement is not going to achieve its desired effect: it cannot successfully establish the foundation of your entire essay. How can you tell if what is crystal clear to you is also being communicated to your audience? Specific word choice in a thesis statement faces a subject head-on, rather than "straddling the fence." For example, the following thesis statement is confusing:

> Many people say that capital punishment is cruel and unusual punishment, and in certain respects this is definitely and undeniably true.

The reader is confused here most of all by the vague phrase "in certain respects this is true" because "in certain respects" does not explain the writer's distinct opinion of the cruelty of capital punishment. Here is a more specific version:

> Theologians and medical experts alike argue that capital punishment is cruel because the victim suffers extreme psychological and physical effects.

There is a world of difference between these two thesis statements. In the second version, readers know without question where the writer will go for the bulk of evidence, and also what specific effects will be detailed.

Other times, although the subject and the controlling idea are clear, the word choices lack the clarity to allow the reader to focus fully on the impact of the thesis statement. Consider the following example:

> Many innovations and technical advances in the last few years in our society have given us a lot more options, but these have cost us something too in the way in which we relate to one another.

After rethinking and working on more specific language, the writer might revise this thesis as follows:

Computers have given us new research and communication capabilities, but they have also depersonalized our daily lives and circumvented human interaction.

While in the first version the writer may have been thinking specifically of computers, readers were unable to picture anything specific with the term *technical advances*. Also, instead of merely indicating vaguely that there are negative as well as positive consequences associated with computers, the writer's second version of the thesis makes the focus clear: the depersonalizing effects of computers.

Practice 4.5   See if you can hone your use of specific language by revising on a separate sheet of paper the following thesis statements. Replace any vague words or terms you find:

1. College can be a strange place for a new student.

2. Our current political system is in need of a big change.

3. Owning a pet can be rewarding.

4. Choosing the right career is really important.

5. Homeless people should not be looked down upon.

◆ ◆ ◆

Establish an Appropriate Tone

If someone were to snarl at you, "Don't speak to me in that tone of voice!" you would know immediately that you had been offensive. In the same way, your attitude comes through not just in *what you say* but also in *how you say it* in your thesis. And this tone can encourage your reader either to give you the benefit of the doubt, or to decide before reading any further that you're not to be trusted. Consider this thesis:

Television commercials are worse than worthless—they are the most despicable examples of blatant, deceptive, sexist, hard-sell tactics in the advertising world today.

Although the thesis has an interesting subject, a controlling idea, and specific language, the writer might want to reconsider both purpose and audience. It is possible that some, perhaps many, readers enjoy television commercials on occasion; some readers might be advertising executives or work in some related way in the television commercial industry. It is commendable that the writer has found a subject he feels strongly about, but perhaps a more reasonable tone would help the thesis. Examine this revised version and ask yourself which version of these two promises a more rational, thoughtful writer:

> While television commercials are often entertaining and sometimes informative, they seldom tell the whole truth but instead lure the viewer with false claims.

Perhaps you responded to this second version of the thesis more readily because the writer's tone in this thesis is reasonable and straightforward. Since tone is so important to an effective thesis, you want to make sure of the following:

- That your tone is appropriate for your audience.

- That your tone is helpful for your purpose.

While your journal entries, E-mail, and letter writing to close friends will be informal, the college essay requires a more formal tone; you don't share the same level of familiarity with your reading audience that you do with a close friend. In addition, particular writing situations call for differing levels of formality, although all require you to use reasonable, nonconfrontational language in order to gain your reader's trust.

Practice 4.6 First read the following essay-writing situations. Then in a few words, describe the most appropriate tone for the reader to take in each situation. The first activity has been done for you.

Audience	Situation	Tone
Highly educated professionals	Inform of dangers of second-hand smoke	_Fairly formal, serious_
Fellow college students	Make fun of procrastinators	_____
President of the United States	Persuade to increase spending for education	_____
Junior high students	Inform of dangers of second-hand smoke	_____
Subscribers of community newspaper	Express disapproval of city council action	_____

◆ ◆ ◆

Test and Reverse

If you have drafted several versions of your working thesis, how do you decide which one will provide the strongest foundation for your essay? A good strategy for determining the effectiveness of your thesis is *reverse testing*—a process in which you test your thesis statement by reversing your position on your subject, and determining what the opposing viewpoint might be. You can try this with all versions of your thesis to see which one works best. To take a look at reverse testing in action, recall Greg Smith's thesis presented at the beginning of this chapter:

> Living in a large city has become increasingly challenging due to higher costs of housing, more crowded roads and freeways, and increasing crime rates.

If Smith were to reverse test, he would think about the opposing viewpoint and come up with something like this:

> Living in a large city has become more desirable due to increased job opportunities, greater number of cultural activities, and efficient and economical public transportation.

This reverse thesis would clue Smith in to an opposing opinion. He might choose to alter his thesis to anticipate counterarguments, as in the following thesis:

> Although living in a large city has become more desirable for several reasons, it has also become increasingly challenging due to higher costs of housing, more crowded roads and freeways, and increasing crime rates.

You can see that reverse testing helps you predict the opposing viewpoint. You can then determine if your own thesis will stand up to that opposition.

Practice 4.7 Write an opposing version of the following thesis statements in order to test the thesis.

1. All college students should be required to take a basic psychology course in order to have an elementary understanding of human behavior.

_____

_____

2. Lack of handgun control has led to increased crime, injury, and murder across the United States. _____

_____

3. Giving college athletes special help and privileges in college courses creates an atmosphere of injustice among college students and faculty.

_____

_____

◆ ◆ ◆

STRATEGIES FOR WRITING THESIS STATEMENTS

1. **PURPOSE** Consider your audience and purpose when selecting and narrowing your subject. In drafting a working thesis, establish a tone that encourages your audience to trust you as a writer.

2. **FOCUS** Limit your subject by including a controlling idea in your thesis statement.

3. **MATERIAL** Delete any material that makes your thesis sound like an announcement. Reverse test to determine the opposing point of view and get peer feedback. Make necessary adjustments.

4. **STRUCTURE** Experiment with the arrangement of the subject and controlling idea in your thesis statement. If breaking your subject into parts will allow readers to follow your ideas more easily, include a plan of development.

5. **STYLE** Check to see that your thesis uses specific language to convey a clear word picture to your audience.

You may find a working thesis during prewriting, or you may still be trying to adjust and narrow the subject to shape a thesis as you enter the second stage of the composing process: drafting.

CHARACTERISTICS OF DRAFTING

After you have experimented with one or more prewriting techniques, determined your audience and purpose in writing, gathered material, and responded to your prewriting, it is time to begin drafting your essay. Remember from Chapter 2 that a draft is a rough preliminary version of a piece of writing. A first draft, or **preliminary draft,** is only one of what will probably be many drafts before you produce the **final draft,** which you will present to your reading audience. Peter Drucker, a well-known business author, refers to his first draft as "the zero draft"—after that he can start counting! And writer and teacher Anne Lamott tells her writing students jokingly that the first draft is the "down" draft—you just get it down on paper, while the subsequent drafts are the "up" drafts—you work on fixing them up.

If you approach drafting as an opportunity to put your planning into action and experiment with various ways of getting your ideas across to your reader, *knowing that you can revise the draft later,* you'll feel more comfortable about this stage of the writing process. To get a better idea of what a first draft might look like, let's examine one student's preliminary draft. (To examine the instructor's comments on this draft, a later revised draft, peer response on this draft, and the student's final draft, see Chapter 7, pp. 172–184.)

MODEL WITH KEY QUESTIONS

Margarita Figueroa's assignment involved reading an essay about dishonesty in America, agreeing or disagreeing with the author's thesis, and then writing an essay that supported her position with specific examples. Once Figueroa had completed prewriting and had developed a working thesis, she decided she had enough material to begin drafting. As she wrote this first draft, Figueroa kept her working thesis and the informal outline on p. 97 next to her computer keyboard. Figueroa noted when she had finished the draft that although she had not communicated all of her ideas as clearly as she had hoped to, she was exhilarated to have transformed all the information from her prewriting into a first draft. Figueroa experienced that tremendous sense of accomplishment that many writers have when they get their first drafts on paper.

DISHONESTY
Margarita Figueroa

Margarita Figueroa decided in the first weeks of her writing class that learning to write clearly would be crucial to her future profession, nursing. Throughout the semester, she worked hard not only on getting first drafts on paper but also on revising and polishing them. Margarita confides that right now she has little free time, but when she does have a few hours, she enjoys reading mysteries.

1   I was reading an essay written by Marya Mannes called "The Thin Grey Line." It was a very interesting article, separating honesty from dishonesty. It made me really think about if people are dishonest or honest. I feel that dishonesty is more characteristic of our society than honesty.

2   Well, first there is the fake car accident that results in getting money out of auto insurance companies. For instance, I had friends that would get together and collaborate with one another and would report to the insurance company about an accident that they were involved in, but it wasn't a real accident. It was a fraudolent claim. They even had a friend who was a lawyer that would help them set everything up as if it was a legitimate accident. They used their own cars, license plate numbers, and insurance companies, and each person received an out-of-court settlement of five hundred dollars. Another reason for dishonesty is when an opportunity arises for an individual to become dishonest.

3   The circumstance that occurs and causes an indivual to become dishonest. For example, my sister told me about an incident that happened to her at Burger King. My sister had ordered burgers, fries, and drinks for her family. After she placed her order, the woman who works at Burger King rang the order up, but meanwhile my sister and the woman were having a conversation about kids. Then, my sister saw the total amount due, which was $14.83, so she gave the woman a twenty dollar bill and the woman gave my sister her order and then gave her the change due to her. This is when the woman made a mistake and gave her back the total amount due, which was $14.83, instead of $5.17, which was the change due. My sister noticed the mistake the woman made, but she didn't say anything. She walked out of Burger King, got in her car, and went home.

4   Dishonesty can also occur between two people in a relationship. It can result in blaming others for mistakes made by someone else. I have a friend that lives in the apartment complex where I stay. Her husband one day was backing up his car into his stall underneath the carport, when all of a sudden he hit one of the wooden poles that holds up the carport and moved it out of place. Then he called the owner of the building and explained to him about the incident that occurred, but instead of taking the blame for hitting the pole, he put the blame on his wife. Every time someone asked him what happened to the pole next to his car, he would reply, "Oh, my wife hit the pole when she was parking the car."

5   Finally, I do agree with the article "The Thin Grey Line" and Marya Mannes' opinion separating honesty from dishonesty because if we really take a close look at different situations, we would probably find a little dishonesty here and there. I feel that everyone has had some sort of dishonesty once in their lives, whether it was a little white lie or not, but dishonesty is a way of life for some people. We

need to be more responsible for our dishonest decisions and behaviors, but most of all, we need to strengthen our moral beliefs because dishonesty can have a major effect on everyone involved.

KEY QUESTIONS

1. **PURPOSE** What seems to be the writer's purpose in this draft? What kind of audience does she appear to be addressing? _____

   _____

2. **FOCUS** Find and underline Figueroa's thesis. Does it have the four characteristics discussed earlier in this chapter for an effective thesis? Which ones are missing or could be improved? _____

   _____

3. **MATERIAL** Where does the writer get her material? Could she use more examples or different ones? In which paragraphs could additional or different material help? _____

   _____

4. **STRUCTURE** How has Figueroa ordered or arranged the material?

   _____

   _____

5. **STYLE** Which phrase seems most effective in getting across the writer's thesis? _____

   _____

GUIDELINES FOR DRAFTING

In writing drafts of essays for previous assignments, Figueroa had stared at a blank computer screen for what seemed like an eternity. Because she did not want to be plagued again with writer's block, she decided to try some of the following suggestions for drafting.

Assess Material

After completing one or more prewriting activities, spread out all the material you have gathered in front of you. If your prewriting was completed on computer, print out all your notes—it's easier to assess material on a printed page. Make sure you have enough paper and pens or pencils. Having all supplies and notes within easy reach will give you greater concentration and fewer interruptions.

Practice 4.8 To determine a strategy for beginning a draft, find in the text the two supplies Figueroa used when drafting. Write these items in the following space.

_____

_____

Now list all the supplies, outlines, and so forth you recall using when you drafted your last essay. Which items were most useful? What items or resources will you add to this list?

_____

_____

◆ ◆ ◆

When you have all of your notes in front of you, assess the information to decide what to use in this first draft. Evaluate your material with your purpose and audience in mind. Ask yourself which details, facts, and examples most effectively support your working thesis for your reader. Make a tentative selection, setting aside (for now) any material that you won't use right away.

Order Material

Each writer needs to discover what works best for him or her—especially during the drafting stage. Your preliminary draft will probably include a working thesis, some support for that thesis, and a tentative method of organizing this support. Some writers begin to draft by jumping right in and writing an introduction that includes their thesis statement. Beginning with an introduction, no matter how rough, may give you a strong sense of having formally begun to write.

Other writers find it more useful to begin drafting in what will become the middle of their essay. Using their working thesis statement as a guide, they begin to develop and organize the examples, details, and other supporting materials that will provide the body of the essay and will support their working thesis.

The following are common ways of organizing material:

- Chronological order
- Spatial order
- Logical order

When you arrange your material in **chronological order,** you're choosing to proceed based on the time order in which events occur. For example, if you're writing an essay describing an event or observing someone or something over a progression of time, chronological order would be a good choice. You would be telling the events or situations in the order in which they occurred. If, on the other hand, the subject of your essay is physical—for example, a computer set-up and operation, or the layout of an efficient office, you might prefer **spatial order,** in which you would proceed from left to right, top to bottom, or front to back. Finally, if your essay deals with ideas and concepts rather than with time or space, you might choose **logical order.** Examples of logical order include **exemplification,** or explanation through the use of examples, cause and effect, comparing and contrasting, proceeding from a general statement to a particular one, or from a minor detail to the whole picture. For more information and for practice in identifying and choosing an order for your draft, see the section in Chapter 5 on organizing your support.

Outline

Once you have an idea of how your essay should be organized, you may want to develop an **outline**—a structural plan that uses headings and subdivisions to present the main points and subpoints of an essay. An outline can serve as an easy-to-read checklist and visual guide, and it can be as formal or as informal as you like. Think of your outline as a blueprint; you will refer to it frequently as you draft your essay to remind you what to do next.

The Informal Outline

The **informal outline** is meant for your use only and can be simply a list of the main ideas you want to develop. This type of outline should be easy to create based on your notes and prewriting, and it can help you decide what should come first, second, and third in the development of your material. To see an example of an informal outline, examine the one that Margarita Figueroa used in preparation for drafting "Dishonesty":

Thesis: I feel that dishonesty is more characteristic
      of our society than honesty.
Dishonesty in groups
      friends and fake car accident
Dishonesty in individuals
      Burger King incident
Dishonesty in not accepting responsibility
      man who shifted blame to his wife

The Formal Outline

Later in the semester, Figueroa's instructor assigned a research-based essay. With her instructor's permission, Figueroa decided to explore more thoroughly the concept of dishonesty. She was asked by her instructor to create a **formal outline** for the research-based essay. The formal outline is one that conforms to certain rules for numbering, lettering, and general format. A formal outline can help you examine the organization of a longer essay or research-based writing to determine if your essay will be logical and complete. Figueroa created the formal outline below. Notice its format.

Thesis: The thin line separating honest from dishonest behavior in America is becoming blurred because families, schools, and public as well as private institutions are neglecting responsibilities and accepting corruption as natural.

I. Families fail to enforce appropriate values.
   A. Mothers and fathers allow children instant gratification, denying them nothing.
      1. Parents give in to all material desires of their offspring.
      2. Children are not expected to work for what they want.
   B. Parents do not model honest behavior for their children.
      1. Many adults engage in dishonest behavior by cheating on taxes or bribing officials.
      2. Other adults refuse to take responsibility and be a "hero" when they witness corrupt behavior in others.
II. Schools either try to teach values and fail or refuse to recognize responsibility.
   A. Programs designed to teach values have been instigated.
      1. These programs have cost taxpayers lots of money and teachers much classroom time.
      2. The programs have accomplished little or nothing in the way of changing the behavior of students.
   B. Many school districts have refused to participate in the programs to teach values.
      1. These districts cite the meager success rate of the programs.
      2. They also stress the high cost of the programs.
      3. They feel it is not the responsibility of educators, but of parents, to teach values.
III. American institutions are rife with dishonesty and corruption.
   A. People who work in public institutions exhibit dishonest behavior.
      1. Politicians, law enforcement officers, and city officials engage in corrupt activities.
      2. Lower ranking officials in institutions may be guilty of small deceptions.

B. People who work for private institutions also engage in dishonesty on the job.

   1. Many business persons pad their expense accounts, take extra long lunch breaks and frivolous "business trips."

   2. Office staff and temporary or part-time office staff are also guilty of corrupt behavior.

You can see that the formal outline follows this format:

- It begins with a thesis.

- It indicates with uppercase Roman numerals the main points (I, II, III, IV).

- It identifies subcategories of topics with uppercase letters (A, B, C, D).

- It distinguishes support or evidence related to these subcategories with Arabic numbers (1, 2, 3, 4).

- It indicates (if the writer wishes to include additional information) specific details with lowercase letters (a, b, c, d).

Figueroa found that using a formal outline for a longer, more complex essay helps to organize material and maintain focus during drafting.

Practice 4.9   Turn to "Responding to Writing: Practice in Outlining" (p. 105) and complete the activities, or find an essay draft that you prepared for another assignment. Create either a formal or an informal outline of the main points and support in your draft.

◆ ◆ ◆

Begin in the Middle

While some writers like to begin drafting with the introductions, others prefer to begin drafting with the body paragraphs, saving the introduction and the conclusion until later. If you discover that this approach works for you, you should know that you're in good company—Richard Wright had almost finished drafting his powerful novel *Native Son* when he discovered, through development of the novel's characters, exactly what to write in his introductory pages. If, like Wright, you're staring at a blank page or screen and you feel hesitant or confused about the introduction, jump right in and proceed with your thesis and supporting material. You can always come back to the introduction later.

You'll have a much greater feeling of accomplishment if you work through your draft in sections rather than try to complete the entire essay in a short period of time. Try drafting a paragraph or two and then taking a short break.

This will allow you to get a little distance—you'll be able to see what you've written with "new eyes" when you come back and review your writing before moving on.

Define All Terms

Regardless of the subject matter of your essay, part of keeping your audience and purpose in mind as you're drafting requires that you define any unfamiliar or possibly confusing terms that you use. If you're telling your reader how to install "woofers" in a sound system or you make reference to the "operatory" where the patient is reclining, the average reader is going to be confused unless you briefly but clearly define these terms. (For more information on definition, see Chapter 9.)

Draft Multiple Versions

When you do come to a section of your draft that poses a problem or that you're unsure about, try drafting at least a couple of different versions of the section. Later, when you review your draft, you can judge which version seems to work better. For example, Figueroa decided to check her working thesis by reverse testing. She experimented by switching the original order of paragraphs 2 and 3.

Reserve Technical Considerations

Don't let spelling, grammar, or punctuation errors slow you down in your drafting stage—these concerns will be addressed in good time in revising and polishing. Instead, focus all your energies on getting your ideas on paper. This may be especially difficult advice to follow, for you may want to write "the perfect essay." Just remember that this is a draft. Your goal is to get ideas down on paper—later on you'll fix them up. If you are distracted at this stage by things like spelling and commas, you'll get sidetracked from what you're trying to communicate to your reader.

Share Drafts with Peers

Although many of us get butterflies in the stomach at the thought of someone else reading our writing, the feedback that we get from instructors, tutors, and peers can be very helpful. **Peer response,** also called **peer editing,** involves sharing your draft (this could be a first, second, or almost final draft) with another class member or within a small group. Your instructor may have a particular system for peer editing, or you may want to initiate a peer editing session yourself by suggesting it to another student. While all feedback is helpful, you will want to evaluate carefully the quality of feedback from student editors.

Practice 4.10 To get a better idea of how peer feedback can help you in drafting, locate a preliminary draft of an essay that you are working on or one that you've kept from a past assignment. Exchange essays with another student in your class. Turn to the peer editing activity in Chapter 7 (p. 195). Answer all "key" questions on a separate sheet of paper.

◆ ◆ ◆

STRATEGIES FOR DRAFTING

1. **PURPOSE** As you draft, don't worry about spelling, grammar, or other technical considerations. Do consider what your audience already knows about the subject and define all unfamiliar terms. Draft multiple versions of troublesome sections to determine which version best suits your purpose.

2. **FOCUS** Begin drafting based on a working thesis that includes a subject, controlling idea, specific language, and appropriate tone. Glance back often at your thesis and make sure that what you are writing relates clearly to it.

3. **MATERIAL** Before starting to draft, assess your material from prewriting and make sure you can access all notes easily.

4. **STRUCTURE** Work from an outline, either formal or informal, to give your draft a logical structure. Experiment with various drafting strategies, such as breaking the draft into smaller chunks or beginning in the middle.

5. **STYLE** Seek out peer or instructor response to gauge the effectiveness of your draft.

JOURNAL WRITING: FROM IDEA TO ESSAY

The following activities will help you to focus on your own drafting process. You'll also practice the process of moving from the shaping of ideas to the framing of a clear thesis.

1. If you have been keeping a reading log as suggested in Chapter 1, return to your log and review what you've written. Choose one journal entry and reread your notes. Can you zero in on what seems to be the most interesting note on the reading? Pick the one direct quote from the left-hand side and your response to it on the right-hand side. For example, let's suppose you've read and kept a reading log for "Stuttering Time" (p. 105). After looking at your log, you find that you've noted the following passage on the left-hand side of your journal: "feels like the canary that miners used to carry into a mine." On the right-hand side of your journal, you've written these words: "Remember reading that these birds were used to see if miners were safe or if they would die. Does Hoagland mean that his stuttering friend is a test case for the rest of us?" Once you've found a particular response of yours that you'd like to experiment with, write a working thesis based on the response that you could support in an essay. In the previous example, here's what might result:

   > The stutterer in Hoagland's essay "Stuttering Time" serves to warn us of the dangers of an increasing detachment that is a scary result of our new technology.

   As you use your journal notes to create a thesis, refer back to the guidelines (p. 85).

2. For this exercise, examine your drafting process. Thinking about the last essay you wrote, respond to the following questions in your journal:

   - What did you do to get ready to draft?

   - How did you go about assessing your material?

   - Did you work from an outline? Did it help? Even if you didn't work from an outline this time, should you try it with the next essay?

   - Did you "begin in the middle" or did you write the introduction first? How did this technique work for you in drafting?

   - Did you try to tackle small sections at a time or did you write from the beginning of the essay to the end?

   - Did you attempt to draft multiple versions of difficult sections to see which versions seemed to work best? How did this strategy for drafting work for you?

   - Did you save technical concerns for later or did you find yourself getting bogged down with spelling, grammar, and punctuation problems while drafting?

   - Did you share your draft with peers, your instructor, or a tutor? How did you feel about having somebody else comment on your writing? Did you agree with the feedback you received? What points did you disagree with?

USING THE COMPUTER: OUTLINING YOUR PAPER AND VISITING WEBSITES

1. After you have chosen one of the Options for Writing in the section that follows, type up and then print out an informal outline. Evaluate this first version, then mark any changes you want to make on the hard copy and use the editing functions (*cut, copy, paste*) to make the changes on screen. If your word-processing program offers an *outline* function, open a new file with a blank outline. Move the information from your informal outline file into the computer's version of a formal outline. Did you have to rearrange anything in your informal outline to make it fit in the computer's formal outline? Which version do you prefer?

2. Do you plan to continue your education at another college or university? Do you have a friend, or a relative, who is planning to apply to college? Nearly all schools now have their own Websites, where you can get information about financial aid, campus communities, transfer requirements and fields of study; download (print out) applications; and even write to college staff for further information. After you visit at least one of the following sites, answer the questions below.

CollegeEdge (⟨http://www.collegeedge.com/COLLEGE⟩): This site is designed to help you choose a college to apply to, based on your academic and professional goals and other factors.

College Bolt (⟨http://college.bolt.com⟩): A planner and guide to financial aid, taking the SATs, campus life, and other issues. Links to web pages of individual colleges and universities.

Student.Com (⟨http://www.student.com⟩): Links to campus newspapers, discussion groups about college life, and coverage of news events from the perspective of college students.

What college or university would I like to learn more about?

_____

What is its Web address (URL)? _____

What did I learn from visiting this school's Website that I didn't

know before? _____

OPTIONS FOR WRITING

Once you've chosen a writing option or have been assigned one by your instructor, begin by using a discovery strategy (p. 69) to generate material. When you have a working thesis and feel ready to begin drafting, review the strategies for drafting (p. 101). Think about how you want to structure your essay. You might create an informal outline. While you're drafting, the outline will help you get your ideas on paper and stay on track with your organization; you can also create a different outline and "audition" an alternate structure for your main points.

1. After rereading the essay "Dishonesty," decide whether you agree or disagree with Figueroa's working thesis. Although Figueroa explores everyday dishonesties, you might want to write about dishonesty in high places or unlikely places. If you've had experience in another community or environment, you could compare that level of dishonesty with what you've witnessed in your current situation. You can gather more material by polling your friends, relatives, and fellow students. Do you think there are circumstances when it is better—perhaps kinder—to lie? If so, you might want to write an essay in defense of dishonesty. Develop your opinion in an essay containing an effective thesis.

2. In "We Are, Like, Poets" (p. 107), Frederick begins his essay by referring to himself as a member of the "twenty-something generation, Generation X, the MTV generation." He feels that his generation has been wrongfully labeled lazy and illiterate. What about your generation? Does your age group carry with it certain stereotypes or preconceived notions? Do these stereotypes lead to snap judgments or misunderstanding of your generation by others? Discuss the traits or stereotypes associated with your age group in an essay.

3. In two essays in this chapter—"Dishonesty" and "We Are, Like, Poets"— the writers use the same element of American popular culture—a Burger King fast-food restaurant—as an example to support one of their main points. Frederick also refers to two other elements of our popular culture: MTV and shopping malls. In an essay, identify one or more elements of American popular culture and explore the impact that this element has on you or on your acquaintances.

4. In "Stuttering Time" (p. 105), Edward Hoagland asserts that technology has lessened society's tolerance for certain handicaps. However, others assert that technological advances, particularly in the areas of medical and computer technology, have greatly increased the quality of life for many people with physical and other handicaps. Do you know of anyone personally who has been helped or hindered by technological breakthroughs? Are there students on your campus who use a computer for physically challenged individuals? Students who benefit from motorized wheelchairs or telephone communications systems for the hearing impaired? Write an es-

say in which you agree or disagree with Hoagland. If possible, interview one or more people on your campus.

¶ 5. In "Stuttering Time," Hoagland mentions a friend who stutters and the intolerance he encounters as a result of his handicap. His friend feels with advancing technology, the intolerance may well become worse. He knows that he will have to figure out new ways to cope with his handicap. Perhaps you have a physical obstacle or know someone who does. Think about how you or this other person "rose to the occasion" and turned a seemingly hopeless situation into a positive one. In one paragraph, discuss and give examples of this turnaround.

RESPONDING TO WRITING: PRACTICE IN OUTLINING

Practice in outlining will enable you to understand how other writers organize their material in support of a thesis. This understanding will permit you to organize material in your own drafts more effectively. Read the following essay by Edward Hoagland, an American writer well known for his essays, fiction, and travel books. Notice that Hoagland begins with a clear thesis: he asserts that technology may lead to decreased tolerance for disabled individuals. Hoagland supports this thesis by describing the ways that technology might lead to intolerance for any individual differences. After you have read Hoagland's essay, complete the outline that has been started for you.

Stuttering Time

Edward Hoagland

1   We have a friend who stutters; and while he notices no increase in rudeness or sarcasm from people in person, he does hear more impatience from telephone operators, secretaries, businessmen, switchboard personnel, and other strangers whom he must deal with over the phone. As he stands at a phone booth or holds on to the devilish device at home, the time allotted to him to spit out the words seems to have markedly shrunk; perhaps it has been halved in the past half-dozen years. This alarms him because at the same time the importance of the telephone in daily transactions has zoomed. Indeed, many people use answering machines to consolidate their calls, and soon voiceprinting may become a commonplace method of identification. Imagine, he suggests, stuttering into a voiceprinting machine.

2   Bell system [telephone] operators, who used to be the most patient people he encountered, now often seem entirely unfamiliar with his handicap. They either hang up or switch

him to their supervisors as a "problem call" after listening for only a few seconds, interrupting a couple of times to demand that he "speak clearly, please." They seem automated themselves, as if rigged to a stop clock that regulates how long they will listen to anything out of the ordinary, though twenty years ago, he says, they practiced their trade with a fine humanity.

3   But it is not just individuals in individual occupations who have changed. The division between personal life and business life has deepened, and the brusqueness of business gets worse all the time. At the bank, one can no longer choose one's teller but must stand in a single line. (The tellers seem to work more slowly, having less responsibility individually for the length of the line.) And inevitably, as we all become known more and more by account numbers, doing business will become still more impersonal, and any voice that doesn't speak as plainly as digits entering a computer will cause problems.

4   We have no solutions to offer. We have brought up the subject only because our friend sometimes feels like the canary that miners used to carry into a mine. He believes his increasing discomfort foretells a worsening shortness of breath in other people—even those who started out with no handicaps at all.

◆ ◆ ◆

Thesis: Technology and an increasingly depersonalized society have resulted in less humanity and tolerance.

  I. A stutterer has noticed more curt and rude responses in telephone transactions.
    A. He is allowed less time to try to frame his words.
      1. He notices this in phone booths.
      2. He notices this also when making calls from his home.
    B. He is alarmed because the telephone grows ever more important in daily life.
      1. More people use answering machines to make their calling more efficient.
      2. Voice printing may soon become the norm.
      3. A person who stutters feels at a disadvantage with such technology.

  II. _____

      _____

    A. _____

      1. _____

      2. _____

B. _____

III. _____

_____

A. _____

1. _____

2. _____

B. _____

IV. _____

_____

A. _____

B. _____

You have seen how to use outlining in your writing to organize support for your thesis during the drafting stage. Outlining is also a useful study strategy. Making an outline of an essay you have read can help your understanding of a writer's main points and organizational plan.

READING AND ADDITIONAL ACTIVITIES

Jim Frederick is a magazine editor and writer in New York. He wrote the following essay in 1993 while he was a college student. As you read, notice that Frederick delays his thesis—you won't find it in the first paragraph. Also examine the way Frederick clearly identifies his audience and establishes an appropriate tone from the very outset of the essay.

We Are, Like, Poets

Jim Frederick

1   Our elders would have us believe that we—the twenty-something generation, Generation X, the MTV generation—are doomed to fail, not in the least by our supposed grammatical ineptness. Paramount to our problems, they claim, is a tendency to pepper our dialogue with the word *like* as if it were a verbal tic, demonstrating our abysmal vocabularies and utter lack of neurological activity.

2   Don't believe it. Much more than the random misfire of a stunted mind, *like* is actu-ally a rhetorical device that demonstrates the speaker's heightened sensibility and offers the listener added levels of color, nuance, and meaning.

3   Take the sentence, "I can't drive you to the mall because, like, my mom took the car to get her hair frosted." Here, *like* is a crucial phonic punctuation mark that indicates: "Im-portant information ahead!" In our frenetic society, where silence is no longer powerful but completely alien, the dramatic pause doesn't carry much rhetorical clout. We employ *like* to replace that now-obsolete device.

4   Or consider: "The human tongue is, like, totally gross." The use of *like* acknowledges that the tongue is not *exactly* totally gross but something *similar* to totally gross. It shows awareness that an indictment this harsh needs tempering. We repeatedly display such lin-guistic savvy in everyday observances: "My dad is, like, an anal-retentive psycho." . . .

5   In a new, ingenious usage, the word *like* becomes a verb form employed to recount an earlier conversation. Consider, "And she was like, 'You told us all to meet in *front* of the Burger King.' And I was like, 'What*ever*, you liar. Why would I when I knew it was going to snow?'" The difficulty here in determining what was actually said is not a limitation, but rather the strength of *like* as a dialogical indicator. It allows us to present the complete ex-perience of a conversation, not just one of its component parts. *Like* is more than a shabby substitute for *said* (as is commonly supposed), but a near equivalent of the word *meant*.

6   Also, *like* is often a broker of diplomacy. In the sentence, "Tiffany, you, like, still owe me that $10, you know," the skillful inclusion of *like* eases a potentially confrontational statement. The British do this sort of thing all the time with words like *rather, quite,* and *actually,* and no one complains.

7   Our generation is not nearly as bad off as we have been told. Hardly a generation of jacked-in, zoned-out illiterates, we the bike couriers, the paralegals, the skate punks, and the mall rats are actually a generation of poets. With a sublime sensibility to the power of *like,* we view our lives, indeed human existence itself, as a grand, eternal, and ever-changing metaphor.

QUESTIONS ON CONTENT

1. What is a "verbal tic" referred to in paragraph 1? (Use your dictionary if

necessary.) _____

_____

2. How many different uses of the word *like* does Frederick discuss?

_____

3. Find and annotate the essay for the meanings of the following words: *paramount, abysmal* (paragraph 1), *rhetorical nuance,* (paragraph 2), *frenetic, obsolete* (paragraph 3), *indictment, anal-retentive* (paragraph 4), *dialogical* (paragraph 5).

4. What kind of generation does Frederick feel he represents? Describe it in

your own words. _____

_____

QUESTIONS ON STRATEGY

1. Describe Frederick's target audience from his clues in paragraph 1.

_____

2. Underline and label Frederick's thesis. Does it have the four elements— subject, controlling idea, specific language, appropriate tone—necessary for an effective thesis? _____

_____

3. If you were to describe the order used by the writer to organize his material, would you say this essay was organized chronologically, spatially, or logically?

_____

4. Find an example in Frederick's essay of specific language that paints a clear word picture and write it here._____

_____

5. Describe Frederick's tone in a few words. _____

_____

Explain whether or not you feel his tone is appropriate for his audience and subject. _____

_____

CRITICAL THINKING IN CONNECTING TEXTS

In "We Are, Like, Poets," Jim Frederick asserts that other generations misconstrue his generation's use of the word *like* as a "verbal tic." In "Stuttering Time," Edward Hoagland warns that telephone operators and voiceprinting machines display decreasing tolerance for people who stutter or have other speech differences. Is our modern society becoming less or more tolerant of differences? With a small group of students, discuss people's treatment of groups perceived as "different" because of their race, age, physical or mental challenges, or ability to communicate in English. You might examine other kinds of differences as well. In your group, discuss the impact that the media has on our levels of tolerance and understanding. Do television, films, magazines, and newspapers serve to increase or decrease our tolerance for differences? See if you can reach some form of agreement within your group. Then, if time permits, collaborate in creating a thesis and informal outline for an essay developing these ideas.

**For more writing resources, be sure to see the
Longman English Pages Website at
http://longman.awl.com/englishpages**

Using Body Paragraphs to Develop Essays

> [A paragraph is] a collection of sentences with unity of purpose.
>
> —*Alexander Bain, from* English Composition and Rhetoric

Preview

In this chapter you will learn

▶ to recognize the characteristics of effective body paragraphs: topic sentence, sufficient support, clear order, precise language

▶ to determine when to paragraph

▶ to compose body paragraphs with topic sentences and adequate detail using chronological, spatial, or logical order

▶ to use repetition and parallel structure in body paragraphs

▶ to use cue words within body paragraphs and from one body paragraph to the next

▶ to identify ground rules for peer editing and to peer edit body paragraphs

Just as the paragraph is a "collection of sentences," each body paragraph, individually and in connection with other body paragraphs, supports and develops the thesis of the college essay. This chapter focuses on the essential paragraphs that are found between the introduction and the conclusion of essays. Body paragraphs include a writer's main points and most of the details and information to support these main points. Although certainly there is information in an essay's introduction and conclusion, body paragraphs form the bulk of the college essay. Put another way, if the essay's thesis is its spine, as we saw in Chapter 4, the body paragraphs are the real muscles of the essay.

CHARACTERISTICS OF BODY PARAGRAPHS

Body paragraphs vary tremendously in purpose, length, style, and subject matter, but almost every effective body paragraph contains the following characteristics:

- It makes one main point.
- It contains sufficient support, using from one to many kinds of evidence to develop its main point.
- It proceeds according to a clear organizational plan.
- It contains no material that does not relate to its point.
- It employs precise language.

In addition, the separate body paragraphs work effectively together within an essay if they possess the following traits:

- Each moves clearly and smoothly from one main point to the next.
- Each makes use of the organizational plan that suits the writer's purpose, logically follows the previous paragraph, and clearly leads to the next paragraph.

MODEL WITH KEY QUESTIONS

Jeremy Smith was eager to share his interpretation of a particular word with readers. As you read his essay, see how many of the characteristics of body paragraphs you can identify in paragraphs 2 through 6 of Smith's essay.

RELATIVITY
Jeremy Smith

....

Jeremy Smith wanted to be creative in his essays and "express my perspective on ideas or events that I feel passionately about." Sometimes Jeremy found that phrases and whole sections of essay drafts that seemed clear to him would not be clear to another reader. Peer editing and instructor conferences helped him to "re-see" his earlier drafts. Jeremy reports that he loves children and is working part-time at a day care center now. He hopes to transfer to UCLA's film program soon.

1   Is New York far from California? Is China far from America? Many people to-day think of the word *far* in terms of distance from point A to point B. And while the word does have that meaning—"to, at, or from a considerable distance" according to Webster, a considerable distance today stretches much farther outward both physically and symbolically than when the word was first used. As times have changed, so has the meaning of this term *far.*

2   The term *far* used to refer to geographical distances we now consider the opposite—*close.* In 1492 when Columbus sailed to the Americas, he was said to have traveled very far, embarking on a journey that was to take him and his crew many months to complete. The approximate distance of his travels was over six thousand miles—an unheard-of distance during Columbus' time. In contrast, today we can travel this same distance in well under a day; if we can afford a Concorde flight, we can make the trip in little over a half-day. Modern technology has transformed far into close.

3   On July 20, 1969, a man named Neil Armstrong set foot on the moon—a destination that we in the nineties still consider far. However, even though the moon is some 300,000 miles away from the earth, I fully expect my grandchildren to be making a lunar or other planetary voyage during their lifetimes. In the future, I predict that distances we now still consider far will be regarded as close.

4   In the same way that we have pushed the envelope for the term *far* as it relates to geographical distances, we have also expanded our vision of far to refer to the advances a person makes in his or her life. We have perhaps heard the expression, "You will go far in life." In the time of Columbus, not everyone received an education—those not fortunate enough to have been born to noble parentage had to struggle just to make ends meet. For this person, "You will go far" might have meant "you will be fortunate enough to feed and clothe your children—you may even have a little nest-egg put aside." However, today, at least in America, this same forecast may be uttered about anyone, regardless of race, creed or sex. Furthermore, in our day, "You will go far" might foreshadow financial success, political or artistic fame, celebrity status in sports or entertainment, or many other possibilities.

5   Contrary to what we currently mean by the expression "You will go far," in some distant future this expression might be directed not to the way the outside world regards any given individual, but instead to the way the individual regards himself or herself. It is possible that civilization will know a time when a shepherd on a hill, living a pure life of self-sacrifice, meditation and moderation, but living this life dressed in rags and living in a humble cottage, will be regarded by his contemporaries as "having gone far."

6   Finally, computer technology has served to change my personal definition of the term *far,* and I believe that this technology will continue to have an impact on the next generation. If I want to call my friends overseas, I have always been able to pick up the phone. But if I wanted to correspond with them, in the past, I have waited up to three or four weeks for my letter to get to them and then for them to return my mail. By the time I received their letter, in many cases the information that they shared was no longer current. In contrast, with the advances offered by E-mail, I can send off a detailed explanation of what has been happening with me and pretty well expect to get a response the same day—sometimes within a few minutes or hours. Perhaps this is why some experts say that the "global village" has arrived; no place on earth is remote or far.

7   *Far* is a word that will continue to change, I'm positive. Although I feel inadequate to predict the extent of these changes, I know one thing that I can predict: mankind will go far with time—we're well on our way and the distance is no longer considerable.

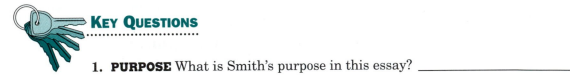

KEY QUESTIONS

1. **PURPOSE** What is Smith's purpose in this essay? _____

_____

2. **FOCUS** What is the thesis of the essay?_____

_____

Annotate the essay by finding and underlining the sentence in each body paragraph that states the main point for that paragraph.

3. **MATERIAL** What are two examples of specific support in two different body paragraphs? _____

_____

4. **STRUCTURE** Are the body paragraphs clearly organized? _____ Choose any body paragraph (2 through 6) and explain how the writer organizes the material. _____

_____

5. **STYLE** Reread the essay. Can you find one or more words that take the reader from one idea to the next? Are there important words that the writer repeats? Write these down in the following space._____

_____

GUIDELINES FOR BODY PARAGRAPHS

Determine the Paragraph's Purpose

Before you begin working on your separate body paragraphs, consider how each body paragraph relates to your broader purpose in writing the entire essay. For example, if you take another look at Jeremy Smith's essay, you can see that the writer's purpose in paragraph 2 is to persuade his audience that the meaning of the term *far* has changed over the centuries. His purpose in paragraph 3 is to convince readers that the term will change yet again in the future.

Practice 5.1   Reread paragraphs 4, 5, and 6 of Jeremy Smith's essay. In the margin of the essay, write what you think the writer wants his audience to think, feel, or do as a result of reading these body paragraphs.

◆ ◆ ◆

Use Topic Sentences

Just as your essay needs a thesis that states the main point of the entire essay, each body paragraph requires a **topic sentence.** This sentence states the overall idea or point you're trying to make in the paragraph. Each topic sentence should be clearly related to your thesis for the entire essay.

Make sure that your topic sentence for each of your body paragraphs does the following:

- It names the main point of the paragraph.

- It contains a **controlling idea.**
  The controlling idea reveals your attitude—what you, the writer, think about your main point—or it limits the main point by telling what particular aspect of the point you will discuss in the paragraph.

For example, look again at the topic sentence for paragraph 2 in Smith's essay "Relativity":

The term *far* used to refer to geographical distances we now consider the opposite—*close.*

Smith's sentence tells his audience that the main point in this first body paragraph is geographical distances. His controlling idea—the limitation Smith puts on this main point—is how these distances have changed over time.

Practice 5.2 Examine the following topic sentences. Annotate each one, circling the main point and underlining the controlling idea. If the sentence does not contain both, put a check by it to indicate that it needs to be rewritten. On a separate sheet of paper, revise those topic sentences in need of more work.

1. Last fall I went on a vacation to the East Coast.

2. College students who work part- or full-time must organize their time efficiently.

3. Buying some basketry supplies can be the beginning of a fun and lucrative hobby.

4. The college library is available for all students.

5. There are many different kinds of friends.

◆ ◆ ◆

Body paragraphs usually begin with a topic sentence, giving the audience the chance to absorb the writer's main point and controlling idea before getting the detailed information to support this main point. If you look again at Jeremy Smith's essay, you'll see that the writer has placed his topic sentence for paragraph 2 at the beginning of his body paragraph. Sometimes, however, you may prefer to use a different type of organization by withholding the subject and controlling idea until details have been absorbed by your readers. This type of organization can give your body paragraph dramatic impact.

The writer of the following body paragraph decided to place her topic sentence at the end of the paragraph. What is the effect of this strategy?

First, the parking lot was far away from the court building and I had to take a shuttle to the building. The bus driver would not let me in unless I had a juror's badge, which I had forgotten. After I showed him my summons and he let me on the bus, he dropped all of us off at the criminal court building. I didn't know where to go, so I followed the crowd that was on the bus to the entrance. I then realized that I would have to go through the metal detector, and I was detained and asked to empty my purse. Then I took the elevator to the seventh floor, and I saw huge crowds of people standing around.

These people looked confused, just like me. It turns out that they had all been summoned. All in all, appearing for jury duty was not at all what I had expected.

—Leah Ford, student

Implied Topic Sentences: Proceed with Caution

Instead of stating the main point of the paragraph outright, a writer may decide to hint at the main idea of the paragraph. This hint is referred to as an **implied topic sentence.** In these cases, all the details in a body paragraph relate clearly enough to one obviously understood subject, as is the case with the following paragraph:

She had on a kind of dirty-pink—beige maybe, I don't know—bathing suit with a little nubble all over it and, what got me, the straps were down. They were off her shoulders looped loose around the cool tops of her arms, and I guess as a result the suit had slipped a little on her, so all around the top of the cloth there was this shining rim. If it hadn't been there you wouldn't have known there could have been anything whiter than those shoulders. With the straps pushed off, there was nothing between the top of the suit and the top of her head except just *her,* this clean bare plane of the top of her chest down from the shoulder bones like a dented sheet of metal tilted in the light. I mean, it was more than pretty.

—John Updike, from "A and P"

Updike's implied topic sentence in this paragraph could be stated as something like the following:

The shoulders of the girl in the bathing suit (main point) were captivating (controlling idea).

If you do want to try an implied topic sentence, make certain that your audience will clearly understand your hints. Every sentence must clearly develop your unstated main point. Otherwise, you may find yourself with a paragraph that makes perfect sense to you but will appear to your reader to have no main point.

Practice 5.3 Read Barbara Ehrenreich's "Zipped Lips" (pp. 135–137). Underline the topic sentences in each of the body paragraphs. If you encounter a paragraph that appears to have no topic sentence, ask yourself if the topic sentence could be implied and then annotate the paragraph by writing the implied topic sentence in the margin.

◆ ◆ ◆

Practice 5.4 Develop each of the following topics into a topic sentence for a body paragraph. Be sure that each topic sentence includes both a main point and a controlling idea.

1. A local park or monument: _____

_____

2. Final exams: _____

_____

3. Cigarette advertisements: _____

_____

4. Plastic surgery: _____

_____

5. Family bonding: _____

_____

6. Interracial dating: _____

_____

7. Drive-by shootings: _____

_____

8. Freedom of speech: _____

_____

9. Live performers in concert: _____

_____

10. Clothing styles: _____

_____

◆ ◆ ◆

Develop Supporting Details

The supporting material for your body paragraphs can come in a variety of forms and from many different sources—your memory, personal interviews, observations, readings, outside research, even your imagination if appropriate for the essay assignment. Even though the type of support may vary tremendously from body paragraph to body paragraph and from essay to essay, the material you use should possess the following characteristics:

- It should relate clearly to your topic sentence. This means that you should omit any information, no matter how exciting or valid, that veers off the subject of the body paragraph.

- It should be stated as clearly as possible. This means using precise rather than vague words. It may also mean defining any unfamiliar terms for your audience.

- It should be reliable. You want to use details that come from your first-hand knowledge or the knowledge of trustworthy sources rather than hearsay. You also want to use information that is current rather than dated unless your subject is one for which dates have no importance.

- It should be sufficient. You need enough information to convince your audience of the main point you are making in the body paragraph. Underdeveloped body paragraphs are perhaps the most common weakness of many college writers. To make sure you have enough information, try to gather *more* than enough, and then you can be selective later with what you decide to use.

The following body paragraph includes sketchy, underdeveloped support material:

Saturday night's party at Tom's house became so crowded that disaster soon followed. Everybody was packed together. The noise was really deafening and the smells were intense. Later some furniture got hurt and the floors were ruined.

—Mitch Wexler, student

Although Wexler has a good topic sentence for the paragraph, he doesn't really paint a clear picture of the disaster, as his topic sentence promises. We don't have too much specific information about the noise or the smells; we don't know what furniture gets hurt, or even what "hurt" means—did something break or did it tear, or did someone spill something on it? Finally we're left unsatisfied about how the floors were ruined. Here's how Wexler revised his underdeveloped body paragraph after receiving helpful comments from his instructor and a peer editor:

Saturday night's party at Tom's house became so crowded that disaster soon followed. People were pressed body to body from the walls to the center of the rooms, and they had to scream at each other to be heard over the pulsating, drum-heavy beat of the band. In spite of the open windows, through which people now climbed because the front door had been locked, the place reeked. The hardwood floors were slick and sticky from drinks and pizza spills; around nine o'clock, there was a cracking sound like a baseball when it makes contact with a bat as a kitchen chair snapped and its two occupants scrambled to avoid hitting the floor.

Practice 5.5 Annotate both the earlier and later versions of Wexler's paragraphs by underlining the main point and the controlling idea in each. In the second paragraph, circle all words or phrases that create a clear picture of his main point.

◆ ◆ ◆

Practice 5.6 To gain experience in developing clear, reliable, and sufficient support in your body paragraphs, choose one of the ten topics that you expanded into topic sentences in Practice 5.4. After writing the topic sentence on a separate sheet of paper, use any prewriting strategy to come up with enough material for an effective body paragraph.

◆ ◆ ◆

Stay on Topic

Remember that every piece of information and every detail in a body paragraph needs to relate to and develop the topic sentence. It's easy to get **off-topic** without realizing it. You are off-topic when your supporting details no longer clearly relate to your topic sentence. For instance, when Mitch Wexler began to revise his underdeveloped paragraph, he found he could add many details that would allow his audience to envision the wild party scene. In his enthusiasm, Wexler included information about the actual songs being played by the band—their specific titles, the names of the original performers for each song, and those songs that were his personal favorites. After rereading his paragraph, Wexler discovered that these details about the songs should be deleted because they did not develop the main point in his topic sentence.

In revising your essay, make sure that each detail in the paragraph clearly supports the paragraph's main point.

Practice 5.7 Read the following paragraph and underline the main point and the controlling idea in the topic sentence. Next, reread the paragraph, crossing out any sentences or phrases you find that do not support the topic sentence.

Location is critical for a successful garage sale. Just getting to the sale must be made as difficult as possible to enhance consumer excitement. If the directions the consumers receive send them in circles, they will feel that this garage sale must have some hidden treasures and anticipation will build! Signs are an important ingredient. Make sure the signs are made from a sturdy and dependable cardboard, tough enough to withhold the strains of rainy or windy weather. Another hot tip is flyers. Drive over to a copy shop and make about a thousand flyers to hand out at a local mall. My favorite copy shops are the ones that stay open twenty-four hours. Some of these offer discounts on week-ends. While you're handing out the flyers at the mall, be sure to eat lunch because you won't be able to take a break during your garage sale.

—Brian Morton, student

◆ ◆ ◆

Use Precise Words

Make sure that each detail in your body paragraphs is as precisely stated as possible. Some essay writers may get several sentences about a subject down on paper, but they don't take the time to make sure that they're not repeating themselves or being vague or "fuzzy" in their writing. In your revising stage, give yourself the time—and if possible, the help of another editor—to ensure that each body paragraph contains the vivid, specific, and effective words that develop your subject by painting as clear a verbal picture as possible.

Practice 5.8 To recognize vague development, read the following early draft of a body paragraph. Work with a partner to revise the underlined vague expressions. You can write in your text or use a separate sheet of paper.

Certain athletes become obsessive and really take sports <u>too far</u>. For example, some football players really get competitive <u>out there</u>. The guys on the team are always <u>trying</u> to show their strength and be better than the player next to them, but when a player will do anything to be better than the other teammates, there is a <u>problem</u>. Also, certain weight trainers and track stars obsess on their sport so much and their success in their sport that they resort to <u>bad practices</u>. They may take <u>some drugs</u> to make them stronger or faster, but these drugs may be illegal and unhealthy. Finally, there are even some examples of competitive athletes cheating in their events. A track person took a short-cut in a big race and she ended up disqualified because of her actions.

—Nicoll Grijalva, student

◆ ◆ ◆

Organize Your Support

Once you have your topic sentence for your body paragraph and you have decided which details will support that topic sentence, think about what might be the most effective organizational plan for that material. It isn't enough to scatter the material randomly among your body paragraphs. In developing your body paragraphs into an essay, you might want to work from an informal outline as discussed in Chapter 4 and to use again the three options for arranging the order of your material: chronological, spatial, and logical. In addition, many patterns of essay development covered in Part Two of this book can be applied to the development of individual body paragraphs as well as entire essays.

Chronological Order

If the supporting details in your body paragraph unfolded over a period of time, you might do well to arrange your support in **chronological order.**

To illustrate, notice that the writer of the following paragraph has organized his material according to time progression. He begins with the first event that relates to the topic sentence:

> I felt that the most scary part of the date was about to happen and things were now out of my control. Once inside the house, I went through the official handshakes and greetings with the parents. Immediately after I introduced myself, a creepy silence fell upon the room. I began to feel sweaty and uncomfortable. I didn't know what to say, but I could feel the parents eyeballing me from head to toe, just looking for the slightest flaw. Then my nightmare came true. The father started to interrogate me. He asked me questions like, "So, do you work?" and "So where exactly are you two going tonight?" and finally, "So, what time are you planning on bringing her home?" At this point, I was willing to accept any curfew the parents were willing to give us as long as I got out before I turned to Jello.
>
> —Keith Siegman, student

Practice 5.9   Reread and then annotate the above paragraph by numbering events in the order in which they occurred. To recognize instances in which you might use chronological order in developing a body paragraph, return to the list of topic sentences you created in Practice 5.4. Put a "C" by any of these topics that could be developed in this manner.

◆ ◆ ◆

Spatial Order

If the main point of your body paragraph concerns a person, place, or object that has physical properties, use **spatial order,** in which the supporting details can be arranged in a visual pattern, such as from left to right, top to bottom, or front to back.

Practice 5.10 To get a better idea of how to use spatial order to organize material, read the following body paragraph:

> As my mother and I enter the lobby of the movie theatre, we are always struck by familiar sights and sounds. The quick and efficient ticket-takers are at the front doors to take our tickets. About twenty feet away and to the right are the food counters, with three smiling uniformed helpers standing in front of brightly lit popcorn in glass cages, popping and giving off a buttery aroma. My eyes are caught by the shiny, colorful candy wrappers displayed in these glass counters: Snickers, Crunch, KitKat, and Reese's beckon me. At the far left edge of the counter are little brown baskets for people to place trash. Many are filled with gum and old receipts. On the right end of the counter are ketchup, relishes, and other condiments for hot dogs.
>
> —Desirea Espinoza, student

Work with a partner after rereading the paragraph and draw a quick map of the space Espinoza describes. To identify situations in which to use spatial order in body paragraphs, look again at your list of topic sentences in Practice 5.4 and mark an "S" by those topic sentences that could be developed with spatial organization.

◆ ◆ ◆

Logical Order

Some main points do not exist as physical objects or take place over a period of time. To develop this kind of topic sentence, you might want to consider **logical order**—organizing the details of your paragraph in the most sensible and reasonable manner possible. The logical order you determine will depend on your main point in the paragraph:

- If you're writing about a situation, you might want to start with causes and proceed to effects.

- If you're comparing two subjects, you might want to progress from similarities to differences or vice versa.

- If you're using examples, you might want to begin with your weakest example and save your most powerful one for the end.

As you read the following illustration of logical order in a body paragraph using examples, note that the writer has chosen to save her most powerful examples for last:

> Many of our city parks today are unsafe and could be hazardous to the health of our children. Some parks have potholes on the ground or cracks in pavement which are dangerous for a child to run on. Others have unsanitary

restrooms where toilets don't flush, walls are covered with graffiti, and the smell is disgusting. Even more potentially hazardous to young children is the poor condition of the park equipment: dirty swings, rusty monkey bars, and old slides invite disaster. Trash, cigarette butts, and dog droppings are also common sights in these parks. Finally, because many of our city's parks are frequented by gangs, children must contend with drive-by shooting and fights among gang members. Because parks are important for the development of children, we should think more seriously about how we can make them safer, more inviting places.

—Grethel Peralta, student

Although Peralta's topic sentence mentions a place, she decided to use logical rather than spatial order because she did not want to discuss the physical details of any one park. Instead, she wanted to make the point that many parks are unsafe. Notice that after offering her final detail, this writer repeats her topic sentence as a wrap-up at the end of her paragraph. Since the paragraph offers quite a bit of detail, Peralta felt she wanted to reinforce her main idea by repeating it at the conclusion of the body paragraph.

Know When to Paragraph: Some General Rules

If you remember that each body paragraph focuses on one main point, you should not have a problem knowing when to begin a new paragraph. As a rule, each new point or subject needs to have its own paragraph. As you are drafting, you may notice that not all your paragraphs are the same length. Don't let the difference in length bother you, as long as each paragraph includes enough support for its topic sentence. The difference in length may occur for several reasons. Some main points are more complicated than others, or some main points may require the writer to define unfamiliar terms. There are, however, a few generally acknowledged rules for paragraph length.

Overlong Paragraphs

As a courtesy to readers, try to avoid paragraphs that go beyond three quarters of a typed, double-spaced page, and never write a paragraph that goes beyond a full typed page. You do not want to delete valuable material to make the paragraph shorter. Instead, one solution is to break your subject into two clear parts, thus breaking one body paragraph into two. Even if this revision calls for you to write an additional topic sentence and perhaps to rearrange your material, by all means do it. You will be allowing your audience to follow the development of your ideas much more easily.

Practice 5.11 Read the following two body paragraphs, which have been typed incorrectly to make them appear as one. Place a mark in the spot where you think the paragraph break should logically go and then fill in the missing topic sentence for the second paragraph in the space provided.

Keeping long work hours will affect grades of high schoolers and may cause them to stop going to school altogether. A friend named James worked for a fast food franchise—his hours were 11 in the morning to 9 in the evening on the weekends, and from 5 to 9 on weekdays. When Monday rolled around, he just didn't have the energy for school work most Mondays. From the time he got his job, his grades started to drop and he didn't graduate from high school. Instead, when he discovered that he was failing his classes, he gave up going to school and dropped out. I have another friend who works for a different fast food franchise, and he is learning only how to set a timer for French fries, how to heat up burgers already cooked by somebody else, and how to collect money from customers. He says that none of these skills will mean anything on his resume and that he has not learned anything he can transfer to any job other than fast food. He even says that if he got another fast food job, he would probably have to learn these same skills differently, because each franchise has its own food preparation methods.

—Peter Huang, student

Missing topic sentence:

_____

_____

◆ ◆ ◆

Just as you want to break up paragraphs that are over a page long, you also want to expand short body paragraphs if they are underdeveloped, as mentioned earlier. The only exceptions are body paragraphs that are short because they are transition paragraphs—they actually move the readers from one main point to the next instead of offering a discussion of a new subject.

Topic Sentence in Wrong Paragraph

When drafting your paragraphs, be careful not to place a topic sentence for your next body paragraph in the body paragraph that you're just wrapping up. While it might seem like a good idea to "preview coming attractions," this only confuses your readers. To see an example of a misplaced topic sentence, read the following two paragraphs:

Dishonest behavior on our city streets is on the rise. On the freeways, there are more and more cars traveling above the speed limit. And people feel picked on when they do get a ticket rather than feeling guilty about being dishonest in breaking a law. Also, many drivers speed through yellow lights rather than slow down and stop. Instead of regarding the yellow light as a warning to slow down, many people take this as a signal to go faster and they step on the gas even harder. Other examples of dishonest behavior on streets include illegal U-turns, illegal parking, and lane changes without signaling. However, it's not just on our city streets that we witness dishonest behavior. Deceptive behavior is also becoming more and more common in the workplace.

People "borrow" supplies from the company without telling anyone—this is sometimes just pens, pencils, little items, but oftentimes more expensive equipment, such as typewriters or video cameras are "borrowed." Many workers think nothing of calling in "sick" when they really just want a vacation day. And countless people on the job take extended lunches and coffee breaks, often to run personal errands on company time. Another deceptive behavior involves the use of the company telephone for personal calls, sometimes even costing the company lost business because the clients can't get through or are ignored by the office staff.

—In Sung Song, student

Practice 5.12 Find the topic sentence in Song's first paragraph that relates to the material in the second paragraph. Underline the sentence and draw an arrow where you think the sentence best fits in the second paragraph.

◆ ◆ ◆

Signal Shifts in Thought

Cue words or **transitions** are words or phrases that allow readers to anticipate what's to come in the body paragraphs of an essay. If you use cue words effectively, your audience will follow your thought process more easily from one detail or main point to the next. Cue words are thus useful not only within body paragraphs but throughout the entire essay. Additional details are discussed in Chapter 7, where you will find an extensive list of cue words to help you signal to your reader that you are moving from one detail or main point to the next.

Practice 5.13 Improve the following paragraph, which has no transitions, by inserting any cue words from the list in Chapter 7 (pp. 187–188) that might help the reader follow the writer's ideas.

I have several good reasons for missing class today. My car was totaled in

an accident yesterday afternoon, and I have no way of getting to school. My

dog ate my homework, and my instructors will never believe that this really happened. My favorite soap opera is featuring a guest star this week whom I absolutely adore and cannot miss, and the VCR is on the blink so I can't tape the show for later viewing. I have no doubt that all of my instructors will understand my situation and take pity on me.

◆ ◆ ◆

Repeat Important Words

You can keep your body paragraphs focused on the main point by using appropriate repetition of important words and phrases. To avoid becoming monotonous in your writing and to make your repetitions more interesting, use **synonyms**—substitute words that have the same or almost the same meaning as the original word.

Practice 5.14 To examine repetition of important words in a body paragraph, read the following example, in which repeated words have been underlined.

> Secondhand smoke is another possible cause of Sudden Infant Death Syndrome. Smoking during pregnancy and smoking around the baby after it is born increase the risk of SIDS compared to infants not exposed to cigarette smoke. Studies show that "infants exposed to 1 to 10 cigarettes a day were 2.4 times as likely to die of SIDS as unexposed infants, while those exposed to 11 to 20 cigarettes a day were 3.6 times as likely to die" (Maugh A-1). The more smoke infants inhale and are exposed to, the higher the risk of their dying from SIDS. Parents should lessen the risk by not smoking at all before pregnancy and after. Those who cannot quit should cut down on the amount and try to smoke away from the infant, so the child won't be affected.
>
> —Letictia Elder, student

In the following space write one synonym that you found.

_____

◆ ◆ ◆

Practice 5.15 Return to Jeremy Smith's essay "Relativity" (pp. 113–114). See if you can identify at least two important words used several times throughout the essay. Write these in the following space.

_____

◆ ◆ ◆

Use Parallel Sentence Structures

Similar ideas can be effectively, and sometimes quite dramatically, linked by using **parallel sentence structures.** Parallel sentence structures repeat a sentence pattern for dramatic effect.

To see how parallel sentence structure works in body paragraphs, read the following example. The repeated sentence structures have been underlined:

> A woman who has had a tough childhood ends up on the streets, working as a prostitute, and she becomes the victim of prejudice. <u>She desperately wants to turn her life around. She wants to go to school; she wants to get a job.</u> But she can't, for when people find out she is a prostitute, no one is interested in hiring her. <u>She wants a decent place to live; she wants to go out on a regular date; she wants to go to church.</u> But she can't find a neighborhood, a date, or a church that will accept her. Why? Because <u>no one wants to live next to an ex-prostitute, no one wants to go out with someone with her reputation, and no one wants to sit next to a woman like that in church.</u> And these are all people who say, "I'm not prejudiced."
>
> —Corona Reynolds, student

Practice 5.16 Underline all repeated sentence structures you find in the following paragraph:

> But although I was initially disappointed at being categorized as an extremist, as I continued to think about the matter I gradually gained a measure of satisfaction from the label. Was not Jesus an extremist for love: "Love your enemies, bless them that curse you, do good to them that hate you, and pray for them which despitefully use you, and persecute you." Was not Amos an extremist for justice? "Let justice roll down like waters and righteousness like an ever-flowing stream." Was not Paul an extremist for the Christian gospel: "I bear in my body the marks of the Lord Jesus." Was not Martin Luther an extremist: "Here I stand; I cannot do otherwise, so help me God." And John Bunyan: "I will stay in jail to the end of my days before I make a butchery of my conscience." And Abraham Lincoln: "This nation cannot survive half slave and half free." And Thomas Jefferson: "We hold these truths to be self-evident, that all men are created equal. . . ." So the question is not whether we will be extremists, but what kind of extremists we will be.
>
> —Martin Luther King, Jr., from "Letter from Birmingham Jail"

◆ ◆ ◆

STRATEGIES FOR BODY PARAGRAPHS

1. **PURPOSE** Know what you want to accomplish in each of your body paragraphs as well as the broader purpose of each paragraph in relation to your entire essay. When revising, check to see that each body paragraph has achieved its individual purpose and also works with the other body paragraphs to support the essay's thesis.

2. **FOCUS** Use a topic sentence (or an implied topic sentence) to focus on a main point and connect all details in each body paragraph. Make sure your topic sentence names the main point and has a controlling idea. In your support material for each body paragraph, omit or revise any information that does not clearly relate to the topic sentence, or rephrase the topic sentence so that it relates to the support material you have presented.

3. **MATERIAL** Check your draft to see that each body paragraph has clearly stated, reliable, adequate support for the topic sentence. Revise any vague or underdeveloped paragraphs.

4. **STRUCTURE** Use an organizational plan for each body paragraph that seems to work best for your material—chronological, spatial, or logical order. Create a new paragraph when you move on to a new main point. Insert cue words to signal a change in direction or level of detail, both within each body paragraph and from one body paragraph to the next.

5. **STYLE** Reread, respond, and revise all body paragraphs so that they use the most precise words possible. Make sure you repeat important words and use parallel sentence structures.

JOURNAL WRITING: FROM IDEA TO PARAGRAPH

This activity will help you identify topic sentences in nonacademic writing—writing that can be described as informal or casual. This journal entry will also allow you to explore some topics of current public interest, generating material that could be useful in the body paragraphs of an essay.

1. Find and read an article in a current newspaper, popular magazine, or Website. (You can check out the editorial page of the newspaper for more in-depth articles.) Choose any paragraph and identify its topic sentence. (Note that newspaper and magazine body paragraphs tend to

be shorter than the body paragraphs in college essays. However, even short paragraphs have topic sentences—and these may be found at the beginnings as well as the ends of paragraphs, or they may be implied.) In a journal entry, copy the topic sentence you've chosen, and then write your evaluation of it. Is it a good topic sentence for the paragraph? Does it state the main point and controlling idea? Finally, write your reaction to the entire body paragraph, explaining whether it is adequately supported.

2. If this part of the journal entry prompts you to write more about the subject, continue to write about your reaction. If not, locate another topic sentence in another body paragraph of the same article or a different one and begin another journal entry.

USING THE COMPUTER: MOVING FROM PREWRITING TO PARAGRAPHING AND EDITING

1. Drafting on a computer makes it easy to experiment with different ways of ordering paragraphs. Open a prewriting file that you've saved on disc or hard drive and print it out. Next, referring back to the guidelines and strategies for body paragraphs in this chapter, open a new file and type in two or more body paragraphs of an essay based on the prewriting. (Don't worry about your introductory or concluding paragraphs for now.) Identify the topic sentence for each body paragraph and highlight it by changing the type to either *bold* or *italic*. Next, experiment with the most effective placement for this topic sentence by using the *copy, cut,* and *paste* edit functions to move this sentence to other places or even to take it out of the paragraph entirely. Print out each different version and compare them. Which is most effective?

2. Precise, well-chosen words can help convey a feeling or idea to an audience. A quick way to discover what all your word choice options might be is to use a *thesaurus,* a useful tool available on many word-processing programs. Open your essay draft file or a prewriting file. Locate a word that doesn't seem as interesting, precise, or unusual as it could be. Highlight it using your mouse (or click on it), and then click on your program's thesaurus option. The program will suggest alternative words to you. If your word-processing program doesn't have a thesaurus option, or if you'd just like to see if there are more possibilities, you can visit an interactive thesaurus at ⟨http://www.thesaurus.com⟩.

OPTIONS FOR WRITING

As you work through any of the following writing options, focus on developing effective body paragraphs, each with a topic sentence and sufficient supporting details clearly related to the main point. Have a plan for organizing your material. In responding to your draft and revising, consult the Strategies for Body Paragraphs (p. 129).

¶ **1.** Choose one of the ten topics listed in Practice 5.4 and develop your ideas on the subject into a paragraph.

¶ **2.** Prewrite to discover three activities you like to engage in to relax, relieve stress, or refresh yourself. Explain each of these activities and their effect on you.

¶ **3.** As a college student, you probably have many tips for how to survive the first semester or at least the first few weeks of college life. Share these survival strategies with an audience of new college students.

4. In Jeremy Smith's essay (pp. 113–114), the writer discusses a term whose meaning has substantially changed over time. Write an essay focusing on another term, word, or expression that used to mean one thing and now means something quite different.

5. After reading Barbara Ehrenreich's essay (pp. 135–137), agree or disagree that democracy is at risk when employers have free speech rights but employees don't. In your thesis, take a clear position on the issue of free speech in the workplace. In your body paragraphs, support your stand by developing separate main points. For each main point, you could examine and discuss the examples in Ehrenreich's essay or you could use examples based on your own work experience or the experience of people you know. (*Caution:* Dress codes in the workplace become a free speech issue *only* if, as in the cases Ehrenreich mentions, the clothing item in question contains a slogan or phrase.)

6. In his paragraph in the section that follows, Carlos De Jesus reports that female police officers find "lewd comments made to them" on the job examples of sexual harassment. In the essay "Zipped Lips," Barbara Ehrenreich asserts that college faculty often have greater freedom of speech than their students. Interview your college's dean of students or faculty members to discover the content of the college's sexual harassment policy. In an essay, summarize the official position of the college on sexual harassment. Discuss any limitations on the freedom of speech of students, faculty, and other college personnel.

RESPONDING TO WRITING: PEER EDITING BODY PARAGRAPHS

Body paragraphs from three student essays appear below. You will be asked to edit each paragraph. Review the following strategies before reading the paragraphs, and refer back to them when needed to complete these or future peer responding activities.

STRATEGIES FOR PEER EDITING

If you are responding to another student's draft:

- Respond with seriousness, even though the draft may have many errors or not be the kind or quality of draft that you would write.

- Withhold both your judgment and your comments until you have read the entire draft.

- Make all comments specific; avoid general remarks that will not help the writer in revising.

- Resist the urge to fix sentence errors, rewrite sentences, or correct punctuation. Instead, just circle or underline problematic areas so the writer will be sure to notice them.

If you are sharing your draft with a peer editor:

- Find someone who will not hesitate to give you honest feedback about your essay; close friends may not be the best peer editors.

- Give your peer editor a clean, legible copy of your draft, typewritten if possible; use double or triple spacing so the peer editor will have room to write comments.

- Give your peer editor a fairly complete rather than a partial draft of the assignment.

- Give yourself time to reflect upon your peer editor's comments before revising. If you are confused by the comments, ask for an explanation or consult your instructor or another peer editor for a second opinion.

After you have read the following body paragraphs, respond to each one by answering the peer editing questions that follow.

5. **STYLE** Search the paragraph for instances of precise word choice, repetition of important words, and use of parallel sentence structure. Jot down an example of effective use of one or more of these items. _____

_____

Which of these concerns of style, if any, do you feel could be strengthened?

_____

What are your suggestions? _____

_____

Choose a paragraph you completed for the Options for Writing section. Complete a draft of the paragraph assignment and ask an editor to respond to the editing questions for your paragraph. You can use these questions when you share your drafts in the future.

 **READING AND ADDITIONAL ACTIVITIES**

Even though America has long held sacred an individual's freedom of speech, that same individual cannot yell "Fire!" in a crowded public building, jeopardizing the lives of others when there is no real danger. The following essay, which appeared in *Time* magazine in 1995, explores the prickly question of freedom of speech and its limitations in the workplace. Author Barbara Ehrenreich, highly respected for her political and social commentary, has written essays for many magazines and newspapers. As you read this essay, first locate Ehrenreich's thesis and then examine each of her body paragraphs to determine their separate purposes and their relationship to the other body paragraphs and to her essay as a whole. Pay particular attention to the various kinds of support she uses for her topic sentences in each body paragraph.

Zipped Lips

Barbara Ehrenreich

1   Earlier this month a fellow named Sam Young was fired from his grocery-store job for wearing a Green Bay Packers T-shirt. All right, this was Dallas, and it was a little insensitive to flaunt the enemy team's logo on the weekend of the N.F.C. championship game, but

Young was making the common assumption that if you stay away from obscenity, libel, or, perhaps in this case, the subject of groceries, it is a free country, isn't it? Only problem was he had not read the First Amendment carefully enough: It says *government* cannot abridge freedom of expression. Private employers can, on a whim, and they do so every day.

2   On January 10, for instance, a Peoria, Illinois, man was suspended from his job at Caterpillar Inc. for wearing a T-shirt bearing the words DEFENDING THE AMERICAN DREAM, which happens to have been one of the slogans of the United Auto Workers in their seventeen-month strike against Caterpillar. Since the strike ended in early December, the firm has forbidden incendiary slogans like "Families in Solidarity" and suspended dozens of union employees for infractions as tiny as failing to shake a foreman's hand with sufficient alacrity. A fifty-two-year-old worker who failed to peel union stickers off his toolbox fast enough was threatened with loss of retirement benefits.

3   It is not just blue-collar employees who are expected to check their freedom of speech at the company door. In mid-December, Boston physician David Himmelstein was fired for going public about the gag clause in his employer's contract with doctors, forbidding them to "make any communication which undermines or could undermine the confidence . . . of the public in U.S. Healthcare . . ." or even revealing that this clause is in their contract.

4   So where are the guardians of free speech when we need them? For the most part, they are off in the sunny glades of academe, defending professors against the slightest infringement of their presumed right to say anything, at any volume, to anyone. Last fall, for example, history professor Jay Bergman was reprimanded by his employer, Central Connecticut State University, for screaming at a student he found tearing down a flyer he had posted. Now the Anti-Defamation League and the National Association of Scholars are rallying to have the reprimand rescinded. Reprimand, mind you, not firing or suspension.

5   Or, in 1991, you would have found the New York Civil Liberties Union defending crackpot Afrocentrist professor Leonard Jeffries of New York's City University. Thanks to such support and the fact that CUNY is a public-sector employer, Jeffries still commands a lectern, from which he is free to go on raving about the oppression of blacks by "rich Jews" and how melanin deficiency has warped the white brain.

6   Most workers, especially in the private sector, have no such protections. Unless their contract says otherwise, they can be fired "for any reason or no reason"—except when the firing can be shown to be discriminatory on the basis of race, sex, or religion. In addition, a few forms of "speech," such as displaying a union logo, are protected by the National

Labor Relations Act, and the courts may decide this makes Caterpillar's crackdown illegal. But the general assumption is, any expansion of workers' rights would infringe on the apparently far more precious right of the employer to fire "at will." So the lesson for America's working people is: If you want to talk, be prepared to walk.

7   Obviously there are reasonable restrictions on an employee's freedom of speech. A switchboard operator should not break into Tourette's-like torrents of profanity; likewise, professors probably *should* be discouraged from screaming at students or presenting their loopier notions as historical fact. But it's hard to see how a Green Bay Packers T-shirt could interfere with the stocking of Pop-Tarts or how a union sticker would slow the tightening of a tractor's axle. When employers are free to make arbitrary and humiliating restrictions, we're saying democracy ends, and dictatorship begins, at the factory gate.

8   So we seem to have a cynical paradox at the heart of our political culture: "Freedom" is our official national rallying cry, but *un*freedom is, for many people, the price of economic survival. At best this is deeply confusing. In school we're taught that liberty is more precious than life itself—then we're expected to go out and sell that liberty, in eight-hour chunks, in exchange for a livelihood. But if you'd sell your freedom of speech for a few dollars an hour, what else would you sell? Think where we'd be now, as a nation, if Patrick Henry had said, "Give me liberty or give me, uh, how about a few hundred pounds sterling?"

9   Surely no one really believes productivity would nose-dive if employees were free to wear team logos of their choice or, for that matter, to raise the occasional question about management priorities. In fact, the economy could only benefit from an increase in democracy—and enthusiasm and creativity—on the shop floor. Or does the "free" in "free market" apply just to people on top?

10   When employers have rights and employees don't, democracy itself is at risk. It isn't easy to spend the day in a state of servile subjugation and then emerge, at five P.M., as Mr. or Ms. Citizen-Activist. Unfreedom undermines the critical spirit, and suck-ups make lousy citizens.

QUESTIONS ON CONTENT

1. What is the First Amendment, in your own words? _____

_____

2. According to Ehrenreich, why would Caterpillar object to particular T-shirt slogans? _____

_____

3. What is meant by a "gag clause" in paragraph 3? _____

_____

4. According to the author, what differences are seen in free speech rights on campuses and in the private business sector? _____

_____

5. What is the paradox mentioned in paragraph 8 that is "at the heart of our political culture"?_____

_____

_____

QUESTIONS ON STRATEGY

1. What kind of support does Ehrenreich use in her first body paragraph?

_____

2. What is the purpose of paragraph 8? _____

_____

Does the author achieve her purpose in this body paragraph? (Support your answer with specific comments.) _____

_____

3. Does paragraph 5 lose focus and veer off-topic, or does it support Ehren-reich's thesis in the essay? _____ Explain your answer.

_____

4. What important words does Ehrenreich repeat for emphasis in several of her body paragraphs? Find two or more. _____

_____

5. Why do you think Ehrenreich's style becomes more informal in her concluding sentence?_____

_____

Is this concluding sentence effective? _____ Explain your answer.

_____

CRITICAL THINKING IN CONNECTING TEXTS

In "Relativity" (pp. 113–114), Jeremy Smith explores the concept of distance. Smith notes that E-mail, for example, has changed notions of distance by allowing us to communicate quickly with people all over the world. However, some critics favor limitations on freedom of speech in cyberspace. In "Zipped Lips" (pp. 135–137), Barbara Ehrenreich asserts that although America has a commitment to personal freedoms, current legislation does not limit the right of employers to curtail freedom of speech for their employees. Working with a partner or small group, decide where we should draw the line. Should employers have the right to restrict employees' speech? Should chat groups and other Internet communications be monitored or censored? What about the rights of professors in the classroom? Should college students or faculty be permitted to use "hate speech" or racist speech in the name of the First Amendment? Should advertisers be allowed to deceive or mislead consumers in print and on television? Should a film or television producer be required to restrict offensive language? If time permits, share your findings with the rest of the class.

For more writing resources, be sure to see the Longman English Pages Website at http://longman.awl.com/englishpages

Creating Effective Introductions and Conclusions

> Great is the art of beginning, but
>   greater the art is of ending.
>
> —*Henry Wadsworth Longfellow, from "Elegiac Verse"*

Preview

In this chapter you will learn
- ▶ how to recognize and evaluate introductory strategies
- ▶ how to identify voice and tone in introductory paragraphs
- ▶ how to write a compelling introduction
- ▶ how to identify and evaluate concluding strategies
- ▶ how to write a memorable conclusion

Think of the introduction to an essay as a tantalizing appetizer—whetting the readers' appetites for the main course, and the conclusion as the dessert—satisfying, flavorful, and essential to a complete essay meal. This chapter offers helpful pointers on beginning and ending essays. As you read the information on introductory and concluding paragraphs, keep in mind that *when* you write these two important parts of your essay is a matter of personal preference. Some writers complete the introduction and conclusion when revising, while others prefer to sketch out these two parts with the preliminary draft, knowing that they will revise later. You'll discover which composing process works best for you.

CHARACTERISTICS OF INTRODUCTIONS

First impressions count! Employers decide whether to hire in the first few seconds of job interviews; readers decide just as quickly whether to read on or put the page down. An eye-catching introduction is crucial if you want to have a successful essay. While introductions to college essays vary in length from one to several paragraphs, an effective introduction contains the following characteristics:

- It captures the attention of the reading audience through the use of a particular strategy.
- It guides the audience smoothly into the subject.
- It sets the tone for the entire essay.
- It either states or moves toward the thesis.

MODEL WITH KEY QUESTIONS

Tommy Honjo wanted to explain a simple task that he felt could save car owners money and result in better road performance. Honjo worried about how to get the reader's interest in a mechanical procedure that the average person might not understand. As you read his introduction, see which characteristics of effective introductions you can identify. When you've read the brief summary of Honjo's body paragraphs and his conclusion, evaluate the success of the introductory paragraph in leading the reader smoothly into the subject.

DON'T BE AFRAID TO POP THE HOOD
Tommy Honjo

A very logical thinker, Tommy Honjo consistently wrote well-organized essays. He confided that he enjoyed writing to explain mechanical processes and technical procedures. Throughout the semester, Tommy worked on solving problems with verbs. Tommy's future plans include a four-year degree, but currently he is an undeclared major, leaving his options open.

1   Have you ever been stuck on the side of the road because your car has broken down? Supposing you could save between twenty and thirty dollars and decrease the likelihood that you'd have car trouble in the future by learning a simple, easily grasped procedure, would you try it? If you're like most people who own cars, once

or twice a year, provided you remember, you take your car to a shop that does a quick oil change. You hand over your money, and your car is filled with recycled oil or possibly incorrect oil for your car, which could damage your engine. However, even though you know little about cars and have never popped the hood, you can easily learn to change your car's oil yourself, save money, and have better automotive performance. To complete this important tune-up procedure, you simply need to track down a few tools and follow several steps.

[Four body paragraphs discuss the necessary parts for the procedure and the items useful in preparation for the oil change, followed by a step-by-step explanation of the procedure and several precautions and recommendations.]

6   Now you may be saying to yourself, "Hold it! This is more complicated than I thought!" But actually the entire oil change should take only an hour or less, and once you have purchased the wrenches, your only expense is the oil and filter. The next time you see a motorist stranded by the side of the road, remember that it's more than likely this person did not change the oil in his or her own car. In the long run, if you're willing to pop the hood and learn to change your car's oil, you might be saving a lot more than the twenty or thirty dollars—you might be saving yourself a substantial tow and car repair bill.

 **KEY QUESTIONS**

1. **PURPOSE** What sentence or phrase in the introductory paragraph first indicates Honjo's purpose in writing this essay?_____

_____

2. **FOCUS** Locate Honjo's thesis and state it in the following space.

_____

_____

3. **MATERIAL** What kind of material does Honjo use in the introductory paragraph to capture the attention of his audience? _____

_____

4. **STRUCTURE** Describe in a few words the organization of the introductory paragraph. After Honjo opens with a general question, how does he move his readers smoothly toward his thesis? _____

_____

5. **STYLE** How does the concluding paragraph "frame" the essay? That is, how does it tie back to the introductory paragraph and offer a satisfying closure for the reader? _____

_____

GUIDELINES FOR INTRODUCTIONS

Hook Your Audience

The first sentence of your introductory paragraph should hook your audience—it should seize their attention and then pull them into the subject. You need to give readers a reason to read more of your essay, and there are many introductory strategies available to you to hook your audience. Seven of these introductory strategies follow with sample introductory paragraphs. The strategies are set off from the rest of the introductory paragraphs with italics.

Background Information

Many subjects for college essays benefit from a brief historical overview or some concise background information on the situation to be discussed. The strategy here is to explain background circumstances so that the reader's appetite is whetted to learn more about the subject. Here is an example of this type of introductory technique:

> *Up until the 1960s, African-Americans, Latinos, and other people of color as well as women were blatantly discriminated against in the American workplace and college admissions for no other reason than their gender or the color of their skin. When Affirmative Action was implemented, it was designed to help minorities and women gain greater representation in jobs, promotions, college admissions, and business contracts.* Today, however, because Affirmative Action has resulted in misunderstanding, bitterness, and verbal warfare, the program should be reviewed and revised.

> —Cenovio Maeda, student

Question

Another introductory strategy involves asking your readers a provocative question or series of questions. Look again at "Don't Be Afraid to Pop the Hood," the model essay at the beginning of this chapter, and you will see that Honjo asks the readers two questions which serve to involve them actively with the subject. Here is another example of this introductory strategy:

> *Are you one of many people who dream of becoming a recording artist? Are you stymied because you have the talent but not the first idea of how to get started in the recording business? If so, get out that music and practice those scales, because you're going to learn how to record your own demo tape. Making a demonstration tape and sending it off to record companies could be the first steps in making your dream of vocal stardom come true.*

Story or Incident

This strategy involves opening the essay with a story or anecdote that directly illustrates the main idea. If you use this strategy, be sure that you keep the length of the story under control—remember that your purpose is to heighten the readers' interest and curiosity in your subject, not to digress into a lengthy narration. The following example uses a story as an introductory strategy:

> *I was eight years old when my parents moved to a new apartment located in Bourj-Hamoud, Lebanon, a beautiful city that used to be called "Little Paris." When I first saw this big building, I thought we were going to live on a boat, so much did the building resemble a boat. What I remember most was our two-hundred-foot-long balcony, wrapping all around our apartment. The first few days after we moved in, I was afraid to venture out on this balcony because it was so large. As the days passed by, the balcony became the place where I spent all my time and where I learned about the outside world.*
>
> —Lucy Mardirossian, student

Statistic, Fact, or Statement

Oftentimes you can command your readers' interest by beginning with a startling statistic or fact. Notice that the writer of the following introductory paragraph uses a specific amount of money to appeal to his audience's regard for wise spending:

> *Last year over half of the nation's computer users spent 50 dollars or more on phone calls and books for technical support related to problems installing or running computer programs.* This money could have been saved

if computer users had a better knowledge of how to install a program. And program installation is not as complicated as many people believe. Most programs require three fairly simple steps, each accompanied by a few precautions.

—Peter Huang, student

Quotation

You may decide to use a quotation to open your essay. Every chapter of this text begins with a brief quotation that introduces the subject to be explored in the chapter. If you use this introductory technique, you need to identify the source unless the quote is a generally known proverb or saying. Libraries have books of quotations listed by subjects, so you might try looking up your subject to see if you can find a thoughtful quotation. If you are writing an essay about a particular book, story, or article, you may choose to begin your introductory paragraph with a quotation from the source you're discussing, just as the following student does in this example:

"A stranger blocked her path, but she passed him blindly. He had to touch her arm before she would look up." The woman was Mrs. Ardavi, arriving from Iran, and the stranger was Hassan, her son, whom she had not seen in over ten years. Both Ardavi and Hassan are characters in the short story "Your Place Is Empty" by Anne Tyler. Both Mrs. Ardavi and her son Hassan must come to terms with differences in culture, personality, religion, and age.

—Cinthya R. Martinez, student

Definition

If your essay focuses on a subject that might not be readily understood by your audience, you may want to ease the readers into the topic by defining any confusing terms first. If you do choose this strategy as your hook, avoid the overused "according to Webster's" or "the dictionary defines" phrasing. The following example of definition as an introductory device was chosen because the writer's subject—artificial bait—is relatively obscure for the average reader. Notice that this author tries to introduce his audience to his subject gently and whet their curiosity at the same time:

If you enjoy prime fishing, you should know that the northern states have excellent fishing lakes. And if you do plan a visit, it will help you to be familiar with Rapalas and their use in game fishing. *What exactly is a Rapala? It is an artificial bait which is tied to the end of a fishing line in place of a basic fishing hook. It is hand crafted of either cedar or balsa wood with two sets of hooks attached to its cigar-shaped body.* If you want to take home a freezer-full of the best largemouth bass, northern pike, walleye, or the highly valued muskellunge, you should learn how and when to use Rapalas.

—Robert Amerson, student

Examples or Details

You may want to arouse audience interest and introduce your subject by giving a series of examples or details associated with the subject. The following introductory paragraph uses this strategy:

Unless you have felt like an outsider, been singled out by resident advisors, stayed up for hours studying for finals, been denied financial loans, failed a test, sat in the wrong class by mistake, read the wrong pages for homework, become sick from cafeteria food on campus, experienced writer's block, paid over three hundred dollars for books, bought the wrong books and could not return them—unless you have experienced at least some of these situations, you have not known the "joys" of being a college student. But though college may be one big pain and one of the greatest challenges you'll ever face, without a college education you are dead.

—Monifa Winston, student

Practice 6.1   For practice in identifying introductory strategies, work alone or with a partner and examine introductory paragraphs from any four essays in this textbook. In the following spaces, write the name of the essay, the page on which you found it, and then the strategy used by the writer to hook the interest of the audience.

_____

_____

_____

_____

◆ ◆ ◆

Introduce the Subject

In addition to capturing the interest of the reader, the essay's introduction should also introduce the subject. Return to the introductory paragraphs used as examples earlier and you will notice that each also introduces the subject.

Practice 6.2 Reread each introductory paragraph you have chosen from this text. Annotate it by circling the first indication of the writer's subject.

◆ ◆ ◆

Establish a Voice and Tone

Every effective introductory paragraph sets up the voice and tone for the remainder of the essay. **Voice** refers to the writer's personality and the way this personality comes through in the essay. **Tone** refers to the writer's attitude toward a subject and to the writer's perception of an audience and relationship with them. If you reread Tommy Honjo's introductory paragraph, you'll notice that the writer's voice is informal: he uses conversational phrases such as "stuck on the side of the road," "hand over your money," and "pop the hood." Honjo's tone is helpful—he communicates to his readers his wish to help them learn a money-saving procedure. A strong, easily recognizable tone in your introduction establishes a firm relationship with your reader and helps you to maintain consistency throughout the body and conclusion of your essay.

Examine the following introductory paragraphs to get an idea of differences in voice and tone.

> Rape is an outrage that cannot be tolerated in civilized society. Yet feminism, which has waged a crusade for rape to be taken more seriously, has put young women in danger by hiding the truth about sex from them.
>
> —Camille Paglia, from "Rape and Modern Sex War"

Notice that the author's voice is fairly formal—she does not use "I" or address the reader directly by using "you." This voice reveals that she prefers her writing personality to be somewhat removed from her reader. In addition, her tone is serious, as indicated by such word choices as "outrage," "crusade," and reference to putting women "in danger by hiding the truth." Paglia's introductory paragraph establishes a tone of warning that will be used throughout the essay.

Now take a look at another introductory paragraph dealing with the same subject.

> I thought of the old "blue balls" defense—you remember, that's the one where backseat Romeos claimed they couldn't halt their sexual advances because their aching gonads imperiously demanded relief—went out with air raid shelters and doo wop. But now there are those like Camille Paglia who are bringing back blue balls with a vengeance. According to Paglia and her cohorts, men really *can't* control their urges. Rape for men is just doin' what comes naturally. And gals, don't bother fighting it—just get used to it again.
>
> —Helen Cordes, from "The Blue Balls Bluff"

Notice this writer's more informal voice—she addresses the audience with "you remember," and she uses the conversational "doin' what comes naturally." This voice establishes a more direct, personal relationship with the writer's audience. Cordes's sarcasm in the phrase "men really *can't* control their urges" helps to signal the reader that the tone of the essay will be mocking.

Practice 6.3   To gain some practice in identifying voice and tone, return to the introductory paragraphs used as examples (pp. 143–146). Annotate them by writing a word or two about the writer's voice and tone in the margin.

◆ ◆ ◆

State the Thesis

After capturing the attention of your audience and indicating the subject, your introduction should either state the thesis for the essay or move toward a more focused subject. The thesis is most often found within the introductory paragraph, as is the case with each of the previous introductory paragraphs.

Practice 6.4   Reread the paragraphs on pages 143–146, and annotate each paragraph by underlining and labeling the thesis in each one.

◆ ◆ ◆

Avoid Truisms or Generalized Questions

Hastily composed introductory paragraphs often result in **truisms**—statements that, while true, are all too obvious or general. For instance, on first draft the opening line, "Love is important to everyone" might seem like a great beginning for an essay on neglected children. However, a second, more critical glance at this opening line should alert you that the average reader might respond with a yawn, putting the essay down without another glance. Don't use the introduction to tell your audience anything they already know. By the same token, don't base your introduction on generalized questions that are meaningless, for which the answers are all too obvious, or questions that are total "set-ups" as leads into the subject. For instance, scrap anything like the following: "Have you ever wondered what the world would be like if there were no disagreements?" or "Do you know the difference between a successful college student and a floundering one?" or "Have you ever experienced discrimination?" When thinking about opening sentences for your introductory paragraph, you should take the time to experiment with different strategies to see which leads most smoothly into your subject.

Practice 6.5 Read the following essay assignments and first lines for an essay. Working with a partner, come up with a better introductory sentence for the subject.

1. (*Assignment:* Focus on the inappropriate disciplining of teenagers by overly strict parents.) "Parents are annoying at times." _____

_____

_____

_____

2. (*Assignment:* Discuss lifestyle differences between college graduates and high school drop-outs.) "Have you ever wondered what a big difference a college education will make in your life?" _____

_____

_____

_____

3. (*Assignment:* Explore some negative effects of television for teenagers and children.) "Have you ever thought that television might be bad for children and teenagers?" _____

_____

_____

_____

4. (*Assignment:* Take a stand on the issue of illegal immigration.) "Immigration is a very controversial issue today." _____

_____

_____

◆ ◆ ◆

STRATEGIES FOR INTRODUCTIONS

1. **PURPOSE** Make sure that your introduction hooks your audience, indicates your purpose, and establishes a voice and tone appropriate for your audience and subject.

2. **FOCUS** Move smoothly from your introductory strategy to a clear thesis.

3. **MATERIAL** Regardless of which introductory strategy you choose, use specific and interesting information rather than truisms or generalized questions or statements.

4. **STRUCTURE** Organize the material in your introduction so that you heighten reader interest and convey all necessary background information.

5. **STYLE** Use words and compose phrases and sentences carefully to lead the audience from indication of subject to clear statement of thesis.

CHARACTERISTICS OF CONCLUSIONS

While the introduction to an essay is important because it determines whether the reader will read further, the conclusion forms the last impression—the final and most lingering memory—of your writing. If you return to Tommy Honjo's essay (pp. 141–142), you'll see that the final paragraph has the following characteristics of an effective conclusion:

- **It conveys a feeling of completion.**
  Notice that rather than bring up any new steps in the process of changing oil, Honjo comments on the ease of the entire process, signaling the reader that he has communicated all necessary information.

- **It "frames" the essay by tying all the main points together and wrapping up any loose ends for the reader.**
  Honjo repeats (from his introductory paragraph) that the procedure will save the reader money and will improve the car's performance. He also makes a prediction, an effective concluding strategy: "you might be saving yourself a substantial tow and car repair bill."

GUIDELINES FOR CONCLUSIONS

Offer Closure

If you've ever been disconnected during a phone conversation, then you know the frustration that accompanies an abrupt and untimely ending. In the same way, your essay should not end with your last main point or with a detail related to a main point. Conclude instead with a few sentences which signal the reader that the essay is ending.

Practice 6.6 Turn to any student essay in this text and read the entire essay, except for the last paragraph. Record your impressions on a separate sheet of paper. Go back to the essay and read the concluding paragraph. Record in the following space the words or phrases signaling that the writer is drawing to a close.

_____

_____

◆ ◆ ◆

Frame the Essay

Much as a frame forms a finite border for a painting, an effective conclusion brings together the contents of an essay for the reader. Successful framing makes use of any of a number of concluding strategies. The introductory strategies mentioned earlier in this chapter can also be used to create effective conclusions. In addition, there are five concluding techniques that could be helpful.

Summary

This common strategy works best for essays that are longer than three typewritten pages. Summarizing a shorter essay is unnecessary—in fact, your audience may be insulted that you doubt their ability to remember this amount of material. On the other hand, if your essay deals with complex or technical material, or if the essay is, say, a ten-page research paper, your audience might appreciate a recap of the information.

To illustrate, the following conclusion summarizes the information from the entire essay:

Overall, although having a part-time job can crowd a teen's schedule and limit study time, this job may be exactly what the teen may need. Learning to meet responsibilities on the job, growing to respect and get along with employers and co-workers, and developing the maturity to budget money are three skills that more teens should acquire.

—Patricia Crippen, student

Recommendation

One effective way to end an essay is to make a recommendation to your readers. To see the impact a recommendation might have on an audience, read the following example:

So now that you've been behind the scenes to see what a waitress has to cope with and juggle during every working hour, perhaps the next time you visit a restaurant or coffee shop, you'll view your waitress with different eyes. As she approaches your table smiling with composure and good humor, try to respond with the same courtesy to this person who does much more for you than just serve up the food.

—Deanna McAmis, student

Prediction or Warning

Using a prediction or issuing a warning can be a dramatic and memorable way to end your essay. For a better idea of how this concluding strategy works, read the following final paragraph:

If parents continue to ignore the suggestive sitcoms, films, and music videos their children watch, and if they fail to monitor their children's viewing, there will be more irresponsible sex and mindless violence in our society. Now more than ever, parents need to teach their children right from wrong. If parents leave this teaching to the media, our society will become even more toxic to young people.

—Carmen Tull, student

Call to Action

The call to action as a concluding strategy challenges the audience to become involved by doing something about a situation or problem. Notice that Tull's concluding paragraph in the previous example hints at an action: increased involvement of parents and the monitoring of television programs. The following is an example of a concluding paragraph with an even more obvious plea for action:

These many examples of unclear wording in our college's sexual harassment policy point out the need for a policy review. Every student on this campus, every faculty member and every staff member—all of us should write, call, or visit the board of trustees and urge them to revise the current sexual harassment policy so that the language is clear, easily understood, and fair to all parties involved.

—Edwin Ksiezopolski, student

Reference to Introductory Strategy

An interesting and satisfying concluding strategy involves referring back to the introductory example, story, statistic, quote, or other device and elaborating or connecting the information, tying the end to the beginning of the essay. The introductory and concluding paragraphs that follow demonstrate this strategy.

I can remember a time when I could play in my own back yard without fear of harm. Today, however, my children do not feel safe in our yard, not because they live in a different community, but because they are growing up in a different time. After reading "A Child's Tragedy Is a Grown-Up's Failure" by Robin Abcarian and "Get It If You Can" by Roy Rivenburg, I agree with the authors that we live in a toxic society.

[Body paragraphs develop three main points with examples relating to a toxic society.]

Although I'm glad I don't have to be a child growing up in this society, I worry and fear for my children. I also wonder if there isn't more that parents, educators, and lawmakers can do to help my children and the children of others feel safe from harm in their own back yards.

Practice 6.7 Look again at each of the following essays from various chapters in this text. Working with a partner, identify which of the five concluding strategies each writer uses and write it next to the title in the space below. Rank the effectiveness of each conclusion, assigning the number 1 to the strongest and 4 to the weakest.

"Zipped Lips" (pp. 135–137): _____

"McDonald's Is Not Our Kind of Place" (pp. 305–307): _____

"We're Lying: Safe Sex and White Lies in the Time of AIDS" (pp. 160–168) _____

"The Second Coming of Poetry" (p. 193–194) _____

◆ ◆ ◆

Avoid Pitfalls

Whatever concluding strategy you decide upon, you'll want to avoid three potential pitfalls.

New Material

Resist the urge to introduce new material, such as another main point or another detail, in your conclusion. Remember that this is the time to wrap up what you have said before and to bring together all your main points previously made into a coherent closing statement.

Apology

Never weaken your position by apologizing—even in your concluding paragraph. For example, your audience will be confused and possibly offended if you conclude with something like the following: "Although I don't know everything about this problem, . . ." or "I may not be one hundred percent right, but I think. . . ."

Moralizing

Avoid the preacher's pulpit in your concluding paragraph. Although some students have the mistaken idea that essays should end with a moral or lesson learned, this is not a good strategy to use. Leave the lesson or moral for the reader to decipher—your essay will be much more memorable if you hint or suggest a lesson rather than forcing one upon your audience.

For example, the following writer might decide in a revised draft to delete the italicized last sentence of this paragraph:

> Today everyone in our family is working. We can now buy ourselves the things we need to get by. There are no more money problems and everyone is happy. Learning to pull together has taught all of us a lesson. Without communicating and helping each other, we wouldn't be able to get by. Everybody appreciates one another for all their hard work. We managed to get closer to one another. Responsibility counted a lot but we've all learned to deal with it. *Times are tough but not impossible if you learn to work together.*
>
> —Ginell Cabanilla, student

STRATEGIES FOR CONCLUSIONS

1. **PURPOSE** Be sure that your conclusion gives readers a sense of completion, framing the entire essay and reinforcing your purpose in writing it.

2. **FOCUS** Choose a concluding strategy that works well with the rest of the essay.

3. **MATERIAL** Avoid introducing any new material in the form of main points or supporting details. Do expand material to include a warning, specific recommendation, prediction, or call to action if appropriate.

4. **STRUCTURE** Organize the concluding paragraph so that your most memorable or arresting statement comes at the end of the conclusion.

5. **STYLE** Revise your conclusion if your tone sounds apologetic or preachy.

JOURNAL WRITING: EXPERIMENTING WITH VOICE AND TONE

For this journal entry you will need to locate any essay you've written—this can be an essay-in-progress or one you've already completed.

1. Read the essay over carefully with special attention to the first and last paragraphs. After reviewing the information on voice and tone earlier in this chapter, focus on the voice and tone you used and then complete the following activities:

   • Imagine a completely different purpose for your essay. Then choosing a new voice and tone but keeping the same subject matter, rewrite your introductory paragraph in a journal entry. For example, if you were Tommy Honjo, writer of the essay "Don't Be Afraid to Pop the Hood," you might decide to address a friend and adopt a flippant, offhand voice and use a lighthearted, confidential tone. Or you could use a much more formal voice and employ a distant, reserved tone.
   • In a second journal entry, rewrite the concluding paragraph of the same essay. Use the same voice and tone that you employed for your first rewritten introduction.

2. When you've completed the journal writing, compare the introductory and concluding paragraphs of your essay with the new versions you've just written in your journal. Think about the appropriateness of each for academic writing, and ponder when you might want to use a different voice and tone in your writing. Notice that once you establish a particular voice and tone in your introduction, your reading audience has a right to expect this voice and tone to be used throughout the essay.

USING THE COMPUTER:
CRAFTING CONCLUSIONS AND ONLINE RESEARCH

1. What was the last blockbuster movie that you saw? Did it have an especially scary, dramatic, or romantic ending? Chances are that ending wasn't in the original script. Many big movie studios these days will show multiple endings of movies to test audiences to see which will be the most popular—and make the most money. You might not be writing for big box office dollars, but can you try the following exercise on your word processor to "test" the effectiveness of different kinds of conclusions on your essays.

   Open a file that contains an essay draft or an essay that you have already completed. Make a copy of this file, and *close* the original. If you already have a conclusion to this essay draft, evaluate it. What kind of concluding strategy did you use? (Review "Frame the Essay," pp. 151–153.) Was it effective? Now, split the screen, and open a new file. In this new file, use any of four strategies—summary, recommendation, prediction or warning, or call to action—to write at least two alternative conclusions to your essay. Would these alternative conclusions be more effective, or less effective, for your essay? Do any of these strategies seem wrong for your audience and purpose?

2. Meghan Daum's essay "We're Lying: Safe Sex and White Lies in the Time of AIDS" (pp. 160–168) describes what it's like to be a young person in the age of AIDS. She contrasts the messages she hears from public health officials and school counselors about "safe sex" with the actual behavior and attitudes of people her age. However you feel about Daum's experiences, AIDS has been a powerful influence both internationally and within your own community. There are many excellent sites on the Web to find more information about AIDS. Two resources are the following:

   • *The Body: A Multimedia AIDS and HIV Information Resource* (⟨http://www.thebody.com⟩): This site includes discussions and stories from people worldwide living with or affected by the HIV virus. Log on to read their stories, follow their arguments, and share your own opinions and experiences. You can also explore the site's resources to find out more about AIDS education and prevention.

   • *AIDS Education Global Information System* (⟨http://www.aegis.com⟩): This site provides a wealth of information, both accessible and more technical, about AIDS education, treatment, and prevention. Visit one or both of these Websites, and in your journal record information or summarize postings that you think people in your community need to know. Report back to the class with your findings.

OPTIONS FOR WRITING

In your drafting and then revising of an Option for Writing, pay particular attention to your introductory and concluding paragraphs. Use the guidelines offered in this chapter to hook your audience with an effective introductory strategy and later, to frame your entire essay with a satisfying and memorable conclusion.

1. Write an introductory paragraph for an essay about a beginning or ending in your life—perhaps related to a relationship or a job, your education, where you live, or how you live your life. You might want to contrast the way you viewed yourself before and the way you see yourself or the world now. Search a book of quotations or find a quote by a favorite author to use as a dramatic opening quote related to your experience.

2. In "Don't Be Afraid to Pop the Hood" (pp. 141–142), Tommy Honjo explains how to perform a procedure that saves money and promotes better automotive maintenance. Write an essay explaining how to do or complete a project, task, hobby, or chore. Choose something that the average person might not know how to do, and in your introduction, be sure to convince the reader of the value of the activity.

3. In "We're Lying: Safe Sex and White Lies in the Time of AIDS" (pp. 160–168), Meghan Daum asserts that she and many of her peers have lied to themselves and perhaps to others. Write an essay detailing a lie you told or were told by someone else. Explain why and what happened to cause the lie, or what happened as a result of the dishonesty. In your concluding paragraph, resist the urge to moralize.

4. In the third paragraph of "We're Lying: Safe Sex and White Lies in the Time of AIDS" Daum states that the unsafe sex practices that she and her peers sometimes engage in are like "putting a loaded gun to our heads every night." Write an essay exploring the causes for potentially self-destructive, dangerous behavior in our society. Track down a statistic or fact that will hook your audience in your introduction.

5. In the second paragraph of her essay, Meghan Daum mentions college health service counselors who would "give us the straight talk." Pay a visit to the health service on your college campus. Ask for any available information about HIV and other sexually transmitted diseases. If possible, interview a college nurse or health service employee. Write an essay discussing your findings.

RESPONDING TO WRITING: BEGINNINGS AND ENDINGS

Read the following introductory and concluding paragraphs. On a separate sheet of paper for each paragraph, answer the set of questions on page 159–160.

Introductory Paragraphs

Paragraph A

When you leave your apartment or house, do you begin to feel better? If you leave for a week-long trip, do you find your head clears, your migraine disappears, dizziness stops, your aches and pains subside, depression fades away, and your entire attitude is better? If so, chemical pollution of the atmosphere in your home may be making you ill.

—Marshall Mandell, from "Are You Allergic to Your House?"

Paragraph B

On seeing another child fall and hurt himself, Hope, just nine months old, stared, tears welling up in her eyes, and crawled to her mother to be comforted—as though she had been hurt, not her friend. When 15-month-old Michael saw his friend Paul crying, Michael fetched his own teddy bear and offered it to Paul; when that didn't stop Michael's tears, Michael brought Paul's security blanket from another room. Such small acts of sympathy and caring, observed in scientific studies, are leading researchers to trace the roots of empathy—the ability to share another's emotions—to infancy, contradicting a longstanding assumption that infants and toddlers were incapable of these feelings.

—Daniel Goleman, from "Researchers Trace Empathy's Roots to Infancy"

Paragraph C

[This introduction by Margaret Atwood and paragraph F belong to the same essay.]

The noses of a great many Canadians resemble Porky Pig's. This comes from spending so much time pressing them against the longest undefended one-way mirror in the world. The Canadians looking through this mirror behave the way people on the hidden side of such mirrors usually do: they observe, analyze, ponder, snoop and wonder what all that activity on the other side means in decipherable human terms.

—Margaret Atwood, from "Through the One-Way Mirror"

Concluding Paragraphs

Paragraph D

Periodically my pilot and I climb into our aircraft and head out over the Minnesota wilderness, following a succession of electronic beeps that lead to some of the last remaining wolves in the lower 48 states. We hope that the data we collect will provide a better understanding of the wolf. We especially hope that our work will help guide authorities into a management program that will insure the perpetuation of the species in the last stages of its former range.

—L. David Mech, from "Where Can the Wolves Survive?"

Paragraph E

I who am blind can give one hint to those who can see—one admonition to those who would make full use of the gift of sight: Use your eyes as if tomorrow you would be stricken blind. And the same method can be applied to the other senses. Hear the music of voices, the song of the bird, the mighty strains of an orchestra, as if you would be stricken deaf tomorrow. Touch each object you want to touch as if tomorrow your tactile sense would fail. Smell the perfume of flowers, taste with relish each morsel, as if tomorrow you could never smell and taste again. Make the most of every sense; glory in all facets of pleasure and beauty which the world reveals to you through the several means of contact which Nature provides. But of all the senses, I am sure that sight must be the most delightful.

—Helen Keller, from "Three Days to See"

Paragraph F

Americans don't have Porky Pig noses. Instead they have Mr. Magoo eyes, with which they see the rest of the world. That would not be a problem if the United States were not so powerful. But it is, so it is.

—Margaret Atwood, from "Through the One-Way Mirror"

1. What introductory or concluding strategy does the writer use?

_____

2. What appears to be the subject of the essay? _____

_____

3. Describe the writer's tone._____

_____

4. Write down the most memorable word or phrase. _____

_____

5. With reference to the five "keys," evaluate the introductory or concluding

paragraph by commenting briefly on its effect on a reading audience.

_____

You can use these same questions in responding to your own or a peer's introductory and concluding paragraphs. Identify strengths and respond to weaknesses in your beginnings and endings of essays by making the necessary changes.

READING AND ADDITIONAL ACTIVITIES

When the following article appeared in the *New York Times Magazine* in 1996, the subject and controversial opinion of writer Meghan Daum prompted much discussion and a number of letters to the editors of the magazine. As you read, ask yourself what introductory strategies the writer uses to grab the attention of her audience. When you've finished reading the essay, evaluate the effectiveness of Daum's conclusion.

We're Lying: Safe Sex and White Lies in the Time of AIDS

Meghan Daum

1   We grew up with simple, cozy absolutes. Our high school educators knew what they were doing. They taught what they were taught to teach. When it came to keeping us from harm's way they treated the exceptional like the given, presented the anomalies as the facts of life. They told us how to act like the "adults we were becoming," never to drink and drive, never to "experiment" with "cannabis," and never to have sex or even go to third base as the result would be emotional trauma of unimaginable proportions, not to mention pregnancy which could mean nothing other than ruined lives,

missed proms, the prophecy of the sack of flour we carried around for health class finally realized.

2   It wasn't until college that I heard the AIDS speeches. Suddenly we were on our
own and didn't have to bring the car back by midnight, so it seemed incumbent upon
all those dorm mothers and counselors to give us the straight talk, to tell us never, ever
to have sex without condoms unless we wanted to die, that's right *die,* shrivel
overnight, vomit up our futures, pose a threat to others (and they'd seen it happen, oh
yes they had.)

3   Suddenly, pregnancy's out the window concern-wise. It's a lesser evil, a math class
rather than a physics class, Chaucer and not Middle English survey. Even those other
diseases, the ones they had mentioned in health class, like gonorrhea and even the in-
curable herpes, seem inconsequential. AIDS is foremost in our malleable minds, a
phantom in our not-yet-haunted houses. They tell us we can get it, and we believe them
and vow to protect ourselves, and intend (really, truly) to stick by that, until we don't
because we just can't, because it's just not fair, because our sense of entitlement ex-
ceeds our sense of vulnerability. So, we blow off precaution again and again and then
we get scared and get an HIV test and everything turns out okay and we run out of the
clinic, pamphlets in hand, eyes cast upwards, saying we'll never be stupid again. But of
course we are stupid, again and again. And the subsequent testing is always for the
same reasons and with the same results and soon it becomes more like fibbing about
SAT scores ten years after the fact than lying about practicing unsafe sex, a lie which
sounds like such a breach in contract with oneself that we might as well be talking
about putting a loaded gun to our heads every night and attempting to use our trigger
finger to clean the wax from our ear.

4   I have been tested for HIV three times; the opportunities for testing were there, so I
took them, forgetting, each time, the fear and nausea that always ensues before the results
come back, those minutes spent in a publicly funded waiting room staring at a video loop
about "living with" this thing that kills you. I've been negative each time, which is not surprising in retrospect, since I am not a member of a "high risk group." Yet I continue to go
into relationships with the safest of intentions and often discard precaution at some random and tacitly agreed-upon juncture. Perhaps this is a shocking admission, but my hunch
is that I'm not the only one doing this. My suspicion is, in fact, that very few of us—"us"
being the demographic frequently charged with thinking we're immortal, the population

accused of being cynical and lazy and weak for lack of a war draft and altogether unworthy of the label "adult"—have really responded to the AIDS crisis in the way the federal government and the educational system would like to think. My guess is that we're all but ignoring it and that almost anyone who claims otherwise is lying.

5   It's not that we're reckless. It's more that we're grasping at straws, trying like hell to feel good in a time when half of us seem to be on Prozac and the rest of us have probably been told that we need it. When it comes down to it, it's hard to use condoms. Even as a woman, I know this. Maybe the risk is a substitute for thrills we're missing in other areas of life. Maybe there's something secretly energizing about flirting with death for a night and then checking six months later to see if we've survived. This, at least, constitutes intensity of experience, a real, tangible interaction with raw fear. It's so much more than what we get most of the time, subject as we are to the largely protected, government approved, safety first-ness of American society. For my peers and myself, it's generally safe to assume that our homes will not be bombed while we sleep, that our flight will not crash, that we will make the daily round trip from our beds to the office and back again without deadly intervention somewhere in between. We live in the land of side impact air bags, childproof caps on vitamins, "do not ingest" warnings on deodorant bottles. We don't intend to die in childbirth. Even for those of us, like myself, who live in cities, who read in *USA Today* polls that we'll probably get mugged eventually, who vaguely mull over the fact that the person shot on the corner last week could have been us, fear continues to exist in the abstract. We've had it pretty cushy. We've been shielded from most forms of undoing by parents and educational institutions and health insurance. But AIDS is housed in its own strange caveat of intimate conversations among friends and those occasional sleepless nights when it occurs to us to wonder about it, upon which that dark paranoia sets in and those catalogs of who we've done it with and who they might have done it with and oh-my-god-I'll-surely-die seem to project themselves onto the ceiling the way fanged monsters did when we were kids. But we fall asleep and then we wake up. And nothing's changed except our willingness to forget about it, which is, in fact, almost everything.

6   I experience these nights every so often. The last one occurred after listening to a call-in radio show called Love Phones, in which barely articulate yet shockingly precocious

teenagers call up a hip, throaty-voiced psychologist and ask questions ranging from prom dates to the latest bondage techniques. One night a 15-year-old girl called and said she'd just been told that a former lover, with whom she'd engaged in unprotected sex, had recently tested HIV positive, and that she herself had so far learned she had chlamydia and was awaiting her own HIV results. The psychologist, Dr. Judy, who usually steers her answers in the direction of promoting her recent book, *Generation Sex,* actually encouraged the audience to pray. I thought this was a curious and unnerving response, especially coming from a shrewd, cutting-edge therapist who had counseled a previous female caller to "go for it" in terms of pursuing a lesbian threesome with two cheerleading squad mates from Floral Park. Over the FM waves that night, Dr. Judy sounded on the brink of tears, and I lay under my covers, horribly concerned, but mostly regretting that I had listened to Love Phones that night, because I wasn't in the mood to face one of these fearful falling asleep sessions. Like witnessing a car accident in which someone's bleeding or screaming, I wish I had taken another road. I wish I hadn't heard that call. I had to be up early the next morning.

7   And in the morning I did feel better because I convinced myself that the caller must be someone living in an altogether different world from mine and the guy was probably either some 25-year-old junkie she'd picked up in a dance club in Queens or a bisexual pretty boy of the sort whose effeminacy is enticing to 15-year-olds for its apparent safety and that Love Phones had probably never before received such a call and its producers had patched her through as a way of shaking up the audience and proving to the sponsors that the show was not only entertainment but something *essential.* These were the reasons that I could go on with my life, that plus the fact that I really had no other choice anyway.

8   But even when we turn off the radio, the media makes it hard for us to go on. A few days after hearing the caller on Love Phones, I saw a movie called *Kids,* photographer Larry Clark's cinema verité foray into the drug-ridden world of a group of unsupervised New York City teenagers. In the film we watch blond, waif-like Chloe get back a positive HIV test result, try unsuccessfully to call her unavailable mother, and then wind her way through the barbaric, trash talking landscape of her "friends" in an effort to seek out Telly, the barely pubescent, sex obsessed marauder who deflowered her and gave her the virus. He, in the meantime, has spent his day soiling another naïf, stealing money from

his mother, and viciously attacking someone who looked sideways at his skater buddies before wooing another virgin to his poisoned loins. *Kids,* with its apocalyptic heavy-handedness, tells us that life has surely gone down the tubes. We're goaded into believing that today's youth is so removed from compassion, so alienated from joy, that even the most intimate acts have become as routine as flicking a cigarette, the ashes of which are likely to land in a bed of chemically treated dry leaves that will ignite and burn down the whole block.

9   Much of the discourse surrounding AIDS in the early 1990s was informed by a male homosexual community, which, in the interests of prevention, assumed an alarmist position. In a *Village Voice* review of two books about the AIDS crisis and gay men, writer Michael Warner described HIV negative status as "living around, under, and next to crisis for that indefinite, rest-of-your-life blank stretch of time." And even though he is speaking largely of the crisis as it relates to gay men, he points out that for homosexuals and heterosexuals alike, "negative status is always in jeopardy and has to be preserved through effort." These sorts of statements are, in many ways, a legitimate tactic for HIV prevention in the gay community, which has been devastated by the disease in staggering proportions. But when words like "crisis" and "effort" are aimed at the heterosexual population as well, a lot of us tend to stop listening. What constitutes strenuous effort for one person may be routine behavior for another. For better or worse, guidelines for HIV prevention among straight people are often a matter of interpretation. *Kids* insinuates that it's scarcely possible to make it through a day without exposing oneself to the virus, especially if one is young, trusting and vulnerable to the smooth talk of boys like Telly, whose slurred lines like "I think about you all the time" are enough to make 13-year-olds lead him to their ruffled beds. The message here is a troubling one: that AIDS exposes itself to those who expose in themselves some kind of emotional neediness, who possess some semblance of romanticism (even in its uniquely post-modern form of fifteen minutes of sweet talk.)

10   At least two questions immediately pop into viewers' minds while watching *Kids.* Why are the boys such assholes? And, why are the girls such pushovers? That old standby the biological imperative certainly begs to serve as part of the answer. If we are to believe that the predatory sexual instincts of men are equivalent to women's

needs to "relate," to be told that someone "has been thinking about them all the time," then the human standards for interpersonal contact, at least by *Kids'* example, is rapidly descending. When men have reached a point where mindlessly groping a spaced-out child stands for a sexual experience and women hearing a few scripted lines from a boy who speaks as if he's got a retainer in his mouth connotes intimacy, it seems tempting just to chuck the whole interpersonal scene. And while *Kids* remains an egregious display of how-bad-it-could-be-if-we're-really-as-blasé-about-sex-as-we-seem, the memorandum to the audience at large remains unequivocal: "It's ugly out there. Don't bother."

11   The message is that trusting anyone is itself an irresponsible act, that having faith in an intimate partner, particularly women in relation to men, is a symptom of such profound naiveté that we're obviously not mature enough to be having sex anyway. That this reasoning runs counter to almost any feminist ideology—the ideology that told us, at least back in the 70s, that women should feel free to ask men on dates and wear jeans and have orgasms—is an admission that few AIDS-concerned citizen are willing to make. Two decades after *The Joy of Sex* made sexual pleasure accessible to both genders and the pill put a government approved stamp on premarital sex, we're still being told not to trust each other. Women are being told that if they believe a man who claims he's healthy, they're just plain stupid. Men are wary of any woman who seems one or more steps away from virginhood. Twenty years after the sexual revolution, we seem to be in a sleepier, sadder time than the 1950s. We've entered a period where mistrust equals responsibility, where paranoia signifies health.

12   Since I spent all of the 1970s under the age of ten, I've never known a significantly different sexual and social climate. Supposedly this makes it easier. Health educators and AIDS activists like to think that people of my generation can be made to unlearn what we never knew, to break the reckless habits we didn't actually form. But what we have learned thoroughly is how not to enjoy ourselves. Just like our mothers, whose adolescences were haunted by the abstract taboo of "nice" girls versus some other kind of girl, my contemporaries and I are again discouraged from doing what feels good. As it was with our mothers, the onus falls largely on the women. We know that it's much easier for women to contract HIV from a man than the other way around. We know that an "unsafe" man generally means someone who's shot drugs or

slept with other men, or possibly slept with prostitutes. We find ourselves wondering about these things over dinner dates. We look for any hints of homosexual tendencies, any references to a hypodermic moment. We try to catch him in the lie we've been told he'll tell.

13   What could be sadder? When I was a young teenager, around the age of Chloe and Telly, I looked forward to growing up and being able to do what I wanted, to live without a curfew, to talk on the phone as long as I wanted, and even to find people whom I could love and trust. But trust is out of vogue. We're not allowed to believe anyone anymore. And the reason we're not isn't because of AIDS but because of the lack of specificity in the anxiety that ripples around the disease. The information about AIDS that was formerly known as "awareness" has been subsumed into the unfortunate—and far less effective— incarnation of "style." As in *Kids,* where violence and ignorance are shown so relentlessly that we don't notice it by the end, AIDS awareness has become so much a part of the pop culture that not only is it barely noticeable, it is ineffectual. MTV runs programs about safe sex that are virtually identical to episodes of "The Real World." Madonna pays self-righteous lip service to safe sex despite basketball star Dennis Rodman's claim that she refused to let him wear a condom during their tryst. A print advertisement for the Benetton clothing company features a collage of hundreds of tiny photographs of young people, some of whom are shaded and have the word AIDS written across their faces. Many are white and blond and have the tousled, moneyed look common to more traditional fashion spreads or even yearbooks from colleges like the one I attended. There is no text other than the company's slogan. There is no explanation of how these faces were chosen, no public statement of whether these people actually have the disease or not. I called Benetton for clarification and was told that the photographs were supposed to represent people from all over the world and that no one shown was known to be HIV positive. Just as I suspected, the advertisement was essentially a work of art, which meant I could interpret the image any way I liked. This is how the deliverers of the safer sex message shoot themselves in the foot. By choosing a hard sell over actual information, people like me are going to believe what we want to believe, which, of course, is the thing that isn't so scary. So, I turn the page.

14   I personally don't know any white female with AIDS. Nor have I ever heard of a man who contracted the virus from a woman. And because of this there have been some situa-

tions where I haven't taken precautions and I don't necessarily think I was unwise. This is a difficult admission and it may be stupid logic, but it is the truth. For me and many of my peers, we're simply not seeing AIDS in our community. We're not going to sacrifice the thing we believe we deserve, the experiences we waited for, because of a Chloe or a caller on Love Phones.

15   This is where I get called a racist, an elitist, an idiot. This is where my college alumni association, chagrined that I didn't absorb all the free information the institution dispensed, removes me from the mailing list. However, I'm speaking for my community, which does make me an elitist in that my community is white, middle-class, educated, and generally prefers to attain some semblance of "relationship" before leaping unshielded on to the futon. I'm speaking for myself, who is not promiscuous, who has said no on more than one occasion, who has been careful on other occasions, but who still lies awake at night and wonders if I'll die.

16   But the inconsistent behavior continues, as do the hushed confessionals among friends and the lies to health care providers during routine exams because we just can't bear the terrifying lectures that ensue when we confess to not always protecting ourselves. Life in one's twenties is fraught not only with the financial and professional uncertainty that is often implicit in the pursuit of one's dreams, but with the specter of death that floats above the pursuit of a sex life. And there is no solution, only the conclusion that invariably finishes the hushed conversations: the whole thing simply "sucks." It's a bummer on a grand scale.

17   Heterosexuals are being sent vague signals. We're being told that if we are sufficiently vigilant, we'll probably be all right. We're told to assume the worst and not to invite disaster by hoping for the best. We're encouraged to keep our fantasies on tight reins, otherwise we'll lose control of the whole buggy, and no one will be able to say we weren't warned.

18   But I've been warned over and over again and there's still no visible cautionary tale. Since I'm as provincial and self-absorbed as the next person, I probably won't truly begin to take the AIDS crisis personally until I see either someone like me succumb to it or concrete statistics that show that we are. Until then, my peers and I are left with generalized anxiety, a low grade fear and anger that resides at the core of everything we do. Our attitudes have been affected by the disease in that we're scared, but our behavior

has stayed largely the same. The result of this is a corrosion of the soul, a chronic dishonesty and fear of ourselves that will, for us, likely do more damage than the disease itself. In this world, peace of mind is a utopian concept.

QUESTIONS ON CONTENT

1. What does Daum mean by "demographic profile" in paragraph 4?

_____

2. Name at least two lies "going around" according to the author.

_____

3. What specific support does Daum give for her assertion that AIDS awareness has become a part of pop culture? _____

_____

4. What is it that advertisers have done with the AIDS problem, according to Daum? _____

_____

Do you agree or disagree with her?_____

_____

5. Why do the people in Daum's group continue to disregard the message that "sex kills"?_____

_____

6. Daum asks in paragraph 13, "What could be sadder?" Do you agree or disagree that not being able to trust one's intimate partner is one of the terrible effects of the AIDS crisis? (State your reasons for your position.)

_____

_____

QUESTIONS ON STRATEGY

1. Describe in a few words Daum's voice and tone in the introductory paragraph. _____

   _____

2. What introductory strategy does the author use to grab the audience's attention? _____

   _____

3. What are two images used in the introduction to help the reader visualize the scene? _____

   _____

4. Throughout the essay, Daum targets a particular audience. When she repeatedly uses "we," to what group is she referring? _____

   _____

5. The following expressions are found in Daum's conclusion: "low-grade fear," "chronic dishonesty," and "corrosion of the soul." What is her strategy in concluding with these images?

   _____

   _____

CRITICAL THINKING IN CONNECTING TEXTS

In "We're Lying: Safe Sex and White Lies in the Time of AIDS" (pp. 160–168) Meghan Daum asserts that advertisers have been less than completely honest about the AIDS problem. In "A Black Athlete Looks at Education" (pp. 34–35), Arthur Ashe claims that the media advance the false

continued

CRITICAL THINKING IN CONNECTING TEXTS   *continued*

image of athletes as overnight successes and proper role models for young-sters. Working in a small group, draw up a list of other areas of public con-cern—for instance, how do advertisers and television spokespersons handle alcohol consumption? What about ethnic stereotypes? Environmental con-cerns? Once you have a list of issues, choose one and come up with a plan for reform—a plan for more responsible, honest handling of the issue by the media. If time permits, share your findings with the rest of the class.

**For more writing resources, be sure to see the
Longman English Pages Website at
http://longman.awl.com/englishpages**

Revising and Polishing the Essay

> What makes me happy is rewriting. . . . It's like cleaning house, getting rid of all the junk, getting things in the right order, tightening things up.
>
> —*Ellen Goodman, syndicated newspaper columnist*

Preview

In this chapter you will learn

▶ how to revise a preliminary draft—responding to peer and instructor comments by rethinking the draft and then adding, cutting, substituting, or rearranging information

▶ how to polish a revised draft—rereading to trim and clarify, inserting cue words, creating a title, proofreading, and employing correct manuscript format

▶ how to work through revisions with the "keys" in mind

▶ how to identify weak spots and design personal revision strategies

▶ how to be an effective peer editor and how to use peer editing to strengthen your own essays

Have you ever reached a snap decision, slept on it, and changed your mind the next morning? Do you recall dropping a letter in the mailbox, leaving a voice-mail message, or dashing off an E-mail, only to wish you could reclaim your words later, once you had a chance to cool down and reflect on your actions? If you've experienced any of these scenarios, then you know something about the importance of *revision* (literally, *seeing again*) for the writer. The composing process does not end with drafting—it continues with revising and polishing. In the revising stage of the composing process, you reevaluate your essay draft in order to make both major and minor adjustments. This chapter will explore specific strategies for revising and then polishing the final draft of your essay.

171

CHARACTERISTICS OF REVISING

Many writers revise as they compose. Examine any essay draft that you've worked on, and you'll probably see crossed out words, arrows moving sentences or phrases around, question marks in the margin, and other notations and changes made while you were in the process of writing. You may actually track changes (such as insertions, deletions, or rearrangement of material) from draft to draft, especially if you have drafted and saved your drafts on the computer and used your word-processing program's editing functions.

But in addition to making changes while you're drafting, revising also involves responding to your draft by standing back and re-seeing your essay as a whole—how does it all come together to accomplish your purpose? In the revising stage, you question and evaluate the thesis, structure, and material of your essay. Finally, when you polish your revision, you evaluate such issues as sentence structure, grammar, punctuation, and spelling.

MODEL WITH KEY QUESTIONS

Chapter 4 presented the first draft of an essay by student Margarita Figueroa, who shared that preliminary version with her instructor. The draft was returned to her with several comments. As you reread Figueroa's first draft, now with her instructor's responses, notice that the instructor uses the five "keys"—purpose, focus, material, structure, and style—to evaluate Figueroa's draft. Be on the lookout as you read for places where Figueroa might want to add, cut, substitute, or rearrange her material.

DISHONESTY
Margarita Figueroa

Margarita Figueroa discovered that instructor and peer feedback helped her in the revising and the polishing stages of her writing. She continued to work on the draft you may recall reading in Chapter 4 (pp. 93–95). and she was pleased with the result of her efforts. Almost finished with her writing classes at this point in her college career, Margarita asserts that she will continue to use her writing skills when she becomes a nurse.

Dishonesty

Margarita Figueroa

make your purpose clear in intro

1   I was reading an essay by Marya Mannes called "The Thin Grey Line."
    What in particular interested you? Focus on subject
    It was a very interesting article, separating honesty from dishonesty. It

made me really think about if people are dishonest or honest. I feel

that dishonesty is more characteristic of our society than honesty.
*Narrow the focus in thesis —don't forget controlling idea
+ specific language —should you break down dishonesty?*

2   Well, first there is the fake car accident that results in getting money

out of auto insurance companies. For instance, I had friends that

would get together and collaborate with one another and would report

you have lots of material —try to structure your material with a major point first, and then your details?

to the insurance company about an accident that they were involved in,

but it wasn't a real accident. It was a fraudolent claim. They even had

a friend who was a lawyer that would help them set everything up as if

it was a legitimate accident. They used their own cars, license plate

numbers, and insurance companies, and each person received an out-

of-court settlement of five hundred dollars. Another reason for

dishonesty is when an opportunity arises for an individual to become

dishonest.

style problem — rephrase so reader can understand statement

3   The circumstance that occurs and causes an individual to become

dishonest. For example, my sister told me about an incident that
                              Is this material necessary?
happened to her at Burger King. My sister had ordered burgers, fries,

and drinks for her family. After she placed her order, the woman who works at Burger King rang the order up, but meanwhile my sister and the woman were having a conversation about kids. Then, my sister saw the total amount due, which was $14.83, so she gave the woman a twenty dollar bill and the woman gave my sister her order and then gave her the change due to her. This is when the woman made a mistake and gave her back the total amount due, which was $14.83, instead of $5.17, which was the change due. My sister noticed the mistake the woman made, but she didn't say anything. She walked out of Burger King, got in her car, and went home.

Again, you have lots of material, but rethink and remember your purpose and specific focus = dishonesty among individuals.

are these exact amounts necessary to make your point?

Your structure is clear – good paragraph breaks

4   Dishonesty can also occur between two people in a relationship. It can

not clear – rephrase or explain?

result in blaming others for mistakes made by someone else. I have a friend that lives in the apartment complex where I stay. Her husband one day was backing up his car into his stall underneath the carport, when all of a sudden he hit one of the wooden poles that holds up the carport and moved it out of place. Then he called the owner of the building and explained to him about the incident that occurred, but instead of taking the blame for hitting the pole, he put the blame on his wife. Every time someone asked him what happened to the pole next to his car, he would reply, "Oh, my wife hit the pole when she was parking the car."

I might be more convinced if you had other examples rather than so much info on one isolated incident.

possibly losing focus?

For a college essay, try omitting "I," "me," "my" throughout?

5   Finally, I do agree with the article "The Thin Grey Line" and Marya

check for style –rephrase

Mannes' opinion separating honesty from dishonesty because if we really take a close look at different situations, we would probably find

vague?

a little dishonesty here and there. I feel that everyone has had some

sort of dishonesty once in their lives, whether it was a little white lie or

be specific?

Aha —Good idea to mention possible solutions in conclusion —can you tie this back to your thesis and your overall purpose —are you trying to persuade us to change our behavior? I'm not quite clear.

not, but dishonesty is a way of life for some people. We need to be

more responsible for our dishonest decisions and behaviors, but most

of all, we need to strengthen our moral beliefs because dishonesty can

have a major effect on everyone involved.

Margarita —

You're headed in the right direction with this draft.

For now,

1 Re-read the Mannes essay —this would help you remember what it was about dishonesty that struck you so strongly.

2 Rethink & narrow your thesis —what's your point of view about all this dishonesty?

3 Re-examine your structure + the material you've chosen for paragraphs 2, 3, and 4. Each one of these paragraphs can really build a strong case for your thesis.

Good job with the first draft.

I look forward to reading your revised draft!

KEY QUESTIONS

1. **PURPOSE** Name one change Figueroa might make in paragraph 1 in response to her instructor's comments. _____

   _____

2. **FOCUS** Why has Figueroa's instructor circled the use of exact dollars and cents? What should Figueroa consider doing with these amounts in her revised essay draft? _____

   _____

3. **MATERIAL** What do the instructor's comments indicate about Figueroa's material in paragraph 4? _____

   _____

4. **STRUCTURE** If Figueroa considers her instructor's comments, will she change or maintain her present structure for the essay? _____

   _____

5. **STYLE** Rephrase the first sentence in paragraph 3 so that readers can understand the thought more clearly. _____

   _____

GUIDELINES FOR REVISING

Allow Time for Reflection

When you have completed your preliminary draft, your first thought may be, "At last, I'm finished with that essay." Resist the impulse to accept this version as your final draft, even though to you the first draft may *look* pretty good. This is doubly true if you are drafting on a computer because the final, clean look of the typeset letters may fool you into thinking your draft is ready for its intended audience. Instead, try to allow a day or two, or at least a few hours, in which to reflect on your preliminary draft. As you go about your other activities during this time, allow yourself time to think about your draft, jotting down any ideas that come to mind. This way, when you begin to revise, you'll be more likely to re-see your draft with objective eyes. Thoughtful revision involves scheduling enough time to reflect on your writing. Ideally, you could take all the time you need to stand back and evaluate what you've written; realistically, you have deadlines to meet.

Use Peer Editing and Instructor Response

Peer editing can be a helpful tool in the revising stage of the composing process. Although you may think your ideas are coming across clearly in a draft, there's nothing like the honest reaction of an unbiased reader to put you in touch with what is and is not working in your essay draft. Your instructor may have a specific format for peer editing, or you may be free to structure peer evaluations on your own. If the latter is the case, find another student whose feedback you value and ask the student to read and respond to your essay.

Here are a few popular methods of structuring peer response:

- *Readaround or workshopping:* Students divide into groups of three or four and each student brings an extra copy of a draft to share with the group. During an alloted time, the group members silently read all essays circulating within their group and jot comments on them or on a separate sheet of paper.

- *Read aloud:* Students divide into small groups, each student reading an essay out loud while others respond on paper with constructive comments for revision.

- *Anonymous peer editing:* Students turn in drafts to instructor or submit drafts using E-mail with only a student body number (no name) on the draft; instructor distributes essays at random to class or circulates them via E-mail for evaluation and anonymous comment.

- *Peer response worksheet:* Instructor distributes to the class specific sets of questions for students to respond to when reading and evaluating another student's essay. To see an example of such a worksheet, turn to page 182.

In revising, you will often have the advantage of your instructor's response to a draft. This can be a helpful complement to self-evaluation and peer editing for three reasons:

- Your instructor is obviously familiar with your assignment—your primary purpose in writing the essay.

- Your instructor has expertise not only in writing but also in objectively commenting on student essays in a way designed to help you in revising.

- Your instructor wants to help you succeed both in this course and also in your future college writing.

Rethink the Draft

Once you have additional feedback from a peer or your instructor, you can rethink the draft. This rethinking can take you in a variety of directions in your revising process.

For example, let's say that your instructor, after reading your draft, suggests that your thesis is too broad and that just one of your supporting points could actually be the basis for an entire paper. You think about this comment and decide that you agree that your subject would be more focused if you limited the thesis. You could then include material in support of this thesis that would be much more convincing and specific than the material you now have. This rethinking of your essay results in a shift in your focus. And now as you begin to work on your new thesis, you won't be using some of the material from your first draft. As a result, you may need to return to the discovering stage to gather more material in support of your new thesis.

This example of rethinking involves a significant adjustment on your part. Other adjustments that occur after rethinking the draft also characterize the revising stage. For many writers these adjustments include adding, cutting, substituting, and rearranging.

Add to the Draft

If your instructor or a peer editor feels that you left some vital information out of your draft or that some point needs further clarification or explanation, you will want to add more material to your draft where appropriate.

Cut What Is Not Working

You may find that you need to cut a part of your draft—to delete words, sentences, or even large sections because they don't pertain clearly to your thesis, they don't suit your primary purpose in the essay, or they repeat what has already been stated. Although cutting may be hard because you've put so much time and effort into finding the material in the first place, cutting repeated, off-topic, or unnecessary information can substantially strengthen an essay.

Make Substitutions

Often after you cut inappropriate material, you find you need to replace what is now missing with new material. This can involve inserting substitutions—words, sentences, whole groups of sentences, or even paragraphs. You may need to return to prewriting to discover more material for your revised draft.

Rearrange Material

Upon rethinking your draft, you may feel—or your peer editor or instructor may have commented—that your material, although supportive of your purpose, should be rearranged. A restructuring of material might result in a more logical flow of ideas. A different way of organizing could also give the essay more dramatic punch.

Practice 7.1 Reread Margarita Figueroa's first draft of "Dishonesty" (pp. 173–175), along with her instructor's comments. Annotate the draft by indicating where she might want to add, cut, make substitutions, or rearrange material.

◆ ◆ ◆

STRATEGIES FOR REVISING

1. **PURPOSE** Distance yourself from your draft for a few hours or a day or two, then reread it, asking yourself if it achieves its purpose.

2. **FOCUS** Check and, if appropriate, adjust your thesis based on instructor or peer comments.

3. **MATERIAL** Search for places in the draft where additional information would help make your point. Delete any material that doesn't clearly relate to your thesis.

4. **STRUCTURE** Experiment with different ways of arranging material and get feedback from your instructor or peers.

5. **STYLE** Be sure that you have an introduction that grabs the interest of your audience and a conclusion that offers closure and ties up loose ends. Check to see that every word and sentence works to communicate your subject clearly to readers. Revise any vague words or phrases.

CHARACTERISTICS OF POLISHING

If you've ever polished a car or a treasured piece of furniture or jewelry, you know the satisfaction that comes from pride of ownership—you've taken something you love and made it even more wonderful. When you polish an essay, you refine it—you check for flaws on its surface, correcting mistakes as well as adding those finishing touches that will make your writing really sparkle.

Polishing is the final stage in the composing process, a crucial stage, but one that is often overlooked by students in their haste to meet an assignment deadline. But polishing is an important stage that can make all the difference in the impact your essay has on its audience. While the revising stage of your writing involves in the "big picture"—rethinking your draft in terms of what ideas you want to add, delete, and rearrange—the polishing stage demands that you use a mental magnifying glass to scrutinize every detail of your revised draft, to search out inappropriate or weak words and phrases as well as grammatical, spelling, and punctuation errors. This stage concludes when you present the final draft of your essay in the correct format indicated by your instructor.

MODEL WITH KEY QUESTIONS

Margarita Figueroa's preliminary draft appears on pages 173–175. When Figueroa completed her second draft, she brought this revised draft to class, where she received feedback from a peer editor. First, read Figueroa's revised draft of the essay, and then examine her peer's response. Notice that the peer editor wrote directly on Figueroa's draft as well as on the peer editing sheet. Next, read Figueroa's final draft, retitled "Practicing What We Preach," which incorporates many peer editor's suggestions and the fine-tuning Figueroa gave to her essay in polishing it.

Dishonesty

Margarita Figueroa

1 Lots of people cheat on their taxes and lie to their loved ones, or don't mention an error when they receive change if that means they would get the benefit of extra money. If we read an essay by Marya Mannes called "The Thin Grey Line," we'll be forced to examine the issue of dishonesty in our society. Although it is not a pleasant thought, *Thesis* dishonesty seems to be winning over honesty in our personal lives, when we go to work, and in our dealings with strangers.

To whom?

2 Even as we stress the importance of dishonesty, many adults don't

"practice what they preach." For example, one partner in a marriage

may be cheating on another by having an affair or playing around on

Save face?

the sly. Or perhaps pride challenges a husband or wife to tell a lie. For

instance, a neighbor's husband lies when his car hits a wooden pole

holding up a carport. He then calls the owner of the building who lives

down the street, putting the blame on his own wife, he even

persuades his wife to go along with his lie that "my wife hit the pole

when she was parking the car."

You could use a transition here.

3 Deception appears in the workplace also. How many times have we or

those we've known "borrowed" supplies from the company we work

or leaving work early? more examples?

for? And what about taking an extra hour for lunch? Possibly the most

dangerous form of dishonesty in the workplace occurs when we are

asked by an employer to deceive a customer, many of us have been

told, "If he calls, just tell him I'm not in." *Add material?*

4 Finally, dishonesty occurs in our day-to-day encounters with total

Not always! Explain when?

strangers. For example, there are those who collaborate to report a

fake car accident in order to get money from auto insurance

companies. Lawyers help with deceptions, urging out-of-court

settlements for hundreds of dollars. Also, people confide that when

given wrong change at fast food establishments, they deceive the

casheer by saying nothing. Instead these people get in their cars and

laugh. *? Clarify this —why do they laugh? What if the error means they get cheated out of money?*

5 Perhaps if we could strengthen our morals and be examples of

honesty, our children wouldn't be as likely to be dishonest.

Your conclusion needs work. Try to link these remarks somehow with your examples of dishonesty in intro. paragraph?

PEER EDIT WORKSHEET

Your name or
student number: _Tommy Cheng_

Writer's name or
student number: _Margarita Figueroa_

1. **PURPOSE** Does the introduction grab your attention? _sort of so-so_ Are you clear about this essay's purpose? _yes_ Is it to express, inform, or persuade? _persuade_ In which sentence does the writer's purpose first become apparent? Write the sentence in the following space: _"Lots of people cheat ...lie... extra money."_

2. **FOCUS** Find the writer's thesis and underline it on the draft. Does this thesis have a suitable subject, controlling idea, specific language, and appropriate tone? _Good 3 areas_ Which of these elements needs more work? _Could make "when we go to work" sound like the other 2 pts._

3. **MATERIAL** Is the material in the essay clear and effective in developing the thesis? _yes_ _a couple of suggestions on essay itself_ Where could the writer add more material? Delete material? Substitute material? (Indicate by writing directly on the draft.)

4. **STRUCTURE** Can you follow the development of ideas clearly from sentence to sentence and from one paragraph to the next? _yes_ _most places_ What might help? (Indicate on draft rearranging, adding cue words, etc.)

5. **STYLE** Jot down in the following space a word group or word that is especially effective. _adults don't "practice what they preach"_
Find in the essay any examples of vague, inappropriate, or incorrect words and circle these on the draft. Indicate one weak area that this writer might check more carefully in proofreading for mistakes. _sentences run together ¶s 2 and 3 and spelling_

Does the writer's conclusion effectively close the essay and tie back to the thesis with effective phrasing? _No-this needs polishing up - it seems abrupt_

After taking time to evaluate her peer editor's comments, Figueroa worked through the polishing stage for this essay. She had planned to spend several days on the entire composing process, and she was much happier with her final draft for this essay than she had been with earlier assignments for which she had devoted less time.

As you read Figueroa's final draft, notice in particular that in polishing her essay, she made changes based on her peer editor's comments and her own evaluation of her draft. Figueroa noticed that Tommy Cheng, her editor, found a particular phrase, "practice what they preach" memorable, so she decided to use the phrase in her revised title. She also refined her introduction and conclusion, two weaker areas noted by Cheng. Figueroa wanted the final draft to move more smoothly from one idea to the next, so she inserted cue words where they would be helpful. Finally, Figueroa checked her spelling, repaired some grammatical errors, and improved her word choice in certain paragraphs noted by Cheng as needing a little polishing.

PRACTICING WHAT WE PREACH
Margarita Figueroa

1   How many people cheat on their taxes? Lie to their loved ones? Fail to mention an error in receiving change when the error happens to be in their favor? Reading an essay by Marya Mannes entitled "The Thin Grey Line" forces us to examine the issue of dishonesty in our society. Although it is not a pleasant thought, dishonesty seems to be winning over honesty in our personal lives, our professional lives, and our day-to-day interaction with total strangers.

2   Even as we stress to our children the importance of honesty, many adults don't "practice what they preach." For example, one partner in a marriage may be cheating on another, having an affair or playing around on the sly. Or perhaps pride challenges a husband or wife to "save face" by telling a lie. For instance, a neighbor's husband lies when his car hits a wooden pole holding up a carport. He then calls the owner of the building, putting the blame on his own wife and even persuading the wife to go along with his lie that "my wife hit the pole when she was parking the car."

3   Unfortunately, deception doesn't stop with personal relationships—it also appears in our professional lives. How many times have we or those we've known

"borrowed" supplies from the company we work for? And aren't we crossing that "thin gray line" every time we leave from work early, come in late, or take an extra hour for lunch? Possibly the most dangerous form of dishonesty in the workplace occurs when we are asked by an employer to deceive a customer. Many of us have been told, "If he calls, just tell him I'm not in," or, "Don't mention a refund if the client doesn't ask."

4   Finally, dishonesty occurs in our day-to-day encounters with total strangers if circumstances or greed motivate us to lie. For example, there are those who collaborate to report a fake car accident in order to get money from auto insurance companies. These fraudulent claims sometimes involve lawyers who help with the deceptions, urging out-of-court settlements for hundreds of dollars. Also, people confide that when given incorrect change at fast food establishments, they deceive the cashier by saying nothing if an error is made in their favor. Instead, these individuals get in their cars, drive home, and pocket their newfound money.

5   If we really take a closer look at different situations in our personal and professional lives and our daily interactions with strangers, we will find more than a little dishonesty. Why? Perhaps if we could strengthen our morals and be examples of honesty to our children, the next generation wouldn't be as likely to cheat on taxes or lie to their loved ones.

KEY QUESTIONS

1. **PURPOSE** What appears to be the writer's purpose in this final, polished draft of the essay? _____

   _____

2. **FOCUS** Explain whether or not Figueroa's revised conclusion focuses more clearly on her thesis. _____

   _____

3. **MATERIAL** What new example has Figueroa added in paragraph 3 as a result of her editor's comments? _____

   _____

4. **STRUCTURE** Which new cue words help Figueroa's audience follow her main points as she develops them?_____

_____

5. **STYLE** Find one example of a new word or phrase that Figueroa uses in her polished, final draft. _____

_____

GUIDELINES FOR POLISHING

Reread Your Revised Draft

Even after you've revised a first or second draft, resist the temptation to consider your work complete. Instead, read the draft out loud slowly. You'll often be amazed at what you discover. Writer and teacher Eudora Welty read aloud everything she wrote because she believed that "the sound of what falls on the page begins the process of testing it for truth."

You can also try reading your essay backward, not word by word but sentence by sentence. Although your sentences may make little sense in relation to your thesis, you can more easily spot errors in grammar, punctuation, spelling, missing words, and typos by reading backward.

Use Your Tools to Improve Weak Spots

Do you have an "Achilles heel"? (Achilles was a mythological Greek warrior who had one area of vulnerability—his heel—in an otherwise mighty body.) Today, we use the expression to refer to an individual weakness or trouble spot. Do instructor or peer comments indicate that you have a tendency to misspell words? To use vague words instead of specific ones? To write incomplete sentences? If you have a recognized weakness, you can use this knowledge to your best advantage as a writer. Be on the lookout for this vulnerable area and polish your essay by addressing the problem.

Once you've identified a particular weakness, consult the appropriate section in the handbook in Part Four of this book and complete the exercises and activities. If you notice or suspect any spelling problems, or if you're not completely sure of the meaning of a word that you're using, remember that your dictionary can help. In addition, a computer's spell checker can certainly help you catch many spelling errors, but you should know that it does not correct misspellings caused by word confusion—for example, misuse of *their* for *there* or *accept* for *except*. For a complete list of similar sounding words and their meanings, see page 468 in the handbook.

Practice 7.2 To help you identify troublesome areas in your own writing, consult a few assignments you've submitted to your writing instructor. After looking over the evaluation, markings, and comments, jot down in the following space two trouble spots connected with grammar, spelling, punctuation, word choice, or usage for which you could use some additional help and practice.

_____

_____

◆ ◆ ◆

Use Peer Editing and Instructor Response

Just as feedback from both your instructor and your peers was an important part of revising your first draft, new feedback on your revised drafts will help you continue to refine your essay in the polishing stage. By all means, share your second and third drafts, and then respond thoughtfully to the comments of your readers.

Trim and Clarify

One important way you can polish your essay involves making certain that every word you use is necessary, specific, and clearly understood by the reader. Go through the essay sentence by sentence and see if you can find any words or phrases that could be trimmed or made more accurate or descriptive.

Practice 7.3 Annotate the following concluding paragraph of an essay draft by trimming or replacing words or word groups where appropriate:

So to make a long story short, trying to find the right mate is like trying to find a needle in a haystack. At this point in time, we can only hope that dating services will grow more efficient at matching guys with chicks according to their true interests and personalities rather than according to some touched up photos or carefully rehearsed videos. It is a crying shame that some enterprising person hasn't seen the light and established just such a service. Perhaps somewhere out there in the great beyond of cyberspace there is a perfect match for each of us.

◆ ◆ ◆

Insert Cue Words

When you're putting those finishing touches on your essay in the polishing stage, you want to make sure (if you have not considered this in an earlier draft) that your audience can follow the flow of your ideas smoothly and effortlessly. Have you ever careened around the streets with an erratic driver—one who presses hard on the gas pedal and then, seconds later, without warning, slams on the brakes? This kind of car ride is jerky and unpleasant, in much the same way that an essay that jerks the reader roughly and without warning from one point to another may fail to achieve its purpose. It is intimidating to the reader not to know what to expect next.

You can solve this problem with the use of **cue words,** words or phrases that signal the reader that some shift in thought is taking place. Cue words tell the reader you're moving from a main point to a specific detail, from comparison to contrast, from cause to effect, and so on. Refer to the list of cue words, found in the box, when you're searching for just the right cue word for your essay.

CUE WORDS

- **Try using these if you want to signal a change in time:**

then	after a while	in the future	afterward
finally	in the past	now	previously
currently	meanwhile	immediately	in the meantime
at last	earlier	soon	simultaneously
formerly	next	until now	eventually
suddenly	before now	at the same time	later
after this	presently	at length	subsequently

- **Experiment with these if you want to show some order, progression, or a series of steps (not necessarily time-oriented):**

first, second	finally	last	in addition
next	another	furthermore	further
also	moreover	besides	not only . . . but also

- **Work with these to cue a contrast or change in what has been said before:**

in contrast	on the other hand	regardless	nevertheless
conversely	however	on the contrary	despite, in spite of
but	even though	still	although
yet	instead		

continued

CUE WORDS *continued*

- **To show a similarity or comparison with what you have stated before:**

similarly	in the same way	in a similar manner	just as
likewise	in comparison	as well as	equally important

- **To signal that you are going into more detail or elaboration:**

for example	for instance	as an illustration	to illustrate
to explain	in particular	to expand on this	

- **To signal repetition:**

again	in other words	to repeat	as has been noted

- **To show emphasis or stress:**

basically	more important	without question	most important
truly	without a doubt	moreover	undeniably
essentially	above all	indeed	

- **To signal some cause/effect relationship:**

because	as a result	since	consequently
thus	accordingly	for this reason	therefore

- **To cue the reader that you are concluding:**

finally	in conclusion	on the whole	all things considered
in brief	to summarize	in summary	in closing

Practice 7.4 Read the following paragraph and insert appropriate cue words from the list.

I have several good reasons for missing class today. _____, my car was totaled in an accident yesterday afternoon, and I have no way of getting to school today. _____, my dog ate my homework, and the instructor will never believe this really happened. _____, my favorite soap opera is featuring a guest star this week whom I really want to see, and the VCR is on the blink so I can't tape it for later. _____, I have no doubt that any intelligent instructor would take pity on me and allow me to make up any class work that I have missed.

◆ ◆ ◆

Create a Captivating Title

Some writers like to have at least a working title right from the moment they begin to draft the essay; others prefer to wait until the final polishing to create a title. You'll want to experiment with what works best for you. Keep in mind that a title is important—it is your reader's first impression of your essay and will help you forecast your particular point of view as well as the subject you'll be discussing. Finally, avoid using a complete sentence as a title. Titles cannot function as thesis statements; instead, try to create a title from one to several words long.

Practice 7.5 To see how titles can communicate to a reader, turn back to the table of contents for this text (pp. xi–xxvi), and scan the essay titles. From those essays that you have read, find a title that you find particularly effective and write it down along with a brief explanation of why you found it effective.

_____

_____

◆ ◆ ◆

Check for Correct Manuscript Format

Manuscript format refers to the general layout of a final draft, including name and title placement, margins, and page numbers. If your instructor does not specify a particular layout, you can follow the most common format, which is to doublespace your essay on 8½ by 11-inch white bond paper, setting one-inch margins on the top, bottom, and sides of the page, indenting paragraphs five to eight spaces, and centering the title.

STRATEGIES FOR POLISHING

1. **PURPOSE** Make certain that every word you use is the best one to support your essay's purpose. As you polish, delete and replace cliches, jargon, undefined terms, wordy expressions, and vague words.

2. **FOCUS** Check your thesis to be sure that the wording clearly communicates your subject to your audience.

3. **MATERIAL** Be certain that each main point is supported by clearly phrased, easy-to-read sentences and that paragraphs are of an appropriate length (see Chapter 5).

4. **STRUCTURE** Find any places within and between paragraphs where cue words would help lead your readers from one idea to the next. Insert appropriate cue words.

5. **STYLE** Ask yourself if your title and introduction engage your audience. Be sure your conclusion offers closure and ties up all loose ends. Finally, proofread the essay carefully for spelling, punctuation, grammar mistakes, typos, omitted words, and correct manuscript format. Do not rely solely on a computer's spelling or grammar correction functions. Repair all mistakes.

JOURNAL WRITING: A REVISION DIALOGUE

Writing in your journal about your experiences when revising and polishing a draft will allow you to explore your feeling about the various activities in these two stages. After Margarita Figueroa read her instructor's comments on her essay (pp. 173–175), she gave herself time to reflect on her drafting process. She wrote in her journal that she had been pleased to read the positive comments made by her instructor, but she had also felt nervous and a little confused about what to do first in revising her draft. After a day of reflection, Figueroa returned to her journal, read her entry of the previous day, and decided on a revision plan.

Journal writing can furnish you with a record of what did and did not work for you, so that in the future you can repeat effective strategies.

1. Locate a final draft of one of your essays, along with all prewriting and earlier drafts. Answer at least five of the following questions in a journal entry.

   • How much time did you allow for the revising stage of this essay? Was this enough, too much, or about right?

   • Did you work from an outline? Did your plan for structuring the essay work? Did you experiment with changing the structure?

   • If you received peer or instructor response to a draft, how did you react to the comments?

   • Did your original thesis change?

   • In your drafts, what material did you add? Delete? Substitute?

   • Did you keep your original title? Introduction? Conclusion?

   • Did you use a checklist in revising? In polishing?

   • Did you read your draft out loud to spot mistakes?

   • Did you try reading the essay backward, sentence by sentence? Was this helpful?

   • Did you use a dictionary and the handbook section of this text when polishing?

   • Did you proofread your essay on the computer screen or on hard copy?

2. Examine the essays you've written for this course. Based on your instructor's comments and your own evaluations, write a list of your strengths and weak spots as a writer. Or, if you prefer, create a personal checklist of problems that seem to recur from essay to essay. Then write a plan to deal with these problems in future essays. You might set up a conference with your instructor or with the writing center on your campus to discuss this plan.

If you find these journal entries helpful, return to this page after you've worked through the composing process for your next essay and answer other questions.

USING THE COMPUTER: REVISING AND POLISHING

1. Although using a computer can facilitate your revision, studies show that students who revise on hard copy (the printed page) write better essays. Many professional writers and editors also prefer to revise using hard copy. To make revising hard copy easier, print out a triple-spaced version with extra wide margins for a draft you're currently revising. You'll have lots of room to evaluate and experiment with adding, deleting, substituting, and rearranging information. Practice revision strategies on this draft or ask a peer editor to respond to the draft, making suggestions between lines and in the margins of the draft.

2. Many word-processing programs offer options for annotating and questioning text. While it is easy to simply change the appearance of words on the screen (as in the exercise above), you might find it more effective to use *annotating, revising, strikeout/strikethrough, insert, comment,* and other *text editing* commands. First, use your program's *Help* function to see which of these commands is available. Practice using a sample or draft text. In most programs, *annotating* allows you to make comments on the screen that are visible to you on the screen but do not show up when a document is printed. Many peer editors find this function especially useful. *Strikeout/strikethrough* makes lines through words that you think of deleting, without actually erasing them from the screen. This is a good way to keep track of changes that you are thinking of making, or that a peer editor has suggested. Try this in your draft.

3. To track down words that you think you may have used too often or incorrectly, use *search* to locate and change those words. For effective editing, you might be on the lookout for vague words like *thing, very, society,* or *really.* When you find these words, reread the sentence in which they appear. Do you "really" need the word? Is there a more interesting, accurate word you could use instead? The *search/replace* function can help you save time in revision. If you notice that you've used the wrong spelling or format throughout your essay—for example, you've typed *effect* where you should have typed *affect*—search/replace will automatically find all the errors and make the correction.

4. Although a *spell checker* can be a terrific help as you polish your essay, it should be your last resort. A spell checker looks at each word

continued

Using the Computer: Revising and Polishing   *continued*

individually and pays no attention at all to context. This might not seem like such a big deal, until you realize just how many homonyms (words that sound exactly alike but mean different things) there are in the English language. Incorrect usages of apostrophes and pronouns also tend to glide uncorrected right through a spell checker. Here are some sentences that a spell checker would let you get away with—but your instructor would not find so funny:

- Although their was a report of piece, gorilla warfare continues.
- The nurse had many patience hear in the hospital.
- Sam was board with the teacher's lessen.
- I would like to meat you, but my voice is horse today and I'm afraid I wouldn't be herd.

To see just how random a spell checker can be, type the names of several friends on a blank screen and have your word processor "check" it. Most programs will give you a list of words that it thinks you should use instead. How silly are some of these suggestions? So how do you use a spell checker? Very carefully, and never by itself. It can help you in early stages of writing by catching the obvious mistakes, and if you're uncertain of your typing, it can help in final polishing. But always be sure to check your spelling yourself.

5. Looking for a word? Want to impress your friends with a really obscure new term? Many publishing companies and search engines have online dictionary sites that go beyond providing definitions. Some provide a "word of the day" or snippets of language history. Does your search engine have a dictionary? Use it to look up a word. Or go to ⟨http://www.m-w.com⟩, the Merriam-Webster Dictionary site.

OPTIONS FOR WRITING

The following options ask you to practice revising and polishing one or more drafts of your earlier essays. Roald Dahl, the creator of *James and the Giant Peach, Willy Wonka and the Chocolate Factory,* and many other children's books, candidly revealed his writing process: "By the time I'm nearing the end of a story, the first part will have been reread and altered and corrected at least 150 times. . . . Good writing is essentially rewriting." You won't have the chance to complete

150 revisions of your essays for this course, but in the following options you will have the opportunity to choose one or more essay drafts that you'd like to revise and polish.

1. After reviewing the "Guidelines for Revising" (p. 176), reread an essay that your instructor has commented on, and then rethink your draft. You may need to readjust your thesis accordingly. When you have worked through a revised draft, use the Peer Response Sheet shown on (p. 195), adding your own questions, if you like. Ask another student to read and comment on your revised draft. After you have read that student's peer response, take some time to rethink your draft again and review the Guidelines for Polishing (pp. 185–186). Now polish your draft, making necessary changes.

2. Review "Trim and Clarify" (p. 186) and the list of cue words on pages 187 and 188. Choose a draft of one of your essays and read the draft aloud, underlining or highlighting any vague or ineffective words or phrases and inserting cue words where helpful to guide the reader. Then write a more polished draft of the essay, consulting the Strategies for Polishing (p. 189).

3. Select a few of your essays that have been graded or evaluated by your instructor and analyze them using the checklists for revising and polishing. Write a paragraph focusing on your strengths and weaknesses in writing and your plan for strengthening future essays.

RESPONDING TO WRITING: PEER EDITING

Peer editing can help you revise and polish your essay. As a writer, you have a right to agree or disagree with how a peer, or even an instructor, responds to your writing. As your writing course continues, you and your classmates will become more effective peer editors. To practice editing, first read the student essay presented here, and then answer the questions that follow.

Student Essay
(Photo Not
Available)

THE SECOND COMING OF POETRY
Anthony Diaz

1 "All they talk about in rap music is violence, guns and disrespecting women. Those rap singers promote gang activity and drug use." I seem to be hearing this a lot lately from the older generation in our society. It upsets me that they think that way; they feel like that because that is the only rap music they hear. The media only projects the negative aspects of hip hop. The only time you see a rap artist on TV is when he is being arrested or thrown in jail. The older generation

seems to think that Snoop Doggy Dog and Warren G are the only rappers, or that all hip hop artists sound the same.

2   When I first moved to Hawthorne my dad expressed his feelings and showed his ignorance about hip hop. He thought that all rappers were gang members doing nothing but cursing and talking about how bad they were. This made me mad; he knew nothing about the music. He didn't even try to understand what the artists were talking about. I had to explain to him that there is a lot of violence in hip hop but that is reality. There is a great amount of violence in our society. Rap music is exactly that: A reflection of society, a reproduction of young people's lifestyles and situations.

3   Older people tend to overlook the talents of many m.c.s in fact they often believe they have no talent at all. I have had people tell me that since rappers sample other records they are not creative. Some don't even recognize them as artists. What they don't realize is that hip hop is one of the most technically complex forms of music that exists. It's not just some guys rhyming over beats.

4   The thought process that goes into writing lyrics is just about the most difficult task in all of music, rap is poetry. When an m.c. can express himself and get his point across all while reciting poetry to a beat, that is a true display of poetic talent. Poetry is the art of writing stories, poems or thoughts into verse. Not only is rap poetry but it has taken the art form to a whole new level. For example an m.c. by the name of Common Sense says "One day I'm cruzin down a one-way street and I done past fun day three blocks ago, within itself life is an obstacle, as I manuever through the manure I try to be responsible." In this simple stanza he explains the state of his life using the metaphor of the streets. In my opinion these are the types of things that make up the essence of modern poetry. It had appeared that poetry was a lost art, but then rappers took the rules and transformed them into one of the most powerful forms of expression, music!

5   The hip hop community has its own dialect, fashion styles, forms of dance, art, mentors and pioneers. It is much more than just music. Hip hop is a culture.

6   When people think it is going to die, it evolves into a new form and becomes stronger than ever. It has been on the scene for about seventeen years, yet some still don't recognize it as a true form of music, like jazz or rock and roll. Rap music must be paid close attention, because it explains a part of our world that some don't even know exists. As long as people continue to express themselves through poetry, the hip hop legacy will never die.

PEER EDIT WORKSHEET

Your name or   Writer's name or
student number: _____   student number: _____

1. **PURPOSE** Does the introduction grab your attention? _____ Are you

   clear about this essay's purpose? _____ Is it to express, inform, or per-

   suade? _____ In which sentence does the writer's purpose first become

   apparent? Write the sentence in the following space: _____

   _____

2. **FOCUS** Find the writer's thesis and underline it on the draft. Does this the-

   sis have a suitable subject, controlling idea, specific language, and appro-

   priate tone? _____ Which of these elements needs more work?

   _____

3. **MATERIAL** Is the material in the essay clear and effective in developing

   the thesis? _____ Where could the writer add more material? Delete

   material? Substitute material? (Indicate by writing directly on the draft.)

4. **STRUCTURE** Can you follow the development of ideas clearly from sen-

   tence to sentence and from one paragraph to the next? _____ What

   might help? (Indicate on draft rearranging, adding cue words, etc.)

5. **STYLE** Jot down in the following space a word group or word that is espe-

   cially effective. _____

   Find in the essay any examples of vague, inappropriate, or incorrect words

   and circle these on the draft. Indicate one weak area that this writer might

   check more carefully in proofreading for mistakes. _____

   _____

   Does the writer's conclusion effectively close the essay and tie back to the

   thesis with effective phrasing? _____

Now that you've practiced using an editing sheet, find a draft of one of your own recent essays and exchange it with another student, responding to the same peer editing questions or others that you or your instructor create. When your draft and the peer editing sheet are returned to you, read your editor's comments and complete these statements:

1. I agree with the following comments made by my peer editor:

_____

2. I disagree with the following comments: _____

_____

3. I plan to revise my essay in the following way:

PURPOSE_____

FOCUS _____

MATERIAL_____

STRUCTURE _____

STYLE_____

As you become more experienced in peer editing the essays of others and in responding to the suggestions of your peers, remember to read peer comments carefully, evaluate them, and rethink your draft, and then to revise and polish accordingly.

 # READING AND ADDITIONAL ACTIVITIES

Peer editing is not limited to college English classes. Many writers in the workplace have other workers or supervisors examine their writing of reports, memos, letters, and other documents in order to offer suggestions for revision. Nor is peer editing something new. In drafting the Declaration of Independence, one of the most famous of America's documents, Thomas Jefferson sought and heeded the comments of peer editors Benjamin Franklin and John Adams, along with other members of Congress. As you read the rough draft of this document written in 1776, notice the revisions made by Jefferson's peers.

Declaration of Independence

Thomas Jefferson

1   When in the course of human events it becomes necessary for ~~a~~ *one* people to dissolve the political hands which have connected them with another, and to ~~advance from that subordination in which they have hitherto remained, & to~~ assume among the powers of the earth the *separate and equal* ~~equal & independent~~ station to which the laws of nature & of nature's god entitle them, a decent respect to the opinions of mankind requires that they should declare the causes which impel them to *the sep-aration* ~~the change.~~

2   We hold these truths to be *self-evident* ~~sacred & undeniable;~~ that all men are created equal & *they are endowed by their creator with* ~~equal rights, some of which are independent;~~ that ~~from that equal creation they derive in rights~~ inherent & inalienable *rights; that* ~~among which~~ *these* are ~~the preservation of~~ life, & liberty, & the pursuit of happiness; that to secure these *rights* ~~ends,~~ governments are instituted among men, deriving their just powers from the consent of the governed; that whenever any form of government ~~shall~~ becomes destructive of these ends, it is the right of the people to alter or to abolish it, & to institute new government, laying it's foundation on such principles & organizing it's powers in such form, as to them shall seem most likely to effect their safety & happiness. prudence indeed will dictate that governments long established should not be changed for light & transient causes: and accordingly all experience hath shewn that mankind are more disposed to suffer while evils are sufferable, than to right themselves by abolishing the forms to which they are accustomed. but when a long train of abuses & usurpations, begun at a distinguished period, & pursuing invariably the same object, evinces a design to ~~subject~~ reduce them **under absolute Despotism* ~~to arbitrary power,~~ it is their right, it is their duty, to throw off such government & to provide new guards for their future security. such has been the patient sufferance of these colonies; & such is now the necessity which constrains them to expunge their former systems of government. the history of ~~his~~ *†the* present ~~majesty~~ *king of Great Britain* is a history of unremitting injuries and usurpations, among which *appears no solitary fact* ~~no one fact stands single or solitary~~ to contradict the uniform tenor of the rest, ~~all of which~~ *but all* have in direct object the establishment of an absolute tyranny over these states. to prove this, let facts be submitted to a candid world, for the truth of which we pledge a faith yet unsullied by falsehood.

*Dr. Franklin's handwriting
†Mr. Adams' handwriting

3   he has refused his assent to laws the most wholesome and necessary for the public

good:

4   he has forbidden his governors to pass laws of immediate & pressing importance,

unless suspended in their operation till his assent should be obtained; and when

so suspended, he has neglected utterly[1] to attend to them.

5   he has refused to pass other laws for the accomodation of large districts of people

in the legislature

unless those people would relinquish the right of representation, a right

inestimable to them & formidable to tyrants only:

6   *he has called together legislative bodies at places unusual, uncomfortable &*

distant from the depository of their public records for the sole purpose of

fatiguing them into compliance with his measures:

7   he has dissolved, Representative houses repeatedly & continually, for opposing

with manly firmness his invasions on the rights of the people:

[†]*time after such dissolutions*

8   ~~he has dissolved~~ he has refused for a long ~~space of time~~ to cause others to be

elected, whereby the legislative powers, incapable of annihilation, have returned

to the people at large for their exercise, the state remaining in the meantime

exposed to all the dangers of invasion from without, & convulsions within:

9   he has endeavored to prevent the population of these states; for that purpose

obstructing the laws for naturalization of foreigners; refusing to pass others to

encourage their migrations hither; & raising the conditions of new

appropriations of lands:

10   he has suffered the administration of justice totally to cease in some of these

states

~~colonies,~~ refusing his assent to laws for establishing judiciary powers:

11   he has made our judges dependent on his will alone, for the tenure of their offices,

[*]*the*   *and payment*

and amount of their salaries:

12   he has erected a multitude of new offices by a self-assumed power, & sent hither

swarms of officers to harrass our people & eat out their substance:

the

~~without our consent~~   *without ~~our~~ consent of our legislatures*

13   he has kept among us in times of peace standing armies & ships of war:

14   he has effected to render the military, independent of & superior to the civil

power:

15   he has combined with others to subject us to a jurisdiction foreign to our

[†]Mr. Adams
[*]Dr. Franklin

constitutions and unacknoleged by our laws; giving his assent to their pretended ~~acts of~~ legislation,

16   for quartering large bodies of armed troops among us;

for protecting them by a mock-trial from punishment for any murders, which they should commit on the inhabitants of these states;

for cutting off our trade with all parts of the world;

for imposing taxes on us without our consent;

for depriving us of the benefits of trial by jury;

for transporting us beyond seas to be tried for pretended offenses;

for abolishing the free system of English laws in a neighboring province, establishing therein an arbitrary government, and enlarging it's boundaries so as to render it at once an example & fit instrument for introducing the same absolute rule into these ~~*colonies*~~ *states;*

*abolishing our most ~~important~~ valuable laws

for taking away our charters, & altering fundamentally the forms of our governments;

for suspending our own legislatures & declaring themselves invested with power to legislate for us in all cases whatsoever:

17 he has abdicated government here, withdrawing his governors, & declaring us out of his allegiance & protection:

18 he has plundered our seas, ravaged our coasts, burnt our towns & destroyed the lives of our people:

19 he is at this time transporting large armies of foreign mercenaries to compleat the works of death, desolation & tyranny, already begun with circumstances of cruelty & perfidy unworthy the head of a civilized nation:

20 he has endeavored to bring on the inhabitants of our frontiers the merciless Indian savages, whose known rule of warfare is an undistinguished destruction of all ages, sexes, & conditions of existence:

21 he has incited[1] treasonable insurrections of our fellow-citizens, with the allurements of forfeiture & confiscation of our property:

22 *he has constrained others*[2] taken captives ~~*falling into his hands,*~~ *on the high seas to bear arms*

*Dr. Franklin

against their country ~~& to destroy & be destroyed by the brethren whom they love,~~ *to become the executioners of their friends & brethren, or to fall themselves by their hands.*

23 he has waged cruel war against human nature itself, violating it's most sacred rights of life & liberty in the persons of a distant people who never offended him, captivating & carrying them into slavery in another hemisphere, or to incur miserable death in their transportation thither. this piratical warfare, the opprobrium of *infidel* powers, is the warfare of the *Christian* king of Great Britain. *determined to keep open a market where MEN should be bought & sold,* he has prostituted his negative for suppressing every legislative attempt to prohibit or to restrain this execrable commerce ~~determining to keep open a market where MEN should be bought & sold~~ ⌃and that this assemblage of horrors might want no fact of distinguished die, he is now exciting those very people to rise in arms among us, and to purchase that liberty of which *he* has deprived them, by murdering the people upon whom *he* also obtruded them; thus paying off former crimes committed against the *liberties* of one people, with crimes which he urges them to commit against the *lives* of another.

24 in every stage of these oppressions we have petitioned for redress in the most humble terms; our repeated petitions have been answered ⌃*only* by repeated injury.[1] a prince whose character is thus marked by every act which may define a tyrant, is unfit to be the ruler of a people who mean to be free. future ages will scarce believe that the hardiness of one man, adventured within the short compass of twelve years only, ⌃*build* *to* ~~lay~~ *a foundation*[1] *so broad & undisguised for tyranny* ~~on so many acts of tyranny without a mask,~~ over a people fostered & fixed in principles of ~~liberty.~~ *freedom.*

25   Nor have we been wanting in attentions to our British brethren. we have warned them from time to time of attempts by their legislature to extend a jurisdiction over these our states. we have reminded them of the circumstances of our emigration & settlement here, no one of which could warrant so strange a pretension: that these were effected at the expence of our own blood & treasure, unassisted by the wealth or the strength of Great Britain: that in constituting indeed our several forms of government, we had adopted one common king, thereby laying a foundation for perpetual league & amity with them: but that

---

*Dr. Franklin

submission to their parliament was no part of our constitution, nor ever in idea if history may be credited: and we appealed to their native justice & magnanimity as well as to the ties of our common kindred to disavow these usurpations which were likely to interrupt our ~~correspondence~~ *connection &* ~~& connection.~~ they too have been deaf to the voice of justice & of consanguinity, & when occasions have been given them, by the regular course of their laws, of removing from their councils the disturbers of our harmony, they have by their free election re-established them in power. at this very time too they are permitting their chief magistrate to send over not only soldiers of our common blood, but Scotch & foreign mercenaries to invade & ~~deluge us in blood.~~ **destroy us* these facts have given the last stab to agonizing affection, and manly spirit bids us to renounce forever these unfeeling brethren. we must endeavor to forget our former love for them, and to hold them as we hold the rest of mankind, enemies in war, in peace friends. we might have been a free & a great people together; but a communication of grandeur & of freedom it seems is below their dignity. be it so, since they will have it: the road to ~~glory &~~ happiness *& to glory* is open to us too; we will climb it ~~in a separately state,~~[1] *apart from them* and acquiesce in the necessity which ~~pro~~*de*nounces our ~~everlasting adieu!~~ eternal separation!

26   We therefore the representatives of the United States of America in General Congress assembled do, in the name & by authority of the good people of these states, reject and renounce all allegiance & subjection to the kings of Great Britain & all others who may hereafter claim by, through, or under them; we utterly dissolve ~~& break off~~ all political connection which may ~~have~~ *have* heretofore subsisted between us & the people or parliament of Great Britain; and finally we do assert and declare[1] these colonies to be free and independent states, and that as free & independent states they ~~shall hereafter~~ have *full* power to levy war, conclude peace, contract alliances, establish commerce, & to do all other acts and things which independent states may of right do. And for the support of this declaration we mutually pledge to each other our lives, our fortunes, & our sacred honour.

*Dr. Franklin

QUESTIONS ON CONTENT

1. Find Jefferson's thesis in paragraph 1 and write it in the following space.

_____

2. According to the Declaration, what should people do when a government ignores the rights of a people? _____

_____

3. Choose three injuries or injustices listed in the Declaration that you feel are the most serious and name them in your own words. _____

_____

_____

_____

4. How have the colonists tried to avoid a total separation (paragraphs 31–32)? Name two steps taken. _____

_____

QUESTIONS ON STRATEGY

1. Why do you think "equal and independent" in paragraph 1 was revised to read "separate and equal"? _____

_____

2. In paragraph 1, why is "separation" a better word choice than "change"?

_____

3. Find an example of trimming in paragraph 2. Jot down the phrases that were trimmed. _____

_____

4. In paragraph 2, notice the insertion of "they are endowed by their creator" substituting for "from that equal creation they derive." This change in the draft emphasizes the role of God in the rights of the colonists. How might this revision have served Jefferson's purpose—to persuade the reader that the King of England was acting unjustly and that the colonists were right in wanting their freedom? _____

_____

5. Review paragraphs 33 and 34 to look for cue words. Jot down two cue words you find. _____

_____

CRITICAL THINKING IN CONNECTING TEXTS

In her essay "Practicing What We Preach" (pp. 183–184), Margarita Figueroa discusses instances of dishonesty within contemporary America. But modern-day Americans are not the only ones guilty of dishonest behavior. Although the writers of the Declaration of Independence showed great courage and initiative in drafting this important American document, Thomas Jefferson and his peer editors misled many into thinking that the Declaration represented the interests of all Americans. In actuality, the writers of this document were all white, free, male, property-owning Protestants—in short, they were certainly not representative of all Americans living then or now. Working in collaboration with a partner or small group, revise the first two paragraphs of the Declaration of Independence so that all Americans are represented, and try to update the language so that it reflects modern thought and usage. After you revise the draft, polish it and then share it with the rest of the class. Vote for the most effective revision.

**For more writing resources, be sure to see the
Longman English Pages Website at
http://longman.awl.com/englishpages**

PART TWO

Exploring Development Options: Choosing Patterns to Fit Purpose

Writing About Events: Narration

> Time passes and the past becomes the present. . . . These presences of the past are there in the corner of your life today. You thought . . . they had died, but they have just been waiting their chance.
>
> —*Carlos Fuentes, diplomat, essayist, and dramatist*

Preview

In this chapter you will learn
- ▶ **how to identify the characteristics of narration—the recounting of an event to serve a particular purpose**
- ▶ **how to use narration within an essay by employing chronological order, setting the scene, maintaining a consistent point of view, incorporating descriptive detail, specific action, and appropriate dialogue**
- ▶ **how to interview a source to gain narrative material**

This chapter will focus on narration, a strategy that we humans have enjoyed from our earliest existence as cave dwellers to the present day. We are a story-telling species, and as children, no matter what our cultural background, we have begged our parents or loved ones to tell us stories. As we mature, rather than losing this fascination with the telling of events, we seek and find narration in film and television plots, news events reported by journalists, and books of fiction and nonfiction. In fact, every time we recount an event or incident, we're using narration.

However, this chapter will focus not on the fictional stories composed in a creative writing class but rather on the narration of real-life events to explain or prove a point in an essay. Although certainly you may focus on events that you have experienced firsthand, it may also suit your essay's purpose to narrate events of public, civic, or academic importance. For instance, if your thesis focuses on the problems of working while taking a full load of college classes, you might want to narrate your own experiences or those of friends to prove your point. If you are in a lab and want to explain what happens when two chemicals are mixed together, you would narrate the steps in order to document your experiment. In a workplace report, if you want to persuade your client to build a particular office structure, you could narrate the success of developers with similar structures in the area. Because narration can be such a helpful way of making a point about an abstract idea by tying real-life experiences to this idea, you will want to familiarize yourself with the characteristics of this writing strategy.

CHARACTERISTICS OF NARRATION

When you use **narration** in an essay, you recount an event or series of events, usually in chronological order. The selection of specific details related to the place and people involved is critical in allowing the reader to grasp the importance of the event or experience.

To illustrate narration at work to support a thesis, read the following excerpt. The writer, whose Korean mother spoke little English, focuses on the power of language to distance immigrants as outsiders in an "English-only world":

1   One day was unusually harrowing. We ventured downtown in the new Ford Country Squire my father had bought her [the writer's mother], an enormous station wagon that seemed as long—and deft—as an ocean liner. We were shopping for a special meal for guests visiting that weekend, and my mother had heard that a particular butcher carried fresh oxtails, which she needed for a traditional soup.

2   We'd never been inside the shop, but my mother would pause before its window, which was always lined with whole hams, crown roasts, and ropes of plump handmade sausages. She greatly esteemed the bounty with her eyes, and my sister and I did also, but despite our desirous cries she'd turn us away and instead buy the packaged links at the Finast supermarket, where she felt comfortable looking them over and could easily spot the price. And, of course, not have to talk.

3   But that day she was resolved. The butcher store was crowded, and as we stepped inside the door jingled a welcome. No one seemed to notice. We waited for some time, and people who entered after us were now being served. Finally, an old woman nudged my mother and waved a little ticket, which we hadn't taken. We patiently waited again, until one of the beefy men behind the glass display hollered our number.

4   My mother pulled us forward and began searching the cases, but the oxtails were nowhere to be found. The man, his big arms crossed, sharply said, "Come on, lady, whaddya want?" This unnerved her, and she somehow blurted the Korean word for oxtail, *soggori*.

5   The butcher looked as if my mother had put something sour in his mouth, and he glanced back at the lighted board and called the next number.

6   Before I knew it, she had rushed us outside and back in the wagon, which she had double-parked because of the crowd. She was furious, almost vibrating with fear and grief, and I could see she was about to cry.

7   She wanted to go back inside, but now the driver of the car we were blocking wanted to pull out. She was shooing us away. My mother, who had just earned her driver's license, started furiously working the pedals. But in her haste she must have flooded the engine, for it wouldn't turn over. The driver started honking and then another car began honking as well, and soon it seemed the entire street was shrieking at us.

—Chang-rae Lee, from "Mute in an English-Only World"

Notice that Lee's narration contains the following characteristics:

- **A specific event or a series of related events is the focus of the narration and forms the subject of the thesis.**
  Lee's specific event involves his mother's encounter with someone unsympathetic to her limited English.

- **The significance of the event forms the controlling idea in the thesis.**
  Lee tells the reader that the day was "unusually harrowing"—through the unfolding of Lee's narrative we understand why the event was so frustrating, and by the time his audience has finished the narrative, Lee has made clear his unspoken but implied thesis: intolerance in multilingual communities can lead to frustration and rage.

- **The setting, people, and actions connected to the event are described in accurate detail and specific action words.**
  Lee tells his audience that the store window is "lined with whole hams, crown roasts, and ropes of plump handmade sausages," that "an old woman nudged my mother and waved a little ticket," that the butcher stands "with big arms crossed," and that later he "hollered our number."

- **The structure is chronological.**
  Lee's narration begins with the car trip, proceeds to the store and the encounter with the butcher, and then ends with the family's return to the car.

- **A particular point of view is used throughout the narrative.**
  Notice that Lee confides to the reader, "*we* ventured downtown," and then "*we* patiently waited."

To notice how narration works within a college essay, read the following model and see how many of the characteristics just discussed you can identify.

MODEL WITH KEY QUESTIONS

In her narrative essay, Tori Ueda wanted to emphasize an event that eventually led her to a more profound understanding of her mother and the cultural and generation gap many American teenagers experience. As you read, notice how the writer sets the scene, keeps the sequence of events in clear order, and begins as well as ends her essay with a discussion of the significance of the event.

"BRADY BUNCH" WANNA-BE
Tori Ueda

In discovering material for her essays, Tori Ueda found clustering and group brainstorming especially helpful. Tori also reported that she was unsure about the value of peer editing in the beginning, but by the end of the semester she felt that the process had helped in the revision of her essays. In evaluating her writing, Tori stated, "My weak essays were due to my inability to overcome my own personal procrastination." Tori plans to go to law school after receiving her undergraduate degree, and eventually she would like to become a probate attorney.

1   How does the culture of one's childhood lay a distinctive foundation that survives well into adulthood? After seeing *The Brady Bunch: The Movie* a few weeks ago, I was thinking about my adolescent years. As I was transformed to my childhood, years that were filled with the turmoil of living with a traditional Japanese family, I remembered a particular incident because it changed the way I perceived my relationship with my mother.

2   Like many other children, I grew up watching most of the "all American" shows such as "The Brady Bunch" and "Leave It to Beaver." The themes of these programs dealt with children rebelling against their parents and going through phases. In my family, unlike the families of my peers, Dad dished out the scolding, shaming, ridicule, and severe punishments while Mom practiced a therapeutic technique of talking problems out. Being a curious child, one early afternoon I took it upon myself to find out if some of the things I saw on television would work on my parents. Unfortunately I discovered that my mother was not as understanding as the "Carol Brady" mothers I was used to watching.

3   On this afternoon I found myself sitting in front of the television watching an episode of "The Brady Bunch." In the show, Marsha got angry with her mother

and ran to her bedroom, slamming her door. The mother did not get angry with the girl; instead she simply sighed and thought up ways to make her daughter feel better. After the show, I sat on the sofa and thought about how this mother-daughter relationship differed from my own. Then I turned on the radio and began to have the time of my life imagining that I was Madonna—since no one was home, I sang my heart out—I WAS the Material Girl giving a live concert at the Great Western Forum. As the afternoon progressed, I was having so much fun that I totally forgot my responsibility, which was always to clean the house before my mother came home from work.

4   An hour later when my mother did come home, she found the house exactly as she had left it in the morning—dirty dishes from breakfast in the sink, unfolded laundry on the sofa, and toys scattered everywhere. She sternly looked at me for a moment and then started yelling at me, "What have you been doing all afternoon? Why is this house still a mess when you've been home from school for three hours?"

5   When these words rushed out of her mouth, hands on her hips, her body leaning in to me, I wondered where my sweet, understanding mom, the one who would wipe away my tears after Dad handed out the discipline, had gone. I blinked, saying nothing, and next she continued to scold me. I blurted out, "Why don't you just take a chill-pill and calm down?" After these words, I stood there, not believing I had disrespected my mother so. I watched a play of emotions roll over her face. When she finally tried to say something, I turned my face away from her. This was the final insult my mother was willing to take from me. She slapped me—she slapped me hard! The slap stung just like the sting of a bee, and moments later I could feel the skin on my face swelling up. I just stood there face-to-face with my mother, thinking to myself, "She actually hit me, and not my father. But if she hit me, then who's going to comfort me and buy me ice cream and tell me everything will be okay?" Tears began to swell under my eyes, my lips were quivering, and my hands were shaking. And my mouth was paralyzed.

6   Now that I look back on this incident, I believe I was crying not because of the pain of the slap, but because I was filled with regret and embarrassed for my actions. I went to my room and basked in self-pity. In the next few minutes I spent in my room, I aged tremendously. I think that this incident made a lasting impression on me because it was the first time my mother had ever physically punished me. I thought to myself, "Why did Marsha get away with yelling at her mother and slamming the door to her room, while I could not stand up for myself in my own house?" That day in my room I was very angry with my mother, and I suspect that my mother felt betrayed—she had somehow raised a daughter to disrespect an elder—a terrible sin in Japanese tradition.

7   When I think about this experience years later, I understand what had angered my mother so much and why my tantrum had not worked as well as Marsha's. That slap became the starting point towards a mature relationship with my mother; we had bridged the generation and the culture gap in that encounter. I was never to watch "The Brady Bunch" with such naïve eyes. My rite of passage prompted me to think of families on television no longer as a symbol for the way all people live.

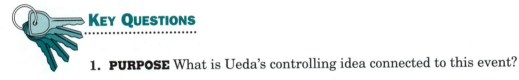

KEY QUESTIONS

1. **PURPOSE** What is Ueda's controlling idea connected to this event?

   _____

2. **FOCUS** What specific event does Ueda narrate? _____

   _____

3. **MATERIAL** Find examples of dialogue. Name one thing you learn about Ueda or her mother from the dialogue. _____

   _____

4. **STRUCTURE** List three cue words or phrases the writer uses to signal a transition and to keep the sequence of events clear. _____

   _____

5. **STYLE** Write two words or phrases that help you visualize the people or the setting of Ueda's event. _____

   _____

   Find and copy a phrase that communicates the writer's personal reaction to the event. _____

   _____

   _____

GUIDELINES FOR WRITING NARRATION

Determine Your Purpose

Narration is an effective writing choice if your purpose in writing your essay will be strengthened by recounting an event or events. Make sure that while your audience is caught up in the event you're narrating—the setting, details, people involved—they also know *why* you're recounting the event. The event you choose to narrate to support your thesis may have involved you personally. For example, you might want to recount your first driving experiences to persuade young readers that driver training is essential before trying to get a driver's license. You may also use narration to describe events that you have researched but could not have witnessed. For instance, a history assignment might require you to narrate the experiences of Alexander the Great in ancient Greece in order to share information or prove a point.

The event itself need not be dramatic or earthshaking—what is important is why you want to share the event with your audience. What is the meaning of the event in relation to your thesis? Determining your purpose will help you select appropriate details for your narration.

Practice 8.1 To identify writing situations in which narration might be a helpful strategy, work alone or with a partner and examine the following list of topics. Write a brief comment explaining how narration could serve the writer's purpose. The first topic has been completed for you.

1. The bombing of the Federal Building in Oklahoma City

Survivors of the Federal Building bombing in Oklahoma City discuss the events that led to their rescue.

2. The physical layout of a local park in your community

3. A refund request for faulty merchandise purchased in a department store

4. The atmosphere of your favorite restaurant

5. Job duties of a payroll clerk

6. The most embarrassing moment in your life

◆ ◆ ◆

Interview Sources If Helpful

Interviews with individuals who witnessed or participated in an event can yield a wealth of essay material for narrative essays as well as for essays using other methods of development. To obtain information for your narration, you can conduct an interview, either in person, by telephone, or online.

To gain the most detailed information from an interview, follow these six steps:

1. Contact your interview subject well in advance of any assignment's due date. Identify yourself as a college student, explain the nature of your assignment, and gain permission to conduct the interview. Assure the person to be interviewed that the information will be used for classroom purposes only.

2. Agree with your interview subject on an appropriate date and time for the interview.

3. Agree on a time limit, possibly thirty minutes. Establishing a limit will allow you adequate time for questioning and note taking, and it will assure your interview subject that the interview will not drag on.

4. Draw up a list of questions connected with the event you wish to narrate. You may want to use the journalists' questions from Chapter 3: *Who? What? Where? When? Why? How?* Send the list of questions to the person to be interviewed early enough to allow the subject sufficient time to think about the questions and responses.

5. During the interview, take notes and ask **follow-up questions**— questions that arise in your mind because of what the interview subject has answered to your original set of questions.

6. As soon as possible after the interview, take some time to review your notes, writing down any additional details that come to mind.

Practice 8.2 Interview a friend or student about life's most embarrassing moment. Follow the six steps for an interview and, if time permits, develop the material from this interview into an essay employing narration.

◆ ◆ ◆

Frame Thesis Around Significance of the Event

If you are writing an entire essay using narration, the event you're recounting serves as your subject, and the impact or significance of the event becomes your controlling idea. To illustrate, return to the topics on page 213. Assume that in the case of the first topic, the survivors of the Federal Building bombing, you want to write an essay for your psychology class. You might come up with a thesis such as this:

<u>**Subject**</u>

The individual reactions of the survivors of the Federal Building bombing.

<u>**Controlling Idea**</u>

Reveal a curious aspect of human behavior under extreme stress.

Practice 8.3   Examine topics 3 and 6 from the list on page 213. Working with a partner, create a thesis for an essay using narrative development. Write each thesis in the space below. Check to make sure you have a subject and a controlling idea, as well as specific language and an appropriate tone.

1. _____

2. _____

◆ ◆ ◆

Set the Scene for Your Audience

William Shakespeare's famous line "All the world's a stage" certainly applies to narration. In recounting any event, it is thus helpful to think in terms of "staging" your material for the reader. Any background information that allows readers to visualize the event will help your narration come alive. In "'Brady Bunch' Wanna-be" (pp. 210–212), the writer creates a vivid scene— "dirty dishes from breakfast in the sink, unfolded laundry on the sofa, and toys scattered everywhere"—in paragraph 4.

Practice 8.4   To identify scene-setting elements, reread "'Brady Bunch' Wanna-be" and write down three more details that allow you to visualize the scene.

_____

_____

◆ ◆ ◆

Choose and Maintain a Consistent Point of View

Decide which point of view you will employ and maintain it throughout your narrative. If you choose the **first person,** you will use the words *I, me, my* or *we, us, our.* First person stresses the writer's involvement in the event; often this point of view is used when it suits a writer's purpose that the audience connects with the writer's feelings about and reactions to the event. If you choose the **third person,** you will use the words *he, him, his* or *she, her, hers.* This will indicate that the story is being told by someone other than the person involved in the event. It might be more appropriate to use the third person point of view if, for instance, you're narrating the history of bagel production in America.

Practice 8.5 Examine the following writing situations and then decide whether first person or third person would be more appropriate.

  1. An essay for a political science class on the early childhood of Bill Clinton.

  2. An essay for college admittance on an obstacle or hardship you've overcome.

  3. A report detailing how the company you work for has used grant money in the past two years.

  4. An essay for a philosophy class on the persecution of Socrates.

◆ ◆ ◆

Follow a Clear Order

Narration usually makes use of chronological order—relating events in the order in which they happened or are happening. In a narration, the **past tense** describes actions that have occurred, the **present tense** describes actions that are occurring, and the **future tense** describes events that have not yet occurred. For example, if you were asked on a college or employment application to write an essay about your work experience, you would choose the past tense. If, on the other hand, the application asked you to describe your present volunteer or community service involvement, you would choose the present tense. If you were asked to detail your career plans and goals for the next five years, the future tense would be your choice. Once you've chosen a tense appropriate to your subject and purpose, be consistent throughout your narration.

Practice 8.6 Read "A Hanging" (pp. 223–227) or "The Discovery of Coca-Cola" (pp. 229–230), underlining the action words and noting the sequence of events and the tense used by the writer.

◆ ◆ ◆

Use Cue Words

As you draft your narrative, keep the sequence of events clear for readers by using cue words. Consult the table of cue words (pp. 187–188), noting especially those words signaling a change in time. Try to work these time markers into your narrative where they will help take your reader from one action or detail to the next.

Practice 8.7 Read the following paragraph from a student narrative and insert the appropriate cue words in the blanks, consulting your list if you need to.

As my dad walked downstairs to say hello to my mother, I began to think this was the best day of my young life. _____ it was not to remain a happy day. About five minutes after sending my father away, I began to hear an argument forming in the downstairs kitchen. _____ piercing words flew from both my parents' mouths. _____ my mother yelled about how my father was always gone, and that he was never there when his family needed him. _____ my father retorted by saying that my mother was making a big deal out of nothing, that she worried and nagged too much. _____ I passed this off as one of their normal fights, in which they stayed mad for a little while and then apologized to each other. _____ I just quietly shut my door and minutes later, I heard a shrill, piercing scream. _____ this was followed by another lower toned scream. I thought that if I played with my new bus real hard and real well that they would stop fighting. _____ it was too late; creaking footsteps soon became audible on the staircase.

—Courtney Risdon, student

◆ ◆ ◆

Incorporate Descriptive Detail and Specific Action

If you take another look at the narratives in this chapter, you will notice that they all employ descriptive detail and specific action words to make the event come alive. We can visualize the "ropes of plump handmade sausages" in the butcher shop Lee describes (pp. 208–209); we feel Ueda's pain when she writes "tears began to swell under my eyes, my lips were quivering, and my hands were shaking" (pp. 210–212).

Practice 8.8 Read the following excerpt and then annotate it by underlining all words or phrases that describe something or show action. Mark all descriptive words with an "n" for noun and an "a" for adjective, and mark action words with a "v" for verb. (For help in recognizing nouns, adjectives, and verbs, refer to the handbook in Part Four of this book.)

> The ramifications of this biological invention were endless. Plants traveled as they had never traveled before. They got into strange environments heretofore never entered by the old spore plants or stiff pine-cone-seed plants. The well-fed, carefully cherished little embryos raised their heads everywhere. Many of the older plants with more primitive reproductive mechanisms began to fade away under this unequaled contest. They contracted their range into secluded environments. Some, like the giant redwoods, lingered on as relics; many vanished entirely.
>
> —Loren Eiseley, from "How Flowers Changed the World"

◆ ◆ ◆

Use Dialogue If Appropriate

Dialogue, words or sentences spoken by people and set off from the text by quotation marks or indentation, can often help writers of narratives give readers a sense of "being there." Good dialogue conveys meaningful information about a person as well as details about events. No two people have the same way of talking—the same mannerisms, dialects, and particular sentence patterns.

Practice 8.9 To see how dialogue can help in narrative development, read "Delivering the Goods" by Bonnie Jo Campbell (pp. 231–233). Annotate the essay by highlighting all of the dialogue. When you have finished this, read only the dialogue, noting who says what. Now write down any information you learned from the dialogue itself.

_____

_____

◆ ◆ ◆

There are many narrative situations in which dialogue would not be appropriate. For example, if you turn to "The Discovery of Coca-Cola" by E. J. Kahn, Jr. (pp. 229–230), you will see that dialogue would probably not suit the writer's purpose or his audience. While you never want to "insert" dialogue just to include it in your narration, it will help to read through your narrative draft, noting in the margin spots where dialogue might help your reader visualize the scene and the people. For help with punctuating dialogue, refer to the handbook in Part Four.

STRATEGIES FOR WRITING NARRATION

1. **PURPOSE** Determine if narration suits your purpose and audience in the essay.

2. **FOCUS** Frame a thesis using an event or events as the subject and the significance or impact of the event as the controlling idea. Maintain a consistent point of view throughout your narrative and check to see that all details focus on the event and its meaning.

3. **MATERIAL** If you are recounting an event that happened to you, use your memory to gather material in prewriting. Play the scene over again in your mind, taking notes. If you are recounting an event not connected to you personally, be sure you have gathered enough material from sources and interviews to communicate the event. In drafting, include descriptive detail and specific action to help the audience visualize the people and the exact place connected to the event.

4. **STRUCTURE** Check to see that cue words indicate for the reader a clear sequence of events. Make sure that you are proceeding in chronological order.

5. **STYLE** In addition to the usual proofreading you do during polishing, examine your narration for any places where dialogue would help the event come alive for your audience. Ask yourself if your introduction sets the appropriate tone for your event. Finally, make sure your conclusion thoughtfully communicates the connection between the event and your purpose in recounting it.

JOURNAL WRITING: THE AUTOBIOGRAPHICAL ENTRY

While writing in your journal regularly can help you in all of your college reading and writing, journal entries can be of special assistance in collecting material for narration essays. The following activities will focus on material that is **autobiographical**—having to do with the people, places, and events connected to your own life. Choose one or more of these activities to respond to in a journal entry. Later, some of these autobiographical reflections may serve as the basis for a narration essay.

1. Track down photographs of yourself from several years ago. In a journal entry, discuss the person you were then—what you liked and disliked, thought about, hoped for, and feared. Narrate an important event that occurred during that time in your life.

2. Recall an incident that changed the way you viewed yourself or some aspect of your life. In a journal entry, write about your perceptions before the incident, then during and after the event. Be sure to mention all specific details connected with the event as you are recounting it.

3. Think about a time that you felt like an outsider—this could have been because you were new to a school or community, spoke a different language or dialect, looked or acted different from your peers or family members, or felt somehow alienated. In an entry, tell about the events that led to this feeling and how you coped with your difference.

4. Think about writing an **obituary**—a written description of a deceased person's life and accomplishments, usually published in a newspaper. If you were to write your own obituary, what is one event you would choose to illustrate a time in your life when you "rose to the occasion" and acted in a manner that made you proud? In a journal entry, write all the details connected with this particular event.

USING THE COMPUTER: DEVISING AND SHARING NARRATIVES

1. Once you have an event you want to write about, open a file and list in chronological order all of the details associated with the event. Don't forget to set the scene and describe the people involved as you're narrating, using descriptive and action words when appropriate. Include all material connected with the event, and type these events in the order in which they occurred. After you have completed this list of details and saved this information, use the *copy* and *move* functions to change the sequence of details to begin with another point in time, creating a **flashback**—an interruption in the forward chronological movement of a narrative that goes back to some prior time in the sequence of events. Once you have at least two versions, compare them to see which one you prefer.

2. Some online communities provide an opportunity to engage in a fascinating information exchange with others who have narratives to share. Retired citizens are one such source; you can link up with them to ask them questions or engage in a dialogue about an important event in their lives. You may then choose to narrate this event in an essay. First, go to one of these Websites:

- *Senior Net* ⟨http://www.seniornet.org⟩

- *Seniors-Site* ⟨http:// seniors-site.com⟩

- *Blacksburg Electronic Village* ⟨http://www.bev.net/community/seniors/sol.sol.html⟩

- *SCIP CyberPals* ⟨http://www.mbnet.mb.ca/crm/cyberpal/⟩

Explain that you are a student who wishes to interview someone about a meaningful event in his or her life as part of a classroom writing assignment. Be sure to leave your E-mail address, so interested people can contact you. When you have a response from someone you would like to write about, follow the steps for interviewing (p. 214). You might want to begin by E-mailing your interviewee a list of questions to start with. As you exchange E-mail with your online partner, remember to get enough details about the setting and people to help you and the future reader of your essay visualize the event you will narrate. Be sure to send your online partner a copy of the narration you create from your E-mail correspondence.

But remember that with this activity, as with other online communication, you should protect yourself by refusing to share any information of a private nature.

OPTIONS FOR WRITING

The following writing options offer you the chance to recount an event and communicate the significance of that event to your reader. Harriet Doerr, a writer who did not discover her talent for narrative until she went back to college in her seventies, confides, "I have everything I need. A square of sky, a piece of stone, and memory raining down on me in sleeves." In working through any of the options, refer to the guidelines and strategies in this chapter as needed.

1. In her essay (pp. 210–212), Tori Ueda refers to her "rite of passage" and a subsequent change in her relationship with her mother. We all have certain rites of passage—events that alter our lives for better or worse. For example, in some cultures, a particular birthday is viewed as significant; in other cultures, certain events such as graduating from high school or getting a driver's license signify a passage to maturity or a move into a new phase. Whatever the event, quite often as a result we experience an altered sense of perception or "awakening." Write an essay narrating such an event and include its significance for you.

¶ 2. The word *place* can refer not only to a physical setting or location but also to a position or standing in which we feel comfortable. We are all continually involved in this process of finding our place. As we grow, we need to move on to new places or positions. Recall a time when you felt different, "out of place," an outsider, or not taken seriously. Write an essay telling about how you found your place or gained acceptance.

3. One of the purposes of narration can be to help the reader visualize or understand an abstract idea. Choose any one of the well-known statements below or find another one that you prefer. Write a narration essay that illustrates the statement.

   • Pride goes before the fall.

   • The more things change, the more they stay the same.

   • Don't judge a book by its cover.

   • The road to hell is paved with good intentions.

   • Hell hath no fury like a woman (or man) scorned.

4. Use narration in an essay in order to make a point about some injustice in the world—perhaps something that you personally experienced or a historical event that happened long before you were born. You can find a good model for this in George Orwell's "A Hanging" (pp. 223–227), in which the writer narrates an event in order to persuade his audience of the inhumanity of capital punishment.

RESPONDING TO WRITING: EXAMINING NARRATIVE STRATEGIES

In this activity you'll see how several of the narrative strategies discussed in this chapter work for George Orwell, a famous British writer who served in the British Imperial Police in India. When Orwell wrote "A Hanging" in 1950, he wanted to recount an event so that readers could see, firsthand, the cruelty of capital punishment. After you read Orwell's narrative, you'll be asked to examine it again to analyze its effectiveness and then to examine one of your own essays employing narration.

A Hanging

George Orwell

1   It was in Burma, a sodden morning of the rains. A sickly light, like yellow tinfoil, was slanting over the high walls into the jail yard. We were waiting outside the condemned cells, a row of sheds fronted with double bars, like small animal cages. Each cell measured about ten feet by ten and was quite bare within except for a plank bed and a pot for drinking water. In some of them brown, silent men were squatting at the inner bars, with their blankets draped round them. These were the condemned men, due to be hanged within the next week or two.

2   One prisoner had been brought out of his cell. He was a Hindu, a puny wisp of a man, with a shaven head and vague liquid eyes. He had a thick, sprouting mustache, absurdly too big for his body, rather like the mustache of a comic man on the films. Six tall Indian warders were guarding him and getting him ready for the gallows. Two of them stood by with rifles and fixed bayonets, while the others handcuffed him, passed a chain through his handcuffs and fixed it to their belts, and lashed his arms tight to his sides. They crowded very close about him, with their hands always on him in a careful, caressing grip, as though all the while feeling him to make sure he was there. It was like men handling a fish which is still alive and may jump back into the water. But he stood quite unresisting, yielding his arms limply to the ropes, as though he hardly noticed what was happening.

3   Eight o'clock struck and a bugle call, desolately thin in the wet air, floated from the distant barracks. The superintendent of the jail, who was standing apart from the rest of us, moodily prodding the gravel with his stick, raised his head at the sound. He was an army doctor, with a grey toothbrush mustache and a gruff voice. "For God's sake, hurry up, Francis," he said irritably. "The man ought to have been dead by this time. Aren't you ready yet?"

4   Francis, the head jailer, a fat Dravidian in a white drill suit and gold spectacles, waved his black hand. "Yes sir, yes sir," he bubbled. "All iss satisfactorily prepared. The hangman iss waiting. We shall proceed."

5   "Well, quick march, then. The prisoners can't get their breakfast till this job's over."

6   We set out for the gallows. Two warders marched on either side of the prisoner, with their rifles at the slope; two others marched close against him, gripping him by arm and shoulder, as though at once pushing and supporting him. The rest of us, magistrates and the like, followed behind. Suddenly, when we had gone ten yards, the procession stopped short without any order or warning. A dreadful thing had happened—a dog, come goodness knows whence, had appeared in the yard. It came bounding among us with a loud volley of barks and leapt around us wagging its whole body, wild with glee at finding so many human beings together. It was a large woolly dog, half Airedale, half pariah. For a moment it pranced around us, and then, before anyone could stop it, it had made a dash for the prisoner, and jumping up tried to lick his face. Everybody stood aghast, too taken aback even to grab the dog.

7   "Who let that bloody brute in here?" said the superintendent angrily. "Catch it, someone!"

8   A warder detached from the escort, charged clumsily after the dog, but it danced and gambolled just out of his reach, taking everything as part of the game. A young Eurasian jailer picked up a handful of gravel and tried to stone the dog away, but it dodged the stones and came after us again. Its yaps echoed from the jail walls. The prisoner, in the grasp of the two warders, looked on incuriously, as though this was another formality of the hanging. It was several minutes before someone managed to catch the dog. Then we put my handkerchief through its collar and moved off once more, with the dog still straining and whimpering.

9   It was about forty yards to the gallows. I watched the bare brown back of the prisoner marching in front of me. He walked clumsily with his bound arms, but quite steadily, with that bobbing gait of the Indian who never straightens his knees. At each step his muscles slid neatly into place, the lock of hair on his scalp danced up and down, his feet printed themselves on the wet gravel. And once, in spite of the men who gripped him by each shoulder, he stepped lightly aside to avoid a puddle on the path.

10   It is curious; but till that moment I had never realized what it means to destroy a healthy, conscious man. When I saw the prisoner step aside to avoid the puddle, I saw the mystery, the unspeakable wrongness, of cutting a life short when it is in full tide. This man was not dying, he was alive just as we are alive. All the organs of his body were working—bowels digesting food, skin renewing itself, nails growing, tissues forming—all toiling away in solemn foolery. His nails would still be growing when he stood on the drop, when he was falling through the air with a tenth-of-a-second to live. His eyes saw the yellow gravel and the grey walls, and his brain still remembered, foresaw, reasoned—even

about puddles. He and we were a party of men walking together, seeing, hearing, feeling, understanding the same world; and in two minutes, with a sudden snap, one of us would be gone—one mind less, one world less.

11   The gallows stood in a small yard, separate from the main grounds of the prison, and overgrown with tall prickly weeds. It was a brick erection like three sides of a shed, with planking on top, and above that two beams and a crossbar with the rope dangling. The hangman, a greyhaired convict in the white uniform of the prison, was waiting beside his machine. He greeted us with a servile crouch as we entered. At a word from Francis the two warders, gripping the prisoner more closely than ever, half led, half pushed him to the gallows and helped him clumsily up the ladder. Then the hangman climbed up and fixed the rope around the prisoner's neck.

12   We stood waiting, five yards away. The warders had formed in a rough circle round the gallows. And then, when the noose was fixed, the prisoner began crying out to his god. It was a high, reiterated cry of "Ram! Ram! Ram! Ram!" not urgent and fearful like a prayer or cry for help, but steady, rhythmical, almost like the tolling of a bell. The dog answered the sound with a whine. The hangman, still standing on the gallows, produced a small cotton bag like a flour bag and drew it down over the prisoner's face. But the sound, muffled by the cloth, still persisted, over and over again: "Ram! Ram! Ram! Ram! Ram!"

13   The hangman climbed down and stood ready, holding the lever. Minutes seemed to pass. The steady, muffled crying from the prisoner went on and on, "Ram! Ram! Ram!" never faltering for an instant. The superintendent, his head on his chest, was slowly poking the ground with his stick; perhaps he was counting the cries, allowing the prisoner a fixed number—fifty, perhaps, or a hundred. Everyone had changed colour. The Indians had gone grey like bad coffee, and one or two of the bayonets were wavering. We looked at the lashed, hooded man on the drop, and listened to his cries—each cry another second of life; the same thought was in all our minds; oh, kill him quickly, get it over, stop that abominable noise!

14   Suddenly the superintendent made up his mind. Throwing up his head he made a swift motion with his stick. "Chalo!" he shouted almost fiercely.

15   There was a clanking noise, and then dead silence. The prisoner had vanished, and the rope was twisting on itself. I let go of the dog, and it galloped immediately to the back of the gallows; but when it got there it stopped short, barked, and then retreated into a corner

of the yard, where it stood among the weeds, looking timorously out at us. We went round the gallows to inspect the prisoner's body. He was dangling with his toes pointed straight downwards, very slowly revolving, as dead as a stone.

16   The superintendent reached out with his stick and poked the bare brown body; it oscillated slightly. "*He's* all right," said the superintendent. He backed out from under the gallows, and blew out a deep breath. The moody look had gone out of his face quite suddenly. He glanced at his wrist-watch. "Eight minutes past eight. Well, that's all for this morning, thank God."

17   The warders unfixed bayonets and marched away. The dog, sobered and conscious of having misbehaved itself, slipped after them. We walked out of the gallows yard, past the condemned cells with their waiting prisoners, into the big central yard of the prison. The convicts, under the command of warders armed with lathis, were already receiving their breakfast. They squatted in long rows, each man holding a tin pannikin, while two warders with buckets marched around ladling out rice; it seemed quite a homely, jolly scene, after the hanging. An enormous relief had come upon us now that the job was done. One felt an impulse to sing, to break into a run, to snigger. All at once everyone began chattering gaily.

18   The Eurasian boy walking beside me nodded towards the way we had come, with a knowing smile: "Do you know, sir, our friend (he meant the dead man) when he heard his appeal had been dismissed, he pissed on the floor of his cell. From fright. Kindly take one of my cigarettes, sir. Do you not admire my new silver case, sir? From the boxwallah, two rupees eight annas. Classy European style."

19   Several people laughed—at what, nobody seemed certain.

20   Francis was walking by the superintendent, talking garrulously: "Well, sir, all has passed off with the utmost satisfactoriness. It was all finished—flick! Like that. It iss not always so—oah, no! I have known cases where the doctor was obliged to go beneath the gallows and pull the prissoner's legs to ensure decease. Most disagreeable!"

21   "Wriggling about, eh? That's bad," said the superintendent.

22   "Ach, sir, it iss worse when they become refractory! One man, I recall, clung to the bars of hiss cage when we went to take him out. You will scarcely credit, sir, that it took six warders to dislodge him, three pulling at each leg. We reasoned with him, 'My dear fellow,' we said, 'think of all the pain and trouble you are causing to us!' But no, he would not listen! Ach, he wass very troublesome!"

23   I found that I was laughing quite loudly. Everyone was laughing. Even the superintendent grinned in a tolerant way. "You'd better all come out and have a drink," he said quite genially. "I've got a bottle of whisky in the car. We could do with it."

24   We went through the big double gates of the prison into the road. "Pulling at his legs!" exclaimed a Burmese magistrate suddenly, and burst into a loud chuckling. We all began laughing again. At that moment Francis' anecdote seemed extraordinarily funny. We all had a drink together, native and European alike, quite amicably. The dead man was a hundred yards away.

Responding to Orwell's Narrative

1. What specific details about the place and the people help you to visualize the scene in paragraphs 1 and 2? _____

   _____

2. Orwell uses dialogue in several places. Find and copy the most effective use of dialogue in the narrative and explain why it is effective for you.

   _____

   _____

3. What tense does Orwell use in his narrative? _____

   Find and jot down three effective action words._____

   _____

4. Reread the essay, circling any cue words or phrases that serve as time markers to keep the sequence of events clear.

5. Notice that like Ueda, Lee, and other writers of narratives in this chapter, Orwell shares his personal reaction to the event on a moment-to-moment basis. In fact, much of the success of Orwell's narration stems from the writer's communication of feelings both during and immediately after the event. Return to the essay and underline all of Orwell's reactions to the situation.

6. In titling his narrative simply "A Hanging" and in recounting this event by sharing his feelings rather than denouncing capital punishment, Orwell makes his point effectively and accomplishes his purpose. In what way does the concluding paragraph reinforce Orwell's point? _____

_____

_____

7. Does it bother you that Orwell never reveals the man's crime? _____ Explain and support your reaction._____

_____

_____

Responding to Your Own Narrative Draft

Once you have a draft of an essay using narration, respond to your draft by completing the following activities:

1. Find and label in your draft all specific details about the place and people connected with the event you're recounting.

2. Find and label any use of dialogue. (Check the handbook in Part Four to see if this dialogue is correctly punctuated.) If you would like to include dialogue in your draft, experiment by adding a sentence or two of dialogue.

3. Experiment with tense by changing all action words from past to present tense. (Pencil these changes in or keep a copy of your original draft if you are drafting on computer.) Compare the two versions of your essay to decide which tense is more effective for your particular narration.

4. Search your draft for cue words signaling time order for the reader. Circle these and mark any places where the order of events might not be clear. Add cue words and rearrange details if necessary.

5. Reread your draft, noting places where your moment-to-moment reaction to the event would help your audience feel a part of the action. Mark these spots and then add your reaction where appropriate.

6. Examine your draft's title and conclusion. Will the title capture the reader's interest without giving too much away? Will your conclusion offer closure and communicate the significance of the event to your audience just as Orwell's conclusion does? Evaluate and make appropriate revisions.

7. Is there any material that in rethinking the draft you might prefer to cut? For example, in his preliminary draft, Orwell may have mentioned the man's crime; he might later have decided that this information did not relate to the main point he was trying to develop in his narrative. Make necessary deletions in your own draft.

READINGS AND ADDITIONAL ACTIVITIES

The following paragraph is excerpted from E. J. Kahn's book *The Big Drink*. Kahn is a journalist who has written extensively about the American lifestyle. As you read, see what new information Kahn is able to share about America's favorite soft drink.

The Discovery of Coca-Cola

E. J. Kahn, Jr.

The man who invented Coca-Cola was not a native Atlantan, but on the day of his funeral every drugstore in town testimonially shut up shop. He was John Styth Pemberton, born in 1833 in Knoxville, Georgia, eighty miles away. Sometimes known as Doctor, Pemberton was a pharmacist who, during the Civil War, led a cavalry troop under General Joe Wheeler. He settled in Atlanta in 1869, and soon began brewing such patent medicines as Triplex Liver Pills and Globe of Flower Cough Syrup. In 1885, he registered a trademark for something called French Wine Coca—Ideal Nerve and Tonic Stimulant; a few months later he formed the Pemberton Chemical Company, and recruited the services of a bookkeeper named Frank M. Robinson, who not only had a good head for figures but, attached to it, so exceptional a nose that he could audit the composition of a batch of syrup merely by sniffing it. In 1886—a year in which, as contemporary Coca-Cola officials like to point out, Conan Doyle unveiled Sherlock Holmes and France unveiled the Statue of Liberty— Pemberton unveiled a syrup that he called Coca-Cola. It was a modification of his French Wine Coca. He had taken out the wine and added a pinch of caffeine, and, when the end product tasted awful, had thrown in some extract of cola (or kola) nut and a few other oils, blending the mixture in a three-legged iron pot in his back yard and swishing it around with an oar. He distributed it to soda fountains in used beer bottles, and Robinson, with his flowing bookkeeper's script, presently devised a label, on which "Coca-Cola" was written in the fashion that is still employed. Pemberton looked upon his concoction less as a refreshment than as a headache cure, especially for people whose throbbing temples could be traced to overindulgence. On a morning late in 1886, one such victim of the night before dragged himself into an Atlanta drugstore and asked for a dollop of Coca-Cola. Druggists customarily stirred a teaspoonful of syrup into a glass of water, but in this instance the factotum on duty was too lazy to walk to the fresh-water tap, a couple of feet off. Instead, he mixed the syrup with some charged water, which was closer at hand. The suffering customer perked up almost at once, and word quickly spread that the best Coca-Cola was a fizzy one.

QUESTIONS ON CONTENT

1. Why would drug stores in Atlanta close down on the day of John Pemberton's funeral? _____

   _____

2. In addition to the discovery of Coca-Cola, what other memorable events took place in 1886? _____

   _____

3. Name the ingredients in Coca-Cola. _____

   _____

4. Look up the words *dollop* and *factotum* in a dictionary. Write the definitions in your own words. _____

   _____

QUESTIONS ON STRATEGY

1. What strategy does Kahn use in his first sentence to capture the interest of his readers? _____

   _____

2. In which verb tense is the narration written and why? _____

_____

3. Annotate the essay by underlining all of the verbs. Choose two which describe specific actions and write them down. _____

_____

4. Kahn states that Pemberton blended the coke mixture "in a three-legged iron pot" and "swished it around with an oar." How do these details give the reader an unexpected picture of the discovery of this soft drink?

_____

Bonnie Jo Campbell decided to write a book about people's workday experiences. The following narrative essay is taken from her book *Getting By: Stories of Working Lives.* As you read, notice Campbell's use of dialogue in several paragraphs.

Delivering the Goods

Bonnie Jo Campbell

1   Last year, after school was out, I found myself staring six weeks of unemployment in the face. My mother quickly got wind of this and lined up myriad farm chores to occupy me—including mucking out her horse barn. The manure was so deep in some parts that the horses were scraping their heads on the ceilings.

2   "How are we going to get rid of this stuff?" I asked.

3   "We're going to sell it." she said.

4   She put ads in the *Kalamazoo Gazette* and the *Kalamazoo Shopper* offering manure for $35 a truckload. My portion for doing the physical work was $20; Mom got $15 for providing the truck and the product. Right away we got calls. A surprising number of people wanted the stuff we were anxious to get rid of.

5   I spent a lot of time inside that barn with my pitchfork, moving layer after layer of manure and urine-soaked straw. The sweat poured out of me like I was a marathon runner. My mother brought me glasses of iced tea to keep my spirits and electrolytes up. Oddly

enough, I wasn't feeling wretched. As my thoughts wandered, I found myself filled with good cheer. After months of sitting in class listening to professors, I felt like I finally had rejoined the world of the living. Moving my muscles was reviving me.

6   Making the delivery was a little embarrassing at first. The body of my mother's pickup truck was rusting away; the two sides of the bed were held together with shock cords. Some days, with the temperature in the 90s, a half ton of manure in the back, and the truck stuck in a traffic jam on West Main, we made quite a sensation. I put my hand over my face and hoped I wouldn't see anyone I knew.

7   Within a week, however, I began to see the absurdity of our situation as liberating. As we rattled through well-kept neighborhoods in a half-ton pickup full of stinking manure, I hung my leg out the window, and, strangely, felt like the master of all I surveyed. Perhaps this is how a prostitute feels toward a wealthy, respectable client: I might be dirty, but I have something you need.

8   Mom and I provided an excellent-quality product at a fair price to decent folks. They were nice—after all, only very earthy people order manure from the farm rather than buying it in bags at the store. Customers often tried to help me shovel, but after I rebuffed their advances, they stood back and smiled at the cascading dung. Hands on hips, eyes sparkling, they perhaps were fantasizing about midsummer gardens brimming with vegetables.

9   One man was planting a full acre of garden. After I unloaded the truck, he took Mom and me to admire a mound on the other side. "Do you know what that is?" he asked. "That's llama manure. And this pile over here, that's pig manure. And that's chicken." His enthusiasm was touching. I felt proud that our manure was out in the world, mingling with other manures, making things grow.

10   There is no vocation more honest than selling manure. Consider what most people do for a living. They build crap, or sell crap, or move crap, or spin a line of bull over the telephone, all the while pretending that their product is something other than crap. When I delivered a load of manure to someone's garden, the customer and I were both upfront about what we were dealing with. All I had to do was ask, "Where do you want this shit?"

11   This experience made me reflect on the idea of work in general. Any job is an important job, whether it's selling manure or selling insurance. People should take pride in what they do, and not assume that a dirty job makes them second-class citizens. Even the smelliest job, done well, has its rewards.

12   My husband works second shift at a paper-converting plant in town. "What are you doing this afternoon?" he asked me one day as I walked him out to his truck. I told him I was going to pitch manure.

13   "Aren't we all," he said, nodding. "Aren't we all."

QUESTIONS ON CONTENT

1. Explain how the title of the essay relates to its content. _____

_____

2. Why was Campbell at first embarrassed by her summer job? _____

_____

3. What insight has Campbell gained from her job experience?_____

_____

QUESTIONS ON STRATEGY

1. How is the dialogue in paragraph 9 effective in giving readers more information about the man with the garden? _____

_____

What difference would there have been if Campbell had chosen to tell the reader about this man rather than use his own words in the form of dialogue?

_____

2. In which paragraphs does Campbell make use of humor? _____

_____

3. Why do you think Campbell compares herself to a prostitute in paragraph 7?

_____

4. What appears to be Campbell's purpose in the second half of the essay?

_____

5. If reading the essay caused you to recall particular jobs you've held in the past, does Campbell seem to want you to take the next step in your thinking? If so, what would this step be? _____

_____

CRITICAL THINKING IN CONNECTING TEXTS

In this chapter, you've read several examples of narration. Like other methods of development, narration may be used by a writer for an entire essay or for a portion of an essay that uses multiple methods of development. For an example of the latter, turn again to Edward Hoagland's "Stuttering Time" (pp. 105–106). Notice that the writer introduces his essay with a narration—he tells the story of his friend who stutters. Although he uses other methods to develop his thesis in his body paragraphs, Hoagland knows the dramatic impact narration can have on an audience. Working with a partner, refer to other essays in earlier chapters of this text and see how many examples of narrative development you can find, jotting down the titles of the essays that contain narration. See if you can also discover the following for each essay using narration:

- How the narrative supports the writer's thesis

- How the scene is set for the audience

- What point of view and tense are used

- If the writer has employed dialogue

If time permits, share your findings with the class.

**For more writing resources, be sure to see the
Longman English Pages Website at
http://longman.awl.com/englishpages**

Observing the World: Description and Definition

To see a world in a grain of sand
And a heaven in a wild flower,
Hold infinity in the palm of your hand
And eternity in an hour.

—from "Auguries of Innocence" by William Blake,
eighteenth century English poet and artist

Preview

In this chapter you will learn
- ▶ to develop your powers of observation and investigation
- ▶ to recognize the characteristics of effective description
- ▶ to write an essay using descriptive detail
- ▶ to identify the characteristics of effective definition
- ▶ to write an essay using various strategies and sources of definition: from a dictionary and a thesaurus to books of quotations and encyclopedias
- ▶ to differentiate between connotative and denotative words
- ▶ to use comparison to strengthen description and definition

When was the last time that you took the opportunity to *observe* a flower, as Blake suggests, rather than vaguely glimpse it out of the corner of an eye? The last time you went to the bank or worked your way through the check-out line at the supermarket, did you notice the people around you? In our fast-paced world, there is often little time for the rewarding art of careful observation.

This chapter focuses on description and definition, two patterns of essay development that rely on your ability to observe something within your world—to notice it carefully—and then clearly communicate that observation to an audience. Both of these patterns are invaluable in developing sentences, paragraphs, and entire essays.

CHARACTERISTICS OF DESCRIPTION

Description is a writing strategy that depicts an observable subject with vivid sensory details. If you are describing the rose you observed on the walk to your classroom or office, you might convey its smell, texture, exact coloration, and shape, right down to that drop of dew glistening on one freshly opened outer petal.

To get an idea of how description works to develop material, read the following excerpt:

> He and my father went bowling together, and I was sometimes allowed to tag along. I didn't particularly care for the sport, but I loved Castle's Bowling Alley, a dark, narrow (only four lanes) low-ceilinged basement establishment that smelled of cigar smoke and floor wax. I loved to put my bottle of Nehi grape soda right next to my father's beer bottle on the scorecard holder and to slide my shoes under the bench with my father's when we changed into bowling shoes. I loved the sounds, the heavy clunk of the ball dropped on wood, its rumble down the alley, the clatter of pins, and above it all, men's shouts—"Go, go, gogogo!" "Get *in* there!" "Drop, *drop*!" Then the muttered curses while they waited for the pin boy to reset the pins. When I was in Castle's Alley I felt, no matter how many women or children might also be there, as though I had gained admittance to a men's enclave, as though I had *arrived*.
>
> —Larry Watson, from *Montana 1948*

Notice that Watson's description contains the following characteristics:

- **It focuses on an observable subject.**
  For Watson, the subject is Castle's Bowling Alley. The writer informs the audience of the subject early in the description.

- **It employs sensory detail—specific details related to the senses.**
  For instance, Watson's phrase "dark, narrow . . . low-ceilinged basement establishment" uses visual imagery; "smelled of cigar smoke and floor wax" appeals to the reader's sense of smell; "slide my shoes under the bench" incorporates the sense of touch; the phrases "heavy clunk of the ball dropped on wood, its rumble down the alley, the clatter of pins and above it all, men's shouts" appeal to the reader's sense of hearing.

- **It relates the detail in an order that allows the reader to grasp the subject, using cue words to form transitions from one detail to the next.**

Watson moves the reader visually from the ceiling to the bowling lanes and benches with such cue words as "next to," "under," and "down."

To see how description works within a college essay, read the following model and see how may of the characteristics just discussed you can identify.

MODEL WITH KEY QUESTIONS

Brenda Grant wanted to describe an object that has special meaning for her—a photograph of her two granddaughters. In drafting her descriptive essay, Grant referred often to this photo, which is shown here.

MY GRANDDAUGHTERS
Brenda Grant

Brenda Grant retired from the workplace to care for her two grandchildren. Soon she was urged by her adult children to attend college. Quite anxious about her writing skills when she first returned to school, Brenda later asserted, "I've learned that I really can write. Now I rely on my life experiences to help me write my essays." Although Brenda continues to struggle with clear organization of her material in essays, she feels much more confident about her writing. Upon completing community college requirements, Brenda plans to leave retirement to become a child care coordinator.

1   Alexia and Ashley are very important to my life since they are my grandchildren. Alexia is almost four years old, and Ashley, the baby, is a year and a half. They're both beautiful in their youth and enthusiasm for life. I became a part of their enthusiasm when for a while, I was the grandmother who took care of them. When their mother, Tiffany, was in the army and their father, Moses, drove a school bus, out of necessity I became Alexia and Ashley's baby-sitter, cook, and playmate. Today, although the girls live far away from me, I carry a special picture of Alexia and Ashley in my wallet.

2   Whenever I look at this picture of Alexia and Ashley sitting together with smiles on their faces, I remember picture day at Lock Child Care Center. I dressed both girls alike and took them to school. Upon seeing them, the camera-man said, "We will call this picture two sisters in love." In the picture, Alexia wears a white ribbon in her longer, wavy hair, while Ashley's little bit of much curlier hair is held in place on top of her head with a small yellow plastic barrette. Ashley and Alexia both wear white, short-sleeved shirts with small yellow sunflowers. Their pants are blue checked with the same sunflower pattern featured in their shirts. They both wear dark blue tennies. The picture background is a giant yellow crayon box on the left and a huge blue crayon with lighter blue background to the right. Across the girls' legs is a red crayon, which both Alexia and Ashley are holding as they sit on a blue carpeted step.

3   In spite of their almost identical clothing, I can see differences in my grand-daughters' personalities when I look at their facial expressions in this picture. Alexia, who has a larger smile on her face revealing her teeth, is more outgoing and friendly. She's like a playful pup. Ashley, whose eyebrows are raised as she looks up at the cameraman, can be as timid as a mouse around strangers. Al-though both girls enjoy playing with their friends, in this picture Ashley has care-fully positioned her hands in a way that reminds me of how much she likes to be the boss when she is playing. In contrast, Alexia's hand positioning is more care-free, and her bandaged finger reveals one of her traits: she often gets hurt in her play.

4   I remember that right after this picture was taken, Ashley looked around at the school and said to Alexia, "I'm a big girl like you and I want to go to school with you, Alexia." Now that the girls' mother is stationed in Atlanta, Georgia, their father and Alexia and Ashley have also moved to Atlanta so they can all be to-gether. I grew so close to my granddaughters because of my responsibilities look-ing after them, and now I find this picture helps me remember them when I get lonely.

KEY QUESTIONS

1. **PURPOSE** Is Grant's purpose to convey factual information or express a dominant impression of her subject? _____

_____

2. **FOCUS** How does Grant limit her subject? _____

_____

3. **MATERIAL** What kinds of details does Grant use to describe her subject?

_____

4. **STRUCTURE** How would you describe Grant's organization of the material?

_____

5. **STYLE** Find one example of precise word choice that helps in communicating Grant's subject to her audience. Write this word or phrase in the
following space, along with why you find it effective in describing the
subject: _____

_____

GUIDELINES FOR WRITING DESCRIPTION

Consider Audience and Purpose

Whether you use description as a pattern of development for all or merely a
part of your essay, you will be describing in order to convey one or both of the
following to your audience:

- *Factual information about your subject:* In this case your purpose is **objective**—having to do with facts rather than feelings or impressions
about a subject.

- *Dominant impression of your subject:* In this case your purpose is **subjective**—stressing feelings and impressions rather than factual information about your subject.

For example, if you want to describe a particular planet for an astronomy
class, you will be relying on factual information. If, however, you want to express to a group of peers the effect that a certain room or book had on you
when you were a child, your supporting detail would probably be a mixture of
factual detail and sensory impressions. You state your objective or subjective
purpose for a descriptive essay in your thesis. If you are writing a descriptive
paragraph, you state this purpose in your topic sentence.

In "My Granddaughters" Brenda Grant uses factual detail, such as the colors and patterns of the girls' clothing and the arrangement of their hair. Grant also expresses her feelings about her subject when she states, "Today, although the girls live far away from me, I carry a special picture of Alexia and Ashley in my wallet." While Grant's impressions about her subject are appropriate for an audience seeking information about Grant's relationship with her granddaughters, impressions or feelings about a subject presented in astronomy class would be inappropriate for an audience wanting factual information on a planet.

Once you think you have a subject you'd like to explore, make sure that you consider *who* might be interested in learning more about the subject and *why* you want to describe a particular subject. Who will form your reading audience and what overall effect do you want to have on that audience?

Practice 9.1 Work with a partner and examine the following subjects for description, filling in a possible audience and purpose for each. The first example has been completed for you.

Subject	Audience	Purpose
1. The internal organs	A group of pre-med students	Offer factual information
2. The view from the tallest building in the city		
3. An old photograph of a relative		
4. Your favorite restaurant		
5. Jealousy in a relationship		
6. A black widow spider with its prey		
7. Your most meaningful physical possession		
8. An unforgettable person		
9. A necessary piece of equipment for your career		
10. A personalized family ritual		

◆ ◆ ◆

Focus Range of Subject

As you can see from the list in the preceding practice, your subject may be anything that you first observe and then describe. While some subjects from the list are concrete, others are abstract. Both kinds of subjects are capable of being observed and described using the strategies in this chapter.

- **Concrete subjects** possess physical properties—for example, your cousin Jake or the way the street looks from your bedroom window. You observe concrete subjects with your eyes, ears, and the rest of your senses.

- **Abstract subjects** possess no physical properties but still exist as an idea, concept, or principle. For example, democracy and kindness are concepts that certainly exist even though we cannot see, taste, or hear them; we can only observe examples of democracy or the characteristics of kindness.

Practice 9.2 Return to the list in Practice 9.1 and indicate next to each subject "C" for concrete or "A" for abstract.

◆ ◆ ◆

In choosing a subject for description, make sure your subject is limited enough to be described vividly. If you're going to write a two-to-three-page essay about your grandmother's house, you might be most successful if you restrict your focus to say, the kitchen and adjacent backyard—describing all the sights, smells, and sounds associated only with these two areas rather than the entire house.

To illustrate, examine a thesis by one student which forecasts his subject for description and includes the writer's dominant impression:

> I'll always remember my grandmother's kitchen and backyard as a place that made me feel secure, warm, and protected from the outside world.
>
> —Bryant Burns, student

The kitchen and backyard areas form the writer's subject; the dominant impression is Burns' feeling of security, warmth, and protection.

If your purpose is objective, you would want to keep your own feelings minimal and inform your audience with factual information. You might limit your subject as in the following thesis:

> While we know much about our sun, several of the sun's characteristics are yet to be fully understood by scientists.
>
> —Charles Kim, student

Practice 9.3   Return to the ten subjects you listed under "Audience" and "Purpose" in Practice 9.1. On a separate sheet of paper, write a thesis for each subject, considering carefully the audience and purpose you have indicated.

◆ ◆ ◆

Select Important Details

You may find that you adjust the focus on your subject after you begin to prewrite to discover important details. Once you have a list or cluster of details, you'll notice that several of these traits tend to develop one dominant impression or controlling idea. At this point, choose those details that focus on your narrowed subject and put aside those that don't seem to relate.

For example, when Bryant Burns first began to gather details for his final thesis, he included his grandmother's entire house in his tentative thesis. The following is Burns' preliminary listing for his subject:

Grass in front yard so green it looked unreal, neatly trimmed, had a hill we rolled down

Rose bushes near the porch

From kitchen came smell of fresh bread or biscuits, homemade, pot roast, sweet potato pie

Big picture window in living room, fireplace, trophies and awards on mantel

Gigantic chairs in kitchen —we used to sit here with big cups of milk

Old fashioned stove, spice rack with little white jars over stove

Another picture window by kitchen table —looked out on back yard

Dog house in back yard, big lemon tree, gate for neighbor, who was a creepy old lady

Apricot tree, plum tree

Grass here was like blanket tucked perfectly in a bed

Smells of grass, old leaves, over-ripe fallen fruit, buzzing flies

When Burns reviewed this list, he found he had many more telling details connected with his grandmother's kitchen and backyard than he did for the rest of the house. At this point, he sorted and selected the details he would use in his description. He set aside details that did not relate to the kitchen or the backyard.

If you are describing an abstract subject, you won't be able to "observe" your subject by using your senses. But you will be able to think about the subject and how you might focus on a particular aspect of it to describe. Let's say you've been asked to write an essay describing your previous work experience. You could use your powers of observation to note all of the jobs you have ever held. Then you could recall in detail your job duties associated with each position.

Whether your subject is concrete or abstract, be sure to keep gathering information in your prewriting until you have more than enough specific detail. That way, you can be selective with what you later choose.

Practice 9.4   Take a few minutes to observe with all your senses the room you are in now. On a separate sheet of paper, cluster or list details that relate to each other. When you've finished, exchange your cluster or list with a partner, and ask your partner to evaluate the effectiveness of your detail. If the person had never seen the room before, would he or she be able to visualize it based on your information, or is the impression of the room vague? If the latter is true, return to your own list or cluster and gather more information.

◆ ◆ ◆

Follow a Clear Order

If you reexamine Brenda Grant's essay (pp. 237–238), you'll notice a spatial order. Grant begins her detailed description in paragraph 2 with her grand-daughters' hair, and then she describes the girls' shirts, pants, and shoes. At this point, Grant introduces descriptive detail about the background of the photograph. Spatial order works well for this visual description.

In paragraph 3 of Grant's essay, the concrete subject—the photograph of the two granddaughters—is still being described. At this point, Grant wanted to convey to her audience the connection between this concrete subject, the photo, and what it represents to her: the more abstract subject of her granddaughters' personalities. In this paragraph, Grant's order is logical rather than spatial. Grant describes Alexia's large smile and what it reveals about her personality, and then she discusses Ashley's expression with its revelation of her personality. Grant shifts her focus to the hands of each girl, explaining how the hands and their positioning in the photo reveal clues about each granddaughter's personality.

The bottom line for organizing a description is this: consider your subject, audience, and purpose, and then come up with the best organizational plan to communicate your subject to your readers. Whatever order you decide to use, signal your audience with appropriate cue words, referring if necessary to the list on pages 187–188.

Practice 9.5   Review Bryant Burns's thesis (p. 241) and his original prewriting list (p. 242) and then complete the following.

1. Cross out any details in his list that do not clearly relate to his thesis.
2. Number the remaining items on the list in the most effective order for a clear description.

◆ ◆ ◆

Employ Vivid Words

If your subject for description is concrete, use words or phrases that appeal to your audience's sense of sight, hearing, touch, taste, and smell. For example, when Watson describes Castle's Bowling Alley (p. 236), he uses the phrases "the heavy *clunk* of the ball dropped on wood" and "the *clatter* of pins." Notice that these words appeal much more specifically to his readers' physical world than phrases like "the *sound* of the ball" or "the *noise* of the pins" would have.

If, on the other hand, your subject for description is abstract, you will find it helpful to use comparisons, especially similes and metaphors (discussed in Chapter 3, pp. 79–80). Often the thoughtful use of a **metaphor** (a direct comparison of one thing with another) or a **simile** (a direct comparison of one thing with another using *like* or *as*) will enable your audience to get a clear and instantaneous picture of the subject you are describing. Be advised, however, that an overused or "stale" simile or metaphor will not help you communicate your subject. How do you know whether your comparison is stale or fresh? A good test is the following: If you believe that another person reading your simile or metaphor might be able to finish the comparison without actually reading the entire phrase, you know that this comparison has been overused. For example, if you see "gentle as a _____," you think of *lamb* as the missing word. If you were to see or hear "stubborn as a _____, you'd no doubt think of *mule*. In contrast, fresh similes or metaphors allow the reader to think about the comparison and make connections, rather than tune out the much-used expression.

Practice 9.6 Return to Brenda Grant's essay "My Granddaughters" (pp. 237–238) and annotate any similes or metaphors you find by circling them. Decide whether you think the comparisons Grant uses are fresh or could be improved upon. For additional practice with comparisons, see the "Responding to Writing" section at the end of this chapter.

◆ ◆ ◆

STRATEGIES FOR WRITING DESCRIPTION

1. **PURPOSE** Determine your audience, then decide whether you want to share factual information, convey your dominant impression about the subject, or both.

2. **FOCUS** Choose a concrete or abstract subject, observe it carefully, record your observations, and narrow the subject so that you can describe it fully.

3. **MATERIAL** Gather more than enough details; then choose those that most effectively paint a word picture of your subject. Include sensory as well as factual details when appropriate.

4. **STRUCTURE** Let the nature of your subject guide you in organizing your description. Use cue words to signal your readers.

5. **STYLE** Use vivid words whenever possible, and employ effective comparisons, especially when describing abstract subjects.

OPTIONS FOR WRITING DESCRIPTION

Each writing option asks you to use the descriptive strategies you have been practicing. Find a subject for which you have a strong feeling and a fair amount of factual information. In gathering material for your drafts, employ your powers of observation to their fullest. If your subject is concrete, you might begin by using your senses to experience and then record physical features. If your subject is abstract, think about the kinds of comparisons and details that would help make your subject vivid for an audience.

1. Describe a place you have called "home," or a particular part of that home. Use descriptive detail to communicate the impression this special place made on you.

2. Describe a person, place, or animal you have observed over a period of several days. Engage in close observation of your subject, recording your findings in the form of daily notes. Write a descriptive essay detailing your subject.

3. In her essay "My Granddaughters," Brenda Grant describes a photograph that affected her. Search for a photo that moves you in some way—this may be a picture of a relative, friend, or total stranger. Write a descriptive essay in which you include information on the person, the clothing, actions, facial expressions, background, and the person's relationship to other objects in the picture. Tie all this descriptive detail together in your thesis indicating the dominant impression the photo has on you.

4. Visit an art gallery on or off campus or find a good quality reproduction of a painting or drawing. Describe this work of art. You might combine factual information with your dominant impression of the work.

5. Write an essay describing the word *courage*. You might want to describe this term in modern terms and contrast it with a description of the concept in an earlier time, say the nineteenth century.

6. Write an essay describing an object or an article of clothing, jewelry, or furniture that is symbolic of your ethnic culture or your religious background. For example, you might describe a menorah, a statue of the Virgin of Guadalupe, a shawl or jacket given to you by a relative. You can begin by observing the object closely, and then you might want to gather more material by recalling the significance and history of the object. You might even interview a family or community member for additional information on your subject.

7. Write a report describing a particular place on your college campus that is in dire need of repair, remodeling, or redesign. If your purpose is to persuade administrators, student body members, or your board of trustees to consider renovation, you will want to remain objective in your report and provide as much detail as possible.

If both description and definition are based on careful observation, how do these two patterns of essay development differ? Recall the rose mentioned earlier in this chapter. Think again about how you might write a description of a rose: you would want to give your readers so much detail that they could *sense*—see, smell, and feel—that particular rose. Examine the following verse describing two roses:

The red rose whispers of passion
And the white rose breathes of love.

—John Boyle O'Reilly from "A White Rose"

Now suppose that you were asked to define a rose. You might use description as well as other strategies for defining, but your aim would be to set boundaries for your reader—you would want to communicate all of the essential characteristics differentiating a rose from all other flowers. The following definition establishes these boundaries in only a few words:

Any of a genus of shrubs . . . with prickly stems, alternate compound leaves, and five-parted, usually fragrant flowers.

—*Webster's New World Dictionary*

CHARACTERISTICS OF DEFINITION

Definition is a statement of the exact nature of a subject, including what the subject is and is not. Defining involves detailing all distinguishing characteristics clearly—so that your reader readily grasps the difference between an *espresso* and other coffee drinks, for example. In your everyday conversation, you probably use definition without being aware of it. Every time someone asks you, "What is that?" you attempt to explain distinguishing features of concrete as well as abstract terms by defining them. "An espresso is a coffee prepared in a special machine which forces steam," you may answer. And in order to define this subject or any other, you need to observe it from a variety of angles to determine its unique traits.

To see how definition works within an essay, read the following:

In its narrowest sense, violence is defined as an act carried out with the intention of causing physical pain or injury to another. But in real life, severe physical violence is only one extreme of a whole spectrum of aggressive behavior that ranges from "verbal violence"—screaming, shouting, saying vicious, spiteful things—to banging one's fist on the table and slamming doors to actually pushing, hitting, kicking, throwing things at or beating another person.

—Shari Miller Sims, from "Violent Reactions"

Notice that Sims' definition has the following characteristics:

- **It focuses on an observable subject.**
  Just as the subject for description, the subject for definition may be concrete or abstract, but it must be capable of being carefully noticed or studied. Sims' subject is violence, the term she highlights early in the paragraph.

- **It uses a variety of detail to establish boundaries on the subject.**
  For example, Sims defines violence by giving a "narrow" dictionary definition, and then she offers a "real life" definition—her detail here is a series of examples of violent behavior.

- **It helps readers recognize the subject, even in new or different contexts.**
  After reading Sims' paragraph, readers have a better grasp of the term *violence* and they understand what it is and is not.

To see how definition works within a college essay, read the following model and see how many of these characteristics of definition you can identify.

MODEL WITH KEY QUESTIONS

Jinnie Delacruz chose quite a controversial word as the subject of her essay. She wanted to address an audience of college students whom she felt misused and misunderstood this word.

DOLTS, BLOCKHEADS, OR YOU-KNOW-WHAT
Jinnie Delacruz

Jinnie Delacruz confides that taking writing classes has greatly improved her writing abilities. Jinnie recently passed her LVN boards and is working as a licensed vocational nurse. At the same time, she is taking college classes in order to get her B.S. and then her M.S. in nursing, with the eventual goal of becoming a nurse practitioner.

1   We used to think that the word *ass* was a term of profanity. In the past, if a child used this word, soap and water might be applied to his mouth because *ass* was considered a dirty word. A child could be well groomed and intelligent, but once he blurted out a word like *ass,* his character would sink just as the Titanic did. Others would look at him as a hole in a brand-name sweater, a scratch on a new CD, or a mold on a fresh loaf of bread. It is ironic that today, the word *ass* seems to be accepted as part of our everyday language.

2   What exactly is an ass? From experience, we know that the word refers to a rear-end or butt, as in "Get off your ass!" Or, if this is too vulgar, there are other definitions that Webster's accepts: "A type of quadruped, of the horse family, used as a beast of burden; a dull, stupid fellow; a dolt; a blockhead."

3   As we hear *ass* used on the streets and on television, the word is not only a noun; it is also used as a verb. A common phrase around campus is "Man, I'm assed out!" referring to the feeling which the number 13 gives a person—the feeling of failing on an exam, the fear of having one's house broken into. Used as an action word, the term is quite negative.

4   Some people don't even realize they're using the term *ass* while they're talking. They just add the word to another word or phrase for no significant reason. Phrases such as "lazy ass," "smart ass," "mean ass," "tight ass," "nice ass," and "hard ass" all contain the term *ass.* Why? Does *ass* emphasize the adjective that precedes it? These words—*lazy, smart, mean, tight, nice,* and *hard,* seem descriptive without adding *ass* to them. For example, the expression, "You're lazy," sounds more appropriate than "You lazy ass." It is clear that adding *ass* to a word is like using a pen on a Scantron or sipping soup with a fork.

5   The word *ass* is used so increasingly that it is as if we have laid down a welcome mat and invited the word into our very homes. When the television is turned on, parents have to worry about whether the programs will "bleep" out this formerly unacceptable profanity. In one recent episode from a popular sitcom, one character yelled to another, "If you want to sit on your ass. . . ." The word is rarely censored any more. Even more recently on *The Simpsons,* "un-censorship" was practiced. Someone in the family said, "Homer, your ass is pathetic."

6   The about-face in public opinion and acceptance of the word *ass* is a signal that society is becoming ever more tolerant of graphic language in the media and in general. We have to wonder if there are very many words left which will be taboo in the next century. Maybe even more important—how many people will know that *ass* can also mean a kind of horse used as a beast of burden? Oh well—by that time maybe we'll all have become dolts or blockheads, sitting on our . . . you-know-what.

KEY QUESTIONS
....

1. **PURPOSE** What clues tell you that Delacruz is addressing a college audience? _____

_____

By the end of the essay, what have you learned about the word that you didn't know before?_____

_____

2. **FOCUS** Find Delacruz's thesis and underline it in the essay. After reading the essay, do you agree with her main point? (Support your position with specific evidence.) _____

_____

3. **MATERIAL** Name three sources the writer uses for material.

_____

4. **STRUCTURE** How is the essay organized—chronologically, spatially, or logically?_____

5. **STYLE** Find the most memorable phrase and jot it down in the following space. _____

GUIDELINES FOR WRITING DEFINITION

Consider Audience and Purpose

Once you have a tentative subject for your definition, consider the background of your target audience. In your drafting, you will want to think about the level of familiarity your audience has with your subject. If you are defining a term with which your audience is already familiar, such as Smith does with the term *violence* and Delacruz does with the word *ass,* your purpose might be to introduce a new perspective. If your audience is completely unfamiliar with your subject, your purpose might be to educate and inform. For example, you might want to inform by defining sexual harassment to an audience of office workers, defining supply-side economics as part of a research paper for an economics class, defining multiculturalism in an essay for a sociology class, or defining "hip-hop" for a report in a music class.

Practice 9.7 Work with a partner and examine the following subjects for definition, filling in a possible audience and purpose for each. The first example has been completed for you.

Subject	Audience	Purpose
1. The modern family	A group of family counselors and psychologists	Persuade to accept new definition
2. The term *biodegradable*		
3. A yellow-bellied sapsucker		
4. A star (a celestial body)		
5. A star (a celebrity)		
6. A college freshman		
7. Gay rights		
8. A microchip		
9. The French Revolution		
10. Date rape		

◆ ◆ ◆

Determine Range of Subject

If your subject is concrete and your purpose is to inform, you might need only a sentence or two for your definition. Many college essays, however, will ask you to write about abstract ideas and issues. For such essays, you will need more than a few sentences to allow your audience to understand your subject. Depending on your audience and your purpose, you have two kinds of definition strategies to choose from:

- **Simple definition** A brief statement describing the exact nature of a subject in one or two sentences.

  For example, in an essay describing new office technologies for a business class, you might find the following simple definition: "Notebook computers are portable computers, often weighing less than five pounds, that can run on either battery or electrical power and can perform all of the functions of a standard desktop computer."

This one-sentence definition allows the reader to continue the essay without having to stop to look up a technical or specialized term. Simple definitions are often a courtesy to the reader; if your audience is interested in your topic but probably isn't made up of experts, you will want to be alert to places where a simple definition might be helpful.

- **Extended definition** Statements describing the exact nature of a subject and involving several sentences, paragraphs, or even an entire essay. This strategy works if your subject is abstract or complex, or if your purpose in providing the definition is to persuade your audience to understand your subject in a unique way. You might also use several strategies rather than just one to define your term. To see how an extended definition works, reexamine the essays by Jinnie Delacruz (pp. 247–248) and Gloria Naylor (pp. 266–268).

Explore Various Kinds of Definition

In writing definitions, you have available several useful strategies for exploring sources and gathering and organizing material. You can use one strategy or many, depending on the nature and complexity of your subject, your purpose in defining, and your audience.

Dictionary Definition

This strategy is often helpful when you are trying to clarify the distinguishing characteristics of your subject. Jinnie Delacruz decided to use a dictionary definition in paragraph 2 of her essay (p. 248). Notice that she did not begin her essay with "According to Webster's"—she knew that a dictionary definition would not be an exciting way to introduce her subject—but used a dictionary definition to develop information within the body of the essay.

You may wish to consult any one of the following references found in college or local libraries or online:

- **Unabridged dictionary** A book that contains thousands of alphabetically listed words along with their part of speech, definition, origin, and history of usage.

- **Thesaurus** A book that contains an alphabetical list of words along with their **synonyms**—words with similar meaning—and their **antonyms**—words with opposing meaning.

- *Funk and Wagnall's Standard Handbook of Synonyms, Antonyms, and Prepositions*

- *Dictionary of Quotations, Bartlett's Familiar Quotations, and Gale's Quotations: Who Said What*

Practice 9.8 To see what kind of information you can gather in an essay, refer back to the list on page 250 and choose one subject to look up in a dictionary, thesaurus, book of synonyms, or book of quotations. In the following space, write your subject, the information you found, and the source you used. (Be sure to rephrase the information in your own words or use quotation marks to indicate that you found the material in another source.)

_____

_____

◆ ◆ ◆

Historical Definition

If your purpose in defining your subject is to help your audience understand it in an expanded time framework, you could use a historical definition. Let's say that you want to show how a word's usage has changed through several centuries. An unabridged dictionary will give you the original meaning as well as the source of a word. Encyclopedias may offer you additional background information on your subject. For example, if you look up the term *anatomy* in an encyclopedia, you may find a long entry that begins with something like the following:

> *Anatomy:* The structural detail and critical analysis of all living organisms. Before 1543, few scientists had dissected the body.

Practice 9.9 Choose a subject that has been around long enough to have some history. Look up the meaning of the word or words in either an unabridged dictionary or an encyclopedia. Summarize your findings in the following space.

_____

_____

◆ ◆ ◆

Comparative Definition

An excellent way of communicating the distinguishing characteristics of your subject is to compare or contrast it with other closely related subjects. The following sentences illustrate this technique:

> *Cripple* seems to me a clean word, straightforward and precise. . . . *Disabled,* by contrast, suggests any incapacity, physical or mental. And I certainly don't like *handicapped.*
>
> —Nancy Mairs, from "On Being a Cripple"

In another kind of comparative definition, you can explain how the term may be misunderstood by stressing what it is *not*. The following is an example of definition by negation:

Sexual harassment is no joke.

—A.J. Anderson, from "Sexual Harassment Is No Joke"

Practice 9.10 Write a comparative definition to accompany each of the following subjects:

Success _____

Prejudice_____

◆ ◆ ◆

Definition by Example

This popular strategy allows your audience to visualize your subject instantly through illustration. Shari Sims uses this strategy in her definition of violence (p. 246): "screaming, shouting, . . . banging fists on the table." These phrases define by giving examples of behaviors associated with violence.

Practice 9.11 Return to the two subjects in Practice 9.10. On a separate sheet of paper, jot down a couple of examples useful in defining each of these subjects.

◆ ◆ ◆

Practice 9.12 Re-read the essays by Jinnie Delacruz (pp. 247–248) and Gloria Naylor (pp. 266–268). Annotate both essays in the margin indicating the strategies for definition that are used.

◆ ◆ ◆

Follow a Clear Order

When you've gathered enough information to define your subject clearly through the use of one or more strategies for definition, you'll want to establish a clear order for your material. If, for example, you are defining a subject using historical background, you might want to use chronological order, beginning with the oldest use of your word and then showing differences or nuances over time. For an idea of how this order might work, examine paragraph 1 of "Dolts, Blockheads, or You-Know-What" (p. 247). You may find in another essay that spatial order makes a subject easier for readers to understand. For example, if you are defining an object with physical properties—a tornado or a rose—proceeding from bottom to top or from left to right will allow your audience to visualize the subject. Logical order is perhaps the most common method for organizing a definition. You can begin with a simple, easy-to-understand definition and then proceed to more complex strategies, building on your reader's increasing knowledge and ability to handle more intricate material. Refer back to the paragraph on page 246 to see how Sims begins with a simple definition and then introduces examples to expand her definition of the term *violence.*

Employ Precise Words

Denotative Meaning
The **denotative meaning** of a word is its standard dictionary definition. For example, when you say that you live in a *house,* you're using a denotative term for a place of shelter, a residence. When your reader sees the word *house,* information is conveyed; emotions and images are not.

Connotative Meaning
If, on the other hand, you say that you live in your *home,* your reader mentally notes that you refer to a residence or place of shelter. The dictionary definition is similar to the one for *house*—but your audience also pictures a *home*—quite possibly one with a roaring fire, cozy armchairs, smells of freshly baked bread coming from the kitchen. **Connotative** words evoke particular emotional associations. *Home* is a connotative word—a word that involves the reader more directly than a denotative word would. If you're trying to persuade your reader of the impact a place of residence has on a person, you will want to use connotative language. If, however, your definition is intended for an audience of real estate agents or city surveyors, you would want to use denotative language based on facts and impersonal information.

    In drafting and then revising your definitions, be sure that you are using the most effective word or phrase for your purpose.

Practice 9.13   Examine the following list of words. After each word, jot down your reaction—positive, negative, or neutral. Also try to note what you associate or picture with the word. The first item has been done for you.

walk   *(neutral) move forward, put one foot in front of the other.*

amble _____

saunter _____

grin _____

leer _____

smile _____

◆ ◆ ◆

Avoid Circular Definitions

One type of definition strategy to avoid is the **circular definition**—a statement that renames the subject to be defined rather than offering a meaningful explanation. For example, defining *family values* as "the values that families hold dear" is about as helpful as offering no definition at all.

Practice 9.14 Rewrite the following definitions so that they genuinely explain the concept.

1. political correctness—the act of being or seeming correct politically

_____

2. assisted suicide—suicide that is assisted in some way

_____

◆ ◆ ◆

STRATEGIES FOR WRITING DEFINITIONS

1. **PURPOSE** Think about what your readers may already know about a subject, and why you want to provide them with a definition. Do you want to inform them or do you want to present them with a new concept of the subject? Decide whether a simple or an extended definition will allow your audience to grasp your subject more effectively.

2. **FOCUS** Be sure that you have focused on a sufficiently narrow subject to allow you to define it fully; at the same time, make sure that the subject is not too narrow.

3. **MATERIAL** Gather information from a variety of sources: dictionaries, encyclopedias, books of quotations, personal observations, recollection of examples, and your imagination.

4. **STRUCTURE** In an essay using more than one strategy for definition or defining more than one term, organize the material in such a way that you begin with simple definitions and then proceed to the more complex ones.

5. **STYLE** Once you have a draft, review it to make sure that all your words—whether denotative or connotative—are precise, and that they are the best words for defining your subject clearly and distinguishing the subject by specific, limiting characteristics. Make sure to revise and eliminate any circular definitions.

OPTIONS FOR WRITING DEFINITION

The following options will allow you to explore in an essay the guidelines for definition you have been reading about and practicing. After choosing a writing option, you'll be focusing on a subject that is either concrete or abstract, just as you did with your descriptive subjects earlier in this chapter. For this assignment, your goal is to communicate the distinguishing characteristics of your subject.

1. Write an essay defining the same article of clothing, jewelry, or furniture that you described in Writing Option 6 (p. 245). This time, you will be using different strategies; rather than telling about an object, you are reporting its distinguishing characteristics. If you are defining a menorah, for example, what differentiates it from a candelabrum? Feel free to consult specialized dictionaries such as a dictionary of religious practices or a dictionary of customs.

2. Read the paragraph by Monifa Winston in Chapter 6 (p. 146) in which she defines her subject, a college student, by using a series of action words, including the following: "*failed* a test ... *read* the wrong pages for homework, *paid* over three hundred dollars for books, *bought* the wrong books." Write an essay in which you define a subject you know something about from your work experience, college major, or special interest. Try to incorporate as many examples as possible into your essay.

¶ 3. Define one of the following terms (or another of interest to you). In thinking about your purpose and audience, ask yourself if you want to inform or express your personal definition.

winner	quitter	procrastinator	immigrant
freedom	obsession	tightwad	prejudice
sexual harassment	gay rights	family values	

4. After rereading "Dolts, Blockheads, or You-Know-What" (pp. 247–248), write an essay defining a term you feel is misused or in some way misunderstood. Use a variety of definition strategies, including at least one outside printed or electronic source.

5. Write an essay in which you define a subject that is a part of modern American culture, but that might not be understood by people from another culture. For example, you could define *situation comedy, yuppies, body piercing, Super Bowl Sunday,* or *fast food.*

Challenge Option: Combining Patterns

Thus far in Part Two of this book, you have read about and practiced narration, description, and definition as separate patterns that you can use to develop material in your essays. However, many writers use more than one pattern of essay development within a single essay. You will be able to combine patterns of development in your own writing if you choose to write on the challenge option that follows or appears in Chapters 10 and 11.

Writing an essay about a *Shangri-La* will allow you to use three patterns together in an essay—definition, description, and narration.

Shangri-La is defined as "any imaginary, idyllic utopia or hidden paradise." The term came into existence in 1933 as a result of a popular book called *Lost Horizon,* written by James Hilton, in which a place, Shangri-La, became a paradise. Think about the places where you've lived or visited. Pinpoint a special place that seemed like a paradise to you. In prewriting, get down as many details as you can remember. Try to use the following structure for beginning and ending the essay, but arrange the body paragraphs any way you like and don't feel limited to a fixed number of paragraphs if you find you want to expand your material:

- *Introduction:* Hook the audience, mention the subject Shangri-La, and name the particular place that is your personal paradise.

- *Body paragraph:* Define Shangri-La, using strategies for definition covered in this chapter. Consult an unabridged dictionary, encyclopedia, book of quotations, or the 1937 film *Lost Horizon,* directed by Frank Capra.

- *Body paragraph:* Narrate your experience in this special place. Here you will be using chronological order.

- *Body paragraph:* Describe your special place. Try to incorporate sensory detail to help your audience visualize your Shangri-La. You may want to use spatial order in this paragraph.

- *Concluding paragraph:* Tie all three patterns—definition, narration, and description—together by closing with your relationship to the place.

JOURNAL WRITING: SENSORY ISOLATION AND WORD ASSOCIATION

The following activities will help you discover details for description and definition. You will be asked to try to concentrate on each of your five senses, recording your observations.

Description

1. Become a camera and record your observations of your visual world. Christopher Isherwood, a writer well known for his astute observations, confided, "I am a camera with its shutter open, quite passive, recording,

not thinking." First warm up your "telephoto eye" by looking through a real camera lens, zooming in on various objects and people around you. If you don't have a camera handy, look through a pinhole in a piece of paper to focus your field of vision. Once you feel confident that your camera-like vision is functioning efficiently, you can dispense with the camera or pinhole, but continue to use your "camera eye" as you take your journal with you and record the following observations:

- an object in your outside world—a bug, flower, leaf on tree, piece of bark, pet
- objects on your desk—pens, pencils, books, stapler
- a person you know—a relative, friend, spouse, worker
- a person you don't know—someone waiting for a bus, sipping coffee in a coffee shop, standing in line at the grocery check-out counter
- a favorite view

For each of these observations, try visually to "zoom in" and "zoom out" noting as you do so what new details present themselves.

2. It is a fact that our senses become more acute when not all are functioning at the same time. For this activity, close your eyes, relax, and don't cheat by peeking. For each "observation station," keep your eyes closed for at least five minutes. Then open your eyes and record everything you heard, smelled, and felt (as in the tactile sense of feeling the chair upholstery or the carpet on your bare feet) before opening your eyes and moving to the next location for observation. Record sensory detail by completing this activity in the following locations:

- An outdoor area such as your yard, a campus lawn, or a park
- Your room or work area at home
- A place where friends or relatives gather—a kitchen or family room, for example
- A crowded place where you know no one—perhaps a coffee shop or a bowling alley, or the campus cafeteria or student union

Definition

1. Take a look at your journal entries for description. Choose a person, place, or object from these entries that seems most interesting to you. In another entry, observe the same subject from the point of view of one who tries to define the subject. This time, think of subjects that are closely related to yours, but different. What can you say about your subject that

will allow the reader to understand its distinguishing characteristics? If you described a leaf on a tree before, take that same leaf and explore traits that make it unique from other types of leaves in your yard.

2. In another journal entry, freewrite on any words that set off your personal "hot" button. According to a Yale University study, twelve especially potent words in the English language are the following: *save, money, you, new, health, results, easy, safety, love, discovery, proven,* and *guarantee.* What particular words somehow infuriate or inspire you, or perhaps take on special significance? Write down the words and whatever comes to mind in connection with the words without censoring your thoughts.

3. In a third journal entry, take the word you have chosen and think of precise words and effective similes or metaphors that you could use to distinguish your term from others. For example, if your "hot button" word is *health,* you might come up with the images "glowing skin," "sparkling teeth," "shiny hair," "a gait like that of a conditioned athlete."

When you've completed these journal entries, review your findings. You may discover surprising and significant observations that may be of interest to an audience if they were developed in an essay.

USING THE COMPUTER: DEVELOPING DESCRIPTIONS AND DISCOVERING NEW WORLDS ON THE WEB

1. If your subject for description or definition is small enough to be observed by you while you're at the computer, you'll see the immediate advantage of rapid-fire freewriting to record your impressions. You can even turn down the brightness on the screen if you find that "invisible writing" is helpful. In addition, you might want to try the following activity as you work through your drafts for essays using description or definition.

   Ask a friend or peer reviewer to read your draft on screen. The reader should highlight (using *bold, italics,* or another command that changes the appearance of certain words) what she or he thinks is effective sensory detail. Your reader should save the text. Now reread the highlighted version. When you notice any sections or paragraphs that have little or no highlighted phrases, add additional sensory detail (either from your freewriting, your journal, or new observations). Remember to return all highlighted portions to normal type before printing out your final version.

continued

USING THE COMPUTER: DEVELOPING DESCRIPTIONS AND DISCOVERING NEW WORLDS ON THE WEB *continued*

2. If you could travel anywhere in the world, someplace you've always dreamed about but never actually visited, where would you go? Imagine that you are a travel writer for a popular magazine, and you have been sent on assignment there. To help your readers imagine this place, you will need to use sensory descriptions, and you may need to define local customs and foods. For this assignment, you can "travel" to your dream destination using the World Wide Web. To find information on your destination, see if your Web provider already has a "travel" information option. Or you could try a search engine index. Both *Yahoo!* ⟨http://www.yahoo.com⟩ and *The Argus Clearinghouse* ⟨http//www.clearinghouse.net⟩ have many options to get you started. Other interesting travel-related sites include the following:

• *National Geographic Society* ⟨http://www.nationalgeographic.com⟩

• *Mungo Park* ⟨http://www.mungopark.com⟩

Write an article describing an imaginary trip that you take to your chosen destination, using plenty of details and descriptions based on what you learned from the Web. To help organize your article, refer to the "Challenge Option" on pages 256–257.

RESPONDING TO WRITING: COMPARISONS

This activity will improve your writing of description and definition. It will also refresh your memory about two kinds of comparisons, simile and metaphor, which were defined on page 244.

Both model essays in this chapter "My Granddaughters" (pp. 237–238), and "Dolts, Blockheads, or You-Know-What" (pp. 247–248), use simile or metaphor. When Brenda Grant states in paragraph 3 that Alexia is "like a playful pup" and that Ashley can be "as timid as a mouse," these similes give the reader a clear idea of the subject. Jinnie Delacruz uses similes in paragraphs 1, 4, and 5. When she asserts in paragraph 4 that "adding *ass* to a word is like using a pen on a Scantron or sipping soup with a fork," she uses the similes to communicate her feeling about the current misuse of the term *ass*.

For practice in identifying and evaluating the effectiveness of similes and metaphors, read the following descriptions and definitions, and then complete the exercises that follow for each.

My brother's wet clothes made it easy to see his strength. Most great casters I have known were big men over six feet, the added height certainly making it easier to get more line in the air in a bigger arc. My brother was only five feet ten, but he had fished so many years his body had become partly shaped by his casting. He was thirty-two now, at the height of his power, and he could put all of his body and soul into a four-and-a-half ounce magic totem pole. Long ago, he had gone far beyond my father's wrist casting, although his right wrist was always so important that it had become larger than his left. His right arm, which our father had kept tied to the side to emphasize the wrist, shot out of his shirt as if it were engineered, and it, too, was larger than his left arm.

—Norman Maclean, from *A River Runs Through It*

The chief feature of the landscape, and of your life in it, was the air. Looking back on a sojourn in the African highlands, you are struck by your feeling of having lived for a time up in the air. The sky was rarely more than pale blue or violet, with a profusion of light, weightless, ever-changing clouds towering up and sailing on it, but it has a blue vigour in it, and at a short distance it painted the ranges of hills and the woods a fresh deep blue. In the middle of the day the air was alive over the land, like a flame burning; it scintillated, waved and shone like running water, mirrored and doubled all objects, and created great Fata Morgana. Up in this high air you breathed easily, drawing in a vital assurance and lightness of heart. In the highlands you woke up in the morning and thought: Here I am, where I ought to be.

—Isak Dinesen, from *Out of Africa*

I don't mean to put a damper on things. I just mean we ought to treat fun reverently. It is a mystery. It cannot be caught like a virus. It cannot be trapped like an animal. . . . When fun comes in on little dancing feet, you probably won't be expecting it. It fact, I bet it comes when you're doing your duty, your job, or your work. It may even come on a Tuesday.

—Suzanne Britt Jordan, from "Fun. Oh Boy. Fun. You Could Die from It."

1. In the margin of each paragraph, identify the pattern of development as primarily description or definition.

2. Locate and then underline a simile or metaphor used by the writer.

3. Circle the subject being described or defined in the passage.

4. Evaluate the effectiveness of each simile or metaphor in giving the reader a clear picture of the subject. Number the passages in order of effectiveness, assigning 1 to the strongest and 4 to the weakest. Be prepared to defend your choices.

Now return to your own essay drafts for description or definition. Find and underline any similes or metaphors you find. Evaluate their effect—are these comparisons fresh or stale? If you have none, add at least one or two comparisons. If you have used a simile or metaphor, but your comparison is less than vivid, revise and strengthen your essay by making the necessary changes.

READINGS AND ADDITIONAL ACTIVITIES

Description

Guy Trebay lives in New York City and wrote the following essay for the *Village Voice* in October of 1996 shortly after a half-pipe, a ramp, was constructed for skaters in Manhattan's Riverside Park. As you read, notice Trebay's description of the skaters as well as description of the newly constructed half-pipe.

Gravity's Rainbow

Guy Trebay

1   Rahmaan Mazone stands poised at the lip, contemplating his doom. Below him is a 10-foot drop into a steel-plated half-pipe. The arc looks even deeper when you factor in Rahmaan's own six-foot height and the wheels of his in-line skates. Only a handful of local skaters have mastered the knack. Rahmaan wants to be one. "I just love heights to death," he says.

2   "Go!" a skateboarder urges as Rahmaan pauses, hovers, seems to cantilever his bulk out over a volume of empty air.

3   He's ready. He is about to let go. He's almost there and then . . . "Aargh!" Rahmaan groans, collapsing in a heap on the platform. "I don't want to die!"

4   We are in Skate Park, a very recently constructed rectangle of asphalt at 108th Street in Riverside Park. For some time, this place was known as Tuberculosis Park, principally because numerous homeless people were encamped here. Many still inhabit an enclosed arcade beneath the park walkway, and also the park itself, and the Penn Central tunnels where the so-called Mole People live.

. . .

5   Skate Park opened just a month ago; already close to 80 skaters arrive each day. The concept originated with 20 local adolescents guided by the Salvadori Educational Center

on the Built Environment. It was realized with a $50,000 grant from the National Parks Service's Innovations in Recreation Program, matched by an equivalent sum from the Department of Parks and other contributors. "We were eager to meet the needs of teens in Riverside Park," explains Riverside Park administrator Charles McKinney. "And we were searching for a project that would allow kids to design their own place. It was just lucky for us that this place was standing here derelict."

6   Crackheads had taken over. Consequently, "there was very little controversy" about reuse of the park. The project was designed with the help of four teachers who conducted a group visit to a skate park in Shimmersville, Pennsylvania, the creation of scale models, and also of a clay maquette depicting the riverside terrain. Construction took just under five weeks. That, too, was accomplished by students. The yield, besides a huge plywood hulk, was "an enormous jump in these kids' self-esteem," says McKinney. There was something else. "We've designated this area from 100th Street to 111th Street as a place to explore prototypes" for specifically adolescent park use, since "urban park environments frequently deny that the needs of some age groups and cultures exist."

7   The kids in the Salvadori program were considered "at risk," as Andy Kessler points out. "One of the teachers involved said that's ridiculous, because all kids are at risk. People think that they can shelter their kids and keep their kids from getting into all sorts of shit. But these kids already know everything. The best thing you can do is give them something to focus on."

8   Daniel Horowitz, for one, is rapt. The skinny Dalton junior is dressed geeky slacker style. He has his own blue helmet and his brother's oversize board. Wobbling up and down the half-pipe, Horowitz works up almost enough speed to reach the rim of the half-pipe, then falters and skids to his knees. "This is only my second time," Horowitz says, as an expert skater prepares to drop into the pipe.

9   "You know, the good thing here," Rahmaan Mazone remarks, "is, instead of getting dissed, people support you. The advanced people share equally with the newcomers." They flame out equally, too.

10   The guy doing aerials rockets above the lip and his board keeps going. Suddenly he's Wile E. Coyote hanging in midair. When he crashes and skids in a painful heap to the bottom of the tube, Mazone lets out a whistle. "That is mad worse than getting body-slammed."

11   Next up is Gil Boyd, a compact and muscular 24-year-old. Using his leg strength and unusually low center of gravity, Boyd carves a precise path through the pipe. He resembles a surfer and, as Andy Kessler explains, "in its purest form, skateboarding's very close to surfing, although there's not much surfing in these parts, since the Hudson doesn't break too well."

12   Boyd's aggressive approach brings to mind the new technical dynamics of skate, surf, and snowboard, and people who don't so much ride as carve and shred. "I've been doing this since 1978," Boyd explains when his own ride is ended. "And what people are doing a lot of now is aerials and lip tricks. It all looks treacherous, but the danger is over-rated. There's an art to falling. I've never personally seen a broken neck."

13   Even before the Parks Department had hung a sign on Skate Park, the private sector began applying muscle: Nike, Blades, and others offered to "sponsor" the brand-new park. "I was pleased I was on the Parks Department's side with that one," says Kessler, whose salary as the park's full-time supervisor is provided in part, at least through November, by the $3 daily use fee. Kessler was among those who lobbied to forego big corporate subsidies in favor of one-day events. That way there are no permanent banners to disfigure the park. "Keep the parks as parks," he says.

14   And let them evolve. Except for a single half-pipe in the South Bronx, Skate Park is about the only legal place in all five boroughs where, at about three o'clock every afternoon, you'll find intense bands of skaters (both sexes) caught up in the kind of back side-airs, inverts, lip tricks, and grinds that won't necessarily send their parents reaching for Prozac. "It's a great sport," says Kessler. "There is no one best part about it. It just feels great riding. There's really just nothing like it when you drop into that tube."

QUESTIONS ON CONTENT

1. Name two details you learn about Rahmaan Mazone. _____

_____

2. Why was Riverside Park formerly known as Tuberculosis Park?

_____

3. In your own words, explain how and why Skate Park came into existence.

_____

4. Although they are both skaters, how would you differentiate Daniel Horowitz from Gil Boyd on the basis of Trebay's descriptions of each skater?

_____

5. Write a simple definition for the following terms presented in the last paragraph of Trebay's essay (work with a partner or small group if helpful): back side-airs; inverts; lip tricks; grinds _____

_____

QUESTIONS ON STRATEGY

1. Explain how Trebay's use of Rahmaan Mazone in the introduction of his essay reinforces his purpose. _____

_____

2. Annotate the essay by highlighting all instances of dialogue. How many people do you think Trebay interviewed? _____ Write down one question you think he asked his interview subjects._____

_____

3. How does Trebay go about winning over an audience of readers that might possibly harbor hostile thoughts about skaters? _____

_____

4. Is there a dominant impression in Trebay's descriptive essay? What is it?

_____

Definition

A telephone operator while she was in college and later a missionary for the Jehovah's Witnesses, Gloria Naylor became a writer of novels and stories detailing the African-American woman's condition. In the following essay, Naylor examines a word that shocked her when she heard it in her third grade classroom.

The Meanings of a Word

Gloria Naylor

1   Language is the subject. It is the written form with which I've managed to keep the wolf away from the door and, in diaries, to keep my sanity. In spite of this, I consider the written word inferior to the spoken, and much of the frustration experienced by novelists is the awareness that whatever we manage to capture in even the most transcendent passages falls far short of the richness of life. Dialogue achieves its power in the dynamics of a fleeting moment of sight, sound, smell, and touch.

2   I'm not going to enter the debate here about whether it is language that shapes reality or vice versa. That battle is doomed to be waged whenever we seek intermittent reprieve from the chicken and egg dispute. I will simply take the position that the spoken word, like the written word, amounts to a nonsensical arrangement of sounds or letters without a consensus that assigns "meaning." And building from the meanings of what we hear, we order reality. Words themselves are innocuous; it is the consensus that gives them true power.

3   I remember the first time I heard the word *nigger.* In my third-grade class, our math tests were being passed down the rows, and as I handed the papers to a little boy in back of me, I remarked that once again he had received a much lower mark than I did. He snatched his test from me and spit out that word. Had he called me a nymphomaniac or a necrophiliac, I couldn't have been more puzzled. I didn't know what a nigger was, but I knew that whatever it meant, it was something he shouldn't have called me. This was verified when I raised my hand, and in a loud voice repeated what he had said and watched the teacher scold him for using a "bad" word. I was later to go home and ask the inevitable question that every black parent must face—"Mommy, what does *nigger* mean?"

4   And what exactly did it mean? Thinking back, I realize that this could not have been the first time the word was used in my presence. I was part of a large extended family that had migrated from the rural South after World War II and formed a close-knit network that gravitated around my maternal grandparents. Their ground-floor apartment in one of the buildings they owned in Harlem was a weekend mecca for my immediate family, along with countless aunts, uncles, and cousins who brought along assorted friends. It was a bustling and open house with assorted neighbors and tenants popping in and out to exchange bits of gossip, pick up an old quarrel, or referee the ongoing checkers game in which my grandmother cheated shamelessly. They were all there to let down their hair and put up their feet after a week of labor in the factories, laundries, and shipyards of New York.

5   Amid the clamor, which could reach deafening proportions—two or three conversations going on simultaneously, punctuated by the sound of a baby's crying somewhere in the back rooms or out on the street—there was still a rigid set of rules about what was said and how. Older children were sent out of the living room when it was time to get into the juicy details about "you-know-who" up on the third floor who had gone and gotten herself "p-r-e-g-n-a-n-t!" But my parents, knowing that I could spell well beyond my years, always demanded that I follow the others out to play. Beyond sexual misconduct and death, everything else was considered harmless for our young ears. And so among the anecdotes of the triumphs and disappointments in the various workings of their lives, the word *nigger* was used in my presence, but it was set within contexts and inflections that caused it to register in my mind as something else.

6   In the singular, the word was always applied to a man who had distinguished himself in some situation that brought their approval for his strength, intelligence, or drive:

7   "Did Johnny *really* do that?"

8   "I'm telling you, that nigger pulled in $6,000 of overtime last year. Said he got enough for a down payment on a house."

9   When used with a possessive adjective by a woman—"my nigger"—it became a term of endearment for her husband or boyfriend. But it could be more than just a term applied to a man. In their mouths it became the pure essence of manhood—a disembodied force that channeled their past history of struggle and present survival against the odds into a victorious statement of being: "Yeah, that old foreman found out quick enough—you don't mess with a nigger."

10   In the plural, it became a description of some group within the community that had overstepped the bounds of decency as my family defined it. Parents who neglected their children, a drunken couple who fought in public, people who simply refused to look for work, those with excessively dirty mouths or unkempt households were all "trifling niggers." This particular circle could forgive hard times, unemployment, the occasional bout of depression—they had gone through all of that themselves—but the unforgivable sin was a lack of self-respect.

11   A woman could never be a "nigger" in the singular, with its connotation of confirming worth. The noun *girl* was its closest equivalent in that sense, but only when used in direct address and regardless of the gender doing the addressing. *Girl* was a token of respect for a woman. The one-syllable word was drawn out to sound like three in recognition of the extra ounce of wit, nerve, or daring that the woman had shown in the situation under discussion.

12   "G-i-r-l, stop. You mean you said that to his face?"

13   But if the word was used in a third-person reference or shortened so that it almost snapped out of the mouth, it always involved some element of communal disapproval. And age became an important factor in these exchanges. It was only between individuals of the same generation, or from any older person to a younger (but never the other way around), that *girl* would be considered a compliment.

14   I don't agree with the argument that use of the word *nigger* at this social stratum of the black community was an internalization of racism. The dynamics were the exact opposite: the people in my grandmother's living room took a word that whites used to signify worthlessness or degradation and rendered it impotent. Gathering there together, they transformed *nigger* to signify the varied and complex human beings they knew themselves to be. If the word was to disappear totally from the mouths of even the most liberal of white society, no one in that room was naive enough to believe it would disappear from white minds. Meeting the word head-on, they proved it had absolutely nothing to do with the way they were determined to live their lives.

15   So there must have been dozens of times that *nigger* was spoken in front of me before I reached the third grade. But I didn't "hear" it until it was said by a small pair of lips that had already learned it could be a way to humiliate me. That was the word I went home and asked my mother about. And since she knew that I had to grow up in America, she took me in her lap and explained.

QUESTIONS ON CONTENT

1. What does Naylor mean by the sentence in paragraph 2, "Words themselves are innocuous; it is the consensus that gives them true power"? Rephrase this thought in your own words. _____

_____

2. What do paragraphs 4 and 5 have to do with Naylor's subject? Explain.

_____

3. Annotate Naylor's essay by underlining each definition she offers. How does Naylor's hearing of the word *nigger* within her black community contrast with her hearing of the same word by "a small pair of lips that had already learned it could be a way to humiliate me"?_____

_____

_____

QUESTIONS ON STRATEGY

1. Why does Naylor delay the focus on her subject until the beginning of paragraph 3?_____

_____

Does this strategy work? Why or why not? _____

_____

2. What strategy or strategies does Naylor use to define her subject in paragraphs 8, 9, 10, and 11? _____

_____

_____

3. Why does the writer conclude the way she does? What is the impact of this

ending on her audience? _____

_____

4. What is Naylor's purpose in this essay?_____

_____

CRITICAL THINKING IN CONNECTING TEXTS

Return to the opening quotation for this chapter on page 235. In these lines, poet William Blake describes the effects of close observation on a patient and careful observer. Each of the four lines contains a separate metaphor to describe the observer's world. Throughout this chapter, you've read essays and excerpts by writers who have used not only their eyes but also their other senses to observe the world and to convey impressions and information about their subjects. While Grant and Trebay focus on concrete subjects in their essays, Delacruz and Naylor focus on abstract ones.

Working with a partner or small group, brainstorm to come up with two lists: a list for concrete subjects for describing or defining and a list of abstract subjects. Now see if you can agree within your group on a specific purpose, audience, and strategy for describing or defining each subject on your two lists. Continue your brainstorming to come up with at least one metaphor or simile that might be helpful in describing or defining each of the subjects you have listed. Keep a record of this brainstorming session to use as material for future essays.

**For more writing resources, be sure to see the
Longman English Pages Website at
http://longman.awl.com/englishpages**

CHAPTER 10

Making Connections: Process and Cause/Effect

Like narration, process suggests ongoing movement and continuous action. The emphasis in a process theme, however, is on the *how*, rather than the *what*.

—*Frank D'Angelo, writing teacher*

In the question of cause and effect, there can be many people who imagine that lightning is the cause of thunder because the thunder comes after the lightning. . . . But *is* lightning the cause of thunder?

—*Jostein Gaarder, from* Sophie's World

Preview

In this chapter you will learn
- ▶ how to identify the characteristics of process and cause/effect patterns of essay development
- ▶ how to write effective essays using process and cause/effect to tell readers *how* and to show them *why*
- ▶ how to use a cause/effect map to gather information and organize points
- ▶ how to recognize and use combined patterns of development within an essay
- ▶ how to improve your essays by maintaining an essay progress log
- ▶ how to create a personal time line
- ▶ how use a computer to access information on the World Wide Web

Let's say your health and safety instructor has asked you to write about the recommended procedures for protecting yourself from lightning danger. To explain the steps, you'd want to use a process pattern of essay development. Now let's say your science instructor has asked you to write an essay explaining why lightning occurs, or what happens as a result of a lightning strike. For this essay, you'd choose a cause/effect method of essay development.

As you can see from these examples, process and cause/effect are closely related patterns of thought and essay development. The former explains *how* and the latter investigates *why*. Process and cause/effect allow us to understand, analyze, investigate, and make connections in all aspects of our existence. You might well use both strategies—process and cause/effect—in an essay for a general college audience wanting more information on several aspects of lightning. But you would also use both strategies if you wanted to communicate, either in a conversation or through E-mail, with a group of friends planning a camping trip during a stormy time of year. This chapter will familiarize you with these two patterns of thought by showing you how to apply both process and cause/effect development to your college essays.

CHARACTERISTICS OF PROCESS

Planning a wedding, learning how to create computer files, and changing a car tire are all examples of processes. Like narration, **process** is a writing strategy that presents a series of actions, but rather than focusing on the *what* of events, it explains *how* to do something or how something works. For instance, a narrative focuses on a particular person's experience removing a tree from the front yard in order to communicate the significance of the event for the person involved. A process essay, in contrast, focuses on the steps involved in the tree removal with the intent of informing the reader of the details of the procedure. Process can also explain how something works, for example, how a telephone operates or how a character in a short story is developed. Process writing may include the actions of a person, operations of a machine, or occurrences in nature.

In the following excerpt, the writer implies firsthand knowledge of his subject from personal experience, but his essay is not a narrative because he does not focus on the significance of the experience. Instead, his writing focuses on the process of finding a compatible college roommate:

1   The first step to mastering roommate relations is understanding the process by which housing officials match incoming freshmen. Before school begins, colleges send out roommate questionnaires to find out whether you are a morning or night person, whether you smoke, whether you have ever engaged in acts of bestiality, etc. After careful analysis, the officials then take delight in matching you with people whose answers are the opposite of yours. Once it has been determined that the students in each pair will be entirely incompatible, they are made roommates.

2   At this point, it may seem like the best idea is to answer each question the opposite of how you would normally respond. This is risky, because there's always that rare chance you'll be matched with someone who really *is* a peppy morning person whose hobbies include vacuuming. . . .

3   A better idea is to get matched with that one person to whom you are truly best suited: yourself.

4   To ensure a roommate-free abode, leave your survey entirely blank except for the section below:

> Q: Do you have a medical condition?

> A: Yes, I suffer from severe multiple-environmental-allergy syndrome. I am allergic to dust, air, sounds, and all synthetic or natural materials. That John Travolta Movie of the Week *The Boy in the Plastic Bubble* was based on my life.

5   If by some fluke the above strategy fails, resign yourself to spending the next year living in an enclosed space with a complete stranger, most likely one who does sleep in a plastic bubble. To pave the way for a smooth transition, most colleges advise contacting your designated roommate before you actually meet. This is a good idea; it allows you to ask personal, probing questions to make sure he or she is the right match for you: (1) Do you own a CD player and/or a TV? (2) A car? (3) Do you have wealthy parents who send generous care packages to share with your roommates? (4) Do you have a girlfriend or boyfriend at a nearby school, where you will spend evenings and weekends? (5) Do you require any special breathing apparatus?

6   Of course, you've arrived early enough on moving day to take the bigger closet, the larger desk, and the unstained mattress before your roommate gets there. When he finally arrives, make him feel like a guest in your home. Show him where he'll be sleeping. Then treat him to dinner at the cafeteria to make others think you have a friend.

7   It is especially important to arrive early if you are placed in a triple. When you live as a threesome, it is standard practice for two to team up against the other. If you show up last, your roommates will have already bonded, and you will be outnumbered.

8   What if you do arrive late on moving day? Seize the opportunity to snoop through your roommates' personal belongings while they are plotting against you in the cafeteria. Flee the premises at once if you come across any of the following warning signs: framed prom picture, Garfield memo board; feathered roach clip; stuffed unicorn; alarm clock; broken glass vial and hypodermic needle.

—Dan Zevin, from "Roommatism"

Notice that Zevin's process demonstrates the following characteristics:

- **The importance, range, or difficulty of the process is clearly indicated.**
  Zevin begins with a thesis that includes the importance of the process: "The first step to mastering roommate relations is understanding the process by which housing officials match incoming freshmen."

- **The process is structured or broken down into a series of separate steps.**
  Zevin outlines the first step in the process in paragraph 1: understanding the process that officials use. In paragraph 2, he proceeds to the second step, filling out the questionnaire. In paragraph 5, Zevin moves from the questionnaire to contacting the roommate; in paragraphs 6, 7, and 8, he continues with the moving day. Zevin uses cue words to delineate each step in the process for his readers. Beginning with the word "first" in paragraph 1, Zevin thoughtfully signals his audience with cue words such as "Before school begins," "After careful analysis," "Once it has been determined," "At this point," "To pave the way," and "When he finally arrives."

- **The writer includes information on any resources needed for successful completion of the process.**
  For Zevin, these materials include a set of specific questions to ask the prospective Roommate. For example, in paragraph 5, he asks, "Do you have wealthy parents who send generous care packages to share with your roommate?"

- **Throughout the explanation of the process, the writer maintains a consistent tense.**
  Zevin uses the present tense to explain his process: "*leave* your survey entirely blank" and "*resign* yourself to spending the next year."

To see another example of process in a college essay, read the model in the next section.

MODEL WITH KEY QUESTIONS

This student wanted to have a little fun with his subject and offer some light-hearted advice to his reader. As you read this "how-to" essay, try to identify the process characteristics just discussed.

SURVIVAL TACTICS FOR A FIRST DATE
Robert Amerson

When Robert Amerson began his writing class, he expressed concern about how long it usually took him to draft an essay. He was under the impression that most writers quickly "hammered out" near-perfect drafts at the keyboard. Over the course of the semester, Robert's classroom experience allowed him to feel more comfortable with his writing process, and he used his knowledge of such subjects as fishing and professional basketball in his essays. Robert plans to pursue a career in economics and looks forward to writing reports related to economic issues.

1   A first date can range from between one of the best experiences of your life to one of the most humiliating episodes you ever experience. My goal is not to guarantee that all your dates will be wonderful romantic encounters. My goal is simply to provide you with five chronological steps to get you through the date alive.

2   The first step is to call your potential date and make arrangements. The first call to your potential suitor is one that has many pitfalls. Preparing for this call involves the same type of planning used to stage a coup. As with a coup, timing as well as skill is essential. This does not mean you must use guerrilla tactics; you may be a great fighter or lover, but if you go in for the kill too soon, you will fail. There are two basic phone call rules: Rule number one is, "Do not call too soon after meeting." Basically, the rule of thumb for your first phone call is to appear aloof and busy, not desperate and lonely. You don't want your date envisioning a night with a potential stalker. To further expound on rule number one, do not call the same night that you meet. Do not call every hour the next day leaving messages. Generally, a good time for calling is between three to four days after your first acquaintance.

3   Remember, rule number two: "Do not appear too eager." This rule is also vital to ensuring that your date will not be washing her hair the night that you plan to go out. Your first phone call is not the time to start planning the wedding or getting the details prepared for a joint banking account. Your first phone call should be like shaving. Be careful, but get it done quickly. After this, you should prepare yourself for the first meeting.

4   The next step in surviving your first date includes your arrival and introduction. You do not want to be too late, or too early. When you arrive, appear confident, but not arrogant. Your introductions should be precise and short. Do not go into a full personal life story when introducing yourself for the first time. It is very important that you leave something for your date's imagination. Try to stay calm and make eye contact even if you are desperate, for no one is attracted to a nervous wreck. If you decide to shake your date's hand, you better be aware if your palms are sweaty because this will be a drastic turn-off and a flag of nervousness. The environment you choose to take your date to will also reflect on your first impression.

5   The next step to surviving your first date is to use proper manners at the dinner table. Do not use your fingers unless it is sushi. You do not want to watch your date eat, because usually this will embarrass the date. More importantly

do not dare help yourself to your date's dinner. When dinner is over and you receive the check, do not get crafty and tell your date you left your checkbook at
home; you should offer to pay, unless you have agreed before to a different
arrangement. By the end of the dinner, you should have some idea of how the
date is going.

6   The fifth step is to make a decision about whether the date should continue.
If your innate feelings are telling you that your date wants to go home right now,
do not insist on prolonging the date. You may continue to a movie, or you may decide your date has lost interest in you. If this is the case, do not lose your in-
tegrity, rushing your partner home at seventy miles per hour. This will only result
in your losing the next date you might have with this person.

7   The last step is the most anxiety-provoking. How do you drop your date off at
home? Should you kiss her? Should you instead just open the car door for her
hoping she exits quickly? The timing for this last step is critical. You need to proceed slowly and cautiously. Do not grab her and kiss her roughly, but instead
watch her reactions carefully as you walk her to her front door and perhaps linger
there for a few minutes discussing the evening. If at this point you think a kiss
would be welcome, go for it! If, on the other hand, you get the feeling that she
never wants to see you again, it's time to get back in your car and cross this experience off of your list. In short, for this last step, expect nothing, and be sensitive to your date's reactions.

8   These steps should be strictly followed to avoid some of the pitfalls of the
first date. While a good first date can be a wonderful, memorable experience, a
bad date can be costly, time-consuming, and terribly embarrassing.

 **KEY QUESTIONS**

1. **PURPOSE** What clues do you find in paragraph 1 to reveal Amerson's target audience and his purpose? _____

   _____

2. **FOCUS** Underline Amerson's thesis. In what way does the thesis limit the
   subject of dating? _____

   _____

3. **MATERIAL** Which step in the process is explained in the most explicit detail and why? _____

_____

4. **STRUCTURE** What steps are involved in the process? Write the steps briefly.

_____

_____

Return to the essay and circle all cue words that take readers from one step to another.

5. **STYLE** Find one piece of useful information the author shares about the process; write it in the following space. _____

_____

GUIDELINES FOR WRITING PROCESS

Identify Your Purpose and Audience

You will want to choose a process pattern of development for your essay if your subject is how a procedure is performed or how a phenomenon works. If you have an accurate sense of the interests and concerns of your audience, you'll be more likely to write a useful "how-to" essay. Ask yourself what your audience might already know about the process and what strategies you might use to make the procedure easier for them to understand. For instance, if you reread Dan Zevin's essay (pp. 272–273), you'll see that his real purpose is not to explain the process of selecting a suitable roommate; instead, Zevin wants to express his opinion and share his humor with readers. For Zevin, process is a writing strategy that he can use to poke fun at some of the practices that college officials and students engage in when they're involved in roommate selection. If you were asked in a psychology class to write an essay focusing on how to find a compatible roommate, your purpose and your audience would be quite different.

Ask yourself questions about your audience: Do you want to stress to these readers the importance, the complexity, or the humorous nature of the process? Are there positive or negative results that they need to know about? Do you want to convince your audience to begin an activity or learn a new skill?

Practice 10.1   Look at the following process writing situations. Write down a few words identifying purpose and the audience's knowledge of the subject. The first example has been done for you.

Subject	Audience	Purpose	Knowledge of Subject
Weight-training	Current trainers	Inform of new procedures	In depth
Weight-training	General (no experience)	_____	_____
Computer use	Current users	_____	_____
Computer use	Nonusers	_____	_____
Forming campus club	College students	_____	_____

◆ ◆ ◆

Focus Your Subject

Once you've identified your purpose and audience, check to make sure that your subject—the process to be explained—is neither too broad nor too limited. For example, let's say that you are experienced in antique refinishing and would like to explain the process to those who might be interested in this hobby. However, as an expert, you become too involved in the prospect of explaining every type of antique refinishing and you wind up trying to write about several different finishes and the steps involved in each. The consequence of your enthusiasm could very well be total reader confusion! Look again at "Survival Tactics for a First Date." Robert Amerson does not attempt to explain the entire dating process but instead focuses on the first date. Similarly, Dan Zevin knows better than to write about all roommates and thus limits his subject to college roommates.

Practice 10.2   Complete the following sentences, thinking about focusing on a subject for process development.

1. One process I may have more information about than the average person is

_____

2. What type of audience might be interested in learning about the process?

_____

3. If the entire process is too complex to write about in an essay, I might focus on

_____

4. What information could I share on this process that might be particularly

useful or enlightening?_____

_____

◆ ◆ ◆

Once you've focused your subject, you will want to create a thesis that names the process and includes a controlling idea. This should include a statement about **range**—the extent of the subject or the boundaries placed on the subject. This controlling idea is the main point you want to make about the process. Looking again at Amerson's essay, you'll see that the thesis in paragraph 1 names the process (going on the first date), and the controlling idea (that it's a feat just to survive the first date).

Practice 10.3 Examine the following subjects and then create a complete thesis—a sentence that names the process (your subject) and includes a controlling idea (indication of the range, difficulty, or importance of the process). The first subject has been completed for you.

Subject: How to re-enter college as an adult student

Controlling idea: Presents some unique challenges

Thesis: Although college reentry presents several unique challenges for an adult, the process can become relatively painless if one follows five simple steps.

Subject: How to plan a dinner party

Controlling idea: _____

Thesis: _____

_____

_____

Subject: How to find employment

Controlling idea: _____

Thesis: _____

_____

◆ ◆ ◆

Structure the Process Using Steps and Cue Words

Have you ever tried to make a cake only to discover that you put the wet ingredients into the dry ones too soon? If you're registering for new classes, what happens if you don't proceed in the required sequence of events? In both cases, this often means starting over again. For successful process writing, a clear step-by-step structure is of the utmost importance to your audience. To make sure that your essay is clearly structured, organize your material by identifying the steps in your process and then ordering those steps in an outline or list. Notice that for Zevin and Amerson, this order is chronological.

Practice 10.4 To test your ability to recognize a sequence of steps in a process, read Craig Swanson's essay "The Turning Point" (pp. 302–303), and complete the series of actions begun in the following list:

Wedge ball of clay about size of cantaloupe

Slice in half on a wire

Slam one half on wedging board

_____

_____

_____

◆ ◆ ◆

When you are organizing your material, try grouping related individual steps into paragraphs. For instance, although Amerson's discussion of first date survival includes many individual instructions, he groups those related to the phone call together in paragraph 2. When Amerson moves on to the steps involved in arriving for the date, he groups them together in paragraph 4. This grouping of material in process development helps your audience to see the main stages or divisions of a whole process, and it can offer you a way to order your paragraphs. Working from an outline that clearly indicates main stages or divisions of a process can also prevent a possibly confusing list of small steps. The larger pattern will help your readers by giving them a sense of the process as a whole.

Practice 10.5 Reread Dan Zevin's excerpt (pp. 272–273). In the following space list the three larger groups that Zevin connects with his process.

_____

_____

◆ ◆ ◆

In addition to using a step-by-step structure, you will want to signal a clear sequence from one step to the next by using cue words and phrases such as *first, second, next, before you add, as you complete this step,* and others found in the table of cue words (pp. 187–188).

Explain Every Step with Precise Detail

You will want to gather enough material about your process to make each step totally clear for your audience. You may find it helpful to go through the process based on your outline or rough draft to see if your instructions are adequate. If you write about natural or technical processes, you may need information from outside sources. For example, if you're explaining the procedure for dissecting a frog, you may want to consult your biology notes or text. If you're explaining a social process, such as the procedure for taking a petition to the state congress, you may need to track down additional information by calling or E-mailing your congressional representative or consulting information in a government booklet or document.

Once you feel that you've gathered enough material to explain your process, use precise language and specific detail to help the reader visualize the process. Notice that Amerson's process is aided by comparisons: "Your first phone call should be like shaving. Be careful, but get it done quickly." Amerson also uses action words; he advises his readers, "Do not *grab* her and *kiss* her roughly, but instead *watch* her reactions carefully."

Check to see that, especially for the more challenging steps of your process, you have given your audience tips, warnings, or concrete suggestions—in other words, any additional information that might be helpful. It's also a good idea to explain *why* certain steps are necessary. For example, rather than just writing, "lay the hubcap on the ground with the screws inside," you might also add, "this will prevent the screws from rolling out into the street or getting lost from your sight."

Practice 10.6 Read Craig Swanson's essay "The Turning Point" (pp. 302–303) and complete the following.

Two effective action words: _____

One comparison: _____

A phrase that provides a helpful tip, suggestion, or warning: _____

_____

◆ ◆ ◆

Maintain a Consistent Tense and Point of View

In drafting your essay, decide on an appropriate tense and point of view, and keep these consistent throughout your writing. If you are offering instructions in your essay, it is best to use the **second person** point of view—*you, your, yours*—and the present tense, as Zevin and Amerson do. If you are explaining a process that you have become familiar with from watching someone else perform it, as Swanson does in "The Turning Point," or if you are explaining how something is done, use the **third person**—*he, his, him* or *she, her, hers*—and the past tense. If you want to emphasize the impersonal nature of the process, use the **passive voice,** a voice in writing in which the subject does not perform any action but instead is acted upon by an outside agent.

To observe the effect of the passive voice, read the following excerpt. Note that the passive voice works for this writer because he wants to convey a sense of helplessness and to convince his audience of the cruelty of the process. The phrases in the passive voice are italicized:

> Off the coast of Costa Rica, the *Maria Luisa,* a tuna fishing boat, sets its net around a school of disporting dolphins. In the eastern tropical Pacific, the presence of dolphins often indicates yellowfish tuna under the surface. A mechanical winch pulls up the net, and a dolphin *is snagged* by its dorsal fin and *raised* high above the ship. The dolphin writhes and twists. The dorsal fin tears off. The net *is pulled* aboard, as more dolphins *are being maimed* and *drowned.* The crew, intent on the tuna catch, rip the mammals from the net. Some are already dead; others still struggle as they *are thrown* into a chute and *dumped* overboard as . . . "food for the sharks." This day, almost 200 dolphins *have been rendered* into shark food in the process of catching only twelve yellowfin tuna, a worse than normal ratio.
>
> —David R. Brower from *Let the Mountains Talk, Let the Rivers Run*

Define All Necessary Equipment and Terms

Imagine your reader's frustration if you fail to mention any supply or tool essential to the process, no matter how small. Such an omission could very possibly hinder the successful completion of the process you're explaining. In addition, any specialized equipment, terms, or words related to steps in the process that your audience might not know will need to be defined or described, and their role in the process clearly explained.

Practice 10.7 Read the following paragraph explaining the embalming process for a corpse, and then annotate the passage according to the directions that follow below.

The next step is to have at Mr. Jones with a thing called a trocar. This is a long, hollow needle attached to a tube. It is jabbed into the abdomen, poked around the entrails and chest cavity, the contents of which are pumped out and replaced with "cavity fluid." This done, and the hole in the abdomen sewn up, Mr. Jones's face is heavily creamed (to protect the skin from burns which may be caused by leakage of the chemicals), and he is covered with a sheet and left unmolested for a while. But not for long—there is more, much more, in store for him. He has been embalmed, but not yet restored, and the best time to start the restorative work is eight to ten hours after embalming, when the tissues have become firm and dry.

—Jessica Mitford, from *The American Way of Death*

1. Circle the words that indicate the tense. Indicate in the margin whether Mitford has used active or passive voice.
2. Find and put a check by any equipment the writer mentions.
3. Find and underline any terms and their definitions.

◆ ◆ ◆

Conclude Thoughtfully

Process can be an enjoyable pattern of essay development to write because sometimes the series of steps seem to "write themselves" once you start drafting. However, one potential pitfall in creating a successful essay using process occurs when writers stop writing with the last step, mistakenly thinking that they are finished.

Try to go beyond the final step in the process to give your audience a sense that they understand not only the procedure but also the significance of the process. It's not enough that your readers have learned from you how to complete the process. Your essay should also affect readers in some meaningful way—it may make them laugh, as in the case of Zevin's essay, or it may make them act differently on a date, as in the case of Amerson's essay. It may also make them think about an issue in a way that they have never thought about it before, as is the case with the process paragraph on tuna fishing, which encourages readers to think about wildlife conservation, or the paragraph about embalming corpses, which forces the audience to consider the expense of death in America.

STRATEGIES FOR WRITING PROCESS

1. **PURPOSE** Identify your intended audience and what you want them to learn from the process you write about.

2. **FOCUS** Limit your subject. In your thesis, name the process and include a controlling idea—a comment on the significance, importance, or scope of the process.

3. **MATERIAL** In prewriting, gather sufficient material to explain the process thoroughly and clearly. In your drafting and revising, elaborate on every step in the process, explain all equipment needed, and define any unfamiliar terms. Be sure to include suggestions for particularly difficult steps as well as warnings of actions to avoid in the procedure.

4. **STRUCTURE** Organize your essay so that you present a sequence of steps in a chronological order or the most helpful order to complete the process. If your process is complicated, break the steps into paragraphs, grouping smaller steps within these larger main stages. Use cue words to take your reader from one step to the next.

5. **STYLE** Use precise, accurate words and phrases that will help your audience visualize all objects and actions connected with the process.

OPTIONS FOR WRITING ESSAYS USING PROCESS

As you work through any of the following writing options, remember to keep your audience interested by conveying the significance of the process as you explain it.

1. Getting a job requires hard work and planning. If you have experience to draw from, write an essay explaining the process. You might include sources such as newspaper ads, employment agencies, or college placement centers. You might also discuss the application and interview process, resumes, and follow-up procedures after the interview.

2. Many of us have tried or want to try some personal improvement program. Perhaps you have some knowledge of body building, aerobics, speed reading, or other program. Explain the process involved in a particular area.

3. If you have a particular recipe or special holiday dish that is reflective of your culture or that has been handed down to you from relative, write an essay detailing the process of creating and serving this dish. If you don't have enough information, interview your relative and get sufficient material to explain the process effectively.

4. Write an essay explaining a process related to your major or hobby. For example, if your major is in a health-related field, you might want to explain the steps in administering CPR. If your hobby is sculpting, you could explain the steps involved in creating a sculpture of the human head.

Challenge Option: Combining Patterns

Robert Amerson's essay (pp. 275–276) explains the process of the first date; Dan Zevin's (pp. 272–273) deals with a different kind of relationship: the one you have with a college roommate. Choose another subject related to interpersonal relationships—for example, surviving a job with a boss you hate, succeeding in a required college class when you dislike the instructor, disciplining a toddler, or coping with a drug-addicted family member. Write an essay in which you use two patterns of development: first, *narration* to tell about your own experience, and second, *process* to explain to your readers how something is done.

CHARACTERISTICS OF CAUSE/EFFECT

While a process pattern of development explains *how,* cause/effect development explores *why.* **Cause** is a writing strategy concerned with why something happens; **effect** focuses on results or consequences. Think about watching a game of pool: one ball (let's say the "cause" ball) strikes another, and then this second ball (the "effect" ball) moves as a result. But what if this "effect" ball then rolls on and strikes another ball? Doesn't it become a "cause" ball at this point? Even in a basic example such as this one, we can see a model for cause/effect thinking and how a kind of chain reaction can change an effect into a cause. Consider the following:

Causes		Effects
too much rain	*leads to*	flooding
flooding	*leads to*	destruction of crops
loss of crops	*leads to*	shortage of product
shortage of product	*leads to*	rise in market price

While these examples may seem easy to grasp, sometimes occurrences appear to be related when they are not. Think about the next to last example: "loss of crops leads to shortage of product." The flooding was hindering the orange crop in California, but perhaps the Florida weather was producing an abundant and high grade orange crop. In this case, shortage of product in California would not lead to a rise in market price nationwide.

A cause-and-effect pattern of development is illustrated in the following excerpt from an essay focusing on college drinking:

1   Since college students have limited responsibilities, they can usually drink heavily without serious repercussions. Drunken college students do sometimes get into trouble, of course. But this is not a drinking problem; it is a drinking *behavior* problem. . . .

2   Students may drink to let off steam, or drink to get drunk, or boast about how much they can drink without puking. But college drinking, by and large, remains social drinking. UO [University of Oregon] students could buy a half-rack of Henry Weinhard's Ale and drink at home. But instead they pay a lot more to drink at [bars like] Rennie's or Max's because they want to be around other people. . . .

3   Drinking isn't only something to do—it's something everyone can do together. It's how many freshmen begin meeting people. "You don't know anybody, and then somebody hands you a beer and pretty soon you're hanging out with a bunch of guys," says Eric, a nineteen-year-old sophomore, remembering his first days in college. Freshmen drink hard early on: a 1995 Harvard study of college freshmen found that 70 percent binge drink in their first semester. But after students find their social circle (and worship once or twice at the Temple of the Porcelain God), many decide to drink infrequently or not at all. . . .

4   Research finds that college students who drink heavily have lower grades than those who drink moderately or not at all. But these students aren't chemistry majors whose grades and classes will be critical for graduate school and future careers. They tend to be business or social science majors who will probably end up in jobs that have little to do with their academic studies. "The truth is that most students can go out drinking several nights a week and get by," says [Carl] Wartenburg, the Swarthmore dean [of admissions].

5   College students get into trouble not because they drink to get drunk but because they get drunk to be irresponsible. "I was drunk" is a get-out-of-jail-free card for college students who act like idiots, get into fights, climb into construction equipment, or behave in other unacceptable or embarrassing ways. It works because friends know that drinking makes people lose control and they may want to use alcohol as an excuse for their own behavior, especially sexual behavior. According to the Harvard study, 41 percent of frequent binge drinkers engage in unplanned sexual activity, as opposed to only 4 percent for non-binge drinkers.

—Ed Carson, from "Purging Bingeing"

Notice that Carson's development of cause and effect demonstrates the following characteristics:

- **The writer presents a reasonable thesis connected to logical cause/effect development. The subject is an event, occurrence or phenomenon, and the writer focuses on cause, effect, or both.**
  Carson's thesis, the last sentence of paragraph 1, includes the subject, college drinking, and then focuses the subject by stating that the real problem with college drinking is the behavior that results. This controlling idea seems reasonable. Notice also that the thesis presents a situation—college drinking—and then focuses on the effects of this situation.

- **The writer uses detail to develop one or more causes or effects connected with an event or occurrence; the writer may focus on causes, on effects, or on a combination of both.**
  In paragraphs 2 and 3, Carson discusses some possible causes of college drinking: letting off steam, getting drunk, being able to boast about drinking capacity, meeting new people, or being quickly accepted at parties. In paragraphs 4 and 5, the focus shifts to the effects of this drinking: lower grades, acting idiotically, getting into fights, performing dangerous feats like "climb[ing] into construction equipment," or engaging in unplanned sexual activities.

- **The cause/effect development has a particular structure.**
  You can see that Carson supports his thesis on the problematic effects of college drinking with an overview of the causes and their connection to *social* drinking in college. This structure helps Carson link the troubling effects of campus drinking to supposedly safer "social" college drinking.

To see how cause/effect works within a college essay, read the model in the next section to determine how many of the characteristics just discussed you can identify.

MODEL WITH KEY QUESTIONS

Student writer Swarupa Reddy has lived in the United States for several years, having come from India as a young woman. Astounded and alarmed by television's impact on American youth, she wanted to share her concern with readers.

TV AS A CULPRIT
Swarupa Reddy

Swarupa Reddy reports that the strategies she learned in her first college writing class helped her "build the foundation to complete freshman composition and other transfer-level English courses." In addition to raising a family, Swarupa is currently taking courses to prepare her for transfer to a four-year university. She intends to pursue a career in one of the health professions.

1   Our minds are rotting away and we might not know it. This is due to a destructive invention, a culprit known as television. Though television has kept families in their homes with countless hours of entertainment, it has also ended up destroying family ritual, affecting academic performance, and promoting sex and violence.

2   One effect of television in our current time is the destruction of family ritual. Once upon a time, so we have been told, families talked with each other. They actually gathered together and shared ideas, interests, and experiences. Since television, this apparently does not occur in most families. Family meals have taken a definite downward toll since the rise of television. At one time families would actually gather around the table for a meal and some family discussion. This was the place and time that families would work out a lot of problems related to school, sports, work, and relations with the opposite sex. Television has changed this, however, with the family members all staring at the tube rather than looking at each other, and listening to television programs rather than talking. No longer is there the shared mealtime ritual of the family.

3   In addition or possibly as a result of the breakdown of family ritual, television has also affected the schoolwork and performance of children and teenagers. Statistics released recently reveal that many more elementary, junior high, and high school students watch television than twenty years ago, and that these children and teens are watching for more extended periods of time than ever before. The results are discouraging to teachers, parents, and school officials. Studies show that those students who watch ten or more hours of television per week—an increasing number—receive lower grades than their counterparts who do not watch television.

4   Finally, television actually promotes sex and violence. Programs that contain sex and violence may impress upon a child the wrong messages, whereas an adult may know how to distinguish between what is proper and what isn't. In a long-term study on the effect of television on young viewers conducted by Stanford University, participants watched certain programs and were then themselves

watched through one-way mirrors. The youngsters "acted out" more violently, hitting, throwing and abusing their toys more frequently after watching such programs. In addition, the carefree and casual use of sex on television has influenced many viewers to want to engage in sex, without acknowledging any of the dangers of unsafe sex. Young viewers in both instances "do as T.V. does," and then they find that actions that work in the television world have different results in the real world.

5   At the risk of becoming social outcasts for criticizing this accepted American phenomenon, we must start to limit the use of television before this culprit brings about even more destruction to our families, our children, and our way of life.

KEY QUESTIONS
....

1. **PURPOSE** What is the connection the writer wants the reader to make between television and family values?_____

_____

2. **FOCUS** In her thesis, does Reddy focus on causes or effects?

_____

Reddy further focuses the subject by including a plan of development in her thesis. What three areas will she explore in her essay?_____

_____

3. **MATERIAL** What outside sources of information does the writer use for evidence? _____

_____

4. **STRUCTURE** Do you think Reddy's ordering of her three points is effective?

_____ Reread the essay and annotate it by underlining all cue words that signal the reader of a cause or effect relationship. Why do you think Reddy ends with sex and violence as her last point?_____

_____

5. **STYLE** In what way does Reddy's conclusion connect to her introduction and offer the reader a sense of closure? Write down specific phrases that reinforce her introduction. _____

_____

GUIDELINES FOR WRITING CAUSE/EFFECT

Determine Purpose and Audience

You will want to choose a cause/effect pattern of development if your purpose in your essay is to show connections—*why* something happens or what *results* from a situation, occurrence, or even an attitude. For instance, why might you want to explore the causes of homelessness in your city? Would your purpose be to inform your audience, or to convince them to vote differently in the next local election? In searching for a subject, think about topics that interest you. Then ask yourself if these topics could also be of interest to a particular audience.

You can use personal experience to discuss causes or effects, in which case you might want to think about changes that have taken place in your own lifetime, or you can write from what you know or can find out about causes or effects related to a particular situation. When you have a few possibilities written down, ask yourself if you care about this subject enough to explore it in an essay, and what your purpose might be in sharing the causes, effects, or both with your audience.

To illustrate, the excerpt from "Purging Bingeing" (p. 286), explores the causes and effects of college drinking. Writer Ed Carson had recently graduated from the University of Oregon at the time he wrote his essay. It's probable that Carson felt college drinking was misunderstood by many readers, and that as a recent college graduate, he had a more realistic perspective. He chose to interview college students, engage in more research, and build a body of evidence to persuade his audience that the behavior connected with college drinking is more of a problem than the drinking itself. Once he had determined his purpose and audience, it was relatively easy for Carson to focus his subject on a working thesis and begin to gather information in prewriting.

Practice 10.8 As an idea-generating activity, think about possible subjects of interest to you—situations, occurrences, happenings, attitudes, or phenomena in the physical world. Write down three subjects that you might consider, along with a particular audience you'd like to address and your purpose in writing.

<u>Subject</u>	<u>Audience</u>	<u>Purpose</u>
1. _____	_____	_____
2. _____	_____	_____
3. _____	_____	_____

◆ ◆ ◆

Focus Your Subject

Once you have an idea of a subject for cause/effect development, ask yourself whether you are more interested in exploring the subject from the point of view of causes, effects, or both. In prewriting it may be helpful to note both causes and effects connected with a situation so that you can better judge which direction to pursue.

Writers can explore two types of cause/effect connections: **immediate connections**—those that have occurred recently and are fairly obvious—and **remote connections**—those that are not so obvious or that might have come about quite some time ago. For example, Swarupa Reddy asserts in her thesis that television viewing may not only destroy family ritual and affect academic performance, but also lead to an increase in teen sexual activity and violent behavior. When Reddy brainstormed ways she could focus on her subject, she noticed that many families don't sit around a table and talk about their day at dinner time. Instead they stare at the television. This negative effect of television on families was immediately visible to the writer. As she continued to explore more remote connections, she remembered reading a study linking violent activities with the viewing of certain television programs, and she decided to pursue this effect also.

Notice that both Reddy and Carson focus on a few specific causes or effects. It would not be practical to discuss all of the causes or the effects of college drinking or television viewing. Ask yourself, "Is this cause or this effect important enough to develop in an essay?" Although Carson knew that two effects of excessive drinking might be throwing up or passing out, he focuses on neither of these all-too-obvious effects. To do so would have distracted readers from Carson's thesis.

Practice 10.9 Return to the subjects you indicated in Practice 10.8. Choose a subject for further exploration and complete the first half of the "Cause/Effect Map" that follows. A **cause/effect map** is a prewriting sheet designed for cause/effect essay planning. Such a map can help you discover and begin to organize your main points. Once you have enough information on your subject, read what you have, decide how you will focus your subject, and write a working thesis in the appropriate space at the bottom of the map.

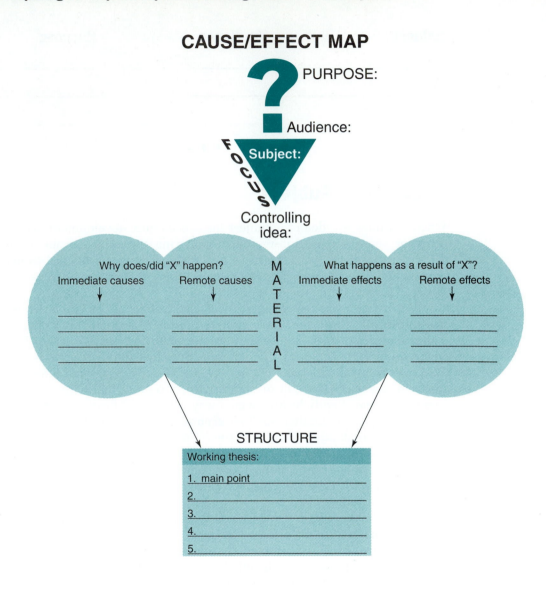

CAUSE/EFFECT MAP

PURPOSE:

Audience:

FOCUS Subject:

Controlling idea:

Why does/did "X" happen?

Immediate causes   Remote causes

M A T E R I A L

What happens as a result of "X"?

Immediate effects   Remote effects

STRUCTURE

Working thesis:

1. main point
2.
3.
4.
5.

◆ ◆ ◆

Sketch Out a Structure: Three Alternate Plans

Once you have a working thesis, you will want to decide on a structure for your essay. Three possible plans—(1) Single Cause/Multiple Effects, (2) Single Effect/Multiple Causes, and (3) Chain Reaction—are shown here.

Plan One: Single Cause/Multiple Effects

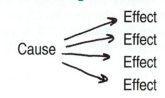

Plan Two: Single Effect/Multiple Causes

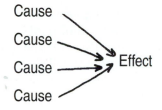

Plan Three: Chain Reaction

Cause ⟶ Leads to first effect ⟶ Leads to second effect ⟶ Leads to third effect

Use the structure, called "Plan One"—which is the one used by Reddy in her essay on the effects of television viewing—if you want to emphasize the effects. How do you decide which effect to put first? You might structure your essay from negative to positive effects, or from obvious effects to more subtle ones, or from local to far-reaching effects. You will want to experiment with order—which cause or effect to put first, second, and so forth.

Notice that the structure called Plan Two is the same as Plan One, only reversed. Use this structure if you want to emphasize the causes of an occurrence or situation. For example, for an economics class essay, this would be an effective way to structure an explanation of the multiple causes of the Great Depression.

Use the structure called Plan Three if your subject has causes or effects that build on each other. For example, if your subject is the celebration of Christmas, your sketch might look something like this:

Original cause for Christmas — Change in holiday to emphasize Santa and gifts — Results in increasing pressure on consumers to spend lots of money — Causes merchants to increase their "hype" and advertising encouraging consumers to spend — Results in new highs in spending, increased stress on celebrants, less emphasis on original cause for celebration.

Practice 10.10 Return to your subject possibilities in Practice 10.9. Examine your notes on causes and effects and choose a structure that you feel would work for your essay. In preparation for drafting, fill in your main points in the order in which you'll first experiment with presenting them.

◆ ◆ ◆

Connect with Cue Words

Because you are seeking to establish a connection between a situation and its causes or its effects, any additional assistance that you can give your audience to allow them to grasp this relationship is helpful. During your writing, refer to the table of cue words (pp. 187–188). Remember that words such as *thus, therefore, because, so, then, consequently, as a result,* and others will help create order in your essay.

Practice 10.11 Read Amitai Etzioni's "McDonald's Is Not Our Kind of Place" (pp. 305–307). Annotate by underlining all cue words you find.

◆ ◆ ◆

Use Specific Details

For every cause or effect you connect with your subject, you will want to use specific details from your own experiences or from outside sources. Notice that when Etzioni asserts that there are multiple effects of teens working at franchises, he supports each effect by giving specific details. For instance in paragraph l0, Etzioni cites the money teens receive as one obvious effect of their working. He continues that while this money may be spent by the poor "to support themselves," middle class students use the money to help pay for college or a car. For many others, the money may provide "an early introduction into trite elements of American consumerism: trendy clothes, trinkets, and whatever else is the fast-moving teen craze."

Avoid Possible Pitfalls

Using cause/effect development successfully in an essay depends not only on your knowledge of a situation but also on your ability to make valid connections between the situation and its causes or its effects. Familiarizing yourself with some common pitfalls of cause/effect writing will make you less likely to make one of these errors in thinking. In reading over your draft or the draft of a fellow student, be sure to point out these errors and revise your draft accordingly.

Oversimplification

One of the most common pitfalls in cause/effect writing is **oversimplification**—attributing only one cause or one effect to a situation. For example, if you tell a friend "I made a horrible grade on the test because I'm bad at multiple choice tests," you're probably ignoring some other factors or causes for your poor performance: you did not study enough, you studied the wrong material, or you were not able to think clearly precisely because you fear multiple choice tests. Quite often we're tempted to oversimplify because we have some bias regarding the subject. To guard against this tendency, avoid subjects that you know you won't be able to approach fairly.

Post Hoc Fallacy

Have you ever washed your car only to have it rain an hour later? You might be tempted to think that it rained *because* you washed your car. You are guilty of what is known as the **post hoc fallacy**—from the Latin phrase *post hoc, ergo propter hoc,* which means "after this, therefore because of this." Don't assume that just because one thing comes before another in time, the first event causes the second to happen. Obviously there will be many times when two events are connected, but when you're writing a college essay, you must be absolutely certain that there is a causal as well as a chronological link in any evidence you present to a reader. For example, when Reddy asserts that television leads to increased sexual activity and violence, she uses the Stanford study of children as a basis of her evidence because these children were observed during the television shows and immediately after. Although Reddy wanted to use an example of a convicted rapist who stated that he had been influenced by television, the writer decided that there was no way of establishing a causal connection in addition to a chronological one.

Practice 10.12 Read the following statements and label them as oversimplification or post hoc fallacy.

1. Increasing numbers of working and single mothers have resulted in uncontrollable and disturbed children. _____

2. Since unemployment has decreased during the present administration, our current President gets credit for employing more Americans than the ex-President._____

3. Because Frank really loves to eat, someday he will be obese.

_____

4. Since Julia was unfaithful to her husband during the same summer she viewed a movie featuring promiscuous behavior, the movie caused her infidelity. _____

◆ ◆ ◆

STRATEGIES FOR WRITING CAUSE/EFFECT

1. **PURPOSE** Identify your audience and what you want them to learn from your exploration of the connections between a situation and its causes or effects.

2. **FOCUS** Once you have a subject, limit your thesis to the causes, effects, or both that you can most effectively develop to support your purpose.

3. **MATERIAL** In prewriting, gather enough material to develop a clear cause/effect relationship. Look for immediate as well as remote connections.

4. **STRUCTURE** Try organizing your essay according to one of the three plans on page 293. Work from a sketch or outline, remembering to insert cue words to clarify relationships.

5. **STYLE** Check your draft for oversimplification and post hoc fallacy, making sure that every word and phrase develops a logical cause/effect connection for your subject. In revising and polishing your introduction and conclusion, be sure that you've captured your readers' interest and made your point about the significance of any causes or effects connected with your subject.

OPTIONS FOR WRITING CAUSE/EFFECT

The following writing options will ask you to use a cause/effect pattern of development in an essay. After you've chosen an option, ask yourself which causes or effects are important and then structure your draft according to one of the alternate plans for this type of development. Examine the draft thoughtfully to identify any pitfalls in reasoning and to determine ways to make the connection between your subject and its causes or effects as clear as possible.

1. Think about a prejudice, attitude, belief, law, or custom that you have questioned. For instance, perhaps you feel the legal driving age should be changed, that women should be allowed in combat situations, or that we should change the way we celebrate the Fourth of July. In an essay, explore possible effects such a change would bring about.

2. Focus on a change or a decision that you've made in your life. What caused you to make the change? Were other people influential in your choice? What happened as a result? In retrospect, are you glad you made the change? Why or why not? In a paragraph, develop the causes or effects connected with your choice.

3. Have you ever fantasized about winning the grand prize in the state lottery—about having millions of dollars to spend? Think about what you would do if this really did happen. Would you travel? Purchase a new car? Spend the money on your family? Make donations to charities? Change the place you live? Quit your job? In an essay, organize the effects of this event into several major changes that would take place and then detail these major changes with specific information.

4. If you have a hobby, pastime, or favorite sport, you know that engaging in this activity gives you pleasure. Write an essay in which you share your reasons for participating in this activity. You can focus on why you became involved, what you get out of the activity, or both.

5. After reading "McDonald's Is Not Our Kind of Place" (pp. 305–307), write a cause/effect essay on the topic of high school or college students working on a part-time or full-time basis. Whether you agree or disagree with Etzioni, you will need to develop causes or effects from your own experience or that of others you know. To strengthen your evidence, you may want to interview other students in your class, asking them to recall the causes and effects of working during their high school years. (For more information on interviews, see Chapter 8.)

Challenge Option: Combining Patterns

Most jobs require employees to perform certain procedures. For example, a salesperson goes through a particular process in assisting a customer, answering questions, executing the sale and completing appropriate paperwork, wrapping or packaging the item that is purchased, and explaining the refund policy of the store. If you have held a job in which you executed a procedure, think and write about the immediate as well as the remote effects of performing this procedure many times in the typical workday. Perhaps one effect was that you developed a particular line of greeting for customers; another may be that you found shortcuts for wrapping the sales item or you discovered that you could keep customers from accidentally taking your pen by attaching it to the sales desk. To use both process and then cause/effect patterns of development, here's how you might want to structure your essay:

- *Introduction and thesis:* Capture audience attention and clearly focus on the process and the effects you'll be discussing.

- *Body paragraphs* (one or more): Explain in detail the procedure you executed on the job.

- *Body paragraph* (one or more): Explore the effects of repeatedly performing this procedure.

- *Conclusion:* Connect the essay's ending to your thesis by thoughtfully commenting on the significance or meaning of these effects on you, on your employers, or on the people you served on the job.

JOURNAL WRITING: CONNECTIONS

Process

Sometimes a mental activity can be clarified by comparing it to a more familiar physical process. Think about some mental activities that you are familiar with, and then see if you can find a physical process with some similarities. For example, maybe studying for an exam is like training for a race; perhaps building your confidence is like weight training. In a journal entry, try to come up with three comparisons. Choose one and write freely about both the overall aspects and the small details, discovering all the connections you can. Try for at least a one-page entry. In another entry, you might respond to this journal writing by noting any new insights or connections you discovered about either the mental activity or the physical process.

Cause/Effect: The Time Line

Remember the billiard balls discussed earlier in this chapter? Now think about an event that happened years ago or quite recently in your own life—one that has caused a sequence of other events to occur. In a journal entry, create a time line, putting approximate dates on each of the effects that resulted from the first event. For example, when you were sixteen you left high school and obtained a full-time, low-wage job. This caused several events:

- Your parents asked you to move out.

- You rented your own apartment.

- You realized after two years on the job that you wanted to go back to school.

- You enrolled in college as a part-time student and received limited financial aid.

Your time line might look something like this:

Left school for job	Got apartment	Quit job	Enrolled in college	Got $ help
	Lived with friend		Decided on major	
January 1995	March 1996	May 1996	September 1997	January 1998

If you find that this entry helps you come up with material for your cause/effect essay, try thinking of another important event in your life and create another time line.

USING THE COMPUTER: CHECKING YOUR GRAMMAR AND FINDING INFORMATION ON THE INTERNET

1. Your word processor probably offers a *grammar check* feature. Experiment with it by applying it to some of your writing. What kinds of "errors" does it catch in your work? If it suggests alternatives to your wording, do you agree with those suggestions? While grammar checkers get mixed reviews from writing instructors and professional writers, they do have the advantage of prompting you to reexamine particular phrases or sentences and consider alternatives. Ask your instructor what she or he thinks.

2. Amitai Etzioni's essay (pp. 305–307) is critical of McDonald's restaurants, especially as places to work. You might have direct experience of your own with working at McDonald's or another fast-food restaurant, and you almost certainly have had experience eating their food! Whether

continued

USING THE COMPUTER: CHECKING YOUR GRAMMAR AND FINDING INFORMATION ON THE INTERNET *continued*

such experiences have been positive or negative, you might be interested in how people have used the Web to promote either a positive or negative image of McDonald's. First, visit McDonald's own Website, *McDonald's.com* ⟨http://www.mcdonalds.com⟩. What do you notice about this site? What kinds of information does it offer? Look up information on employment opportunities. Does what you read sound like your own, or a friend's, experiences with working in a fast-food restaurant? Next, visit *McSpotlight* ⟨http://envirolink.org/mcspotlight⟩. This site includes news, information, discussion groups, and other resources that give an alternative, and mostly negative, view of McDonald's. How is this site different from the "official" McDonald's site? Compare the information both sites offer about a specific issue—the nutrition value of McDonald's food, or working conditions in the restaurants, for example. What do you think?

RESPONDING TO WRITING: KEEPING A PROGRESS LOG

At this point in your English course, you probably have a stash of rough, interim, and final drafts that you have shared with your instructor and perhaps one or more peer editors in your class. In addition, you've probably received written comments on your drafts, verbal comments, perhaps a letter grade, and maybe a list of suggestions. This might be a good time for you to review all your drafts to date and to complete the progress log on page 301. You can then use this information to improve your future essays. The progress log might also form the basis of a writing conference with your instructor.

Before you begin this progress log, find and reread all of your submitted drafts of essays. Note all instructor and peer editor comments. You can now complete each section of the progress log. Enter a plus (+) for any area you feel you've mastered, a minus (−) for any area still needing substantial work, and a check mark (✓) for any area that is basically coming along fine.

When you've completed the progress log, examine it carefully to determine your strengths as well as weaknesses in essay writing. According to your progress log, what appears to be your greatest strength to date?

What area or areas could use improvement?

_____

Refer to this text's table of contents and index to locate information and activities related to essay-writing skills you would like to improve. Review the appropriate sections of your text and ask your instructor for additional information and advice about improving the quality of your essays.

PROGRESS LOG

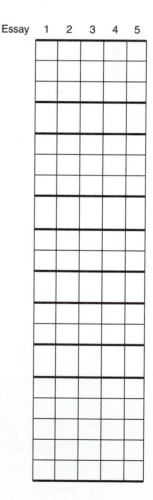

PURPOSE
- Introduction engages audience interest
- Purpose is clear
- Point of view is consistent

FOCUS
- Thesis has subject, controlling idea, appropriate tone
- All main points and details support thesis
- Conclusion connects with thesis

MATERIAL
- Thesis is adequately and clearly supported
- Information reliable, accurate, detailed

STRUCTURE
- Organization of main points is clear
- Cue words signal any shift in thought

STYLE
- Sentence structure is sound and varied
- Word choice is specific and descriptive
- Surface errors are not distracting
- Manuscript format is correct
- Writer's unique voice comes through

Essay   1   2   3   4   5

READINGS AND ADDITIONAL ACTIVITIES

Process

Craig Swanson majored in math and computer science, completed his graduate work in artificial intelligence, and loves to write. He asserts, "If I could write all day long, I'd be a very happy man." As you read the following essay, notice how Swanson combines personal narrative with process: at the same time Swanson tells about his father and what his hobby means to him, he explains how to "throw" a pot, and he also hints at the significance of finding something in life that is really enjoyable.

The Turning Point

Craig Swanson

1 Dad lost his job last summer. They say that it was due to political reasons. After twenty years in the government it was a shock to us all. Dad never talked much about what he did at work, although it took up enough of his time. All I really know was his position: Deputy Assistant Commissioner of the State Department of Education. I was impressed by his title, though he rarely seemed to enjoy himself. Just the same, it was a job. These days it's hard enough to support a family without being out of work.

2 Apparently his co-workers felt so badly about the situation that they held a large testimonial dinner in his honor. People came from all over the east coast. I wish I could have gone. Everyone who went said it was really nice. It's a good feeling to know that your Dad means a lot to so many people. As a farewell present they gave Dad a potter's wheel. Dad says it's the best wheel he's ever seen, and to come from someone who's done pottery for as long as he has, that's saying a lot. Over the years Dad used to borrow potter's wheels from friends. That's when I learned how to "throw" a pot.

3 When I came home for Thanksgiving vacation the first thing I did was rush down to the basement to check it out. I was quite surprised. Dad had fixed the whole corner of the basement with a big table top for playing with the clay; an area set up for preparing the clay, including a plaster bat and a wedging board; the kiln Walt built for Dad one Christmas; one hundred and fifty pounds of clay; nine different glazes; hand tools for sculpting, and the brand

new potter's wheel. It had a tractor seat from which you work the clay. It could be turned manually or by motor, and it offered lots of surface area, which always comes in handy. Dad was right, it was beautiful. He had already made a couple dozen pots. I couldn't wait to try it.

4   The next day I came down into the basement to find Dad in his old gray smock preparing the clay. I love to watch Dad do art, whether it's drawing, painting, lettering, or pottery. I stood next to him as he wedged a ball of clay the size of a small cantaloupe. He'd slice it in half on the wire and slam one half onto the wedging board, a canvas-covered slab of plaster; then he'd slam the other half on top of the first. He did this to get all the air bubbles out of the clay. You put a pot with air bubbles in the kiln, the pot'll explode in the heat and you've got yourself one heck of a mess to clean up. Dad wedged the clay, over and over.

5   When he was finished he sat down, wet the wheelhead, and pressed the clay right in the center of the wheel. Dad hit the accelerator and the clay started turning. He wet his hands and leaned over the clay. Bracing his elbows on his knees he began centering the clay. Steady right hand on the sides of the clay. Steady left hand pushing down on the clay. Centering the clay is the toughest part for me. The clay spins around and around and you have to shape it into a perfectly symmetric form in the center by letting the wheel do all the moving. Your hands stay motionless until the clay is centered. It takes me ten or fifteen minutes to do this. It takes Dad two. I shake my head and smile in amazement.

6   Dad's hands cup the clay, thumbs together on top. He wets his hands again and pushes down with his thumbs. Slowly, steadily. Once he's as far down as he wants to go he makes the bottom of the pot by spreading his thumbs. His hands relax and he pulls them out of the pot. Every motion is deliberate. If you move your hands quickly or carelessly you can be sure you will have to start again. Dad wipes the slip, very watery clay, off his hands with a sponge. It is extremely messy.

7   To make the walls Dad hooks his thumbs and curls all of his fingers except for his index fingers. Holding them like forceps, he reaches into the pot to mold the walls to just the right thickness. He starts at the bottom and brings them up slowly, making the walls of the pot thin and even all the way up, about twelve inches.

8   Dad sponges off his hands, wets them, and then cups his hands around the belly of the pot. Slowly, as the pot spins around, he squeezes his hands together, causing it to bevel slightly. Dad spends five minutes on the finishing touches. He's got himself a real nice skill.

9   It is a rare treat to watch Dad do something that he enjoys so much.

QUESTIONS ON CONTENT

1. How did Swanson's father feel about his job? _____

_____

2. How does Swanson's father feel about his hobby? _____

_____

3. Why is it important to get all the bubbles out of the clay? _____

_____

QUESTIONS ON STRATEGY

1. If the writer's focus is on the process of "throwing" a pot, why does Swanson

begin the essay with a fairly lengthy discussion of his father's job situation?

_____

2. What tense does the writer use in the first five paragraphs?

_____

3. What tense is used for the rest of the essay? _____

_____

4. Why does the author change tense? _____

_____

5. Reread the essay, underlining all words that help you visualize the process

of "throwing" a pot.

Cause/Effect

This essay focuses on high school students working in places such as fast-food franchises. Amitai Etzioni—an associate professor of sociology at Columbia University whose writings on war, peace, and social change have won many awards—states that many teen jobs are worse than uneducational. He contends that they can teach teens to become liars and cheats and to waste their money on trendy fashions. Although Etzioni has lived in the United States for many years, he was born in Germany, and his stand on the issue of teen employment may be a reflection of his European background. While you may disagree with many of Etzioni's assertions, he offers his audience some strong support of his thesis. As you read, see if you can determine any important effects of teen employment that Etzioni fails to mention.

McDonald's Is Not Our Kind of Place

Amitai Etzioni

1   In today's reality you need to look beyond the school itself to examine those factors that hinder or provide opportunities for generating educational experiences that enhance character formation and moral education. Today's high school students spend much time outside the school and within the work environment. It would be shortsighted to ignore the educational effects of this context. As I have stressed, much of the education of children takes the form of experiences; since work has become such an important part of many high school students' lives, it too must be examined in this light: Is it educational?

2   I regret to report that from this viewpoint, McDonald's (and other companies like it, from Roy Rogers to Dunkin' Donuts) are far from benign creations. McDonald's is bad for your kids. I don't mean the flat patties and the white-flour buns. I mean the jobs it takes to mass-produce these delicacies. About two-thirds of high school juniors and seniors these days have part-time paying jobs, many in fast-food chains, of which McDonald's is the pioneer, trendsetter, and symbol. Such employment would seem to be straight from the pages of the Founding Fathers' moral education manual on how to bring up self-reliant, work-ethic-driven youngsters. From lemonade stands to newspaper routes, it is a longstanding tradition that American youngsters hold paying jobs. Here, kids learn the fruits of labor and trade and develop the virtue of self-discipline. . . .

3   Hardee's, Baskin-Robbins, Kentucky Fried Chicken, and the like appear to be nothing more than a vast extension of the lemonade stand. They provide large numbers of steady teen jobs, test the teenagers' stamina, and reward them quite well compared with many other teen jobs. Upon closer examination, however, the McDonald's kind of job is rather

uneducational in several ways. Far from providing an opportunity for self-discipline, self-supervision, and self-scheduling, like the old-fashioned paper route, it is highly structured and routinized. True, students still must mobilize themselves to go to work, but once they don their uniforms, their tasks are spelled out in minute detail. The McDonald's Corporation dictates for thousands of local outlets the shape of the coffee cups; the weight, size, shape and color of the patties; the texture of the napkins (if any); how often fresh coffee is to be made (every eight minutes); and so on. There is little room for initiative, creativity, or even elementary rearrangements. Thus, fast-food franchises are breeding grounds for robots working for yesterday's assembly lines and not practice fields for committed workers in tomorrow's high-tech posts.

4   . . . Although it is true that these workplaces provide income and even some training to such low-skilled youngsters, they also tend to perpetuate their disadvantaged status. Such jobs provide no career incentives and few marketable skills, and they can undermine school attendance and involvement.

5   The hours are long. Often the stores close late, and after closing workers must tally and clean up. There is no way that such amounts of work will not interfere with schoolwork, especially homework. Fifty-eight percent of the seniors at Walt Whitman High School in Montgomery County, an affluent area in Maryland, acknowledge that their jobs interfere with their schoolwork.

6   One study did find merit in jobs at McDonald's and similar places. The study reported that this work experience teaches teamwork and working under supervision. That may be true, but it must be noted, however, that such learning is not automatically educational or wholesome. For example, much of the supervision in fast-food places leans toward teaching the wrong kinds of compliance (blind obedience or being pissed off with the world, as the supervisors often are). Also, such compliance helps very little to develop the ability to form quality-of-work circles, in which employees and supervisors together seek to improve operations.

7   Supervision is often both tight and woefully inappropriate. In the days before industrialization and capitalism, the young were initiated into the world of work in close personal relations such as between a master (adult) craftsman and an apprentice. Even when a young person worked for someone other than his parents, he lived in the master's or farmer's home and was integrated into his family; he was not part of a teen horde.

8   Today, fast-food chains and other such places of work (record shops, bowling alleys) keep costs down by having teens supervise teens, often with no adult on the premises. There is no mature adult figure to identify with, to emulate, or to provide a role model or mature moral guidance. The work culture varies from one store to another: some places are tightly run shops (must keep the cash registers ringing); in other places the employees may "party," only to be interrupted by the intrusion of customers. Rarely is there a "master" to learn from; rarely is there much worth learning. Indeed, far from being places where solid work values are being transmitted, these are places where all too often teen values dominate. Typically, when one of my sons was dishing out ice cream for Baskin-Robbins in upper Manhattan, his fellow teen workers considered him a sucker for not helping himself to the till. Most of them believed they were entitled to a self-awarded "severance pay" of fifty dollars on their last day on the job.

9   The money raises additional issues. The lemonade stand and paper route money was your allowance. Apprentices, to the extent that they generated a significant flow of income, contributed most, if not all, of it to their parents' household.

10   Today's teen pay may be low by adult standards, but it is often substantial. Especially among the middle class, it is largely or wholly spent by the teens. That is, the youngsters live free at home and are allowed to keep considerable amounts of money. Where this money goes is not quite clear. Some use it to support themselves, especially among the poor. Some middle-class youngsters set money aside to help pay for college or save it for a major purchase, like a car. But large amounts seem to pay for an early introduction into trite elements of American consumerism: trendy clothes, trinkets, and whatever else is the fast-moving teen craze.

11   One may say that this is only fair and square: the youngsters are just being good American consumers, working and spending their money on what turns them on. At least, a cynic might add, the money isn't going to buy illicit drugs and booze. On the other hand, an educator might bemoan that these young, as-yet-unformed individuals are driven to buy objects of no intrinsic educational, cultural, or social merit. They learn early and quickly the dubious merit of keeping up with ever-changing mass-merchandising fads.

12   Moreover, many teens find the instant reward of money, and the youth status symbols it buys, much more alluring than credits earned in algebra, American history, or French. No wonder quite a few would rather skip school, and certainly homework, to work longer hours at a Burger King.

QUESTIONS ON CONTENT

1. According to Etzioni, what percentage of high school juniors and seniors have part-time jobs? _____

   _____

2. What advantages does the author cite for these jobs? _____

   _____

3. What disadvantages does he stress?_____

   _____

4. Name three fast-food franchises other than McDonald's that are targeted by Etzioni: _____

   _____

QUESTIONS ON STRATEGY

1. Reread the essay, and note in the space below the places where the writer does give credit to some positive effects of these jobs. _____

   _____

2. Is Etzioni's use of outside sources as well as the experience of his son sufficient to convince you of his thesis? _____ Why or why not?

   _____

3. Do you think the writer has a European bias? If so, where do you find evidence of this bias? _____

   _____

4. Is Etzioni guilty of oversimplification in any part of his essay? If so, in which paragraph? _____

   _____

CRITICAL THINKING IN CONNECTING TEXTS

The essays by Swanson and Etzioni both touch upon employment and what it means to people. In "The Turning Point" (pp. 302–303), Swanson confides, "Dad never talked much about what he did at work." The writer also reveals, "he rarely seemed to enjoy himself." In "McDonald's Is Not Our Kind of Place" (pp. 305–307), Etzioni asserts that "the McDonald's kind of job is rather uneducational in several ways" and later states that this type of job leaves little room for initiative or creativity. Working with a partner or small group, think about jobs that you have held—part-time, full-time, seasonal, temporary. Then broaden your exploration to your immediate family members and close friends. Assign a notetaker as you brainstorm some reasons people get and then stay in jobs they're not satisfied with. What are some of the effects of holding a dull, monotonous job? Think about those people who seem to enjoy their work: What is it they do on the job that makes their work special? How has their job satisfaction affected the rest of their lives? If time permits, share your findings with the rest of the class.

**For more writing resources, be sure to see the
Longman English Pages Website at
http://longman.awl.com/englishpages**

Showing Relationships: Comparison/Contrast and Division/Classification

> Become aware of the two-sided nature of your mental make-up: one thinks in terms of the connectedness of things; the other thinks in terms of parts and sequences.
>
> —*Gabriele Rico,* author of Writing the Natural Way

Preview

In this chapter you will learn
- ► how to identify the characteristics of comparison/contrast and division/classification in essay development
- ► how to use comparison/contrast to reveal similarities or differences
- ► how to identify "one-side-at-a-time" versus "point-by-point" organization in comparison/contrast essay development
- ► how to use division/classification to analyze the relationship of parts to the whole, or to sort and group according to common characteristics
- ► how to find a unifying principle when using division/classification in an essay
- ► how to differentiate between types and stereotypes

You need a new car, and to help you make a decision, you have drawn up a comparative list of features of your two favorite models. In doing so, you're employing a method of thinking—comparison/contrast—helpful in making decisions as well as understanding how experiences connect.

You're putting the clean laundry away. In sorting and placing your items of clothing in various drawers, you're using another crucial method of thinking in our complex world: division/classification.

Comparison/contrast and division/classification are closely related patterns of essay development as well as ways of thinking. They allow writers to explore a subject by breaking it down into smaller parts and examining those parts. In an essay, this sorting and analyzing helps readers understand how objects and ideas relate. Understanding a subject in depth permits readers to evaluate, and if necessary, to choose among alternatives. This chapter explains how to use comparison/contrast and division/classification patterns of development in your essays.

CHARACTERISTICS OF COMPARISON/CONTRAST

Decisions, decisions! Will you order the juicy cheeseburger and fries or the healthy avocado and sprouts on whole wheat? Do you want to major in biology or business? Should you vote to place height restrictions on new housing developments in your neighborhood or oppose these restrictions? No matter what you do or where you go, decisions need to be made. You may make a choice based on instinctive response, or you may decide by using **comparison**—which explores the similarities or likenesses of one choice with another—or **contrast**—which points out the differences.

What subjects might you want to compare or contrast in an essay? Just as choices in real life are limitless, so are the subjects you can choose to write about. You might want to compare or contrast two characters in a short story, two lifestyles, two sports, two movies, two opinions. For an economics class, you might want to compare the past with the present—was our quality of life better or worse in the 1950s than it is now? For a midterm exam in biology, you might contrast two organs in the human body. For a business class, you might compare two management styles. When your essay's purpose is to organize information for clear understanding, to make choices, and to notice qualities of a subject in more detail, comparison/contrast is an effective strategy.

To examine comparison/contrast development, read the following excerpt:

1   As soon as Uncle Frank arrived, his tie loosened and his sleeves rolled up, I felt sorry for my father. It was the way I always felt when the two of them were together. Brothers naturally invite comparison, and when comparisons were made between those two, my father was bound to suffer. And my father was, in many respects, an impressive man. He was tall, broad-shouldered, and pleasant-looking. But Frank was all this and more. He was handsome—dark wavy hair, a jaw chiseled on such precise angles it seemed to conform to some geometric law, and he was as tall and well-built as my father, but with an athletic grace my father lacked. . . .

2   Frank was witty, charming, at smiling ease with his life and everything in it. Alongside his brother my father soon seemed somewhat prosaic. Oh, stolid, surely, and steady and dependable. But inevitably, inescapably dull. Nothing glittered in my father's wake the way it did in Uncle Frank's.

—Larry Watson, from *Montana 1948*

Notice that Watson's excerpt contains the following characteristics:

- **Two subjects from the same general group are compared or contrasted.**
  Watson's two subjects are brothers: the writer's father and Frank, his uncle. The writer introduces his subjects with his early reference to "Uncle Frank" and "my father"; he further signals the focus of his subject when he states, "Brothers naturally invite comparison. . . ."

- **The structure clearly separates one subject from the other.**
  Watson organizes his writing by contrasting the two brothers point by point. He states that his father was "tall, broad-shouldered, and pleasant looking" and then switches the focus to his uncle: "Frank was all this and more. He was handsome—dark wavy hair, a jaw chiseled on such precise angles it seemed to conform to some geometric law."

- **The same features are discussed for both subjects—there is a balance to the comparison or contrast.**
  Watson compares the two brothers in height, body build, facial features, and personality.

- **A conclusion results from the comparison or contrast of the two subjects.**
  Watson hints at this conclusion early in the first paragraph: "when comparisons were made between those two, my father was bound to suffer." At the end of the second paragraph, Watson concludes his presentation of the two subjects with a striking image: "Nothing glittered in my father's wake the way it did in Uncle Frank's."

The technique of comparison/contrast works in another way in the following model. As you read, try to identify the characteristics of this pattern of development.

MODEL WITH KEY QUESTIONS

This student writer had recently read a popular book asserting that men and women have different values. She decided to test the author's theory by contrasting her husband's behavior with her own.

MEN ARE MAKITA, WOMEN ARE MARIGOLDS
Yen Glassman

Yen Glassman is a mother of two young children, so she attends college on Saturdays. Yen reports that she has found the learning center on her campus very helpful. She enjoys writing essays both for her writing classes and for publication in the college literary magazine. Yen has an interest in gardening, but as far as career plans are concerned, she is undecided, keeping her options open.

1   Men and women have opposite views of shopping. However, do-it-yourself home improvement stores are able to attract both customers (men and women), with different intentions and focus. When Keith and I recently visited Home Depot, a local home improvement store, I found out that even though men and women respond differently to the same products and displays in the store, these differences really serve to complement each other.

2   When Keith and I decided to remodel our bathroom, we spent a lot of time discussing items needing work. We would go to Home Depot together. This was a rare occasion because Keith was willing to accompany me on a shopping trip. Usually, he would rather stay home with the children. However, Home Depot drew a different reaction from Keith. He was looking forward to it and actually got ready ahead of me and waited in the car.

3   On the other hand, I always love to go shopping, no matter what the circumstances—I'd rather be in a department store shopping for dresses, but a home improvement store has its own charms. For our remodeling project, Keith and I agreed that we would repaint the walls and change the cabinets of our bathroom. I could hardly wait to compare paint chips.

4   When we arrived at the store, each of us headed in different directions. Like many other men, Keith was immediately attracted to the power tool section where there were live demonstrations of the latest technology. After testing several tools, Keith decided to refinish the bathroom cabinets, and he was excited about purchasing a Makita power saw and sanding machine in order to begin work on the cabinets.

5   In contrast, I went to the wallpaper and faucet sections. After seeing several wallpaper sample books, I decided to wallpaper the bathroom with a flower pattern instead of repainting. In addition, I also wanted to replace our old faucet with new porcelain faucets with two gold-plated handles for hot and cold, despite the fact that these did not fit the existing plumbing of our bathroom.

6   When we regrouped, Keith and I realized that each of us was attracted to different products and we had gotten completely off track from our original project.

Walking around the store, I observed many different responses of men and women in the shopping mode.

7   For example, on the molding aisle, a lady was driving a male employee crazy by putting back every piece of lumber he had chosen if it contained any knots or had the slightest imperfection. On the other hand, a male construction worker had a list of items and quickly and methodically selected various wood materials with not thought to their small imperfections or roughnesses.

8   As John Gray states in the book *Men Are From Mars, Women Are From Venus,* "Men value power efficiency and achievement. Women value beauty and romance." The Home Depot appeals to men through gadgets and new power tools, the objects that help them to achieve their projects and goals. In contrast, the store attracts women with its many items for beautifying the home and decorating to express their feelings.

9   However, even though men and women are different in some of their values, they complement each other like lock and key: one cannot work without the other. In addition, the more we understand our differences, the more we can learn to support and respect each other.

KEY QUESTIONS

1. **PURPOSE** What significant point does Glassman make in paragraph 1 about men's and women's responses to shopping? _____

_____

2. **FOCUS** In her thesis, does Glassman indicate that she will be comparing or contrasting? _____

_____

3. **MATERIAL** Notice that the writer draws from personal experience for her material, but she also relies on two other sources. What are they?

_____

4. **STRUCTURE** Does Glassman develop her essay by exploring all the features of one subject and switching to the other subject, or does she go back

and forth from the first to the second subject? Refer to particular para-graphs in support of your answer. _____

_____

5. **STYLE** In what way does Glassman use John Gray's words to connect her conclusion to her thesis? _____

_____

GUIDELINES FOR WRITING COMPARISON/CONTRAST

Determine Your Purpose and Audience

You will want to choose a comparison/contrast pattern of development in your essay if your purpose involves communicating a significant point about two subjects. Perhaps you want to convince your audience that one career field is better than the other; maybe you want to inform them of the actual differences between two frequently confused mathematical theories or medicines. Employ comparison/contrast to organize information about two closely related sub-jects if you want your audience to be able to make a choice by noticing the fea-tures of each subject in more detail.

Practice 11.1 Take a look at the following ideas for subjects and then fill in a possible audi-ence and purpose for each one. The first example has been done for you.

<u>Subject</u>	<u>Audience</u>	<u>Significant point</u>
1. Two brands of sedans	Potential car buyers	One car is better than the other
2. Two characters in two different short stories	_____	_____
3. Two Italian restaurants	_____	_____
4. Two football players	_____	_____
5. Going to college to obtain marketable skills and going to college to obtain a well-rounded education	_____	_____
6. Emeralds and diamonds	_____	_____

◆ ◆ ◆

Identify Similar Subjects to Compare or Contrast

If you look at the list of subject ideas from the previous practice exercise, you'll notice that the two subjects for each pair are from the same general group. It would be impossible to compare or contrast thoughtfully emeralds and football players, or an Italian restaurant and a short story.

In "Men Are Makita, Women Are Marigolds," Yen Glassman is careful not to contrast men's behavior in a home-improvement center with women's behavior in a different environment, such as a boutique or a grocery store. This would invalidate any meaningful conclusion about her two subjects. There are exceptions to this "similar subject" guideline, but in general, unless your instructor specifies, it's a good idea to choose two subjects to compare or contrast that have enough in common to warrant pointing out similarities or differences.

Practice 11.2 Examine the list below and mark "yes" by appropriate subjects for a comparison/contrast essay. Explain briefly why you think the subjects are appropriate. If you can't mark "yes," change one of the subject choices to make the combination work. The first example has been done for you.

1. A book about coal miners and a movie about coal-miners

yes—similar subjects _____

2. A book about coal miners and a movie about Russian aristocracy

_____

3. A book about coal miners and a book about construction workers

_____

4. High school study skills and high school hang-outs

_____

5. Constructive addictions and destructive addictions

_____

◆ ◆ ◆

Focus Your Subject

In narrowing your thesis for comparison/contrast, try to do the following:

- Name the two subjects to be compared or contrasted.

- Indicate whether the subjects will be compared, contrasted, or both.

- Include a controlling idea in which you mention why you are examining these two subjects. This could be a statement of the significance of the comparison or contrast of the two subjects.

Notice that Yen Glassman's thesis includes her subjects, the limitations of the subjects—different reactions based on gender to a home improvement store visit—and the significant point she wants to make. She states, "I found out that even though *men and women* [subjects] respond *differently* [indication of contrast] to the same products and displays in the store, *these differences complement each other* [controlling idea]."

Practice 11.3 Take a look at the following subjects and audiences. Fill in what you feel could be a controlling idea for each comparison/contrast pair of subjects. The first example has been done for you.

<u>Subject</u>	<u>Audience</u>	<u>Controlling Idea</u>
1. Two brands of sedans	Potential car buyers	One car is better than the other
2. Two characters in two different short stories	Those familiar with both stories	_____
3. Two Italian restaurants	People who like Italian food	_____
4. Two football players	Football fans	_____

◆ ◆ ◆

Practice 11.4 To differentiate between effective and ineffective thesis, read the following thesis statements. On a separate sheet of paper, comment on their effectiveness according to the guidelines just discussed:

1. French television sitcoms are quite different from American sitcoms.

2. Although Echinacea and goldenseal are both North American herbs useful for various physical ailments, we know quite a bit about the first but almost nothing about the other.

3. When I compare the way I lived before I became a college student with the way I live now, I see a big difference.

◆ ◆ ◆

Choose Points and Maintain a Balance

Once you have an effective thesis with a controlling idea, you will want to choose the points you make about your subjects. **Points** are the ideas that will be discussed equally for each of two subjects in a comparison/contrast essay. If you want to influence your friend to buy one brand of car instead of another, you wouldn't just say, "Trust me; I know that the Ford is better—it's just an all-around better vehicle in every respect." Instead, you would want to draw up a list of points to prove that the Ford is superior. You might want to talk about dependability, price, performance, mileage, comfort, body style, service accessibility, and safety features. You would then discuss each of these eight points for both the Ford and the Honda. But to be fair, logical, and clear in your comparison, you would present the same points for the Ford that you present for the Honda, and in the same order. You wouldn't change the order of points as you go from one subject to the other, for this would only confuse your audience.

You also want to be sure to present a *balanced* comparison or contrast—notice that when Watson describes the two brothers, the writer attempts to give his audience equal details about the points—height, body build, facial features, and personality—for each man.

Practice 11.5 Reread "Men Are Makita, Women Are Marigolds" (pp. 313–314) looking for points of comparison or contrast. Complete the following list. The first one has been completed for you.

	Author's husband	**Author**
1. Feelings about shopping trips	Would rather stay home	*Enjoys them*
2. _____	_____	_____
3. _____	_____	_____
4. _____	_____	_____

◆ ◆ ◆

Sketch Out a Structure: Two Possible Plans

You have two options for organizing an essay using comparison/contrast development: the one-side-at-a-time method and the point-by-point method. You can compare the two methods and then decide which one will best serve your purpose. As you are drafting, you may want to experiment by writing two alternative versions and then get feedback from a peer editor or instructor to determine which plan works better.

In the one-side-at-a-time plan, you present all of your information on one subject first and then switch to the "other side"—that is, the second subject being compared or contrasted. Read Joseph Suina's essay "And Then I Went to School" (pp. 337–342), for an example of this structure. Notice that first the writer details his home environment on the reservation—he talks about the sights, smells, and details associated with his grandmother and their adobe home. Halfway through the passage, Suina shifts his focus to the elementary school—again he details the sights and smells associated with this environment. His one-side-at-a-time structure can be outlined as follows:

I. Home environment

   A. Furniture

   B. Foods

   C. Smells

   D. Grandmother's presence—sense of comfort

II. School environment

   A. Teacher's presence

   B. Furniture

   C. Lighting

   D. Cold classroom—sense of confinement

In contrast, both Watson's excerpt and Glassman's essay present the reader with a point-by-point plan—a point is made about one subject and then the same point is used to contrast or compare the other subject. Here is an outline of Watson's structure for the excerpt from *Montana 1948* (pp. 311–312):

I. Height

   A. Frank

   B. Father

II. Shoulders

   A. Frank

   B. Father

III. Face and hair

   A. Frank

   B. Father

IV. Personality

   A. Frank

   B. Father

Notice that as Watson moves from one subject to the next, point by point, he gives approximately the same amount of detail for both subjects on every point he makes.

Practice 11.6 Reread Yen Glassman's essay (pp. 313–314). On a separate sheet of paper, outline the main points of the essay. When you've finished, annotate the essay by labeling it as point-by-point or one-side-at-a-time.

◆ ◆ ◆

Use Cue Words

Signaling your reader that you're moving from one subject to the other is extremely important in comparison/contrast development. If you choose the one-side-at-a-time method, your essay will require fewer transitions than if you employ the point-by-point organizational plan. However, regardless of your organizational plan, make clear exactly which point you're making and which of your two subjects you're talking about by using appropriate cue words, such as *in contrast, on the other hand, in a similar manner, in comparison,* and *in the same way.*

Practice 11.7 Review the table of cue words (pp. 313–314). Look again at Yen Glassman's essay (pp. 313–314) and annotate it by underlining all cue words or phrases you find.

◆ ◆ ◆

STRATEGIES FOR WRITING COMPARISON/CONTRAST

1. **PURPOSE** Think about why you want to compare or contrast two subjects. Consider the audience that would be interested in these two subjects and their level of knowledge about the subjects.

2. **FOCUS** Limit your subject to two situations, people, ideas, or objects. Indicate whether you will develop similarities, differences, or both. Include the significance of the comparison or contrast of your two subjects.

3. **MATERIAL** Choose the same points to compare or contrast for the two subjects, making sure that you gather enough information in prewriting to present meaningful detail on both subjects. Delete any unconvincing or unrelated material.

4. **STRUCTURE** Decide whether your subjects are better suited to a one-side-at-a-time or a point-by-point plan. In revising, make sure you have followed your chosen plan consistently. In polishing, ask yourself where you could insert cue words to help your audience move from one point or subject to another.

5. **STYLE** Polish your introduction and conclusion to ensure that they serve your purpose in comparing or contrasting the two subjects.

OPTIONS FOR WRITING COMPARISON/CONTRAST

You will be using your skills of comparing and contrasting when you think about and choose one of the following writing options. When you decide which option you'd like to explore, think about whether you want to emphasize similarities, differences, or both.

1. In her essay (pp. 313–314), Yen Glassman points out several differences in gender response. Perhaps you disagree; maybe you can think of many similarities men and women share in their responses to specific situations. In an essay, compare the two sexes, supporting or refuting Glassman's and John Gray's claim that men and women have different values.

2. In his essay (pp. 337–342), Joseph Suina contrasts his early childhood environment living with his grandmother on the Cochiti reservation with his subsequent elementary school environment. Can you think of a time you underwent a change from one environment to another? Perhaps you want to contrast your life as a college student with the kind of life you led before. Or

it could be that your current situation living with a roommate or living alone has made for a dramatic contrast from your former situation, perhaps living with your parents or another relative. Contrast the two environments.

3. Reread the excerpt from *Montana 1948* (pp. 311–312). The author focuses on two brothers and their contrasting qualities. Do you know two relatives or close friends who, in spite of their apparent similarities, possess profound differences? What about you and a sibling or close friend? Write an essay developing the differences or the similarities of two people you know well.

¶ **4.** Have you read a good book only to see it turned into a mediocre movie? Or have you read a good book and then been led to seek out others that were similar? Compare or contrast a book with its movie version, or two books on the same subject written from different points of view.

Challenge Option: Combining Patterns

This essay asks you to use first cause/effect and then comparison/contrast patterns of development. Think of two significant events in America's history that are recent enough for you to remember. For example, if you're old enough to remember the first human to walk on the moon in 1969, you could pair this event with the discovery of the possibility of life on Mars in 1997. Or you could pair the Jim Jones mass suicide in Guyana in 1978 with the Heaven's Gate mass suicide in 1997.

Once you have chosen two events or occurrences, gather information in prewriting. As you draft your essay, you might want to follow this structure:

- *Introduction and thesis:* Name the two occurrences, indicate whether you will compare or contrast the two, and include the significance of the comparison or contrast to capture the interest of the audience.

- *Body paragraphs* (one or more): Detail the causes or effects connected with the first occurrence.

- *Body paragraphs* (one or more): Show a contrast or a similarity in the two occurrences by detailing the causes or effects connected with the second occurrence.

- *Conclusion:* Make clear the significance of the similar or different causes or effects connected with the two incidents.

CHARACTERISTICS OF DIVISION/CLASSIFICATION

Perhaps one of the first tasks you perform at the beginning of each semester is to buy subject dividers for your notebooks. Dividing a notebook into sections enables you to find notes, essays, hand-outs, and other class materials easily. When the schedule of classes is published for your college, you can find the course you're interested in quickly because all course offerings are categorized by subject. All of us make use of the organizational strategies of division and classification every day, often without realizing it. Just as sorting and analyzing are automatic human responses to our complex world, so also are they important methods of essay development. Division and classification permit us to grasp relationships between simple and complex subjects.

Although division and classification are distinct methods of developing an essay, they are quite a bit alike and are sometimes used together within the same essay. **Division** is a writing strategy that breaks the subject down into smaller parts and analyzes these parts in relation to the whole. **Classification** is a writing strategy that brings several separate items together under the same "umbrella" or category so that distinguishing characteristics can be closely examined.

To observe how division/classification works, read the following essay written by a former basketball player.

"Five on the Floor, but Is There More?"

Julie Jones

1   I, having played this challenging and somewhat stirring sport for seven years, have had the privilege to observe the numerous talents and diverse personalities of women basketball players. I have categorized these distinct personality traits into categories which fit the many encounters I have had with other participants of the game of basketball. They are the Grunter, the Sissy, the General, the Timorous One, the Faultless One, and the Basket Case.

2   The Grunter: One will usually find this player in the position of the post. She is known for her thunderous grunting while rebounding. She claims that the louder she grunts the higher she jumps. She is an aggressive player and has an amplified voice.

3   The Sissy: This player is known for calling an unauthorized time-out after breaking her nail while passing the ball. She is more worried about if her uniform makes her look fat, how her hair looks, and if her mascara is running than she is about the game. Every time she misses a basket, does not get a rebound, makes a bad pass, or does anything that makes her look anything but wonderful, she falls to the floor shrieking in pain, although she is hardly ever actually hurt. She is not necessarily a bad player, but she does tend to be annoying.

4   The General: This player is the team leader, she is in charge and never seems to be confused. If she is bewildered with a situation, it is her goal to make sure that no one perceives her confusion. She remains calm, cool, and collected, but underneath her surprising equanimity she is just as rattled as her teammates. She will hardly ever release her emotions on the court, but when she does, it is almost certain she will receive a technical for doing so.

5   The Timorous One: This player seems to be very withdrawn on the court. She is afraid to holler for the ball, grunt, or do anything that may make her look less feminine. She does, however, get the ball more often than one would think. She secretly pinches, claws, pushes, or uses any kind of easily hidden strategies to steal the ball from her opponent. She is downright mean on the floor to her challenger, but is the perfect angel in her teammates' eyes.

6   The Faultless One: This is the player who "never does anything wrong." She is usually the player who annoys her teammates, the referees, the crowd, and her coach. Every time she is called for a foul, traveling, double dribble, or any kind of turnover, she looks at the referee in disbelief and screams, "WHAT?" while making body gestures of various sorts. After screaming at the referee, she then looks at her coach and continues with her various gestures. After getting back on defense, she continues to discuss the call with any teammate that pretends to listen. She would never admit to any wrongdoing, and she is known for accusing the statistician of numerous mistakes.

7   The Basket Case: You can spot this player before the game even begins; she is the one wearing unmatching socks. She has an abundant number of Kleenex stuffed in the drawstring of her shorts (in case her nose would begin to run during the game). During the game she runs from one end of the court to another with the rest of the team, but she has no idea what she is doing. One can tell where she has run by following the Kleenex trail she unknowingly left; one might think it was so she could find her way back to the other end of the court.

8   These are many different types of women basketball players The next time you attend a basketball game, I challenge you to put the players into the categories I have presented or into categories of your own. You may find analyzing personalities of players makes the game even more exciting and interesting. You should watch for those players with "hidden qualities" because there is much more to the game of basketball than what you may see on the surface.

     Notice that Jones' essay demonstrates the following characteristics:

- **A principle or standard is employed for breaking the subject into separate parts or types.**
  Jones tells the reader that her categories are based on "distinct personality traits."

- **The subject is broken down into categories or divisions for separate consideration.**
  Jones states that her subject is "women basketball players," and that these can be sorted into the following groups: "the Grunter, the Sissy, the General, the Timorous One, the Faultless One, and the Basket Case."

- **The classifications or divisions of the subject are logical, clearly developed, and detailed sufficiently to explain and differentiate each one.**
  Jones' categories are all based on her indicated principle of personality traits; she doesn't slip in a category based on looks, for instance, or family background. The categories also proceed in a specific order. Jones places the Grunter next to the Sissy to emphasize the humorous contrast of these two types of players. Finally, in each of Jones's six categories, there are enough specific details to give a real sense of each type. For instance, the vivid phrases, "she falls to the floor shrieking in pain" in paragraph 3 and "Kleenex stuffed in the drawstring of her shorts" in paragraph 7 give the audience a clear picture of these categories.

See how many of the characteristics of the division/classication pattern of essay development you can identify in the following student model.

MODEL WITH KEY QUESTIONS

Student writer Ofoegbu wanted to share his experiences in the world of work by focusing on the subject of co-workers. As you read his essay, notice that some of his work experiences point out cultural differences between America and Nigeria.

CO-WORKERS
Chuks Ofoegbu

Chuks Ofoegbu confides, "My writing process started when I was in high school." Born and raised in Nigeria, Chuks is interested in politics and likes to write about contemporary issues. In drafting his essays, Chuks learned the importance of defining all terms that an American audience might not understand. Chuks is currently working as a paralegal with a law firm and reports that he'll be able to think about long-term career plans when his financial situation is solid.

1   "Your boss is not your mother." That's the good news from one of the books I read recently, *Oedipus Wrecks*, by Brian Desroches. The book was named after Oedipus in the Greek legend who, in ignorance and partly from ambition, killed his

own father and married his mother. The bad news, on the other hand, is that a lot of us feel and act like our managers or bosses are members of our families. The result is that we co-workers may squabble with one another in the workplace for selfish reasons. Based on the way my co-workers interact with other workers and their bosses, I can place them in three groups: the Butter-ups, the Get-alongs, and the Judases.

2   For the Butter-ups, flattery is the only method to get ahead. For the first year of the five years I worked as a cashier in the Ministry of Finance in Nigeria, I encountered the Butter-ups constantly. Their strategy was to compliment the boss excessively in order to win favorable personal evaluation reports which were sent to office headquarters. These compliments came in the form of presents given to the boss on his birthday and wedding anniversary, or presents given to him for his wife's or children's birthdays. This group of Butter-ups was comprised of young men and women who needed promotion and a raise in their salary to enjoy the good things of life. The Butter-ups would give such presents and a shower of praises to the boss even for no apparent reason.

3   Another group of co-workers I came in contact with were the Get-alongs. They just "got along with the boss." They believed in the old fable, "Slow and steady wins the race." I was among this Get-along group. We had a good relationship with the boss because we would often come to work fifteen minutes or more before the official opening hour and we would perform our job assignments efficiently. In spite of the fact that we offered the boss no special gifts or flattery, he had a soft spot for us because our level of neatness in our work, our attire, and our desks was impressive. In addition, our interactions with our co-workers were unruffled.

4   The third group of workers were the Judases, from the Biblical character Judas Iscariot who betrayed Jesus. This group believed in the "divide and rule" method to gain power. These workers created disharmony between the boss and the other co-workers through back-biting and false allegations. They accused other workers of taking gratifications from members of the public, cheating in promotion examinations, and keeping false records in personnel files at headquarters. Why would they do this? The Judases actually wanted to create this disharmony so that the boss would be toppled. They wanted him out because they had a clash of interest with him over staff control and the way office furniture sent from headquarters had been shared among workers.

5   In the end, the Judases were either posted to handle managerial posts elsewhere or reprimanded through letters to desist from their false accusa-

tions. I survived this time of turmoil with the three groups of co-workers. However, colleagues, I would advocate for peace and harmony in the workplace rather than sowing the seeds of disunity and acrimony between co-workers. Just as Oedipus discovered, ignorance and ambition are a dangerous combination.

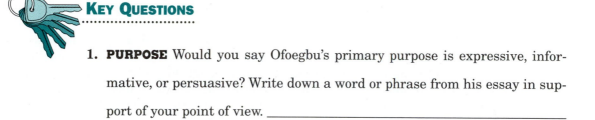

KEY QUESTIONS

1. **PURPOSE** Would you say Ofoegbu's primary purpose is expressive, informative, or persuasive? Write down a word or phrase from his essay in support of your point of view. _____

_____

2. **FOCUS** What basis for breaking his subject into groups does Ofoegbu mention in his first paragraph?_____

_____

3. **MATERIAL** What types of details does Ofoegbu use the most to develop his three categories? _____

_____

4. **STRUCTURE** Why does the writer order the categories with the Butter-ups first and the Judases last? _____

_____

Circle the cue words that take the reader from one main category to the next in the three body paragraphs.

5. **STYLE** Reread the essay, underlining any quoted passages. Now examine these quotations. In what way do they help delineate each category of workers? _____

_____

GUIDELINES FOR WRITING DIVISION/CLASSIFICATION

Connect Subject, Audience, and Purpose

You will want to use a division/classification pattern of development in your essay if you have a complex subject that you want to divide into more manageable parts. Dividing and/or sorting will help you impose order and increase your audience's understanding of your subject. Your purpose may be to express humor, as Julie Jones does (pp. 323–324), or you may want to inform your audience, as Chuks Ofoegbu does (pp. 325–327).

In thinking about your purpose, remember not to bore your audience by presenting them with useless information. Classifying college students' hairstyles into shaved, short, medium, and long would probably result in a real "snoozer" of an essay; separating American freedoms into freedom of speech, freedom of thought, freedom of assembly, and freedom of worship is a nice idea, but unless you offer new information, most readers will tune you out. Once you're assigned a subject or think of an idea for a subject, consider the audience that would benefit from or appreciate having more information on the subject. Then think about how you might break that subject down for this audience.

Practice 11.8 To gain more experience in thinking about division/classification, determine an audience and a purpose for each of the following subjects.

Subject	Audience	Purpose
1. Potential careers for your major	_____	_____
2. Types of people in the student center	_____	_____
3. Categories of customers in a retail store	_____	_____
4. Necessary components in a rock concert	_____	_____
5. Types of computers	_____	_____

◆ ◆ ◆

Identify a Unifying Principle

One potential pitfall for essays using a division/classification pattern involves mixed categories or divisions. Therefore, you will want to make sure you have a **unifying principle**—a basis for breaking down and sorting your subject. For example, in Julie Jones's essay (pp. 323–324), basketball players are sorted into categories on the basis of one unifying principle—on-court appearance and actions.

Practice 11.9 Find the unifying principle for each of the groups below. Cross out the one item that is not categorized as the others are according to the same principle. The first group has been done for you.

1. Swimsuits

a. String bikini

b. Two-piece

~~c. Nylon~~

d. one-piece

Unifying
principle: _suit style_

2. Vacations

a. European

b. South American

c. Asian

d. Summer

_____

3. Workers

a. White-collar

b. Blue-collar

c. Part-time

d. Semi-skilled

_____

4. Roommates

a. Shy

b. Outgoing

c. Comical

d. Messy

Unifying
principle: _____

5. Fitness activities

a. Stress

b. Jogging

c. Swimming

d. Tennis

_____

6. Movies

a. Horror

b. Romance

c. French

d. Adventure

_____

◆ ◆ ◆

Limit Divisions or Categories

Into how many parts should you divide your subject? Julie Jones comments on six basketball types; Chuks Ofoegbu examines four categories of co-workers. Although there is no "correct" number, you will generally want three or more divisions or classifications. You might want to try using as many parts or types as you can develop in sufficient and clear detail for the length of your assigned essay. Also, remember that a few strong components are always preferable to many underdeveloped ones; you don't want your essay to look like a list without any supporting material. The number and quality of these types or categories will determine your plan of development. Be careful not to "invent" a category or a division that doesn't really exist. For example, avoid something like this: "the good friend, the so-so friend, and the best friend."

Your thesis may include the following parts:

- Subject
- Controlling idea—the unifying principle for your division or classification
- Plan of development—an indication of how many parts or categories you've broken your subject into, what these parts or categories are, and the order in which you will discuss them

Notice that Chuks Ofoegbu's thesis for his essay (pp. 325–327) contains these parts:

(Controlling idea — Unifying principle)

"Based on the way my co-workers (subject) interact with other workers and their bosses, I can place them in three groups: the Butter-ups, the Get-alongs, and the Judases."

(Plan of development)

Practice 11.10 Choose one of the subjects on page 329 and see if you can come up with a thesis statement that includes these three parts: subject, controlling idea, and plan of development. Write the sentence here.

_____

_____

◆ ◆ ◆

Determine a Plan

Once you have a working thesis, you will need to gather material in prewriting to make each division or classification clear and distinct. When you have enough material, consider how you might arrange your information. Oftentimes, it is helpful to draft a couple of variations. If you review your purpose and audience, one arrangement will strike you as more effective than the others. It's also helpful to remember that your preliminary organizational plan does not need to be set in stone. For instance, Chuks Ofoegbu reversed his original arrangement of categories because his peer editors suggested that the "Judases" would be a dramatic group to end with.

Practice 11.11 Using the same thesis statement you selected in Practice 11.10, decide on an effective ordering for your subject's parts or types. Write out a brief outline, or complete a list, clustering, or branching on a separate sheet of paper.

◆ ◆ ◆

Polish for Pizzazz

Once you've written a draft, received feedback, and given yourself time to respond to suggestions of others, go back to your essay and polish it to bring out the **piz-**

zazz—the style, energy, spirit, or vigor in writing. Even the most meticulously written draft can get bogged down by mechanical "pigeonholing" of a subject into parts or categories if the writer doesn't give the audience a strong sense of energy and spirit. If you read "How to Produce a Trashy TV Talk Show" (pp. 343–345), you'll see that Kimberly Smith really grabs her reader's attention by opening with a personal experience instead of moving right in to her subject's "ingredients."

Be creative in your introduction. Maybe you'd like to open with a little historical background on your subject, or perhaps you could get the attention of your audience by posing a problem. Check also to make sure that your conclusion is not tedious. Notice that none of the essays using division/classification close with a renaming of the parts or categories. Instead, Chuks Ofoegbu closes with a bit of personal advice to his colleagues, and Jones hints that we can really learn a lot by watching out for "hidden qualities" on the basketball court.

Practice 11.12 To gain experience in polishing an essay for pizzazz, return to the thesis and plan of development which you were working on in Practice 11.11. Think of a creative way you might introduce your subject. Now think of a creative way you might conclude that same essay. (For more information on introductions and conclusions, see Chapter 6.)

◆ ◆ ◆

STRATEGIES FOR WRITING DIVISION/CLASSIFICATION

1. **PURPOSE** Ask yourself what you want to communicate to your audience by sorting a subject into categories or breaking it down into separate parts.

2. **FOCUS** State your subject, the categories or divisions you're using, and your unifying principle. Check for overlapping categories or divisions—each should be unique.

3. **MATERIAL** You can use personal experience, but you may want to do a little research to find out more about your subject. Check to see if you have enough material to develop each of the main parts or types fully.

4. **STRUCTURE** Experiment with the most logical and effective order for your particular subject and purpose in dividing or classifying. Use appropriate cue words to signal movement from one division or classification to the next.

5. **STYLE** Choose descriptive detail and action words that will make your categories or divisions come alive for the reader. Reread your introduction and conclusion, and then polish them for pizzazz.

OPTIONS FOR WRITING DIVISION/CLASSIFICATION

The following writing options will give you an opportunity to use the strategies for division/classification. Choose an option, decide on a unifying principle for breaking your subject down into parts or types, and then make sure you have sufficient information to develop each part or category.

1. In "How to Produce a Trashy TV Talk Show" (pp. 343–345), Kimberly Smith focuses on the ingredients for such shows. Can you think of other subjects that have components or "ingredients"? Perhaps you would like to discuss the ingredients for a successful college student, hero, parent, athlete, or lover. Write an essay explaining each element of your subject.

2. Have you ever felt you were compartmentalized as a person—employee, college student, mother, father, son, daughter, boyfriend, girlfriend, soccer player, amateur bodybuilder, etc.? Select four major roles that you play and write an essay detailing each of these as a compartment. Make each compartment or role clear by indicating the divisions in your body paragraphs.

3. Are you majoring in a field that has several possible career or job opportunities? For example, the field of nursing offers registered nurse, nurse practitioner, licensed vocational nurse, and certified nurse associate. Divide a major into potential careers and discuss each, perhaps mentioning the salary, job duties, level of education required, and any special skills needed. You might visit the career center on your campus for more information.

4. Do you have a hobby or a special skill? Let's say you know a lot about self-defense. You could write an essay discussing three different types of self-defense: kung fu, jujitsu, and karate. Break your hobby into three or more subdivisions and explore the attributes of each type.

5. Do you like to people-watch? Go to a public place—a library, bar, restaurant, park, or the student center at your college—and try to place people into different categories based on their actions and interactions. For example, in the park your categories might include the loners, reading their books or newspapers on the park bench; the lovers holding hands, oblivious to all around them; the young mothers or fathers with their children. Write a paragraph detailing each category.

6. Reading Chuks Ofoegbu's essay "Co-workers" (pp. 325–327) may serve to remind you of past or present jobs in your life. If you've ever been a waitress, waiter, salesperson, clerk, or other, could you classify your customers, co-workers, or bosses based on the way they behave? In an essay, detail these categories of people.

Challenge Option: Combining Patterns

Write an essay using definition and classification. (For a review of definition, see Chapter 9.) Many of us have encountered times on the job, in school, at home with young children, or in a sport or volunteer commitment when we've been tempted to take the day off and just not show up. In other words, at these times we feel we need a "mental health day." Think about the temptation of taking your own mental health day and write an essay on the subject, using the following structure or another arrangement that you prefer:

- *Introduction:* Grab the interest of the audience; focus your subject and use a clear thesis.

- *Body paragraphs* (one or more): Define "mental health" as this term relates to commitments and/or occasional burn-out, frustration, or stress connected to commitments.

- *Body paragraphs* (one or more): Break "mental health" days down into three categories; explore three types of occasions or situations that could make you want to take a holiday from your commitments.

- *Conclusion:* Try to connect your concluding remarks to your introduction and thesis in a meaningful, thoughtful way.

JOURNAL WRITING: TYPES AND STEREOTYPES

Comparison/Contrast

Think about two people whom you know really well—these could be relatives, friends, or co-workers. For a journal entry, draw a line down the middle of your paper, putting one name on the top left side and the other name on the right side. Now think of as many specifics about the person on the left side as you can—looks, personality, way of talking, walking, likes, and dislikes. At the same time, record the corresponding detail for the person on the right side. After you have a page or more of material, review what you've written. Would you say these two people are more alike than different? In what respects are they similar? In what other respects do they differ? You may find that you want to develop your journal entry into a comparison/contrast essay.

Division/Classification

When as a writer you decide to use classification to develop your essays, you break your subject into **types**—into kinds or groups. The word **stereotypes,** however, means something quite different: preconceived notions that place someone or something into a category. Stereotypes sometimes result from human prejudices, and many times victims of stereotyping suffer discrimination. For example, if you see a person in the market who looks unshaven and is wearing dirty, torn clothing, going up and down the food aisles, you might jump to the conclusion that the person is homeless. This might lead to your next conclusion that he or she is looking for food to steal. This person—who may or may *not* be homeless—then becomes the victim of your stereotyping. In a journal entry, write about a time that

- you've stereotyped another by labeling or placing the person into a category without enough evidence.

- you have suffered as the victim of someone else's stereotyping.

In the future, check to make sure you are not stereotyping in your writing, and be on the alert to spot this faulty reasoning in the writing of others.

USING THE COMPUTER: COMPARING AND CONTRASTING INFORMATION AND WEBSITES

1. The *split screen* option can be very useful when you do prewriting for both comparison/contrast and division/classification essays. Set up separate lists to collect and evaluate material for both subjects in your comparison/contrast essay, comparing the two as you go along to make sure you're gathering enough balanced information. For a division/classification essay, use a split screen to work on two parts or categories of your subject at the same time. Later in your drafting stage, the split screen option is useful for both methods of development. Split the screen to view your body paragraphs, and again check for balance and clear order, inserting, moving, and deleting where appropriate. Remember to save your work, printing out any prewriting or drafting if you prefer working from a hard copy.

2. Have you ever seen one of the "trashy TV talk shows" described by Kimberly Smith (pp. 343–345)? Did you see anything that made you want to laugh, or yell back at the television? Many popular talk shows (both the "trashy" shows and the more "legitimate") have sites devoted to them on the World Wide Web. To find these sites, go to ⟨www.yahoo.com/news_and_media/television/shows/talk_shows/⟩, where there is an index of shows by name. Some shows are represented by several Websites—an

"official" site managed by the show and its producers, and "unofficial" sites set up by fans. On both kinds of sites, you may be able to suggest ideas for shows, respond to a particular episode, read more about the host and guests, and participate in chat groups. Choose a show that you have seen on television, and visit at least one Web page devoted to that show. Are the Web pages as "trashy" as the show? Based on the chat groups, or on "unofficial" Web sites for the show, how would you characterize the show's audience? If you find a site that lets you E-mail producers to suggest a topic for a show, work with a partner to come up with a topic. Remember that many of these "trashy" topics are phrased as questions. As part of your E-mail to the show producers, you might want to explain why you think your topic would interest the show's audience, and suggest ways of getting guests on the show as well as questions the host can ask them.

3. By now, you have seen many different kinds of Websites. Some might be very elaborate, with animated characters or even sound and video. Others might be like the newsletters some people send out with holiday cards, describing someone's life and interests for anyone who happens to take the time to read. Setting up a personal Website is like publishing a book that you write. You might not ever know who reads it, and you can choose how much or how little information to reveal about yourself. But if you have interests or experiences that you would like to share, you can use your writing skills to "publish" a web page of your own.

Find out if your school allows students to set up their own Web pages. Often, this service is free to students and staff while they are enrolled. (You might also be able to set up your own web page through a private online service.) Next, sign up for any tutorials or classes your school computer lab offers on setting up a Web page. As with all writing you do, there are issues to consider when you set up such a site:

• Will your page have a main theme or subject? (Besides yourself!)

• Who will your audience be? What information or entertainment can you provide on your Web page that will attract their interest?

• What details and experiences can you provide that will enhance your main points? You might want to link your page to other sites, where readers can find additional information. Or you might want to add photographs or sound to your page.

RESPONDING TO WRITING: A SCAVENGER HUNT

If you've ever been on a scavenger hunt, you know that it is a game in which people compete to be the first to find various items on a list. This activity will challenge you to "scavenge" for items found in the following comparison/contrast and division/classification paragraphs. All of the items listed below each paragraph can be found somewhere in the paragraph, and all have been defined and discussed either earlier in this chapter or elsewhere in your book. Annotate the paragraph by labeling each item as you find it. The first example has been done for you.

Subjects

1. **My parents** took issue over the question of whether it was possible for white people to improve. They assumed that black people were the humans of the globe, but had serious doubts about the quality and existence of white humanity. Thus my father, distrusting every word and every gesture of every white man on earth, assumed that the white man who crept up the stairs one afternoon had come to molest his daughters and threw him down the stairs and then our tricycle after him. (I think my father was wrong, but considering what I have seen since, it may have been very healthy for me to have witnessed that as my first black-white encounter.) My mother, however, *believed* in them—their possibilities. So when the meal we got on relief was bug-ridden, she wrote a long letter to Franklin Delano Roosevelt. And when white bill collectors came to our door, it was she who received them civilly and explained in a sweet voice that we were people of honor and that the debt would be taken care of. Her message to Roosevelt got through—our meal improved. Her message to the bill collectors did not always get through and there was occasional violence when my father (self-exiled to the bedroom for fear he could not hold his temper) would hear that her reasonableness had failed.

—Toni Morrison, from "A Slow Walk of Trees"

subjects

cue word signaling contrast

thesis

one-side-at-a-time plan

specific detail

2. Dr. [Harvey] Milkman, in a theory often cited by those who are stretching the boundaries of addiction, proposed in the mid-1980s that there are three kinds of addiction, each marked by the change they produce in emotional states. The first involves substances or activities that are calming, including alcohol, tranquilizers, overeating, and even watching television. The second involves becoming energized, whether by cocaine and amphetamines,

gambling, sexual activity, or high-risk sports like parachute-jumping. The third kind of addiction is to fantasy, whether induced by psychedelic drugs or, for example, by sexual thoughts.

—Daniel Goleman, from "As Addiction Medicine Gains, Experts Debate What It Should Cover: Critics Argue That Too Many Patients Are Called Addicts"

subject	divisions of subject
thesis	cue words that signal orderx
unifying principle	specific detail

READINGS AND ADDITIONAL ACTIVITIES

Comparison/Contrast

Joseph Suina grew up on New Mexico's Cochiti Pueblo reservation, where he still resides today. Suina teaches in the Multicultural Teacher Education Program at the University of New Mexico. In the following excerpt from an essay, Suina focuses on the differences between his early life on the reservation and his later experience in school.

And Then I Went to School

Joseph H. Suina

1   I lived with my grandmother from the ages of 5 through 9. It was the early 1950s when electricity had not yet invaded the homes of the Cochiti Indians. The village day school and health clinic were first to have it and to the unsuspecting Cochitis this was the approach of a new era in their uncomplicated lives.

2   Transportation was simple then. Two good horses and a sturdy wagon met most needs of a villager. Only five or six individuals possessed an automobile in the Pueblo of 300. A flatbed truck fixed with wooden rails and a canvas top made a regular Saturday trip to

Santa Fe. It was always loaded beyond capacity with Cochitis taking their wares to town for a few staples. With an escort of a dozen barking dogs, the straining truck made a noisy exit, northbound from the village.

3   During those years, Grandmother and I lived beside the plaza in a one-room house. It consisted of a traditional fireplace, a makeshift cabinet for our few tin cups and dishes, and a wooden crate that held our two buckets of all-purpose water. At the far end of the room were two rolls of bedding we used as comfortable sitting "couches." Consisting of thick quilts, sheepskin, and assorted blankets, these bed rolls were undone each night. A wooden pole the length of one side of the room was suspended about 10 inches from the ceiling beams. A modest collection of colorful shawls, blankets, and sashes was draped over the pole making this part of the room most interesting. In one corner was a bulky metal trunk for our ceremonial wear and a few valuables. A dresser, which was traded for some of my grandmother's well-known pottery, held the few articles of clothing we owned and the "goody bag." Grandmother always had a flour sack filled with candy, store bought cookies, and Fig Newtons. These were saturated with a sharp odor of moth balls. Nevertheless, they made a fine snack with coffee before we turned in for the night. Tucked securely in my blankets, I listened to one of her stories or accounts of how it was when she was a little girl. These accounts seemed so old fashioned compared to the way we lived. Sometimes she softly sang a song from a ceremony. In this way I fell asleep each night.

4   Earlier in the evening we would make our way to a relative's house if someone had not already come to visit us. I would play with the children while the adults caught up on all the latest. Ten-cent comic books were finding their way into the Pueblo homes. For us children, these were the first link to the world beyond the Pueblo. We enjoyed looking at them and role playing as one of the heroes rounding up the villains. Everyone preferred being a cowboy rather than an Indian because cowboys were always victorious. Sometimes, stories were related to both children and adults. These get-togethers were highlighted by refreshments of coffee and sweet bread or fruit pies baked in the outdoor oven. Winter months would most likely include roasted pinon nuts or dried deer meat for all to share. These evening gatherings and sense of closeness diminished as the radios and televisions increased over the following years. It was never to be the same again.

5   The winter months are among my fondest recollections. A warm fire crackled and danced brightly in the fireplace and the aroma of delicious stew filled our one-room house.

To me the house was just right. The thick adobe walls wrapped around the two of us protectingly during the long freezing nights. Grandmother's affection completed the warmth and security I will always remember.

6   Being the only child at Grandmother's, I had lots of attention and plenty of reasons to feel good about myself. As a pre-schooler, I already had the chores of chopping firewood and hauling in fresh water each day. After "heavy work," I would run to her and flex what I was certain were my gigantic biceps. Grandmother would state that at the rate I was going I would soon attain the status of a man like the adult males in the village. Her shower of praises made me feel like the Indian Superman of all times. At age 5, I suppose I was as close to that concept of myself as anyone.

7   In spite of her many years, Grandmother was still active in the village ceremonial setting. She was a member of an important women's society and attended all the functions, taking me along to many of them. I would wear one of my colorful shirts she handmade for just such occasions. Grandmother taught me the appropriate behavior at these events. Through modeling she taught me to pray properly. Barefooted, I would greet the sun each morning with a handful of cornmeal. At night I would look to the stars in wonderment and let a prayer slip through my lips. I learned to appreciate cooperation in nature and my fellowmen early in life. About food and material things, Grandmother would say, "There is enough for everyone to share and it all comes from above, my child." I felt very much a part of the world and our way of life. I knew I had a place in it and I felt good about me.

8   At age 6, like the rest of the Cochiti 6-year-olds that year, I had to begin my schooling. It was a new and bewildering experience. One I will not forget. The strange surroundings, new concepts about time and expectations, and a foreign tongue were overwhelming to us beginners. It took some effort to return the second day and many times thereafter.

9   To begin with, unlike my grandmother, the teacher did not have pretty brown skin and a colorful dress. She was not plump and friendly. Her clothes were one color and drab. Her pale and skinny form made me worry that she was very ill. I thought that explained why she did not have time just for me and the disappointed looks and orders she seemed to always direct my way. I didn't think she was so smart because she couldn't understand my language. "Surely that was why we had to leave our 'Indian' at home." But then I did not feel so bright either. All I could say in her language was "yes teacher," "my name is Joseph

Henry," and "when is lunch time." The teacher's odor took some getting used to also. In fact, many times it made me sick right before lunch. Later, I learned from the girls that this odor was something she wore called perfume.

10   The classroom too had its odd characteristics. It was terribly huge and smelled of medicine like the village clinic I feared so much. The walls and ceiling were artificial and uncaring. They were too far from me and I felt naked. The fluorescent light tubes were eerie and blinked suspiciously above me. This was quite a contrast to the fire and sunlight that my eyes were accustomed to. I thought maybe the lighting did not seem right because it was man-made, and it was not natural. Our confinement to rows of desks was another unnatural demand from our active little bodies. We had to sit at these hard things for what seemed like forever before relief (recess) came midway through the morning and afternoon. Running carefree in the village and fields was but a sweet memory of days gone by. We all went home for lunch because we lived within walking distance of the school. It took coaxing and sometimes bribing to get me to return and complete the remainder of the school day.

11   School was a painful experience during those early years. The English language and the new set of values caused me much anxiety and embarrassment. I could not comprehend everything that was happening, but yet I could understand very well when I messed up or was not doing so well. The negative aspect was communicated too effectively, and I became unsure of myself more and more. How I wished I could understand other things just as well in school.

12   The value conflict was not only in school performance but in other areas of my life as well. For example, many of us students had a problem with head lice due to "the lack of sanitary conditions in our homes." Consequently, we received a severe shampooing that was rough on both the scalp and the ego. Cleanliness was crucial and a washing of this type indicated to the class how filthy a home setting we came from. I recall that after one such treatment, I was humiliated before my peers with a statement that I had "She'na" (lice) so tough that I must have been born with them. Needless to say, my Super Indian self-image was no longer intact.

13   My language, too, was questionable from the beginning of my school career. "Leave your Indian (language) at home" was like a trademark of school. Speaking it accidentally or otherwise was a sure reprimand in the form of a dirty look or a whack with a ruler. This punishment was for speaking the language of my people which meant so much to me. It was the language of my grandmother and I spoke it well. With it, I sang beautiful songs

and prayed from my heart. At that young and tender age, comprehending why I had to part with it was most difficult for me. And yet at home I was encouraged to attend school so that I might have a better life in the future. I knew I had a good village life already but this was communicated less and less each day I was in school. . . .

14   I had to leave my beloved village of Cochiti for my education beyond Grade 6. I left to attend a Bureau of Indian Affairs boarding school 30 miles from home. Shined shoes and pressed shirt and pants were the order of the day. I managed to adjust to this just as I had to most of the things the school shoved at me or took away from me. Adjusting to leaving home and the village was tough indeed. It seemed the older I got, the further away I became from the ways I was so much a part of. Because my parents did not own an automobile, I saw them only once a month when they came up in the community truck. They never failed to come supplied with "eats" for me. I enjoyed the outdoor oven bread, dried meat, and tamales they usually brought. It took a while to get accustomed to the diet of the school. I longed for my grandmother and my younger brothers and sisters. I longed for my house. I longed to take part in a Buffalo Dance. I longed to be free.

15   I came home for the 4-day Thanksgiving break. At first, home did not feel right anymore. It was much too small and stuffy. The lack of running water and bathroom facilities were too inconvenient. Everything got dusty so quickly and hardly anyone spoke English. I did not realize I was beginning to take on the white man's ways, the ways that belittled my own. However, it did not take long to "get back with it." Once I established my relationships with family, relatives, and friends I knew I was where I came from and where I belonged.

16   Leaving for the boarding school the following Sunday evening was one of the saddest events in my entire life. Although I enjoyed myself immensely the last few days, I realized then that life would never be the same again. I could not turn back the time just as I could not do away with school and the ways of the white man. They were here to stay and would creep more and more into my life. The effort to make sense of both worlds together was painful and I had no choice but to do so. The schools, television, automobiles, and other white man's ways and values had chipped away at the simple cooperative life I grew up in. The people of Cochiti were changing. The winter evening gatherings, exchanging of stories, and even the performing of certain ceremonies were already only a memory that someone commented about now and then. Still the demands of both worlds were there. The white man's was

flashy, less personal, but comfortable. The Indian was both attracted and pushed toward these new ways that he had little to say about. There was no choice left but to compete with the white man on his terms for survival. For that I knew I had to give up a part of my life.

17   Determined not to cry, I left for school that dreadfully lonely night. My right hand clutched tightly the mound of cornmeal Grandmother placed there and my left hand brushed away a tear as I made my way back to school.

QUESTIONS ON CONTENT

1. In your own words, describe the differences between Suina's home and school environments. _____

   _____

   _____

2. In contrasting his grandmother and his elementary teacher, name two differences the writer mentions. _____

   _____

3. Name one other point of contrast Suina develops beyond differences in physical environment and people. _____

   _____

4. In which paragraph do we see the separation that allows the writer to view the reservation with different eyes? _____

   _____

QUESTIONS ON STRATEGY

1. Find and label one example of one-side-at-a-time development.

2. Find one or more examples of patterns of development other than comparison/contrast. What are they? _____

   _____

3. In paragraph 10, notice Suina's word choice. The walls of the classroom are described as "uncaring"; the writer feels "naked"; the lightbulbs are "eerie" and "blinked suspiciously." These words evoke in Suina's audience a sense of stark dread and coldness. Now reread paragraphs 3 and 4. Write down two words or phrases that are effective in giving the audience the contrasting feeling of warmth and security. _____

_____

_____

Division/Classification

When Kimberly Smith wrote this essay, which was published in her campus newspaper, she was a senior at Boston University. As you read, notice that Smith delays her thesis and concentrates in the first several paragraphs on capturing the reader's attention, offering background information, and establishing an informal, friendly tone. Think about her strategy in doing this and whether you agree that it helps make her essay effective.

How to Produce a Trashy TV Talk Show: The Four Secret Ingredients

Kimberly Smith

1   During winter break this year, I found myself (as I do every year) suffering from way too much time on my hands and way too little to do with myself. While I had planned on a month of rest and relaxation, a time to see all my old friends and accomplish all the projects I had been putting off for the past three months, I soon succumbed to boredom after the first week of my exciting vacation. So, for the long remainder of break, I did what most of you probably did on your vacation: I spent my days sleeping late, moping around the house, complaining to my parents about how bored I was, talking on the telephone to my BU friends, and, of course, watching the tube. This last activity is what I found myself most frequently engrossed in.

2   It never fails to amaze me what a variety of programming is on television these days, especially after spending three months watching the five channels that I receive at school (two networks, two home shopping stations, and the Spanish channel). From twenty-four-

hour up-to-date weather coverage and programs about how to correctly groom your pet to moral chats with Mother Angelics, there are shows geared toward every type of person these days. But despite this vast variety of quality television programming I had to choose from, I found myself most frequently tuned to possibly the trashiest genre of television ever invented: the talk show. What's worse is that since I've been back at school I've continued to be a victim of television talk. It's not that I even really approve of these shows. Personally, I think they thrive on exploiting personal problems for profit and are, quite frankly, an insult to human intelligence. I mean, what does it really say about the people of our nation when hundreds of thousands of Americans tune in to see a program about transvestite makeovers or a couple whose pets come between their relationship?

3   But who am I to talk? For I, like hundreds of other people (and I'm sure many of you), cannot resist tuning into these shows and others like them. It's not something I'm proud of, but I won't deny it either. At least I don't go so far as to set my VCR each day to record Sally Jessy, but if it's on, the topic looks interesting, and I have nothing better to do, then I'm going to watch. So now that I've admitted my fault (my one and only fault), I would like to share the wisdom that I've gained from watching these shows with all those people out there who have managed to resist the talk-show temptation. I give you the formula for the perfect talk show:

4   The first ingredient needed to make a talk show successful is a host who will be adored by his or her fans. There is no special look required of these people, for in the talk-show business, anything goes as far as appearance—fat hosts, bald hosts, old hosts, short hosts, and hosts with trendy red glasses all do equally well. And as far as personality, anything goes as well. An overly-excited-to-the-point-of-being-annoying female host who drools over her male guests is as popular as her sensitive male rival who sends everyone to therapy for free. But in my opinion, there is only one thing required to make a talk show host a success: He or she must be a washed-up celebrity who can find nothing better for work. Take Tempestt Bledsoe, Maury Povich, Ricki Lake, Vicki Lawrence, Carnie Wilson, and Mark Wahlberg, for example.

5   The second factor that goes into creating a great talk show is the right audience. These people must be energetic, enthusiastic, and must worship their host practically to the point of kissing his or her feet. They must also be willing to chant out the host's name in unison at a moment's notice. Most important, audience members must not be afraid to ask the guests questions, as well as express their feelings, beliefs, and expert opinions about the

topic at hand. It does not matter if they give their opinion of guest number one while the host is in the middle of interviewing guest number five, or even if their opinion doesn't appear to be relevant at all. The fact that they are able to express themselves and cause everyone in the audience to clap and cheer is good enough.

6   Another element that contributes to the talk-show formula are the guests: The more odd the guests, the better the ratings. People with thousands of tattoos or other self-inflicted defacements of their bodies, people with strange sexual habits, and people who have had out-of-body experiences seem to be some of the favorites. Guests who do not meet any of these criteria must at least possess a horrible rage for another guest and be willing to verbally—or physically—express this rage on the air.

7   The final secret needed to make a successful talk show is an interesting topic. Again, in this category, pretty much anything and everything goes. And while there is a wealth of creativity as far as show topics go, there are a few tried-but-true ones that work every time. These topics are: surprise engagement proposals; "surprise, I've had a crush on you since second grade"; "my mother-in-law is ruining my marriage"; and "I wish my husband/wife would. . . ." (Anything can be used to fill in this category. Some of my personal favorites are "stop flirting with the opposite sex," "lose 150 pounds," and "get rid of his/her body hair").

8   Well, there you have it: the secret formula for talk-show success, the knowledge that I gained during my productive winter vacation. For those of you who do not tune into this type of television, I hope that I've given you some valuable insight into the talk-show industry. And for those of you who do watch, I hope that you will now admit to your television-trash addiction. Just remember that wherever you are, whatever time of day, there will always be a talk show to tune in to.

QUESTIONS ON CONTENT

1. Smith confides in paragraph 2 that she's a "victim of television talk." Explain her phrase in your own words. _____

_____

2. What is the one requirement for a successful talk show host?

_____

3. What clues do you have that Smith is addressing an audience at least somewhat familiar with her subject? _____

_____

4. In order to maintain the effectiveness of the essay, what details might Smith want to change in a few years? _____

_____

QUESTIONS ON STRATEGY

1. Find and jot down a phrase in which Smith establishes a direct connection between herself and her readers._____

_____

2. Find two specific phrases used by Smith to hint that her tone is not serious but sarcastic or mocking. _____

_____

3. What is Smith's unifying principle—the basis from which she divides her subject into separate parts? _____

_____

4. If you were to help her with the essay, could you come up with yet another part or "ingredient" for a trashy talk show? Jot it down.

_____

CRITICAL THINKING IN CONNECTING TEXTS

Several of the essays in this chapter focus on behavior: In "Men are Makita, Women Are Marigolds" (pp. 313–314), Yen Glassman contrasts male and female behavior; in "Five on the Floor, But Is There More?" (pp. 323–324), Julie

Jones depicts types of behavior on the basketball court; and in "Co-workers" (pp. 325–327), Chuks Ofoegbu classifies workers on the basis of their behavior. The three writers each mention that they have learned something by observing their subjects.

What can we learn about one another, and about avoiding stereotyping, from observing our ethnic, cultural, and subcultural differences? Because America is a land rich in diversity, certain behaviors considered normal by one group of people may be regarded as abnormal by another. For instance, while westerners tend to stand about 18 to 20 inches apart when they talk, people from Saudi Arabia like to stand closer to their subjects—around 12 to 14 inches apart. Someone born in the United States may feel somehow threatened by this "too intimate" behavior and move away from the speaker; at the same time, the immigrant from Saudi Arabia may perceive that the American is unfriendly, distant, and possibly unapproachable. A person from the Southwest may prefer to wear "cowboy" boots, even in the city. This might seem like strange behavior to someone raised in the city, while this city-bred individual's habit of avoiding eye contact with strangers on the street may appear bizarre to the Midwesterner in the boots.

Work with a small group of people or your entire class to discover other examples of behaviors based on cultural or subcultural differences. Think about the people you see in public places, on campus, in your local neighborhoods, and on the job: baby boomers, Generation-Xers, dog owners, cat lovers, business persons, artists, senior citizens, bikers, or joggers. Discuss behavioral differences, including misunderstandings, communication breakdowns, or stereotyping, and then explore possible solutions. Take notes and keep them—you might want to use your notes to write an essay exploring behavioral differences and stereotyping.

For more writing resources, be sure to see the Longman English Pages Website at http://longman.awl.com/englishpages

Taking a Stand: Argument

> Give me the liberty to know, to utter, and to argue freely according to conscience, above all liberties.
>
> —*John Milton, poet*

Preview

In this chapter you will learn
▶ to identify the characteristics of argument
▶ to evaluate arguments on the basis of soundness and validity
▶ to distinguish among logical, emotional, and ethical appeals
▶ to recognize and avoid logical fallacies
▶ to develop skill in writing essays using strategies of argument: stating a claim, supporting the claim with reliable evidence, refuting the opposition, using appeals fairly

CHARACTERISTICS OF ARGUMENT

When you hear the word *argument,* do you envision a disagreement, perhaps one involving shouts, accusations, or maybe even slammed doors? Think back to the last heated exchange you had with a loved one or friend, a boss or co-worker. Were you both behaving logically? Possibly, like many people, you were so emotionally involved that you weren't reasoning carefully or stating your arguments clearly; you might have been too caught up in the heat of the moment.

In contrast to this scenario of the fervent quarrel, the writing strategy classified as **argument** involves persuading an audience to agree with you on a controversial issue. To persuade your readers, you use evidence to support your opinion. And while argumentative essays do often include a writer's personal opinion and revolve around a heated or controversial dispute, they need to be controlled and reasonable in order to be effective. In learning about argument and practicing argumentative writing, you'll draw upon what you've learned about various methods of essay development in other chapters of this text. In addition, you'll be practicing some new skills.

To see how argument can be used to develop an essay, read the following essay, asking yourself what this writer wants from his audience.

Rainforests of the Sea

Kieran Mulvaney

1   To some, the open ocean exists as a vast wasteland, an aquatic desert largely devoid of life beyond the occasional playful dolphin or breaching whale. But this image, though common, is wrong: there is life in the ocean, teeming through the waters in a dazzling array of diversity. Much, however, is invisible: literally, as in the billions of microscopic organisms found throughout the water column, and figuratively, as in the many larger species that dwell in the ocean's darkest depths or the farthest reaches.

2   Coral reefs are a different matter. No need here for any expensive equipment to scan the tiniest water droplets or to plumb the ocean depths. As long as you're on the coast in the right parts of the world, you need nothing more than a mask and snorkel to enter the realm of the reef.

3   And a coral reef can be host to an amazing richness of life. Indeed, reefs are home to by far the greatest abundance of species in any marine ecosystem. A recent estimate suggests that there may be about 93,000 species already described from coral reefs. Many more remain to be identified, and the total number of species on coral reefs could be as high as a million. For example, about one third of the world's marine fishes are found on reefs, and, at One Tree Reef in Australia, nearly 150 species of fish have been recorded in an area of less than $50m^2$.

4   Reefs, both by themselves and in combination with ecosystems such as mangroves and seagrasses, provide important feeding, breeding, and nursery areas for a wide range of marine life. They create sheltered lagoons, protecting coastlines against wave erosion. Millions of people depend on reefs for their livelihood, and the combination of their spectacular array of life and their proximity to the coast has increasingly made them attractive tourist destinations.

5   Unfortunately, this very same combination is also causing reef systems around the world to be degraded and destroyed at an alarming rate. According to the World Conservation Union (IUCN), as much as 10 percent of the world's coral reefs has been degraded beyond recovery, and another 30 percent is likely to decline within the next 20 years. Those

at greatest risk are in South and Southeast Asia, East Africa and the Caribbean, but the problem is widespread: out of 109 countries where reefs are known to occur, significant reef degradation has occurred in 93.

6   The abundant fish life on reefs has long been exploited for food. In earlier times, the scale and nature of the fishing meant that fish populations didn't suffer: but in more recent years, changes in fishing techniques and the commercialization of fisheries have, among other factors, led to sharp declines in many species.

7   Dynamite fishing, for example, takes place in many areas. One blast can destroy an area of reef 10 meters in diameter. More recently, the use of sodium cyanide has become widespread as a means of stunning fish to supply the aquarium trade and also to satisfy increased demand for live fish in Asian restaurants.

8   On reefs around the world, fisheries that once concentrated on valuable fish such as grouper and snapper now yield less desirable parrotfish, triggerfish and damselfish. Many of the spawning grounds of the Nassau grouper, where huge numbers aggregate for a few days each year, have been found by fishermen, who can remove the major part of an entire breeding population in a very short space of time. This species is now scarce throughout the Caribbean and, together with the Napoleon wrasse, was among the first species of coral reef fish to be listed as globally threatened on the 1996 IUCN Red List.

9   The queen conch, once an important part of the subsistence diet in the Caribbean, has also been virtually eradicated from many reefs in the region and is now an expensive, luxury food. Similarly, the giant clam, which filled an important dietary and ceremonial role in the Pacific, has been over-exploited across vast areas by an industry seeking to feed an Asian appetite for sushi and aphrodisiacs.

10   Perhaps even more serious than such direct exploitation, reef habitats are also under enormous threat from construction and development. More than half of the world's population lives on or near the coast, and both the proportion and absolute numbers are expected to continue growing. This increasing crush of people has had predictable consequences for reefs. In some places, new development has literally been built directly on top of reef systems; elsewhere, reefs have been blasted, bulldozed or mined for use as materials in, or to make way for, construction. More than 500,000 tons of coral sand are excavated annually from Mauritius alone.

11   There are other impacts. Pollution from small-scale, but repeated, oil spills, agro-chemical run-off and heavy metals is a problem in many areas. Domestic and industrial pollution from Bangkok and Pattaya, for example, has almost totally destroyed the reefs in

the northern Gulf of Thailand. And, when sewage, animal waste and fertilizer are carried downstream or simply discharged straight into coastal waters, seaweed and phytoplankton thrive, which reduces the sunlight reaching the corals.

12   Sedimentation, which arises from activities such as deforestation and dumping sand to make beaches, is another serious threat. The sediment smothers reefs and reduces the amount of sunlight penetrating the water, which is devastating for corals, whose cells contain photosynthesizing algae. Death for corals can come in a matter of days or even, in extreme cases, hours.

13   Ironically, the growth of the tourist industry in reef regions, prompted by the corals' spectacular beauty, can add to the problems those reefs face. Damage by careless swimmers, divers, and boaters can all destroy chunks of reef; of even greater concern are the additional sewage, wastes and beach erosion resulting from siting tourist facilities and resorts so close to reefs. Coral cover off the western coast of the Gulf of Thailand is reportedly declining by 20 percent annually, due to tourist-related coastal clearing and sewage pollution.

14   A number of steps are being taken to try to limit, arrest, and even reverse reef damage. 1997 has been declared the International Year of the Reef in an attempt to raise awareness and generate support for a global coral reef monitoring program. Because reefs are found in so many different countries and are subject to a varying combination of pressures, each with their own specific social, environmental and economic causes, it is impossible to write a blanket prescription that will cure all corals' ills at a stroke.

15   Scientists, therefore, recommend an integrated approach which includes the establishment of marine protected areas, management of tourism and development activities, education, the generation (where appropriate) of sources of income other than those based on exploiting reefs, and strict regulation of the reef exploitation that does take place.

16   But, even as steps are being taken to address and implement such important measures, the difficulty of the task is highlighted by new problems, while our response is hampered by our poor knowledge of the coral reef world. Since the 1950s, plagues of the crown-of-thorns starfish have been reported from coral reefs across the Pacific. These huge starfish eat coral, and, when they occur in plague proportions, they can destroy an entire reef. Scientists are still unclear as to whether these plagues are entirely natural or have been exacerbated by human activities.

17   A rather different story was observed in the Caribbean in 1983 when an unknown pathogen wiped out the long-spined sea urchin. On some reefs, the effects were devastating.

These urchins are important grazers, and their loss meant the prolific growth of algae, which killed vast areas of coral. The worst effects appeared to be in areas where overfishing had removed most of the grazing fishes, which might have been able to do the work of the urchins.

18   The corals themselves, too, are susceptible to poorly understood problems, such as black-band and white-band disease, which have destroyed vast areas of reef. Another issue of concern is coral bleaching. This is a decline of photosynthetic algae, or algal pigment, in the cells of reef corals, which often results in the coral's death. Though this can occur naturally, for example in coral damaged by storms, it is now happening much more frequently and, at times, over much larger areas. There are a number of possible causes, but the one attracting the most attention is increased sea temperatures as a result of global climate change.

19   Coral reefs have been called "rainforests of the sea," a tribute to the abundance and diversity of life they contain. The comparison is, unfortunately, apt in another way. Unless action is taken soon, and applied widely, reefs, like rainforests, will continue to disappear before our very eyes.

Notice that Mulvaney's argument demonstrates the following characteristics:

- **The subject is debatable.**
  Mulvaney, Senior Editor of SeaWeb, chooses as his subject the endangered condition of the world's coral reefs. He airs an opinion: the coral reefs are "under threat." This statement is an opinion rather than a fact.

- **The thesis makes a reasonable claim, a statement that can be supported by evidence.**
  Mulvaney's thesis comes at the end of paragraph 5: "Unfortunately, this very same combination is also causing reef systems around the world to be degraded and destroyed at an alarming rate."

- **The opposition is acknowledged and refuted.**
  In the first paragraph, Mulvaney states, "To some, the open ocean exists as a vast wasteland, an aquatic desert largely devoid of life beyond the occasional playful dolphin or breaching whale." He effectively refutes this opposing position by explaining in the next several paragraphs why "this image, though common, is wrong: there is life in the ocean, teeming through the waters in a dazzling array of diversity."

- **The argument is developed with reliable and up-to-date evidence.**
  In paragraph 3, Mulvaney cites a "recent estimate" of the number of species in the coral reefs. In paragraph 5, he refers his audience to statistics gathered by the World Conservation Union. In paragraph 8, Mulvaney mentions facts obtained in 1996.

• **Appeals are used to advance the writer's argument.**

When in paragraph 4 Mulvaney asserts that coral reefs "provide important feeding, breeding, and nursery areas for a wide range of marine life. . . . create sheltered lagoons, protecting coastlines against wave erosion," he employs a logical appeal. If coral reefs are destroyed, marine life and coastlines will suffer as a result. When Mulvaney later adds in paragraph 6, "The abundant fish life on reefs has long been exploited for food," he uses emotionally laden words to appeal to his audience's feelings and to arouse a desired response from them.

To observe these characteristics at work in a student essay, read the following model and see how many of the characteristics just discussed you can identify.

MODEL WITH KEY QUESTIONS

In his search for an issue of public concern, Brian Villapudua discovered that he felt strongly about immigration. He decided to gather additional information by consulting online sources and recent articles in periodicals.

LET'S MIX IT UP
Brian Villapudua

Brian Villapudua's essay on the immigration issue reflects the writer's interest in economic affairs. Brain plans to transfer to a University of California campus and to pursue a bachelor's degree in economics with a French minor. He would then like to become a consultant for an international business firm. Brian is presently attending the Sorbonne University in Paris. He is continuing to work on his writing skills, keeping journals of his European trips and the many people he has met in his travels.

1   Immigration is a touchy subject today and very few people in this country are willing to stick their necks out and take a stand on one side or the other. Either way they look at this muffled debate is bound to raise many questions. Let's take, for example, those who side with the anti-immigrationists. They argue that immigration puts a greater stress on the taxpayers to support immigrants. Anti-iimmigrationists say immigrants are taking away jobs from U.S. nationals and rais-

ing rents, and that too many immigrants are entering too fast to assimilate into "American" culture. However, these people appear to have made rash judgments about the issues when making such arguments, which seem to stem from xeno-phobic prejudices. Some of us don't like to deal with things which are unfamiliar to us, but immigrants are an invaluable resource to this great nation, which was created by immigrants. Thus, we should strive to increase the number of legal im-migrants allowed into our country.

2   One argument anti-immigrationists make is that the taxpayers are burdened by the extra expenses for health, welfare, and other non-educational services that are placed on the system by immigrants. But are immigrants really burdening this country? George Borjas, an economics professor at the University of California at San Diego, discovered that even though immigrants receive more in government benefits than they pay in taxes, they actually produce a net gain for the U.S. econ-omy of about four billion dollars a year.

3   What about immigrants taking away our jobs? This is another question asked by anti-immigrationists. In actuality, the jobs that immigrants accept are usually low-paying ones in restaurants, households, agriculture, and in the manufacturing industry. Dr. Larry Bedard, a hospital board member in a wealthy community, ex-plains, "We want them [the immigrants] to clean our houses, rake our leaves, take care of our children, do the scut work of life."

4   Although some argue that immigrants, both illegal and legal, are destroying the prosperity of this country, they cannot totally blame immigrants for the prob-lems that the U.S. is now facing. Part of the problem is the poor service pro-vided by the U.S. Immigration and Naturalization Services, known as the INS. Currently, the individual offices of the INS do not have a standardized operation; instead each office operates as it deems best. In addition, some INS employees have been exerting their prejudices on certain ethnic groups, obviously making it more difficult for some to get through the system than for others. Overhauling the INS to provide better, more efficient service for all immigrants would help stop the influx of illegals by increasing the number of legal immigrants into the country. Also, since immigrants get tired of complicated red tape, getting rid of unnecessary forms could lessen the bureaucratic resistance that affects many immigrants.

5   We as U.S. citizens should remember that immigrants provide this country with an invaluable source of labor as well as help the economy through the con-sumption of goods. If the U.S. is to stop legal immigrants from entering, we are going to lose a part of our country's heritage—the open arms we once stretched out to welcome foreigners during the formative years of our nation.

KEY QUESTIONS

1. **PURPOSE** What is the writer's purpose in discussing the immigration issue?

   _____

2. **FOCUS** Write the writer's claim in your own words. _____

   _____

3. **MATERIAL** Find two examples of evidence used by Villapudua and anno-

   tate the essay by underlining the two examples. _____

   _____

4. **STRUCTURE** Describe the organizational plan Villapudua uses.

   _____

5. **STYLE** Does the introductory paragraph establish the writer as fair

   and ethically motivated? Explain and offer support for your point of

   view. _____

   _____

GUIDELINES FOR WRITING ARGUMENT

Choose a Controversial Subject

When you're picking your brain for a subject for your argument, be aware that certain subjects just won't work for an argumentative essay. You cannot argue about beliefs, preferences, facts, or that which is impossible. Don't "shoot yourself in the foot" by choosing one of these topics. Here is a closer look at four types of subjects that are not appropriate for an essay using argument.

Facts

Since your main purpose in an argument is to persuade your audience to agree with you, **facts**—data that are regarded as true, rather than controversial—do not make appropriate subjects. However, while facts are not appropriate as subjects, they provide excellent supporting evidence to convince your readers to agree with you.

Preferences

Preferences—personal likes and dislikes that are shaped not by reason but by background and emotions—do not make appropriate subjects for argumentative essays. Personal preferences usually can't be changed. In "Rainforests of the Sea" (pp. 349–352) Kieran Mulvaney argues that healthy reef life impacts humans and other marine animals in many positive ways. He does not argue that the life of the coral reef is superior to all other forms of life.

Beliefs

If you've ever tried to discuss religion with another person, you probably know that **beliefs**—ideas that are held to be true for each individual but can't be proved to others—usually don't make good subjects for argument. For example, the subject in "Let's Mix It Up" (pp. 353–354)—U.S. immigration—has nothing to do with the writer's personal beliefs but instead focuses on his opinion regarding this issue.

Impossibilities

Other subjects to avoid in an argumentative essay are **impossibilities**—proposals that are not possible in the real world. For instance, even though Villapudua speaks out in favor of immigration and asserts that immigrants have made tremendous contributions to our country's resources, he does not argue for unlimited immigration into the United States. He knows that trying to convince an audience of this unrealistic position would be as futile as trying to push a huge boulder uphill.

Opinions

What *is* an arguable subject? Opinions that can be debated because they have two or more sides or stands are excellent subjects for argumentative essays, especially if the opinions focus on issues of public concern.

In contrast to facts, preferences, beliefs, and impossibilities, **opinions**—issues, especially issues of public concern, about which a person feels strongly—make excellent subjects for an argumentative essay. It's important to differentiate between a personal preference and a reasonable opinion. To illustrate, "chocolate ice cream tastes better than vanilla" is a preference. In contrast, the opinion that "yogurt is better for people than ice cream" may be supported by specific evidence about vitamins, minerals, caloric content, and testimony from dietary experts.

Practice 12.1 Read the following sentences to see if they contain debatable subjects for an essay. Identify each as F (fact), P (preference), B (belief), I (impossibility), or O (opinion on an issue of concern to others).

1. _____ In the Civil War, both the North and the South lost many lives.

2. _____ If we as a nation would engage in more recycling, we would make the world a better place for future generations.

3. _____ Short hair is more attractive on men than long hair.

4. _____ God watches all of our actions.

5. _____ Elvis Presley, although rich and famous, was a lonely man.

6. _____ Watching musical groups in concert is more enjoyable than watching solo performers in concert.

7. _____ College instructors should never assign homework to their students.

8. _____ In the United States, the voting age is eighteen.

9. _____ Most guinea pigs are smaller than most dogs.

10. _____ The best colleges cost the most money to attend.

◆ ◆ ◆

Assess Your Audience

Once you've found a debatable subject, think about what kind of audience you will be addressing. Notice that both Mulvaney and Villapudua appear to be addressing an audience that does not have any specialized knowledge of their subjects. Although Mulvaney as SeaWeb's senior editor is probably familiar with all reef terms, he attempts to define them for readers. When he mentions the "queen conch" in paragraph 9, he explains that this sea animal was once "an important part of the subsistence diet in the Caribbean." In paragraph 12, Mulvaney takes care to explain sedimentation as an occurrence "which arises from activities such as deforestation and dumping sand to make beaches." In paragraph 4 of "Let's Mix It Up," when Villapudua refers to the INS for the first time he tells his audience that this acronym stands for the Immigration and Naturalization Services.

Ask yourself how much knowledge of the subject your readers possess, as this will influence the type of evidence and the manner in which you present your material in your argument. How would you categorize your audience in relation to your opinion on the subject? Do you think the average reader would be inclined to agree with you? Would your audience be cautious and possibly undecided, capable of siding with you or against you? Or is your opinion one that is so unpopular or controversial that you predict outright reader hostility?

Practice 12.2 To try your hand at assessing an audience, read the following subjects for arguments and the accompanying situations, and then decide whether you would categorize the audience as friendly, neutral, or hostile. Write your assessment next to the subject.

<u>Subject</u>	<u>Audience</u>	<u>Assessment</u>
1. Violence against women resulting from popular song lyrics	Record companies	_____
2. Violence against women resulting from popular song lyrics	Feminists	_____
3. More lenient attendance policy for college classes	Students	_____
4. More lenient attendance policy for college classes	Faculty/administration	_____
5. Importance of self-examination for cancer detection	Insurance agencies	_____
6. Importance of self-examination for cancer detection	High school students	_____

◆ ◆ ◆

Focus Subject with a Reasonable Claim

Once you've determined both a subject and audience for your argument, you'll want to focus your subject with a **claim**—the assertion the writer makes that his or her opinion is valid. The claim forms the thesis statement for an essay using argument, and it sometimes includes a demand or request, using such words as *ought to, should, must,* or *needs.* An example of a claim can be found in the thesis for "Let's Mix It Up" at the end of paragraph 1: "Thus, we *should* strive to increase the number of legal immigrants allowed into our country."

Notice that this thesis contains a subject (legal immigrants) and a controlling idea (we should strive to increase the numbers).

Practice 12.3   Turn the following subjects into claims, making sure that each claim includes a subject and a controlling idea.

1. Capital punishment _____

2. Computers and colleges _____

3. Vitamin E _____

4. Birth parents and adopted children _____

5. Violent crime and city living _____

◆ ◆ ◆

Use a Variety of Reliable, Current Evidence

You will want to compile **evidence**—support material for claims made within an essay. Evidence can consist of any or all of the following:

- **Facts** Information held to be true
- **Statistics** A group or list of numerical facts
- **Expert testimony** Statement by experts in a relevant field
- **Charts, graphs, tables, surveys** Numerical information about a subject
- **Detailed, documented examples** Illustrations or models from life
- **Personal interviews** Meetings with people who know about the subject
- **Firsthand experience** What the writer knows about the subject
- **Observation** What the writer has observed about the subject

To develop a sound argument—one that can withstand scrutiny and convince your reader—you will want to employ a variety of evidence that is both reliable and current. **Reliable evidence** is support material that comes from qualified sources. Notice that Villapudua uses the findings of a university professor of economics in paragraph 2 of his essay. **Current evidence** is support material that comes from sources that have shared information within the last few years. All sources for Mulvaney's "Rainforests of the Sea" are current. When consulting sources and doing research, be sure to check publication dates.

Practice 12.4 Specific types of evidence are presented in each of the following three paragraphs. Identify the claim that each writer makes, and fill in the type of evidence used to support that claim. Refer back to the list of kinds of evidence if you find it helpful.

> Advocates argue that good child care can also benefit employers. Richard Stolley, president of CCAC [Child Care Action Campaign], was instrumental in the development of a day-care center at Time Inc., the large media company where he is editorial director. "It's a productivity issue," he explained. "The number of employees who don't show up or who show up harried because child-care arrangements have fallen through is enormous. Child care is not a women's issue. It has an effect on productivity of men and women, on the whole working family."
>
> —Michael Ryan, from "Who's Taking Care of the Children"

Claim: _____

_____

Type of evidence:_____

_____

> Does hate speech harm the individual to whom it is addressed? I can speak to this myself. My parents came to this country nearly four decades ago from the Middle East. I was born in Texas and later grew up in California's Central Valley. My early years were spent constantly trying to conform and avoid the appearance of being different. As a young person in public schools, I often heard comments, jokes, and insults about my ethnicity and the place my parents had once called home. I can assure you that these comments hurt—and in a different way than they might if reversed against those in more populous numbers. If they caused me some pain as a white male, I could only imagine what they must feel like when directed to those already burdened with discrimination in our society.
>
> —Joseph S. Tuman, from "Hate Speech on Campus"

Claim: _____

Type of evidence:_____

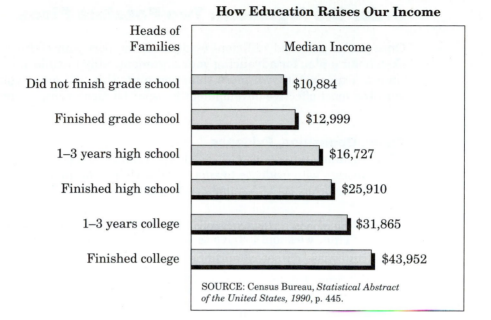

How Education Raises Our Income

Heads of Families	Median Income
Did not finish grade school	$10,884
Finished grade school	$12,999
1–3 years high school	$16,727
Finished high school	$25,910
1–3 years college	$31,865
Finished college	$43,952

SOURCE: Census Bureau, *Statistical Abstract of the United States, 1990*, p. 445.

More positively, . . . education serves a useful function by upgrading prospective workers' skills—human capital—which in turn boosts earning for individuals and promotes economic growth for society. There is growing evidence to support this view. As the illustration "How Education Raises Our Income" (above) shows, education and income are strongly related. . . . Economist Dan Burkhead estimates that a 25-year-old man with a college degree can expect to earn within 40 years $365,000 more than a man with a high school diploma can. A 25-year-old female college graduate also can expect to earn within 40 years $144,000 more than a female high school graduate.

—Alex Thio, from "How Education Raises Our Income"

Claim: _____

_____

Type of evidence:_____

_____

◆ ◆ ◆

Order the Argument: Two Possible Plans

Once you've gathered sufficient evidence to support your claim, you'll want to sketch out a plan for advancing your argument. Stay flexible and give yourself time to experiment with more than one plan; this will allow you to come up with the most effective development for your particular argument.

Claim, Opposition, Evidence

After beginning your essay with a claim, you can then acknowledge the opposition and elaborate with evidence to support your claim. For a model of this plan, look again at "Let's Mix It Up" (pp. 353–354). Here's an outline of Villapudua's structure:

I. Introductory background information and claim (paragraph 1): "Thus, we should strive to increase the number of legal immigrants allowed into our country."

II. Acknowledgment of opposing view (paragraphs 2 and 3): "One argument anti-immigrationists make . . ." and "This is another question asked by anti-immigrationists. . . ."

III. Refutation of opposing view (paragraphs 2 and 3): Expert testimony from Borjas and Bedard.

IV. Evidence to support claim (paragraph 4): Information on INS operations and reform efforts.

Premise, Opposition, Claim

You may also advance your argument by beginning with a **premise**—a specific piece of evidence—proceeding with the acknowledgment of the opposition, offering more evidence that refutes the opposition, and concluding with your claim. For an example of this plan of development, read Derek Humphrey's essay "Offering Euthanasia Can Be an Act of Love" (pp. 272–273). Here's an outline of Humphrey's structure:

I. Premise (paragraph 1): The American Medical Association decided that "artificial feeding is a life support mechanism and can be disconnected from hopelessly comatose patients."

II. Premise (paragraph 2): Courts in two other states have also ruled this way.

III. Premise (paragraph 4): People fear life support equipment use by their loved ones; testimony from Annas about people's rights.

IV. Acknowledgment of opposing view (paragraphs 5 and 6): "Food is a gift from God" and Nazi excesses of the 1930s.

V. Refutation of opposing view (paragraphs 5–8): "A pipe is a manufactured item," not normal feeding; "No terminally ill or comatose person was ever helped to die by the Nazis."

VI. Claim (paragraph 9): Assisting a loved one to die is "good medicine"
and demonstrates a "caring society" willing to demonstrate "an act
of love."

Practice 12.4 Think about sketching out an appropriate argumentative plan. Work with a
partner and compose an outline for the following claim: "Colleges should make
freshman composition a pass/fail rather than a graded course."

◆ ◆ ◆

Use Cue Words to Advance Argument

Check the table of cue words (pp. 187–188) in revising and polishing, to make sure
that you move your audience logically and smoothly from one part of your argument to the next. In addition to the cue words listed in the table, the following
transition words or phrases may be helpful in advancing your argument clearly:

- Phrases that signal that the writer is acknowledging the other side: *my
opponents, the opposition believes, while many people think, there are
some who say, it is often thought that, in all fairness.*

- Phrases that signal that the writer is being fair or attempting to put
some limits on the claims made: *apparently, frequently, appears, most of
the time, sometimes, may, might, on several occasions.*

Include Appropriate, Fair-minded Appeals

In your argument, you will be appealing to your audience to side with you on
the issue being discussed. These appeals can be of three types: logical, emotional, and ethical.

Logical Appeals

Logical appeals are a writer's calls for help based on sound reasoning and
good common sense. These are the appeals that a writer will use to take the
reader from point A to point B, no matter what plan of development will be followed. For example, when Villapudua poses the question, "What about immigrants taking away our jobs?" he answers the question with details from a rep-
utable source. The source states that the only jobs immigrants appear to "take
away" are low-paying ones that few others are willing to take. Villapudua appeals to the reader's ability to think reasonably on this point.

Emotional Appeals

Much of what we read in advertising copy or see in television commercials uses **emotional appeals,** which are often advanced by a writer's choice of words, to persuade an audience. (For more information about the power of word choice, see the sections on connotative and denotative meanings in Chapter 9. For example, when Kieran Mulvaney uses the phrases "smothers reefs" and "devastating for corals" (pp. 349–352) his word choice evokes an emotional response from his audience.

Ethical Appeals

Ethical appeals enlist audience support on the basis of the writer's fairness or sense of moral values. For example, when an advertisement for America's Chemical Industry states, "Landfills, if *properly* designed, operated, and monitored—are one of the best ways to dispose of certain kinds of solid wastes," the writers of the ad appeal to readers by convincing them that they should have faith in the chemical industry since it is ethical enough to act responsibly and design proper landfills.

Which kind of appeal and how many appeals should you include in your argument? This is a sticky question. Throughout your argument, if you use a fair and unbiased tone, you'll be appealing ethically. And certainly you'll want to develop as many logical appeals as you can. Then you can enhance your argument using emotional appeals, as long as you have the logic to back them up. Just make sure the facts justify the emotion you're arousing in your audience.

Practice 12.5 For practice in identifying appeals, read the excerpts from the two essays by Nizer and Johnson on America's drug problem (pp. 369–371). Find an example of each type of appeal and write it here:

1. Logical appeal _____

2. Emotional appeal _____

3. Ethical appeal _____

◆ ◆ ◆

Avoid Logical Fallacies

In your zeal and enthusiasm to influence others, you risk using **logical fallacies**—errors or flaws in reasoning or logical thinking. Although some writers may be guilty of knowingly using a logical fallacy to persuade a reader, more often, writers unknowingly fall into the fallacy trap even though they would like to present a balanced, well-supported argument. Learn to recognize the following fallacies in the writings of others and try to avoid them in your own writing:

- *Ad hominem* A Latin phrase meaning "to the man," this term refers to an attack on specific people associated with an issue rather than addressing the issue itself. For instance, if you were to say that all defense attorneys are untrustworthy because one noted defense attorney lies to the press, you would be guilty of an *ad hominem* argument.

- **Begging the question** A logical fallacy in which the writer repeats a claim rather than offering any real proof to support it. For example, if you state that a certain politician will be controlled by major corporations, but you offer no evidence about any connections, you've given no real proof in support of your claims.

- **Equivocation** A logical fallacy in which the writer uses vague or unclear words to mislead the reader. To illustrate, you might state that the United States has "suffered no *real* loss of money or manpower from the Persian Gulf encounter." What exactly is a "real loss of money or manpower"?

- **False dilemma** Sometimes referred to as the "either/or fallacy," this error leads a writer to present only two sides of a complex issue. You'd be guilty of presenting a false dilemma if you asserted, "If we don't stop using aerosol products, the world will be destroyed by the greenhouse effect."

- **Hasty generalization** A logical fallacy in which a writer jumps to a conclusion without considering all evidence. If you say that "a college's math classes are suffering huge drops in enrollment because the classes must be too difficult for students," you are jumping to a conclusion without considering all factors.

- See also ***post hoc* fallacy** and **oversimplification** (Chapter 10, p. 295.)

Practice 12.6 For practice in identifying logical fallacies, read the excerpts from the two essays by Nizer and Johnson (pp. 369–371) and then answer these two questions.

1. Search for logical fallacies in Nizer's argument. When you've found one, write the phrase and identify the type of fallacy in the following space. Refer back to the list of logical fallacies above for review.

_____

2. Now search for logical fallacies in Johnson's argument. Write down any that you find, also identifying the type of fallacy.

_____

◆ ◆ ◆

STRATEGIES FOR ARGUMENTATION

1. **PURPOSE** Choose a subject of public concern that you feel strongly about—avoid facts, preferences, beliefs, and impossibilities. Define your audience; figure out exactly whom you want to address and why you'd like to advance your argument on the issue.

2. **FOCUS** State your claim, making sure that it is reasonable and that your tone presents you as a fair person.

3. **MATERIAL** Gather enough evidence to advance your argument effectively. Check to see that you use current and reliable sources, including several of the following: facts, statistics, expert testimony, charts, graphs, tables, surveys, examples, personal interviews, firsthand experience, observation.

4. **STRUCTURE** Use the most effective organization of your material to advance your argument. Experiment with alternative plans—from claim to specific evidence and from evidence to claim. Place your acknowledgment of the opposing side wherever this will be most appropriate. Use cue words to move from one piece of evidence to the next.

5. **STYLE** Use logical as well as ethical and emotional appeals. Make sure you have the facts to support these appeals. In revising and polishing, search your draft for logical fallacies, revising when appropriate. In your introduction, make sure you're conveying your stand on the issue clearly to your audience; in your conclusion, ask yourself if you've communicated what action you want your readers to take in response to your essay.

JOURNAL WRITING: AN OPINION INVENTORY

Your journal can be helpful in generating ideas for an essay using argument. In an entry, create an inventory of issues that interest you. First, try to list ten or more issues that you might like to write about. Think about what has been headlined in the papers recently or discussed by television newscasters. Explore your feelings about political situations in the United States and abroad. Don't forget to think about campus issues also. Is your tuition increasing? Is student parking scarce? Are computers hard to find on campus? If you are taking a night class, do you feel safe walking to your car? You might also think about issues of local concern in your community. Do people with loud music or power tools interfere with your peace and quiet? Are your parks or streets in need of repair?

Once you've created a substantial inventory, choose two or three of these issues to explore further. Then in another journal entry, answer the following questions for each issue:

- What is my stand on this issue?

- Why do I feel this way about the issue?

- Who would disagree with me and why?

- What evidence do I already have that I could use to advance an argument?

- What kinds of additional evidence would be particularly helpful in developing an argument on this issue?

Your opinion inventory and the resulting answers to questions associated with issues should help you focus on some exciting subject possibilities for essays using argument.

USING THE COMPUTER: WRITING, DEVELOPING, AND OBSERVING ARGUMENTS

1. Many of the word-processing functions presented in other chapters can be applied to drafting arguments. For example, try using *cut, copy,* and *paste* to experiment with the ordering of claims, opposition, evidence, and premise in your drafts (for review, see pp. 362–363). Use the *split screen* to keep all your notes on evidence available as you draft, and use the *copy* and *paste* functions to move pieces of evidence into your argument. *Annotation* (either *voice* or *text*) can help you or a peer reviewer note places in your argument where you might be using a fallacy.

2. You can use the Internet in developing your argumentative strategies. First, find an ongoing discussion about a controversial issue that interests you and about which you might write an essay. Then, "listen" in on how people are discussing the topic. You might try one of the following chat groups:

- ⟨http://www.talkcity.com⟩

- ⟨http://chat.yahoo.com⟩

- ⟨www.hotbot.com/partners/forumone.html⟩

continued

USING THE COMPUTER: WRITING, DEVELOPING, AND OBSERVING ARGUMENTS *continued*

In addition, many newspapers and magazines have Websites that invite reader response (If a chat room is like a debate on a bus or in a bar, these response forums are more like a letters-to-the-editor page where every response is printed, and the letter-writers can also respond to each other.)

However, some people use the anonymity of the Web to say things that they wouldn't usually admit, and some people can be very crude in their opinions and in their responses to other chat room participants. Does this seem to be an effective way of arguing in an online environment? How do other participants in the chat room respond to rude or arrogant postings?

If you're lucky, though, you will find many new perspectives on an issue being expressed in a chat room. Do you recognize good argument strategies in any of the postings? Print out examples of rude or unproductive arguing, and examples of smart and considerate arguing, and share them with the class. Be prepared to discuss what makes a particular posting an effective or ineffective style of argument.

OPTIONS FOR WRITING ARGUMENT

The following writing options encourage you to take a stand on an issue of public concern. As you work through your essay, think about where you can gather solid, convincing evidence to advance your argument.

1. Euthanasia, life-support systems, living wills, artificial feeding—these terms have today become increasingly controversial. Read the two arguments "Offering Euthanasia Can Be an Act of Love" (pp. 372–373) and "Do Not Go Gentle into That Good Night (p. 374) and then explore the issue both authors consider by making a claim of your own about the subject. Support your claim in an essay. To find more information, you can browse the Web, use an online subject index (see p. 260), use the *Readers' Guide to Periodical Literature* at your college library, or interview a local hospital administrator, nurse, or doctor. Try the keywords *euthanasia, life-support systems, living wills, artificial feeding,* or *Kevorkian* (a doctor who supports and performs euthanasia for his terminally ill patients). In compiling your information, be sure you have found material on both sides of the issue so that you can present a sound, balanced argument.

2. Think about an issue of campus concern that impacts you in some way—for example, student parking, tuition increases, attendance policy, food service, sexual harassment policy, or the need for a child care center. If several of the students in your class are also exploring the same campus issue, you can break into "pro" and "con" teams at random. Engaging in such a mini-debate should allow you to discover specific points for both sides of the issue. Beware of logical fallacies presented by either side. Take notes and then develop an essay arguing for one side of this campus issue. Explore the possibility of interviewing a faculty or staff member, an administrator, or other students about the issue.

¶ 3. While some major corporations and companies promote their products through responsible advertising, many others use misleading or deceptive advertisements and commercials to sell their products. Just flip through any popular magazine or watch an hour of prime-time television, and you can find several examples of blatant deception. Argue for more responsible advertising, more educated and wary consumers, or tighter government controls on advertising. Part of your evidence might come from specific ads and commercials. Find those that make use of emotional appeals with little or no appeal to logic. You might also look for ads that thrive on logical fallacies.

4. Although Louis Nizer in "Low-cost Drugs for Addicts?" (pp. 369–370) and Beth Johnson in "Our Drug Problem" (pp. 370–371) have divergent viewpoints on the issue of drug legalization, both clearly recognize drug use as a major problem in the United States. Write an essay in which you take a stand on the legalization of "street drugs." Feel free to discuss points not raised by either of these writers or to use their material to support your own position.

RESPONDING TO WRITING: ASSESSING STRATEGIES FOR WRITING ARGUMENT

Recognizing the strengths and weaknesses in the strategies of other writers will help you identify strong points as well as troublesome areas when writing argument. Read the following two excerpts at least twice before answering the prompts that follow. As you read these two opposing arguments, keep an open mind and avoid being swayed by any personal beliefs you may have.

The first excerpt is by lawyer and author Louis Nizer.

1   We are losing the war against drug addiction. Our strategy is wrong. I propose a different approach.

2   The Government should create clinics, manned by psychiatrists, that would provide drugs for nominal charges or even free to addicts under controlled regulations. It would cost the Government only 20 cents for a heroin shot, for which the addicts must now pay the mob more than $100, and there are similar price discrepancies in cocaine, crack and other such substances.

3   Such a service, which would also include the staff support of psychiatrists and doctors, would cost a fraction of what the nation now spends to maintain the land, sea and air apparatus necessary to interdict illegal imports of drugs. There would also be a savings of hundreds of millions of dollars from the elimination of the prosecutorial procedures that stifle our courts and overcrowd our prisons. . . .

4   Many addicts who are caught committing a crime admit that they have mugged or stolen as many as six or seven times a day to accumulate the $100 needed for a fix. Since many of them need two or three fixes a day, particularly for crack, one can understand the terror in our streets and homes. It is estimated that there are in New York City alone 200,000 addicts, and this is typical of cities across the nation. Even if we were to assume that only a modest percentage of a city's addicts engage in criminal conduct to obtain the money for the habit, requiring multiple muggings and thefts each day, we could nevertheless account for many of the tens of thousands of crimes each day in New York City alone.

5   Not long ago, a Justice Department division issued a report stating that more than half the perpetrators of murder and other serious crimes were under the influence of drugs. This symbolizes the new domestic terror in our nation. This is why our citizens are unsafe in broad daylight on the most traveled thoroughfares. This is why typewriters and television sets are stolen from offices and homes and sold for a pittance. This is why parks are closed to the public and why murders are committed. This is why homes need multiple locks, and burglary systems, and why store windows, even in the most fashionable areas, require iron gates.

—Louis Nizer, "Low-cost Drugs for Addicts"

1   In the eyes of some, legalizing narcotics is a tantalizing cure-all for America's drug problem. It's time, they say, to stop pouring enormous resources into the war on drugs. The war has been lost. Drug use, they argue, is here to stay. Ignoring evidence that drug legalization can produce a permanent underclass of hopelessly addicted people, as has happened in Holland, they advocate removal of all legal restrictions on drug use. . . .

2   The only thing more costly than continuing the current war on drugs would be the legalization of narcotics; such a measure would claim innumerable human lives. Government figures estimate that crimes involving drug use cost society more than $58 billion a year. Substance abuse is linked with 52 percent of rapes committed; 49 percent of murders; 62 percent of assaults; and 50 percent of traffic fatalities and incidents of spousal abuse. The legalization of narcotics could only push those figures higher.

3   Currently, drug abuse costs American industry as much as $75 billion per year in lost productivity, liability for errors committed by substance-abusing employees, and drug-related injuries. Imagine how that figure would soar if legal restraints were removed. If people didn't have to drive

into a seedy neighborhood, didn't risk arrest and disgrace, how many more would try addictive drugs? Moreover, what would be the fate of addicts if narcotics were available legally? In the words of one cocaine addict, "I'd be dead. . . . I'd just sit down with a big pile of the stuff and snort it until I dropped." . . .

4   Why, then, would anyone recommend legalizing narcotics? The answer has to do with racism, elitism, and sheer indifference to the suffering of others. "These people are going to kill themselves anyway," many middle-class Americans reason. "I'm not going to have my tax dollars used to try to save them. Besides, what does it matter if drugs wipe out a generation—as long as it's a generation of black and Hispanic kids?" . . .

5   Legalizing narcotics, then, . . . is not the solution; it's simply another way of ignoring the problem. Making drugs legal won't make them go away. What is needed is an all-out attack on the conditions that lead to drug abuse. Improved education, more affordable housing, new employment opportunities—these are the only effective weapons against drugs.

                                        —Beth Johnson, "Our Drug Problem"

1. Find and label the claim in each argument. Remember that the claim does

   not always come before the evidence. _____

   _____

2. Find three kinds of evidence used by Nizer to support his argument.

   _____

3. Find three kinds of evidence used by Johnson to support her argument.

   _____

Now that you've examined both arguments on this same issue in greater detail, ask yourself which writer advances his or her point of view more effectively. In responding to your own essays, make sure you recognize any weaknesses that could undermine your stand, and then make necessary changes to strengthen your argument.

READINGS AND ADDITIONAL ACTIVITIES

Derek Humphry takes a strong stand on the issue of euthanasia in his essay. (If you don't know the meaning of *euthanasia,* be sure to look up its meaning in a dictionary.) As you examine the essay, notice Humphry's technique for acknowledging and then refuting the opposition.

Offering Euthanasia Can Be an Act of Love

Derek Humphry

1. The American Medical Association's decision to recognize that artificial feeding is a life-support mechanism and can be disconnected from hopelessly comatose patients is a welcome, if tardy, acceptance of the inevitable.

2. Courts in California and New Jersey have already ruled this way, and although a Massachusetts court recently ruled in an opposite manner, this is being appealed to a higher court.

3. The AMA's pronouncement is all the more welcome because it comes at a time when the benefits of some of our modern medical technologies are in danger of being ignored because of the public's fear that to be on life-support machinery can create problems.

4. People dread having their loved ones put on such equipment if it means they are never likely to be removed if that proves later to be the more sensible course. As medical ethicist and lawyer George Annas has said, "People have rights, not technologies."

5. The argument by the pro-life lobby that food is a gift from God, no matter how it is introduced, and thus to deprive a comatose person of pipeline food is murder, is fallacious. A pipe is a manufactured item; the skill to introduce it into the body and maintain it there is a medical technology. Without the pipeline, the person would die. Food is common to all humans, but taking it through a pipeline is a technique carried out because the person has sustained an injury or suffers an illness which prevents normal feeding.

6. The pro-life lobby also harks back to Nazi excesses of the 1930s and '40s as part of its argument for continued pipeline feeding. True, Nazi Germany murdered about one hundred thousand Aryan Germans who were mentally or physically defective because it considered them "useless eaters," detracting from the purity of the German race.

7. But neither the views of the victims nor their relatives were ever sought: they were murdered en masse in secret fashion and untruths concocted to cover the crimes.

8. No terminally ill or comatose person was ever helped to die by the Nazis. Moreover, their barbarous killing spree took in 6 million Jews and 10 million noncombatant Russians, Slavs, and gypsies. Life was cheapened by the Nazis to an appalling degree. What connection is there between the Nazis then and the carefully considered euthanasia today of a permanently comatose person who might, as Karen Quinlan did, lie curled up for ten years without any signs of what most of us consider life?

9   Helping another to die in carefully considered circumstances is part of good medicine and also demonstrates a caring society that offers euthanasia to hopelessly sick persons as an act of love.

QUESTIONS ON CONTENT

1. On what issue have the courts recently ruled?_____

_____

2. In what paragraph do you find Humphry's claim? _____

_____

3. Why does Humphry point out that a pipe is "manufactured item"?

_____

QUESTIONS ON STRATEGY

1. Evaluate the effectiveness of Humphry's distinction of Nazi murder of "use-less eaters" and his own stand on artificial feeding. Does he make a clear and valid distinction between the two? Explain and support your view. ____

_____

_____

2. Find one or more emotional appeals in the essay and jot it down.

_____

3. Is the emotional appeal used fairly? That is, is it supported by facts?

_____

4. Notice that in paragraph 5, Humphry points out a logical fallacy made by the opposition. Does this strengthen his argument, and if so, how?

_____

_____

Arguments can take many shapes—they can be found not only in essays but also in advertisements, speeches, and poems, for example. In the following example, Dylan Thomas, the famous Welsh poet, has advanced a powerful argument. The poem has remained, since its publication in 1952, a well-loved classic, with an audience of countless readers today. The poetry thus serves as a vehicle to address his aging father, to urge him to fight death to the end. As you read, notice the unique way that Thomas uses outside sources to develop his argument.

Do Not Go Gentle into That Good Night

Dylan Thomas

1   Do not go gentle into that good night,
Old age should burn and rave at close of day;
Rage, rage against the dying of the light.

4   Though wise men at their end know dark is right,
Because their words had forked no lightning they
Do not go gentle into that good night.

7   Good men, the last wave by, crying how bright
Their frail deeds might have danced in a green bay,
Rage, rage against the dying of the light.

10   Wild men who caught and sang the sun in flight,
And learn, too late, they grieved it on its way,
Do not go gentle into that good night.

13   Grave men, near death, who see with blinding sight
Blind eyes could blaze like meteors and be gay,
Rage, rage against the dying of the light.

16   And you, my father, there on the sad height,
Curse, bless, me now with your fierce tears, I pray.
Do not go gentle into that good night,
Rage, rage against the dying of the light.

QUESTIONS ON CONTENT

1. The two words *night* and *light* are used in place of two other words. What word or concept is *night* substituting for? _____ And *light?*

_____

2. List the four types of men mentioned by the poet. _____

_____

3. What do all four types have in common? _____

_____

4. State in your own words the claim that Thomas makes. _____

_____

QUESTIONS ON STRATEGY

1. Who, in addition to the poet's father, comprises the intended audience for
this argument? _____

_____

2. Underline the phrase that is repeated throughout the poem. What is the
poet's strategy in repeating this phrase? _____

_____

3. An *oxymoron* is a figure of speech in which contradictory terms are used
together, for example "cruel kindness" or "sweet sorrow." With this information in mind, find an oxymoron in the poem and then write it down, followed by your explanation of why the poet uses it. _____

_____

4. Reread the poem, underlining all references to nature that you find. Why
do you think the poet uses so many of these? _____

_____

5. What kinds of evidence does the poet use to support his claim?

_____

_____

6. Does Thomas acknowledge the opposition, and if so, in what lines?

CRITICAL THINKING IN CONNECTING TEXTS

Several of the readings in this chapter focus on issues surrounding life, death, and survival. Kieran Mulvaney argues that the ecosystems of the world's coral reefs are in danger; Brian Villapudua mentions that many Americans feel immigrants threaten the future economy of our country. From differing positions, Derek Humphry and Dylan Thomas both explore the end of life for each human being. In a small group, brainstorm to come up with a list of issues impacting on one of the following:

• The survival of humans in your particular area of the world

• The continuance of a local tradition, custom, or law

• An endangered species in your specific region of the United States

When your group has chosen a subject, create a claim about your subject and share it with other groups in the class. Plan a mini-debate in which each group can employ strategies to convince the rest of the class that a particular subject is the most worthy of consideration and action on the part of concerned citizens. Save your notes—they could be of help if you decide to write an essay on this subject.

**For more writing resources, be sure to see the
Longman English Pages Website at
http://longman.awl.com/englishpages**

PART THREE

Exploring Other Options:
A Writer's Toolkit

....

Unit 1 Timed Writing

Unit 2 Portfolios

Unit 3 Research Assignments

Unit 4 Application Letters

Unit 5 Résumés

Timed Writing

Examining strategies for timed writing will enable you to feel more comfortable and more prepared to write under pressure. Throughout your college career, you will be asked on many occasions and in various classes to write in-class essays and short-answer exams. In addition, skills and confidence in timed writing will serve you well in your career path: people in the workforce are often asked to present a report, summarize a situation, or compose a business memo more or less "on the spot."

Although the format may vary tremendously by subject and instructor, each timed writing possesses the following characteristics:

- **It focuses on a subject.**
  You may or may not be given a choice, but you will be asked and expected to respond specifically to the subject of the essay question.

- **It is administered within a fixed, predetermined period of time.**
  For some in-class essays, you may be given three hours; others may be timed writings of ten to fifteen minutes. Whatever the time limit may be, it will help you to know that all students will be feeling the same time constraints. If you do not turn your essay in at the end of the allotted time, it cannot be evaluated.

- **It is usually written by hand, using pen and paper.**
  There are increasing exceptions today with computer labs and personal laptop computers becoming more common in class.

- **It resembles the regular college essay in much of its structure: thesis, development, conclusion.**
  Whether you're asked to write a brief essay response in ten minutes, or a longer one because you are given two hours of writing time, the in-class essay focuses on a thesis, develops that thesis, and then concludes.

SAMPLE TIMED WRITING

The writing instructor who administered the following timed writing asked students to prepare for the assignment by reading and discussing two editorials in the campus newspaper. The editorials focused on whether or not American tobacco makers should be held financially responsible for smoking-related illnesses. A week before the timed writing, the instructor informed students that they would have two hours (the regular class time for this course) to complete the writing assignment, and that they could use no notes or outside sources.

When Russell Fullerton and the other students in his class arrived on the day of the timed writing, they were given the following essay question:

> Should American tobacco makers take financial responsibility for smoking-related illnesses? In developing your essay, discuss the issue by using examples to support your thesis.

Fullerton wrote the following in-class essay in response to the essay question.

COFFIN NAILS
Russell Fullerton

Russell Fullerton confides that he has never found writing difficult but that he really didn't try hard to write clearly until coming to college. Russell states that he has little trouble organizing or developing his ideas. When he's writing on a computer, he knows how to solve most of his spelling problems, but when writing a timed, handwritten assignment, Russell still grapples with spelling errors. Russell describes his interests and prospective major as follows: "Computers, computers, . . . uhm . . . computers."

1   Despite the knowledge that smoking cigarettes has been proven to cause many health problems, millions of people still go through a pack or more a day and many new smokers pick up their first cigarette each day. This is an exercise of their freedom of choice—perhaps not the smartest choice, but their choice nonetheless. There are many products on the market that may not be as addictive or harmful as cigarettes but are, however, destructive to the user: chocolate when eaten in excess, ergonomically-challenged school and office furniture, Haagen-Dasz ice cream, or even roller blades (unsafe at any speed). Even though these products pose health hazards, their manufacturers are not asked to pay for the effect their products have on the people who use them. Yet the tobacco industry is being asked to pay for the effects caused by its product, even though the people who smoke have freely chosen to do so. The American tobacco industry should not be forced to take financial responsibility for smoking-related illnesses.

2   Once the American public did not know exactly how dangerous it was to smoke, but for years now, every thinking person has been aware of the health hazards. My parents had both smoked for twenty-five years before they quit eight years ago—cold turkey. And now, eight years later, they have started smoking again. Both of my parents are fully aware of the risks, but they have chosen to smoke again, most

likely for the rest of their lives. When asked why he started again now, my father says he would rather enjoy himself for the time he has left than live forever and not have any fun. My father, mother, and many other smokers have made an informed choice, and the tobacco industry should not have to pay for this choice.

3   Many parents are angry because tobacco advertisements target children with their cartoon camels and smoking cowboys. These parents claim that their children will be influenced to smoke by these images. They assume that children are not old enough to take responsibility for their choices; in this they are correct. That is why it is illegal for children to smoke. It is the parents' responsibility to guide their children to make the right choices in this confusing world. The tobacco industry is not alone in using advertising to promote potentially harmful products among both children and adults. Images of beautiful and healthy people surround us constantly, guzzling down alcoholic beverages, caffeine, "perfectly safe" diet pills, for example. In a recent McDonald's commercial, a group of children ask Ronald McDonald where hamburgers come from. Instead of taking the children to the slaughterhouse, Ronald takes them to the "hamburger patch" where the talking hamburgers grow on trees. Is what the tobacco industry has done worse than this?

4   Selling cigarettes does not kill people. Smoking cigarettes can kill people—and that's a smoker's responsibility. If we are going to prosecute the tobacco industry for creating the cigarettes, perhaps we should then prosecute the individuals who smoke the cigarettes. They are the manufacturers of the clouds of second-hand smoke, which have proven to be more deadly than the cigarettes themselves. However, when we start prosecuting manufacturers or consumers for making or using products, then we chip away at the freedoms we have fought to preserve for so long. Freedoms come with a responsibility—the freedom to make good and bad choices, and the freedom to live with the effects of those choices. When these freedoms are taken, they are not just taken from the manufacturers, but from the consumers as well.

GUIDELINES FOR TIMED WRITING

Make Preparations

What you do *before* the actual in-class essay day can help you to stay calm and complete an effective timed writing. Go over any notes, review chapters from which you believe information will be asked, and think about the subject and the essay question, if you know them. Ask your instructors what kinds of in-class writing assignments they give, what materials you will be permitted to bring with you, and if they have any suggestions for preparation before the actual day of the timed writing.

Make sure that you have all your supplies ready and in good order: a couple of functioning erasable pens (in case one of them runs out of ink), paper or blue book if required, paperback dictionary if you are allowed to use one, a wristwatch, especially if there is no clock in your classroom, and any other materials you may need and are permitted to bring. Fellow students may not appreciate last-minute borrowing on the in-class essay day.

On the day of the timed writing, make every effort to get to class on time or even five minutes early. Your early arrival could result in that extra few minutes for proofreading at the end of class time. Finally, once you have prepared mentally and your supplies are ready, relax. Once you start reading the assignment and thinking about it, you may even find that you enjoy the challenge of writing under pressure.

Understand the Question

Once you receive the question or writing prompt, read it carefully. If it is written on the board, jot it down quickly on a piece of scratch paper so that you can think about it and refer to it more easily. Underline **directives**—the instructive words, usually verbs, that tell what is expected of you in the timed writing. For example, Russell Fullerton focused on the directives "discuss" and "use examples" before beginning to write his in-class essay. After he underlined these two directives, he knew which strategy he would use to organize and develop his material. The following are some of the most commonly used directives in timed writing along with a brief definition for each:

DIRECTIVES USED IN TIMED WRITING

- **Explain** Show or make clear, establish connections, tell why or how or what, depending on the subject.
- **Compare** Develop the similarities between one subject and another.
- **Contrast** Explore the differences between two subjects, pursuing ways in which the two subjects are not alike.
- **Define** Establish boundaries for, set limits on, a subject. Tell what the subject is by differentiating it from others closely related; possibly tell what it is not.
- **Illustrate** Explain by example and detail.
- **Identify** Distinguish, know, list the various parts of the subject.

- **Describe** Paint a word picture with sensory details. Sometimes instructors use this directive more broadly to mean "discuss" or "explain."

- **Interpret** Share your understanding of the subject. Go into the significance of the idea, event, or process in order to explain its meaning to your audience.

- **Trace** Detail in chronological order events or situations or occurrences connected with the subject.

- **Evaluate** Explore the value of the subject. To evaluate, you need criteria to judge the worth of a subject.

- **Discuss** Literally, this means "talk about." When you get this directive, be careful—even though it may appear that you've been given the "green light" to talk about any aspect of the subject, create a thesis that will steer you away from vagueness and into specific territory that you can support with details.

- **Analyze** Divide the subject into its component parts so that you can take a more in-depth look at each part in relation to the whole.

- **Summarize** Explain the subject briefly in your own words. If you're asked to summarize, the instructor wants to see whether you can recall the important aspects of a subject and put them in your own words.

Allocate Time

Once you know what you will be expected to cover in your timed writing and the strategy your instructor wants you to use, schedule your time to allow you to plan your main points, write the draft, revise it, and then proofread it. If you have only one essay question, as Russell Fullerton did for his essay "Coffin Nails" (pp. 380–381), you might come up with a time allocation like this:

5 minutes to reread the question and decide on a strategy

10 minutes to organize main points and find a thesis

1 hour and 20 minutes to write

15 minutes to revise and polish

   Total: 1 hour and 50 minutes

Resist the temptation to begin writing before you have completed your preparations. The biggest problem students have with in-class essays is not that they write too little, but that too often they write without thinking about the essay question and mapping out a plan first. Often this results in rambling, vague, or off-topic answers.

Find a Thesis and Sketch a Plan

Sometimes you may get an idea for a working thesis after you've read the essay question; other times, you may have no idea for a thesis but you do know that you can make several main points related to the subject and the specific directives. In many cases, you can take your essay question, and with a little careful rewording, turn it into a statement that becomes your thesis. If you reread "Coffin Nails", you will see that Fullerton turned the essay question into a thesis in paragraph 1.

Whether or not an idea for a working thesis comes to you, get started by jotting down your main points in a **scratch outline**—a brief, quickly written outline of main points. If you did not have a working thesis to begin with, you will probably feel more capable of creating one after looking over your scratch outline. To see what a scratch outline looks like, examine Russell Fullerton's scratch outline below, written in preparation for "Coffin Nails."

Sample Scratch Outline

Should American tobacco makers take financial responsibility for smoking-related illnesses? In developing your essay, discuss the issue by using examples to support your thesis.

No!

adult know dangers of smoking
— my parents
— dad's comment

issue of misleading ads
— children —Joe Camel
               Ronald McDonald
               cowboy w/ cigarette

adults + ads
— coffee
— beer
— diet pills
— junk food

Draft and Reread

Working from your scratch outline and thesis, begin to draft your written response. Begin with your thesis, and then launch into your main points and supporting detail. While you're drafting, glance at your watch every now and then to make sure that you're following your allocated schedule. As you write, try to keep the assigned question uppermost in your mind so that you stay on the subject.

Revise and Polish

One major difference between an essay assigned as homework and a timed writing is that the latter does not get worked through multiple drafts. Often you'll have time only for a scratch outline and then one draft. Once you have a scratch outline, write the draft that you are going to turn in, leaving sufficient time for revising and polishing of this draft.

When you have finished the draft, ask yourself if you have answered the essay question thoroughly and clearly. If you find that you've left out something crucial to your development, you can always write this sentence or even paragraph in the margin or on a separate sheet of paper, marking it with an asterisk (*) or drawing an arrow to indicate where the additional information belongs.

After you've read the draft for content, read it again to make sure that your spelling is correct (you may be permitted to use your dictionary), that all sentences are correctly punctuated, and that every word is the most specific word possible for clear communication of your thesis. If you find any errors or off-topic phrases or sentences, correct or delete even if this means crossing out words, phrases, or whole sentences. You can also insert words with a caret (^). Title your essay; check to see that your name is on the essay, and make sure that your pages are in the right order.

STRATEGIES FOR TIMED WRITING

1. **PURPOSE** Read and reread the question or writing assignment, underlining the directives. Think carefully about what is expected of you in the timed writing.

2. **FOCUS** If possible, restate the question in the form of a thesis statement. If this won't work, begin to jot down all main points you can make about the subject. After reviewing your list, draft a thesis that addresses the subject and fits the main points you've listed.

continued

STRATEGIES FOR TIMED WRITING *continued*

3. **MATERIAL** Use a strategy for developing your material suggested by the directives in the essay question. Check the question to make sure that you are using material appropriate to the subject.

4. **STRUCTURE** Before drafting your timed writing, write a scratch outline. Refer to this outline during drafting.

5. **STYLE** In revising, make appropriate and legible additions and deletions. Check word choice to be sure that any vague words are replaced with specific ones. Check punctuation, spelling, title, page order, name placement.

UNIT 2

Portfolios

Your instructor may ask you to submit a portfolio for evaluation. A **portfolio** is a collection of your writing in a folder, notebook, or binder. Portfolios are an excellent way to publish and share your writing with fellow students, friends, and family. In addition to helping you grow as a writer by reflecting on your earlier work, portfolios can furnish you with samples of your writing to submit if you transfer to another college or university.

If you are requested to submit your portfolio to your instructor, you may need to follow a particular presentation format. You may be asked to submit an **evaluation portfolio**—a selection of your best writing samples. Whether or not you are asked to submit an evaluation portfolio, you may want to start and then develop throughout the semester a **process portfolio**—a collection of writing that may include essays, essay drafts, and possibly in-class writings, journal writings, and even poems, short stories, and other pieces of writing you've completed apart from class assignments.

Although portfolio models may vary in content and emphasis, each student portfolio tends to have the following characteristics:

- **It reveals the process as well as the growth of the writer over a period of time.**

- **Its content is diverse.**
  The writer wants to share his or her strengths in a variety of writing situations covering several different subjects.

- **It is the product not just of the writer but of the classroom writing community.**
  Peer editors and the instructor often help to decide what pieces of writing are included, what revision strategies to use, and possibly the order and manner of presentation in the portfolio.

A sample student portfolio, table of contents, and preface follow.

SAMPLE PORTFOLIO
Rebecca Obidi

Rebecca Obidi shares a not-so-surprising secret: "The more I write, the better I get at writing." In her writing class, Rebecca enjoyed writing essays about a wide variety of topics including her home country in Africa, a chemical process she had learned about in a college science class, and the existence of demons and ghosts. Rebecca plans to obtain a degree in medicine.

Table of Contents

Preface

1   I am submitting this portfolio in partial fulfillment for the requirements for English A. I have included all of the essays written this semester, as you requested.

2   As we discussed in our conference, I didn't feel comfortable with my first essay, "How College Has Affected My Reading," but I have attacked the structural problems so the organization is stronger. I revised the longest and worked the most on my two strong essays, "My Father's Farm" and "Culture in West Africa" and my weak essay, "Molisch's Test." I especially worked on adding more descriptive detail to the first essay. I know you advised me that my subject in "Culture in Nigeria" was much too broad, and I've tried to focus on language, religion, nutrition, and appearance for the region in the revised version. Now that I look at it one more time, I think you may still feel that I try to cover too much, but I really wanted to tie these four aspects together. Michael Kern peer edited both drafts for me.

3   My weakest essay was a real disappointment to me, as I told you. I worked so hard in organizing the process and checking with my chemistry teacher to make sure I had it down right, but I couldn't seem to communicate the importance of the subject. Sophie Anugwom edited my revised draft. She agrees that it is much more interesting for the average reader.

4   My biggest surface error, the comma splice, still isn't gone. Now that the semester is over I plan to review my handbook and visit the Writing Center to get some additional worksheets. I think the verb ending problems I had before are under control now. Thank you for your help, advice, and comments during the semester.

GUIDELINES FOR PORTFOLIOS

Keep Progress Logs

If you decide to assemble a portfolio, keeping progress logs for each of your essays will help you identify your writing strengths and weaknesses. Progress logs will also help you reflect on and improve your writing by allowing you to recall what did and did not work in a given assignment. You can use the progress log on page 390 to help with your writing assignments. (For another kind of essay progress log, see Chapter 10, p. 301)

Review All Essays

In order to select and revise writings for your portfolio, you'll want to reread and review all the essays you've written over the course of the semester. If you are turning in an evaluation portfolio, you'll want to look for your best essays and also those that show your range as a writer. Start by putting all essays in chronological order, beginning with your first essay. Then reread each essay, imagining that you are reading it for the first time.

Confer with Instructor

If your instructor uses portfolios for evaluating student writing, he or she will probably want to meet with you at least once during the semester to discuss your portfolio progress. You may wish to meet with one or more peer editors in preparation for your conference. If you haven't been given specific instructions on how to prepare, assemble all your drafts by ranking them from what you feel are the most effective to the least effective pieces of writing. Get the evaluation of a peer editor if possible, and come up with a tentative top three or four choices. Be prepared to explain and justify your choices, any problems you had with them, whether and how you solved these problems, and what you would have done differently if you could write the essay again. Also give some thought to your original goals for the class—did you meet all goals you set for yourself or are there still some you want to work on in the future? Once you've addressed these questions, you'll be more prepared for your portfolio conference.

ESSAY PROGRESS LOG

Title of essay: _____

Date of completion: _____

1. How did you decide on your subject for this essay? Was it the result of journal writing, a specific assignment made by your instructor, or other?

   _____

2. What strategies for prewriting did you use?_____

3. How many drafts did you work through before turning the essay in?

   _____

4. Did you use the computer? _____ If so, how and in what stages of your composing? _____

5. Did you share one or more drafts of this essay with a peer editor? _____ Tutor? _____ Instructor? _____ Other? _____ What did your editor like about the essay?

   _____

   What needed revision?_____

   _____

6. Did you revise the draft or simply retype? _____ What was the most difficult aspect of the revision?_____

   _____

7. What surface errors and other proofreading problems did you solve in polishing? _____

   _____

   What errors eluded you? _____

   _____

8. If you continue to work on this essay, name one change would like to make:

_____

9. What do you think is the greatest strength of this essay?

_____

10. Summarize your writing schedule in working through this essay. How many days elapsed from choosing your subject and beginning prewriting to turning in the completed final draft? _____

If this writing schedule did not work for you, what would you change as far as a writing schedule for your next essay? _____

_____

Although the conference format may vary, you will get feedback and advice from your instructor, and you may be given specific suggestions on content selection for your portfolio as well as revision strategies for your portfolio writings.

Select and Revise

Based on your conference and the advice of peer editors, select the essays you wish to include in your portfolio. Let's say your instructor asks you for your four strongest essays; you would then be turning in an evaluation portfolio, but keeping your process portfolio for your own future reference. To choose the essays you wish to include in an evaluation portfolio, reread each of them at least one more time, and then revise and polish to make sure that all five "keys"—PURPOSE, FOCUS, MATERIAL, STRUCTURE, and STYLE—are working to their best advantage in your final portfolio drafts.

Create a Preface and a Table of Contents

Once you have revised and polished the selections to your satisfaction, you will want to create a portfolio preface and a table of contents. The **preface** is an introductory statement to a work telling its purpose or plan. It provides your instructor and anyone else who reads your portfolio with a brief introduction to your work. You might want to explain how your choices for the portfolio reflect your growth and advancing skills as a college writer. For example, in Rebecca Obidi's "Preface" (pp. 388–389) she mentions her focus in revising and specific problem areas in her essays. She also discusses her strategies for working on sentence boundaries.

You will want to use a separate page for your table of contents. This list should include everything in the portfolio, including your preface, along with the title and beginning page number for each selection. Be sure to number your pages consecutively as soon as you have chosen your contents and decided on an order for your portfolio.

Assemble Your Portfolio

Finally, assemble your portfolio by choosing a notebook or folder. If you prefer, you can make a binder out of sturdy, attractive paper. Bind your portfolio in such a way that the pages are held together and are easy to read. Then decorate or individualize the cover in any way you wish, for example with photographs, drawings, or markers. If you plan to share your portfolio with prospective employers, you might want to give it a more business-oriented appearance.

STRATEGIES FOR PORTFOLIOS

1. **PURPOSE** Decide whether you want to assemble and keep an evaluation portfolio or a process portfolio. Ask yourself who will be reading your portfolio and for what purpose.

2. **FOCUS** Determine whether you want to focus in your portfolio on your growth as a writer, on the range of your writing abilities, or on your final essays. Check to see that your preface clearly communicates your portfolio focus to your readers.

3. **MATERIAL** Following the suggestions of your instructor, the advice of peer editors, and your own reflection and evaluation of your writings, choose the essays and other writing samples that reveal your skills and growth as a writer and that serve your portfolio's primary purpose.

4. **STRUCTURE** Arrange the portfolio in a manner, possibly chronological, that emphasizes the progress you've made in your writing. Be sure to include a table of contents to signal your audience about the organizational plan for your portfolio.

5. **STYLE** Revise and polish the essays and other writings that you have selected for portfolio publication to make sure that each word, phrase, and sentence is the most effective for your purpose. Find and eliminate distracting surface errors or manuscript format discrepancies.

Research Assignments

When you **research** a subject, you look into it further by going beyond what you know to explore various sources. In the **research** process, you collect information from any or all of the following: people, books, magazines, indexes, newspapers, surveys, and electronic sources. You then sift through this data and organize your findings to come up with a conclusion or recommendation.

You'll be utilizing research skills in many settings—in college, on the job and in your personal life. In addition, research essays utilize many skills of successful essay writing that you've been learning and practicing throughout this text: clear thesis, captivating introduction and conclusion, well developed body paragraphs, and logical organization of material. The main difference is that **academic research**—research completed more formally and according to an accepted format for a collegiate audience—requires that you point out your sources in order to share the exact origin of your information. Research essays possess the following characteristics:

- **The subject is worthy of and appropriate for research.**

- **The essay makes use of several sources for information.**

- **The research data are presented in the essay in a variety of ways, including summary, paraphrase, and direct quotes.**

- **The research leads to a particular conclusion.**

SAMPLE RESEARCH PAPER

BLUE SKY, WHY?
Melissa Lombardi

Melissa Lombardi comments, "As a high school student, I did not recognize the benefits of freewriting and getting my instructor's inputs on my rough draft. I was never satisfied with the finished product back then! Now, I begin well in advance, so that I have time to make every paragraph say what I want it to say." Melissa wants to become a physicist and says that her plans have not changed since she researched this career for her essay. However, she confides, "I'll take it a little more slowly so I can spend time with Caroline, my new baby."

1   A physicist is like a small child. Children wonder why the sky is blue; adults never notice the sky because it has always been there, and they never ponder its color, because it has always been blue. Adults are too jaded, and too familiar with the world around them; they are conditioned by it, and just accept it without question. Like a child, a physicist looks at the world through eyes that are not prejudiced by expectations. A physicist must be objective, rational, honest, and above all, curious. In his description of the work of a physicist, James Gonyea, a career counselor on America Online, states that "physicists explore and identify basic principles governing the structure and behavior of matter and energy" (1). Physicists study the most fundamental aspects of the universe—where it came from, what it is made of, what rules it is governed by, and where it is going.

2   Physics is broken down into countless sub-fields; two of the most popular of these at the moment are elementary particle physics and astrophysics (Dodge and Mulvey 4). Elementary particle physicists study matter on the smallest scale; their work focuses on fundamental particles such as quarks and leptons, which are the building blocks of atoms. Astrophysicists, on the other hand, study stars, which are the largest discrete objects in the universe. Within these fields, there are three different types of researchers: experimentalists, theorists, and computational physicists. Experimentalists work in a lab setting, theorists use mathematics, and computational physicists use computer modeling to test their ideas.

3   Physicists generally work in universities or in industry. At a university, a physicist's responsibilities may include researching, publishing papers, teaching, and serving on committees. The research may be pure, meaning that the only goal is knowledge, or applied, meaning that there is a specific, real-world application in mind. In industry, a physicist's primary responsibility is research. Physicists conduct applied research with commercial applications in mind, such as medical applications of lasers.

4   University jobs carry more prestige, but prestige doesn't pay the mortgage. Physicists employed in industry have a median salary of $30,000 higher than physicists employed in universities (Curtin and Chu 1). Dr. Gabriel Lombardi (the author's husband), a physicist at Mission Research Corporation, "chose to work

in industry, even though [he] loves teaching, because it just seemed better all the way around. Faculty positions don't pay as well, and there are very few open at any given time." John Dooley, a physics professor at Millersville University in Pennsylvania, acknowledges that the pay isn't very good, but he loves teaching, and has worked in a school setting throughout his career. Ironically, Dr. Lombardi wonders "if an academic career path would have been more satisfying," and Dr. Dooley "always wanted to work in industry."

5   To qualify for work in either a university or in industry, a prospective physicist must go through college, graduate school, and a post-doctoral research position. This can require up to 10 years of training after completion of undergraduate studies, but according to James Gonyea, "persons with only a bachelor's degree in physics or astronomy are not qualified to enter most physicist or astronomer jobs" (4).

6   The level of career satisfaction among physicists is very impressive. Dr. Bill Shackleford, who is now retired, says that after a 30-year career, he has no re-grets about his choice to become a physicist, and he feels he worked in the "golden age" of physics. Dr. Dooley recognizes that he gets paid to do something he enjoys, and knows that this is "not a common experience." These satisfied physicists are just two of many curious, childlike individuals who are fascinated by what makes the sky blue, as well as other fundamental questions about our universe.

[Note: you always begin a new page for works cited.]

WORKS CITED

Curtin, Jean M., and Raymond Y. Chu. <u>Society Membership Survey: Salaries 1994.</u> College Park, Maryland: The American Institute of Physics, Nov. 1995.

Dodge, Elizabeth, and Patrick J. Mulvey. <u>1994 Graduate Student Report.</u> College Park, Maryland: The American Institute of Physics, Dec. 1995.

Dooley, John. Personal interview via E-mail. 10 Nov. 1996.

Gonyea, James. "Physicists and Astronomers." Interview via E-mail. 11 Nov. 1996.

Lombardi, Gabriel G. Interview via E-mail. 9 Nov. 1996.

Shackleford, William L. Interview via E-mail. 8 Nov. 1996.

GUIDELINES FOR RESEARCH

Pose a Question to Launch Your Investigation

Begin your research by posing a question about a subject that intrigues you. What is it you would be most interested in finding out about the subject? For example, in "Blue Sky, Why?" student writer Melissa Lombardi was curious to find out what a physicist actually does on a day-to-day basis on the job. This question about your subject will serve as a tentative thesis, likely to change as you learn more about your topic.

Identify Your Audience

Once you've posed your question for investigation, you'll need to identify your audience—which in the case of an academic research essay is narrowed to a college community of students and professors. Try to target an aspect of your investigative question that your audience would be most interested in.

Collect Data from Appropriate Sources

Interviews
The **personal interview,** a prearranged meeting with a person in which particular questions are asked, is a good way to gather firsthand information on a research subject. In "Blue Sky, Why?" Melissa Lombardi interviewed several sources by E-mail. (For interview strategies, see p. 214 in Chapter 8.)

Print Sources
Your college or local library is the best place to find printed research sources, which include books, magazine and newspaper articles, articles in scholarly journals, book reviews, pamphlets, encyclopedias, special interest encyclopedias, and various kinds of dictionaries and reference books. You might want to begin your search by consulting either a general encyclopedia, such as *Encyclopaedia Britannica,* or a specialized encyclopedia, such as the *Encyclopedia of Science and Technology* or the *Encyclopedia of Psychology.* An encyclopedia may suggest specific subject headings or direct you to other useful sources.

Indexes to periodicals, or lists of articles organized by subject and author, can also help you find information for your research. The *Readers' Guide to Periodical Literature* lists articles from hundreds of popular magazines. Other more specialized indexes, such as the *Humanities Index* and the *Social Sciences Index,* offer lists of articles in particular fields of study.

You may find that some of the articles you are trying to locate are available in hard copy, while others are kept on **microfilm,** a film on which printed sources are copied in a much smaller size for easier storage. Librarians can help you track down information and use the library's microfilm machines.

Electronic Sources

Many magazine, newspaper, and journal articles can be found in computerized indexes. The *Readers' Guide to Periodical Literature* is available on computer as well as in hard copy in most college and many local libraries. In addition, your college library will probably have at least two other computerized databases that can be helpful if you are researching a subject not covered in general interest periodicals.

If you have computer online access at home or if your college library offers an online service, you can access information through the Internet, interview a subject online, or search encyclopedias or other sources on the Web.

Evaluate Your Data

Before you decide to use any source, appraise it by asking yourself the following questions:

- Does the information relate directly to the subject and focus of my research?

- Is the information current? This is of no importance with certain timeless subjects, for example, the origin of a particular myth, but of the utmost importance with those that rely on recent information, such as career opportunities in physics or possible cures for the ebola virus. For many research subjects, a source that is ten years old or older is considered out of date.

- Is the source objective rather than biased? If a source is reputed to voice an opinion on only one side of the issue, this source is possibly biased. Examine the way the source obtained information on the subject. If studies were conducted, were they conducted fairly and did they include a sufficient number of participants to be valid?

Record Your Data: Three Kinds of Notes

Before you begin note-taking, be sure to record the following information about each source:

- Author or editor of the article or book
- Title of the article or book

- Name of the magazine or journal

- Place of publication for a book

- Publisher for a book

- Publication date (and volume number if this is a scholarly journal)

- Exact page or pages where the information is found

(For electronic sources, the information you'll want to record is slightly different. Ask your instructor for current format guidelines or consult the most recent edition of the *MLA Handbook for Writers of Research Papers*. MLA stands for Modern Language Association.)

Once you've recorded this basic information for each source, you can proceed with note-taking, which usually takes one of three forms: (1) summary, (2) paraphrase, or (3) direct quotes.

Summary

As explained in Chapter 1, a **summary** is a statement of the most important points of a piece of writing. Use a summary note when it's important to get only the main ideas of the source. In "Blue Sky, Why?" (pp. 393–396), Melissa Lombardi used summary in her note-taking. In her first sentence in paragraph 5 of her essay, Lombardi summarizes information from Neuschatz and Mulvey, one of her sources; she condenses several sentences from her source into one sentence of main points, written in her own words.

Paraphrase

When you **paraphrase,** you take the information from a source and put it in your own words without condensing it. When might you take notes in the form of paraphrasing instead of summary? When it's important not to condense the information, but instead to communicate all of the data—specific facts and details—to readers. Although you communicate these facts in your own words, you must still give credit to the source of that information. For instance, when Lombardi uses information obtained from Curtin and Chu at the beginning of paragraph 4, she paraphrases this information by putting it in her own words. She also includes the source and the particular page on which she found the information.

Direct Quote

Sometimes the exact words of the source are dramatic or the language is as important as the source's ideas. In this case, you'll want to use a **direct quote**—the exact words of a source without omissions, changes, or additions and set off from the rest of the text by quotation marks or indentation. For instance, in paragraph 1 of "Blue Sky, Why?" the writer introduces her source and then uses his exact words: "physicists explore and identify basic principles governing the structure and behavior of matter and energy."

If you omit words, you must signal this to your reader with **ellipsis points;** if you add words, you must enclose them in **brackets.** (See pp. 461–462 in the handbook in Part Four for use of these punctuation marks.)

Avoid Plagiarism

Regardless of whether you summarize, paraphrase, or quote, in an academic research essay you should always give credit to your source. Giving credit shows your honesty as a writer, lends authority to what you've written, and helps others who might like to follow up on your research by reading your sources. If you fail to give this credit, you commit **plagiarism**—the act of stealing someone else's words, ideas, or facts without crediting the source. To avoid plagiarism in an academic research essay, always cite your sources. **Citing sources,** also called **documentation,** is a writer's indication in an accepted format that he or she has used the words, ideas, or information from a source or sources.

In "Blue Sky, Why?" the sources are cited both in the text, with the authors and page numbers given for summaries, paraphrases, and quotes, and at the end of the essay in the "Works Cited" section. For most research essays in an English course, you will need to use the Modern Language Association (MLA) format. Here are a few brief examples to familiarize you with this format:

Book with single author
Lamott, Anne. Bird by Bird. New York: Doubleday, 1994.

Book with multiple authors (two or three)
Bentley, Nicolas, Michael Slater, and Nina Burgis. The Dickens Index. New York: Oxford UP, 1990.

Article in a magazine
Ellis, John. "Franklin's Cop-Out." Time 15 June 1997: 42–43.

Move from Notes to a Plan

Read through your notes on your sources, putting aside those that don't seem to relate clearly to your current thesis. This process should help you focus your thesis question. Next, take the notes that you think you can use to develop your thesis and try to sort them into some logical order. You will find an outline helpful for a research-based essay since you may be pulling information together from a variety of sources. (For a review of outlining, see pp. 97–99.)

Incorporate Sources in Your Draft

To begin drafting, follow your outline and try to use material from your note-taking—summarized information, paraphrases, and direct quotes—applying your best judgment as to which points lend themselves to particular ways of conveying the research information.

STRATEGIES FOR RESEARCH

1. **PURPOSE** Once you have a topic, pose a question that you would like to answer in your research. Determine the aspect of the topic that would be of primary interest to your audience.

2. **FOCUS** Compose a flexible thesis, based on your question. Your thesis should change as you gather information from sources.

3. **MATERIAL** Make sure that all of your sources are reliable and current. Try to collect information from appropriate printed, electronic, and interview sources. In note-taking and in drafting, use a mixture of summaries, paraphrases, and direct quotes. Remember to introduce and credit all sources if you are writing an academic research essay.

4. **STRUCTURE** Work from an outline to make sure you're presenting your research in an organized way to your audience.

5. **STYLE** In revising and polishing, check to see that you've identified all sources, and that you've employed quotation marks, ellipses, and brackets where appropriate. Reread your draft to find and correct any places where you've paraphrased or summarized information without giving credit to the source.

Application Letters

Sometimes a prospective employer will ask for specific content and form in an application letter. More often, however, applicants will be expected to know what such a letter should include. A successful application letter possesses the following characteristics:

- **It conforms to standard business letter format.**
  The letter is typed on good quality, plain white or ivory 8½ by 11-inch paper. It contains the complete address of the sender and below this, the complete name and address of the person to whom the letter is written. The letter begins with a salutation and ends with a closing and signature.

- **It is one page or less in length.**
  The application letter should be brief because it is meant to introduce the applicant who is inquiring about a job. It is usually accompanied by a resume, which offers greater detail and is organized for easy reading.

- **It mentions a specific job opening and where or how the applicant learned of the position.**

- **It briefly but clearly explains the applicant's qualifications for and interest in the job.**

- **It requests an interview; if there are to be no interviews, it thanks the reader for the opportunity to be considered for the job.**

SAMPLE APPLICATION LETTER
Jan Mendoza

Jan Mendoza
206 Patterson Drive
Long Beach, California 90815
July 6, 1998

Bill Johnson
Johnson and Associates
10990 Wilshire Blvd.
Los Angeles, CA 90024

Dear Mr. Johnson:

1   I have been away from the workplace for five years while raising my young child. Now, however, I am eager to return to a professional environment. A longtime friend of mine, John Wheeler, praised your firm and suggested that I contact you about employment possibilities. Although my resume reflects work experience in the retail sales field, I have decided to pursue a career in the consulting industry. The MBA program that I completed at California State University Long Beach in 1992 has significantly complemented both my engineering education and skills and my work experience.

2   Armed with a broader understanding of business operations, I embrace change and look forward to any opportunity to improve myself through learning. My ability to analyze given situations and apply problem-solving devices has proven successful in my academic and professional careers.

3   A position with Johnson and Associates would allow me to utilize my talents to satisfy client needs while contributing to the growth and success of your company. As the enclosed resume indicates, my skills are diverse and flexible. I possess excellent analytical, communicative, creative, and interpersonal skills. In addition, my knowledge of various computer applications, and my organizational skills and leadership abilities make me an asset in many situations.

4   I would like the opportunity to discuss my background with you personally. I will call you next week to arrange a meeting. Please feel free to contact me with questions or comments. I can be reached at (310) 555-7732. Thank you for your time and consideration.

Yours truly,

Jan Mendoza

Jan Mendoza

Mike Anderson reports, "My favorite kind of writing is creative writing, but even though it's not as fun, expository writing is something I know I need to do as well. This is the kind of writing most people look at to judge a person's writing skills." Although he hasn't yet decided on a specific major, Mike believes his writing skills will serve him well in a variety of professions. Currently he is keeping a daily journal.

Michael Anderson
2604 Alma Avenue
Manhattan Beach, CA 90266
November 2, 1998

Mr. Kenneth Small, Personnel Director
Surf Concepts Inc.
1225 Main Street
Torrance, CA 90504

Dear Mr. Small:

1 I am responding to your advertisement in the *Daily Breeze* for the summer intern position in the graphic design department. Please consider me a candidate; I feel I have many of the skills and interests you're looking for.

2 I will graduate from high school this June, and I am now awaiting college acceptance letters for next fall. Although I have been concentrating on my studies, I already have some work experience. For two summers, I was a docent for several hours a week at the Cabrillo Marine Aquarium in San Pedro. This past summer, I worked two part-time jobs: I was a service clerk at Smart & Final in Culver City and a shoe salesperson at Barney's New York in Santa Monica.

3 Although I'm undecided at this point about my undergraduate major, I have always loved art and have done quite well in school, completing many art courses, including AP studio art this fall. My AP instructor has been impressed with my work, and she has encouraged me to pursue this interest. In addition, I feel a kinship with your company, Surf Concepts, a company so well known for its ocean gear. I am an avid surfer and bodyboarder, having competed and won prizes through Bodyboarder International Association (BIA).

4 The dates and work schedule that you mention in your advertisement would coincide perfectly with my availability this summer. I have enclosed my resume, my art instructor's reference, and several slides of my artwork. I would appreciate the opportunity to have a personal interview, and I am available any weekday from 3 in the afternoon until your closing time.

5 Thank you for taking the time to look over my materials, and I look forward to hearing from you soon. My home phone has an answering machine: (310) 555-5326.

Sincerely,

Michael Anderson
Michael Anderson

(See page 408 for Michael Anderson's résumé.)

As you have seen in the sample application letters and as you will see in the sample résumés, job applicants' qualifications can range from limited experience and technical skills for those starting out in the job market to those with years of experience and a high level of technical expertise.

GUIDELINES FOR APPLICATION LETTERS

Identify Your Audience

Before composing your letter, think about the company and the person to whom you're addressing your job inquiry. This person will prefer reading a letter that is clearly addressed directly to him or her rather than a "stock" letter that has obviously been written to several prospective employers. Take a moment to consider what you know about the company and the job situation that could help to personalize your application letter.

Generate Ideas Through Prewriting

To discover material for your application letter, you can use one or more strategies for prewriting. Think about information you could convey about yourself, your training, experience, and special interests that relate clearly to the job requirements and that will encourage the prospective employer to read your resume carefully and give you an interview appointment. This is not the time to be overly modest about any accomplishments that you think might set you apart from other job candidates.

Plan and Draft

Work from a scratch outline, cluster, or list as you draft. Make sure that you mention in your draft how you heard about the job: newspaper advertisement, friend, business associate, college career center, counselor, or other. It is also a good idea to mention the specific job title rather than referring to "your job opening." You may also want to refer briefly to your related work experience, special training, or career goals.

Follow Correct Format

When you are writing the final, polished draft, be sure to follow standard business letter format. This means using 8½ by 11-inch white or ivory paper, using a typewriter or word processor, setting off paragraphs by indenting or double-spacing, and employing the headings, salutation, closing, and signature associated with business letters.

Request an Interview

Clearly request a personal interview. To ensure that your employer can contact you, include in your application letter your telephone number, E-mail address, and home address.

STRATEGIES FOR APPLICATION LETTERS

1. **PURPOSE** Identify your prospective employer by finding out as much information as you can about the company and the position you're applying for.

2. **FOCUS** Use the application letter as an opportunity to introduce yourself and offer a brief overview of your qualifications.

3. **MATERIAL** Make sure your letter contains background information on how you heard about the job as well as your qualifications and any special training or skills that are related to the job.

4. **STRUCTURE** Organize your letter so that you proceed from naming the specific position you are applying for and mentioning how you heard about the job to summarizing your qualifications and asking for an interview.

5. **STYLE** Employ standard business letter format.

Résumés

The **résumé** is a written summary that lists information and vital statistics that a prospective employer needs to know about a job applicant. Résumés are organized in an easy-to-read way using headings for different categories of information. There are several formats for résumés, each emphasizing particular aspects of a job applicant's background. However, most résumés include the following information:

- Personal information, such as address and telephone number

- Applicant's education, work experience, and special skills

- Activities and professional memberships as well as volunteer work relating to potential employment

- References

- Career goals or employment objectives (optional)

SAMPLE RÉSUMÉ
Mindy Balgrosky

Mindy Balgrosky reports that she writes regularly as a part of her job duties. Upon entering the workplace many years ago, she was surprised at how easily her college writing skills transferred to her employment. Mindy enjoys working in the travel industry and appreciates the opportunity to see new places and interact with different cultures. In her free time, she enjoys reading.

Mindy Balgrosky
412 Elm Street, Los Angeles, CA 90024
(310) 555-9585
mindyb@email.com

Professional Profile

- Possess in-depth and hands-on experience in the travel industry.
- Demonstrate strategic planning skills in both the agency and client environment.
- Ability to manage complex interpersonal dynamics, including multicultural relationships.

Experience

BATEY ADS USA, Los Angeles, CA   September 1994–Present
Vice President, Account Director

Responsibility for Singapore Airlines and Singapore Tourist Promotion Board North American advertising and marketing programs, including brand and tactical campaigns. Determine strategic positioning of airline in North America and then direct creative development and media placement. Coordinate activity between Singapore and U.S. offices. Develop marketing programs and sales promotions.

J. WALTER THOMPSON, Los Angeles, CA   January 1991–September 1994
Vice President, Management Supervisor

Directed Anglo and Hispanic advertising for Mexicana Airlines with $12MM in billings. Directed team in the strategic development and execution of corporate and retail advertising. Senior contact for agency to both domestic and Mexico clients. Responsible for the 'Disappear to Mexico' campaign and the '$99 Everywhere to Mexico' promotion which were the most successful campaigns of their type in Mexicana's history.

Supervised strategic, creative and media developed for Philippine Airlines, including ethnic advertising. Was senior Account Services team leader for all travel-related new business pitches, including SECTUR, various Fundos Mixtos and the Hawaii Visitors Bureau.

CONTINENTAL AIRLINES, Houston, TX   October 1987–January 1991
Director of Marketing Services

Directed advertising and marketing services for domestic corporate and retail product. Controlled budget of $50MM. Developed and supervised implementation of airport and field sales collateral programs. Responsible for coordinating all marketing projects with internal departments.

Manager of Leisure Marketing

Identified market segments with greatest revenue potential, developed and implemented marketing programs for the domestic leisure product. Developed ad hoc value-added programs with hotel and car rental companies.

WESTERN AIRLINES, Los Angeles, CA   March 1980–April 1987
Manager, Market Planning

Responsible for marketing relationships with code-sharing commuter carriers. Represented airline at FAA/DOT regulatory meetings on airport slots. Coordinated airport slots and promoted marketing relationships with international carriers at IATA conferences. Forecasted system revenue and traffic for Marketing and Finance, including potential new routes.

Education
Graduated from the University of California at Irvine with a B.A. in English, 1973.

SAMPLE RÉSUMÉ
Michael Anderson

Michael Anderson
328 17th Street
Manhattan Beach, CA 90266
(310) 555-5326
michael@email.com

OBJECTIVE: to obtain a summer position that will allow me to use my abilities in art.

WORK EXPERIENCE
Cabrillo Marine Aquarium, San Pedro
Docent and tour guide for South Bay elementary schools

Economics Research Associates, West Los Angeles
     Filing reports, tabulating   June-Sept. 1996
Service Clerk at Smart and Final, Culver City
     Cleaning, stocking shelves, collecting carts   June-Sept. 1997
Barney's New York in Santa Monica
     Sales clerk in men's shoe department   July-Sept. 1997

EDUCATION
Full-time student at Chadwick School, Palos Verdes
     Will graduate from high school June 13, 1998   1994 to 1998

ACTIVITIES, AWARDS, INTERESTS
First Place, Bodyboarder Int'l. Assoc. Amateur Contest
     Dana Point   Sept. 1997
High Honors, Golden State Examination in Geometry   June 1995
Honor Roll, Chadwick School   1994 to present
Senior Docent Award, Cabrillo Marine Aquarium   1994 to 1996
Barton Hill School—weekly volunteer in classroom tutoring
     third graders   1995 to 1997

REFERENCES
Jane W. Bradbury, Co-chair, Fine Arts Department
Chadwick School
Palos Verdes Peninsula, CA 90274
(310) 555-1543

Don Sickel, Store Manager
Smart & Final
10113 Venice Boulevard
Los Angeles, CA 90038
(310) 555-1722

Christie Wagner, Volunteer Coordinator
Cabrillo Marine Aquarium
3720 Stephen M. White Drive
San Pedro, CA 90732

GUIDELINES FOR RÉSUMÉS

Gather Material

An effective résumé includes details on the following subjects: work experience, education, special activities, interests, and awards, memberships in professional organizations, references, and, in some cases, career objectives. In addition to this information, you will also want the names, titles, addresses, and phone numbers of three people who know you well and who have agreed to furnish you with a reference should a prospective employer contact them.

To gather material for your résumé, you may need to consult your address book, calendar, companies for which you have worked, and other appropriate sources to make sure that all details are accurate.

Match Format with Purpose

Once you have compiled all information for your résumé, consider your immediate employment objective as well as long-range career goals, if you have them. You should also look over the information you have gathered and consider your strengths and weaknesses. In your placement of the headings on the résumé page, you might want to begin with your strongest point, whether it is education, work experience, or special activities.

On the other hand, if you apply for a position for which your specialized education might give you an advantage over other job candidates, you might want to begin with your educational history. Be sure to include any special skills or training that a prospective employer might like to know about—for instance, knowledge of computers, or operation of a cash register or a fork-lift.

The heading for references is usually reserved for the last part of your résumé. You may choose to list three references with the pertinent contact information or you may instead write "References available on request." Either way, be sure to contact three references to obtain their permission as well as their current titles, business addresses, and phone numbers.

STRATEGIES FOR RÉSUMÉS

1. **PURPOSE** Identify your immediate employment objectives so that you can determine your potential audience.

2. **FOCUS** Use underlined, boldfaced, or capitalized headings to focus the reader's attention on separate categories of information.

continued

STRATEGIES FOR RÉSUMÉS   *continued*

3. **MATERIAL** Be sure you have headings for all important categories: work experience, education, special activities and skills, and references.

4. **STRUCTURE** Organize your headings on the page so that your stronger job qualifications come before your weaker ones.

5. **STYLE** Make sure that you give correct and current addresses, telephone numbers, and dates in your resume.

USING THE COMPUTER: DISCOVERING A CAREER

1. See if your word-processing program offers *templates,* or *model documents* for résumés, memos, letters and other businees documents. A template provides all the basic structure and formatting for a document, freeing you to fill in the blanks with relevant information. You might find this especially useful for producing a résumé. Choose a template. Following the guidelines and strategies for résumés presented in this chapter, create your own résumé or update an earlier version of it.

2. Whether you are just beginning to plan your career or are contemplating a midlife career shift, there is a wealth of resources available to you on the World Wide Web. The following two sites are particularly comprehensive:

   • *Monster Board* ⟨http://www.monsterboard.com⟩ may have a scary name, but it includes profiles of thousands of companies, information on career fairs, job search assistance, and advice on career planning. Use this resource to find out if a particular company is hiring, or who you should contact at that company if you want to send a résumé and cover letter. Be sure to look up that company's profile before you draft your cover letter and résumé. You may find particular information and details that will make your cover letter more interesting and specific.

   • *About Work* ⟨http://www.aboutwork.com⟩ also includes company profiles and employment opportunities, as well as chat groups on specific work-related issues and articles on workplace concerns. A special section, *StudentCenter,* is designed for college students beginning their career planning, and includes information on internship opportunities, choosing courses relevant to your career goals, and advice on creating effective résumés and cover letters.

3. To determine what kinds of computer programs you will need to know in your intended career, visit your college career center or job counselor. Make a note of the following:

My dream job _____

Programs I'll need to know _____

At your campus computer lab, find out if these programs are available and if free sessions on how to use them are offered. (You might also be able to run through program tutorials on your own.) Sign up—and within weeks you'll have new skills for your résumé!

4. Most commercial search engines (Lycos, Yahoo!, Microsoft Internet Explorer, etc.) help you find information on the Web by offering a general subject index. For example, if you're interested in finding out more information on career counseling, you can speed up your search by clicking on an index link to "employment" sites. If you get on the web through your school's computer lab, ask a lab worker to recommend a search engine that has an index. Write the name of that search engine and its URL here _____. Or you could explore on your own. Here are some popular subject indexes for the Web:

- *The Argus Clearinghouse* ⟨http://www.clearinghouse.net.
- *The Internet Public Library* ⟨http://www.ipl.org⟩
- *Library of Congress World Wide Web Home Page* ⟨http://Lcweb.loc.gov⟩
- *WWW Virtual Library* ⟨http://vlib.stanford.edu/overview.html⟩

**For more writing resources, be sure to see the
Longman English Pages Website at
http://longman.awl.com/englishpages**

PART FOUR

Editing Essays:
A Concise Handbook

- ■ **Reviewing Parts of Speech**

- ■ **Writing Sentences**

- ■ **Sentence Combining**

- ■ **Solving Sentence Problems**

- ■ **Solving Verb Problems**

- ■ **Solving Pronoun Problems**

- ■ **Solving Adjective and Adverb Problems**

- ■ **Solving Modifier Problems**

- ■ **Solving Punctuation Problems**

- ■ **Solving Mechanics Problems**

- ■ **Solving Spelling Problems**

(Turn to next page for a more complete guide to the handbook.)

GUIDE TO THE HANDBOOK

Editing Essays: A Concise Handbook

REVIEWING PARTS OF SPEECH

We can label all words according to the way we use them in sentences. The eight labels we use, called the **parts of speech,** are nouns, pronouns, verbs, adjectives, adverbs, prepositions, conjunctions, and interjections. The three words *a, an,* and *the* are not parts of speech; they are called **articles.**

Nouns

Nouns refer to persons, objects, places, or ideas.

Common nouns are general words for persons, objects, places, or ideas: *student, beeper, corner, advantage, suggestion.* Do not capitalize common nouns.

Proper nouns are specific names of persons, objects, institutions, places, or ideas: *Jerry Seinfeld, Pepsi Cola, Venezuela, Protestantism.* Always capitalize proper nouns.

Singular nouns refer to one person, object, place, or idea: *a student, a beeper, the corner, an advantage.* **Plural nouns** refer to two or more persons, objects, places, or ideas: *students, beepers, corners, advantages, suggestions.*

Pronouns

Pronouns take the place of nouns. Pronouns come in six categories.

Personal pronouns include all forms of *I, we, you, she, he, they,* and *it,* as well as the reflexive pronouns *myself, ourselves, yourself, yourselves, himself, herself, itself,* and *themselves.*

Possessive pronouns show ownership. They include *my, mine, your, yours, his, hers, its, our, ours, their,* and *theirs*

Indefinite pronouns are words that refer to a number of persons or things, like *everyone, something, all, many,* and *each.*

Relative pronouns introduce clauses that relate to or modify other parts of a sentence. These pronouns include the forms of *who,* as well as *which* and *that.*

Interrogative pronouns, used to begin questions, include *who, which,* and *what.*

Demonstrative pronouns point out persons, places or things. Demonstrative pronouns include *this, that, these,* and *those.*

Verbs

Verbs designate action or a state of being. **Action verbs** include words like *swim, drive, dance,* and *write.* **State of being verbs** include *be* (in all its forms—*is, was, were,* etc.), *seem, become, feel, look, remain, seem, smell,* and *taste.* In number, verbs are either singular (referring to one: the boy *runs*) or plural (referring to more than one: the boys *run*). In person, verbs refer to the first person (*I, we*), second person (*you,* either singular or plural), or third person (*he/she/it, they*). In tense, verbs indicate time periods: present, past, and future—and shades of differences within each category.

Adjectives

Adjectives describe or modify nouns. Some adjectives, like *green, heavy, beautiful,* and *happy,* tell what kind of person or thing is being described. Others, like *twenty, few,* and *innumerable,* tell how many persons or things are being described. A few adjectives, like *this, that, these,* and *those* (which are pronouns when they stand alone), identify which person or thing is being described.

Adverbs

Adverbs describe verbs, adjectives, and other adverbs. Adverbs can designate how, when, or where an action occurs. Many adverbs, like *quickly, permanently,* and *happily,* are formed by adding *ly* endings to adjectives.

Prepositions

Prepositions are small words or word combinations that show relationship or direction. Prepositions include words like *in, of, on, above, beneath,* and *through,* as well as word combinations like *by means of, on behalf of,* and *in re-*

gard to. **Prepositional phrases,** such as *of the students, in the film,* or *with an attitude,* contain prepositions and their objects (the nouns or pronouns that come after them).

COMMON PREPOSITIONS

Some of the most common prepositions are listed below:

about	between	on
above	by	onto
across	for	over
along	from	past
among	in	through
at	into	to
before	like	toward
behind	next to	under
beneath	of	with
beside	off	

Conjunctions

Conjunctions are connectors that link words, phrases, or clauses.

Coordinating conjunctions (*for, and, nor, but, or, yet,* and *so,*) join equal parts of a group of words, such as two words (bread *and* butter), two phrases (above the ankles *but* below the knees), or two clauses (she wanted to apply for the job, *yet* she had doubts about it). Coordinating conjunctions are used to join parts of **compound sentences.**

Correlative conjunctions, such as *either/or, not only/but also,* and *both/and,* are used in combination to join words, phrases, or whole clauses.

Subordinating conjunctions, such as *because, when, if, although,* and *since,* connect **independent clauses** with **dependent clauses** in **complex sentences** (*Since it was raining, they decided to go to a movie.*)

Interjections

Interjections are inserted exclamations. These are short words like *oh, well, yes,* and *sure,* and phrases like *good heavens!* or *good grief!* that express strong feeling or surprise. Put commas or exclamation points after interjections.

Practice in identifying words by how they are used in a sentence will help you in checking your own writing for correct sentence formation. Label each word in the following sentences (omitting *a, an,* and *the*) by writing the part of speech just above the word. Use abbreviations for the eight parts of speech: *n.* (noun), *pro.* (pronoun), *v.* (verb), *adj.* (adjective), *adv.* (adverb), *prep.* (preposition), *c.* (conjunction), *i.* (interjection). The first sentence has been done for you.

      n.   *n.*   *v.*   *n.* *prep.*   *n.*   *c.*   *v.*

1. Dolores Whittaker placed the plant in the sun and waited.

2. Immediately after Jay logged on, his computer froze and he screamed, "Great!"

3. Pamela Nguyen announced her new and exciting job offer to the board members.

4. Professor Matson wanted to plant a seed of curiosity in the minds of her students, so she ended the class with three questions.

5. You have only one choice: come before the board with the whole story or re-sign your position.

6. The college lawn was the scene of much merriment last Thursday during activity hour.

7. Well! I waited in line patiently for over an hour!

8. This college has had a sexual harassment policy in place for ten years.

◆ ◆ ◆

WRITING SENTENCES

Every sentence contains a subject and a verb.

Subjects

The **subject** of a sentence names the person or thing the sentence is about. Subjects are usually nouns or pronouns.

Sentences with Noun Subjects:

A *degree* in hotel management makes you eligible for the job.

These *videotapes* belong to the college library.

Sentences with Pronoun Subjects:

We discovered a new way to drive to New Orleans.

After much thought, *she* entered the bike race.

Verbs

A **verb** is a word that shows an action or a state of being.

Sentences with Action Verbs:

The members of the Spanish Club *eat* lunch together every Tuesday.

The space shuttle *orbited* the earth before descending.

Sentences with State of Being Verbs:

The Edmonton Oilers *are* ahead of the Dallas Stars by one goal.

Jay Leno *became* host of the *Tonight Show* in May 1992.

To be complete, action and state of being verbs sometimes must be accompanied by one or more **helping verbs,** like a form of *be* (*be, is, are, was, were, will*), *have* (*have, has, had*), and *do* (*do, does, did*). Other helping verbs include *can, could, may, might, must, shall, should,* and *would.* A main verb with its helping verbs is called a **verb phrase.**

Sentences with Verb Phrases:

In the manual, you *will find* the most frequently asked questions.

They *could have seen* a silent movie at the film festival.

Do the prices on the menu *include* dessert?

Clauses

A **clause** is a group of words that has a subject and a verb. An **independent clause** can stand alone and function as a complete sentence.

Independent Clauses (Complete Sentences):

subject   verb
Action *movies give* Ronald a headache.

subject   verb
Stretching *exercises are* helpful before distance running.

A **dependent clause** has a subject and a verb but does not express a complete thought and therefore cannot function as a complete sentence.

Dependent Clauses:

Although the three brothers grew up in different families.
[The word *although* makes the clause dependent. We are "dependent" on another thought to understand what happened.]

Although the three brothers grew up in different families, they all loved to read.
[It is now a complete sentence.]

People who write films.
[The dependent clause is *who write films.* The subject of the clause is *who,* and the verb is *write,* but *who write films* does not express a complete thought.]

People who write films have special talents.
[This is now a complete sentence.]

Types of Sentences: Simple, Compound, Complex, Compound-Complex

Simple Sentences

A **simple sentence** has one independent clause, with one subject-verb combination.

subject   verb
Jennifer works in a restaurant on weekends.

Compound Sentences

A **compound sentence** has two independent clauses joined together. Each clause has its own subject-verb combination.

subject   *verb*   *subject*   *verb*
Stephanie buys lottery tickets every week, but *Franklin spends* his money on compact disc recordings.
[The sentence contains two independent clauses joined by but.]

Complex Sentences

A **complex sentence** has one independent clause and one (or sometimes more than one) dependent clause. Each clause has its own subject-verb combination. The dependent clause can appear before, after, or in the middle of the independent clause.

Dependent Clause before Independent Clause:

Because the divorce rate has increased, many families are headed by one parent.

Dependent Clause after Independent Clause:

We arrived at Danceteria *before the crowds made dancing impossible.*

Dependent Clause between Independent Clause:

We *who are about to die* salute you.

Compound-Complex Sentences

A **compound-complex sentence** has two or more independent clauses and one or more dependent clauses.

dependent clause
Although many people are interested in space exploration,

independent clause   *independent clause*
most underestimate the vastness of space, and some cannot tell the difference between a planet and a star.

SENTENCE COMBINING

Knowledge of the four types of sentences just covered will allow you to build sentences in varied and interesting ways. With this knowledge, you can convey to your reader relationships between two or more ideas. If you want to present two or more ideas or pieces of information as having equal importance, you can use **coordination.** If you want to make an idea or piece of information less prominent than another, you can use **subordination.**

Coordination

coord

A compound sentence can be formed by **coordination**—joining two independent clauses with a comma followed by a coordinating conjunction. The coordinating conjunctions are the short connecting words *for, and, nor, but, or, yet,* and *so.* The first letters of the coordinating conjunctions spell FANBOYS, which is an easy way to remember the words.

Two Independent Clauses (Sentences):

A comet appears small in the night sky.

It can be millions of miles long.

Compound Sentence:

A comet appears small in the night sky, *but* it can be millions of miles long. [Two independent clauses are joined by a comma and the coordinating conjunction but.]

Two Independent Clauses (Sentences):

Courses in technical writing are useful.

They can lead to high-paying jobs.

Compound Sentence:

Courses in technical writing are useful, *for* they can lead to high-paying jobs. [Two independent clauses are joined by a comma and the coordinating conjunction *for.*]

Subordination

sub

A complex sentence can be formed by **subordination**—joining two independent clauses with a subordinating conjunction. The subordinating conjunction makes one of the clauses dependent on (subordinate to) the other.

COMMON SUBORDINATING CONJUNCTIONS

after	because	until
although	before	when
as	if	where
as if	since	while

Two Independent Clauses (Sentences):

The concert conflicted with commencement exercises.

The date of the concert was changed.

Complex Sentence:

Because the concert conflicted with commencement exercises, the date of the concert was changed.
[The addition of the subordinating conjunction *because* makes the first clause dependent. When the first clause is dependent, it is almost always followed by a comma.]

Two Independent Clauses (Sentences):

Utility bills go up.

Air conditioning consumes a large amount of electricity.

Complex Sentence:

Utility bills go up *when* air conditioning consumes a large amount of electricity.
[The addition of the subordinating conjunction *when* makes the second clause dependent. When the dependent clause comes second, usually no comma is needed.]

You can also use a relative pronoun, like *which, that, who, whoever,* or *whomever,* to create complex sentences.

Two Independent Clauses (Sentences):

The students felt nervous.

They had an exam that morning.

Complex Sentence:

The students *who* had an exam that morning felt nervous.
[The addition of the relative pronoun *who* makes the second clause dependent. No commas set off the dependent clause because the clause is crucial for the meaning of the sentence.]

Two Independent Clauses (Sentences):

At the party I met someone from my old high school.

That high school was torn down years ago.

Complex Sentence:

At the party I met someone from my old high school, *which* was torn down years ago.
[The addition of the relative pronoun *which* makes the second clause dependent. A comma precedes *which* because the dependent clause is not crucial to the meaning of the sentence.]

Problem-solving Practice 2

On a separate sheet of paper, use coordination (a coordinating conjunction) or subordination (a subordinating conjunction or a relative pronoun) to combine each of the following pairs of sentences.

1. Experts once predicted that computers would make books obsolete. That has not happened.

2. The computer age began in the 1960s. Book publication has grown.

3. The use of computers itself has increased the number of books. Many of the books have been written about computers.

4. Books on word processing appear every month. They have become too numerous to count.

5. Other areas of activity have expanded as well. Computer technology has had an impact on them.

6. Teachers once feared they would be replaced by computers. They have discovered that their role is even more important than before.

7. Computers have enhanced rather than eliminated teachers' jobs. Teachers can use computers to take over repetitive drills.

◆ ◆ ◆

SOLVING SENTENCE PROBLEMS

Fragments

frag

A **fragment** is an incomplete sentence. To be a complete sentence, a group of words must contain a subject and a complete verb, and express a thought that can stand by itself. To solve a fragment problem, either rewrite the sentence or connect the fragment to a complete sentence.

Fragment: Picked up a virus last week.
[The sentence is missing a subject. *Who* or *what* picked up a virus?]

Corrected: *Jeanne's computer* picked up a virus last week.

Fragment: The skunk-ape, which is a foul-smelling creature.
[The sentence is missing a main verb. What does the skunk-ape *do?*]

Corrected: The skunk-ape, which is a foul-smelling creature, *has surprised* fishermen in Florida since the 1920s.

Fragment: Because the siren made an ear-splitting sound.
[The subject is *siren,* and the verb is *made.* The word *because,* however, makes the thought incomplete. We don't know what happened as a result of the siren's ear-splitting sound.]

Corrected: The siren made an ear-splitting sound.
[The sentence has been rewritten to omit *because;* the sentence now expresses a complete thought.]

Corrected: Because the siren made an ear-splitting sound, *the cyclist veered toward the oncoming traffic.*
[The fragment has been attached to an already complete sentence.]

Problem-solving Practice 3

Write F next to all fragments and S next to all complete sentences. On a separate sheet of paper, turn the fragments into sentences.

1. _____ People in the suburbs who carpool to work.

2. _____ After allowing for tuition and books.

3. _____ Along the highway were many annoying billboards.

4. _____ Because Spanish 2 has a prerequisite.

5. _____ In February, we usually go skiing in Vermont.

6. _____ Except for those who travel by bus.

7. _____ The governor and his wife appearing on camera together.

8. _____ During the last episode of a soap opera I saw recently.

9. _____ When spring comes, the water level rises.

10. _____ Having passed the bar exam, she felt exhilarated.

◆ ◆ ◆

Run-ons and Comma Splices

A **run-on** is two (or more) sentences run together without any punctuation between them.

> Brazil became independent in 1828 it was called an empire until 1889.

A **comma splice** is two (or more) sentences linked by commas instead of being separated by periods.

> Emil attends the University of Texas, he finds his courses stimulating.

Advice: Do not attempt to solve a run-on sentence problem by inserting a comma between two complete sentences. To do so will only turn a run-on into a comma splice.

Here are five ways to correct either a comma splice or a run-on.

1. Use a period to separate the sentences. Remember to start the second sentence with a capital letter.

   Comma splice: Kepler's Law explains the motion of the planets around the sun, most astronomy students master the concepts early in their studies.

   Run-on: Kepler's Law explains the motion of the planets around the sun most astronomy students master the concepts early in their studies.

   Corrected with a period: Kepler's Law explains the motion of the planets around the sun. Most astronomy students master the concepts early in their studies.

2. Use a semicolon to make one long sentence with two parts. Begin with a lower-case letter after the semicolon.

> **Comma splice:** A float rolled slowly toward the middle of the field, it was circled by cheerleaders and a marching band.

> **Run-on:** A float rolled slowly toward the middle of the field it was circled by cheerleaders and a marching band.

> **Corrected with a semicolon:** A float rolled slowly toward the middle of the field; it was circled by cheerleaders and a marching band.

3. Use a comma and a coordinating conjunction: *for, and, nor, but, or, yet, so.* (Don't forget the acronym FANBOYS, which can help you remember the seven coordinating conjunctions.)

> **Comma splice:** The tenants sent many letters to the landlord about the lack of heat, he did not reply.

> **Run-on:** The tenants sent many letters to the landlord about the lack of heat he did not reply.

> **Corrected with a coordinating conjunction:** The tenants sent many letters to the landlord about the lack of heat, *but* he did not reply.

4. Use a subordinating conjunction, such as *after, although, because, before, if, since, when, where, while.* The subordinating conjunction turns one of the sentences into a dependent clause.

> **Comma splice:** I returned home from work last night, someone had already made dinner.

> **Run-on:** I returned home from work last night someone had already made dinner.

> **Corrected with a subordinating conjunction:** *When* I returned home from work last night, someone had already made dinner.

5. Use a relative pronoun, such as *that, which, who, whose.*

> **Comma splice:** Computer experts refer to Moore's Law, it says that the speed of personal computers doubles every eighteen months.

> **Run-on:** Computer experts refer to Moore's Law it says that the speed of personal computers doubles every eighteen months.

> **Corrected with a relative pronoun:** Computer experts refer to Moore's Law, *which* says that the speed of personal computers doubles every eighteen months.

Problem-solving Practice 4

Correct all comma splices and run-ons, using one of the five solutions above. If a sentence is correct, write C next to it.

1. Scientists disagree about what caused dinosaurs to become extinct.

2. One theory is that dinosaurs vanished about 65 million years ago an asteroid crashed into the earth.

3. Plants, the dinosaurs' main food supply, may have died out, the collision darkened the sky for months.

4. Geologists believe that such a catastrophe might have eliminated half of all life on earth.

5. They have even found a layer of underground clay containing iridium, it is an element often present in objects from outer space, it matches the period when dinosaurs disappeared.

6. There is evidence to support the asteroid theory some scientists think that dinosaurs died out gradually.

7. Some evidence indicates that dinosaurs became extinct before the collision supposedly occurred the asteroid theory cannot be considered proven.

8. More exact methods of dating fossils may be discovered then we may know more about what happened.

◆ ◆ ◆

Faulty Parallelism

Faulty parallelism results when similar thoughts are expressed in dissimilar ways. To make your sentences flow smoothly, use parallel constructions whenever possible.

> **Faulty parallelism:** The marathon went *along the avenue, over the suspension bridge,* and *then it turned into the park.*

Corrected: The marathon went *along the avenue, over the suspension bridge,* and *into the park.*
[Each description of the marathon's course is expressed as a prepositional phrase.]

Faulty parallelism: The party was *wild, noisy,* and *it had a note of hilarity.*

Corrected: The party was *wild, noisy,* and *hilarious.*
[Each description of the party is expressed as an adjective.]

Mixed Construction

Mixed constructions result when someone's writing process and thinking process don't quite match. Solve mixed-construction problems by rethinking and then rephrasing the sentence for clarity.

Mixed construction: I wondered was she the right girl for me.

Corrected: I wondered if she was the right girl for me.

Corrected: Was she the right girl for me?

Mixed construction: By agreeing to their demands was a sure way to invite further demands.

Corrected: Agreeing to their demands was a sure way to invite further demands.

Corrected: By agreeing to their demands, we will surely invite further demands.

Problem-solving Practice 5

In the space at the left of each sentence, write "FP" for faulty parallelism, "MC" for mixed construction, or "C" for correct sentence. On a separate sheet of paper, revise all the incorrect sentences.

1. In studying the review sheets helped him do well on the test.

2. After growing up in San Francisco was why she liked art and culture.

3. They wanted to advance in their jobs, earn a lot of money, as well as enjoying their work.

4. The visit to Eastern Europe left her better informed, more tolerant, and an optimist.

5. Tony wanted to know did they believe everything they heard on television.

6. I got a headache from too little sleep and because I was anxious about the examination.

7. Murphy's Law states that whatever can go wrong will go wrong.

8. The vehicle started, stopped suddenly, and was going in reverse.

◆ ◆ ◆

SOLVING VERB PROBLEMS

Verb Tenses

There are three basic verb tenses.

Present:	Phyllis *enjoys* racquetball.
Past:	Phyllis *enjoyed* racquetball.
Future:	Phyllis *will enjoy* racquetball.

Present Tense

In the **present tense,** most verbs take *s* endings (third person singular) or no endings (first and second person singular; all plural forms).

	Singular	**Plural**
First person:	I succeed	We succeed
Second person:	You succeed	You succeed
Third person:	He, she, it succeeds	They succeed

Forms of *Be, Have,* and *Do*

The irregular verbs *be, have,* and *do* have more forms than other verbs. Instead of just adding an *s* ending, *be* has these forms in the present tense:

	Singular	**Plural**
First person:	I am	We are
Second person:	You are	You are
Third person:	He, she, it is	They are

Have has two forms in the present: *has* for third person singular and *have* for all other subjects.

Do also has two forms: *does* for third person singular and *do* for all the others.

Past Tense

In the **past tense,** verbs fall into two categories: **regular verbs,** which take *d* endings, and **irregular verbs,** which change their spelling and do not take *d* endings.

Regular Verbs

Present	**Past**
discuss	discuss<u>ed</u>
doubt	doubt<u>ed</u>

kiss	kiss<u>ed</u>
stampede	stamped<u>ed</u>
succeed	succeed<u>ed</u>
walk	walk<u>ed</u>
wander	wander<u>ed</u>

Irregular Verbs

Irregular verbs never take *d* endings. Instead, they change in different ways—*go* changes to *went, think* to *thought,* and so on.

The irregular verb *be* will take different forms than other verbs in the past tense. These forms include the following:

	Singular	**Plural**
First person:	I was	We were
Second person:	You were	You were
Third person:	He, she, it was	They were

OTHER IRREGULAR VERBS

Present	Past	Present	Past
become	became	make	made
begin	began	meet	met
bring	brought	pay	paid
buy	bought	put	put
choose	chose	quit	quit
cost	cost	rise	rose
cut	cut	seek	sought
do	did	sell	sold
feel	felt	send	sent
fly	flew	shine	shone
get	got	sing	sang
give	gave	spend	spent
go	went	stand	stood
have	had	steal	stole
hear	heard	swim	swam
keep	kept	take	took
know	knew	teach	taught
lay	laid	tear	tore
lead	led	think	thought
lie	lay	throw	threw
lose	lost	write	wrote

Future Tense

All verbs form the **future tense** by adding the helping verb *will* to the main verb *with no ending*.

will be	will register
will deliver	will spend
will do	will study
will have	will succeed
will jog	will work

Subject/Verb Agreement

If the subject of a sentence is singular, the verb must be singular. If the subject is plural, the verb must be plural.

> *singular   singular*
> *subject   verb*
> *Paula* usually *arrives* on time.

> *plural   plural*
> *subject   verb*
> *We,* on the other hand, often arrive late.

Compound Subjects

Two or more subjects joined by *and* are called a **compound subject.** A compound subject takes a plural verb.

> *compound   plural*
> *subject   verb*
> *Manuel and I* usually *invest* our money in mutual funds.

Either/Or (Neither/Nor)

Two or more subjects joined by *either/or* or joined by *neither/nor* take a singular verb if both subjects are singular.

> *singular subjects   singular*
> *with neither/nor   verb*
> *Neither Jack nor Melanie plans* to videotape the performance.

If one subject is singular and the other is plural, the verb agrees with the subject that is closer to it.

> *plural subject   plural*
> *closer to verb   verb*
> Either Kamal or his *brothers are going* to represent the family at the ceremony.

singular subject singular
closer to verb verb
Either the brothers or *Kamal is going* to represent the family at the ceremony.

Collective Nouns

Collective nouns name groups that act together: for example, *class, committee, company, family, group, jury, school, team.* A collective noun usually takes a singular verb.

collective singular
noun verb
Our *family meets* for a reunion every year.

collective singular
noun verb
The *committee has reached* its decision.

If the group does not act as a unit, however, the collective noun takes a plural verb.

collective plural
noun verb
The *jury disagree* about what happened on the night in question.
[The members of the jury have different opinions.]

collective plural
noun verb
The *team are taking* their places on the field.
[The team members act individually.]

Singular Nouns Ending in *s*

Nouns ending in *s* that have a singular meaning take a singular verb.

singular singular
subject verb
Physics has intrigued me ever since childhood.

singular singular
subject verb
The *news* of her appointment to the court *is* exciting.

Indefinite Pronouns

The indefinite pronouns *anybody, anyone, everybody, everyone, nobody, no one, somebody,* and *someone* are singular and take a singular verb:

singular singular
subject verb
Everybody wants to help you find your watch.

singular   *singular*
subject   *verb*
Somebody has spotted it.

Other indefinite pronouns (*each, one, neither, none*) are often separated from the verb by a prepositional phrase that includes a plural noun. The verb must be singular to match the singular subject.

singular   *singular*
subject   *verb*
Each of the laid-off workers *has found* a new job.

singular   *singular*
subject   *verb*
One of the stations on the express line *was closed* last week.

The indefinite pronouns *all, half, some, most,* and *more* usually take a plural verb.

plural   *plural*
subject   *verb*
All of the visitors *have* badges.

plural   *plural*
subject   *verb*
Some of the customers *find* the restaurant's prices too high.

When the indefinite pronouns *all, half, some, most,* and *more* refer to a singular noun or pronoun, they take a singular verb.

All of the cake *has been eaten.*
[The indefinite pronoun all refers to the singular noun cake; therefore, all takes the singular form has.]

Half of the fee *is* due tomorrow.
[The indefinite pronoun *half* refers to the singular noun *fee;* therefore, *half* takes the singular verb *is.*]

Sentences Beginning with *Here* or *There*

The words *here* and *there* are adverbs, not nouns, and therefore are never the subject of a sentence. Look for the true subject to determine whether the verb should be singular or plural.

There *are* many *reasons* for her decisions.
[The subject of the sentence is *reasons.* To agree with the subject, the verb, *are,* must be plural.]

Here *comes* the *band!*
[The subject of the sentence is the collective noun *band.* To agree with the singular subject, the verb, *comes,* must be singular.]

Inverted Subjects

When the usual sentence order of subject followed by verb is reversed, the verb must still agree with the subject.

> From understanding, respect, and kindness *grows love.*
> [The sentence begins with a prepositional phrase instead of with the subject. The singular verb *grows* agrees with the singular subject, *love.*]

> Under the apple tree *lie you and I.*
> [The sentence begins with the prepositional phrase *under the apple tree.* The plural verb *lie* agrees with the plural compound subject, *you and I.*]

Relative Pronouns

When a verb follows a relative pronoun (*that, which, who*), the verb agrees with the antecedent of the pronoun (the noun to which the pronoun refers).

> The *paper that is* single-spaced should be reformatted.
> [The relative pronoun *that* refers to the singular noun *paper;* therefore, the verb, *is,* must be singular.]

> Monica is one of those *people who surf* the World Wide Web daily.
> [The relative pronoun *who* refers to the plural noun *people;* therefore, the verb, *surf,* must be plural.]

Problem-solving Practice 6

Underline the subject or subjects and circle the correct form of the verb in parentheses.

1. Half of the money (has, have) already been spent.

2. Most of the assistants in the program (is, are) graduate students.

3. A stimulating environment with caring family members (contribute, contributes) to an infant's healthy development.

4. Inside the entrance to the business school (hangs, hang) pictures of two former deans.

5. Physics (is, are) a course I want to take before I leave school.

6. Graduates who (donate, donates) large amounts of money are invited to attend the honors convocation.

7. Either cable television channels or the local radio station (announce, announces) school closings during snowstorms.

8. Jerry is one of those students who (miss, misses) the homework assignment because he leaves class early.

9. Here (is, are) the first batch of applications we have received.

10. The company changed (its, their) logo last month to project a more up-to-date image.

◆ ◆ ◆

Tense Shifts

Tense refers to the time frame (past, present, future) of a verb. Keep your verbs in the same time frame unless you deliberately want to signal a time change.

Unnecessary shift from past (first sentence) to present (second sentence): When I *got* up this morning, I *felt* excited. I *know* I *have* an exam at eleven o'clock, but I *am* ready for it because I *study* hard the night before.

Corrected (all verbs in past): When I *got* up this morning. I *felt* excited. I *knew* I *had* an exam at eleven o'clock, but I *was* ready for it because I *had studied* hard the night before.

Unnecessary shifts within each sentence: This story *is* about two girls who *lived* in the South. Although they *are* sisters, one of them *was* cheerful while the other *complains* all the time. The mother *tries* to be a good parent to both, but she *could* not treat them the same way.

Corrected (all verbs in present): This story *is* about two girls who *live* in the South. Although they *are* sisters, one of them *is* cheerful while the other *complains* all the time. The mother *tries* to be a good parent to both, but she *cannot* treat them the same way.

Voice

Passive voice means that the subject of the sentence does not perform the action of the sentence. **Active voice** means that the subject carries out the action.

Passive voice: The question was answered by both contestants simultaneously.
[The subject of the sentence, *question,* does not perform the action.]

Active voice: Both contestants answered the question simultaneously.
[The subject, *contestants,* performs the action: *contestants answered.*]

For strong writing, use the active voice whenever possible.

Weak: Loud rock music *was heard* on the bus.

Stronger: Everyone on the bus *heard* the loud rock music.

Weak: Much dissatisfaction *is being felt* over the new city tax.

Stronger: Citizens *feel* much dissatisfaction over the new city tax.

Sometimes, however, the person(s) or thing(s) performing the action are not as important as the person(s) or thing(s) acted upon. In such a case, use the passive voice for emphasis:

Weaker (active voice): The police *took* three suspects to police headquarters for questioning.

Stronger (passive voice): Three suspects *were taken* to police headquarters for questioning.

Faulty Predication

pred

Avoid writing sentences with a subject and a verb that don't belong together. Mismatched subjects and verbs can result in illogical or meaningless statements.

Faulty predication: *Increases* in federal funds for education *are expected to rise* next fall.
[*Increases* don't rise. The word *increases* itself means the act of rising.]

Corrected: Federal funds for education *are expected to increase* next fall.

Corrected: *Increases* in federal funds for education *are expected* next fall.

Faulty predication: A *bounced check* is when there are not enough funds in an account to cover payment of the check.
[*A bounced check is when* does not make sense. A check is a *thing.*]

Corrected: A bounced check is the result of overdrawing funds in an account.

Corrected: A bounced check results from overdrawing a checking account.

Correct unnecessary tense shifts, inappropriate passive voice, and faulty predication in the following sentences. Cross out the errors and insert your corrections.

1. Because people were worried about the authority of police meant that all law-enforcement officers had to leave their guns at headquarters.

2. The poem was read aloud in class by Margaret.

3. His personal computer was given to Sampson by his parents.

4. The moon was landed on by the Apollo 11 crew in 1969.

5. He hit the ball and runs to first base.

6. The athletes were putting on their uniforms and jokes with each other.

7. A stranger approaches and slipped a flyer under the door.

8. Satisfaction with this product is expected to appease customers in the future.

◆ ◆ ◆

SOLVING PRONOUN PROBLEMS

pro agr

Pronoun Agreement

A pronoun is a word that takes the place of a noun. Use pronouns that agree in number and gender with the nouns to which they refer.

> *John* lost *his* book.
> [The pronoun *his* agrees in number—singular—and gender—male—with the noun to which it refers, *John.*]

> Both *companies* changed *their* names.
> [The pronoun *their* agrees in number—plural—and gender—neuter—with the noun to which it refers, *companies.*]

Use singular pronouns with *everyone, everybody, anyone, someone, each,* and *nobody.*

> **Incorrect:** Everyone among the women here knows this is true for *them.*

> **Correct:** Everyone among the women here knows this is true for *her.*

Incorrect: *Each* of the apples must be carefully polished and then put in *their* container.

Correct: *Each* of the apples must be carefully polished and then put in *its* container.

Avoid sexist language by using *one, he or she, him or her,* or *his or her* if the gender of the noun in question is unknown. You can also change your subject to the plural if you feel that repeated use of *he or she, him or her* or *his or her* will become distracting.

Incorrect: A *firefighter* who stays on the force for twenty years receives *his* retirement benefits.

Correct: A *firefighter* who stays on the force for twenty years receives *her or his* retirement benefits.

Correct: *Firefighters* who stay on the force for twenty years receive *their* retirement benefits.

Incorrect: *Anyone* who does that is putting *his* life at risk.

Correct: *Anyone* who does that is putting *his or her* life at risk.

Correct: *Those* who do that are putting *their* lives at risk.

Pronoun Case

If a pronoun is the subject of a sentence, use the subjective case: *I, you, she, he, it, we, they,* or *who (whoever).* To determine how the pronoun is used in a sentence, mentally delete any nouns that are joined to the pronoun. Then try reading the sentence with the intervening words deleted.

Incorrect: *Him* and Sheryl gave voice lessons to the children.
[Mentally delete the words *and Sheryl.*]

Correct: *He* and Sheryl gave voice lessons to the children.

Incorrect: *Us* three applicants will hear about the job tomorrow.
[Mentally delete *three applicants.*]

Correct: *We* three applicants will hear about the job tomorrow.

The verb *to be* in all of its forms always takes the subjective case.

Incorrect: *Whom* will be the captain of the team?

Correct: *Who* will be the captain of the team?

case

If the pronoun is an object of a verb or a preposition, use the objective case: *me, you, her, him, it, us, them,* or *whom* (*whomever*).

> **Incorrect:** The employment officer interviewed *we* three applicants.
> [Mentally delete the words *three applicants.*]
>
> **Correct:** The employment officer interviewed *us* three applicants.
>
> **Incorrect:** The professor gave voice lessons to Alan and *she.*
> [Mentally delete the words *Alan and.*]
>
> **Correct:** The professor gave voice lessons to Alan and *her.*

Turning questions into statements can help you decide whether to use the subject *who* or the object *whom.*

> **Incorrect:** *Who* will Mr. Jones hire?
> [Turn the question into a statement: Mr. Jones will hire . . . The verb needs an object, not a subject.]
>
> **Correct:** *Whom* will Mr. Jones hire?

Sometimes you may need to mentally complete a sentence to know whether to choose a subject or an object pronoun.

> **Incorrect:** Franco likes Chinese food more than *her.*
> [Complete thought: Franco likes Chinese food more than she does. Otherwise, the sentence means that Franco like Chinese food more than he likes the woman.]
>
> **Correct:** Franco likes Chinese food more than *she.*
>
> **Incorrect:** Lucy is taller than *me.*
> [Complete thought: Lucy is taller than I *am.*]
>
> **Correct:** Lucy is taller than *I.*

Pronoun Reference

ref

Make sure that any pronoun you use clearly refers to another noun or pronoun. Sometimes you can solve unclear pronoun reference problems by replacing a pronoun with a noun.

> **Incorrect:** When Betty put the rich cake on the table, *it* fell.
> [It is unclear whether the cake or the table fell.]
>
> **Correct:** When Betty put the rich cake on the table, the *table* fell.
> [For clarity, a noun is used instead of a pronoun.]
>
> **Incorrect:** Because the writer's tone is ironic and his settings are symbolic, *this* sometimes frustrates readers.
> [It is unclear whether *this* refers to the tone, the setting, or both.]

Correct: The writer's ironic tone and symbolic settings sometimes frustrate readers.
[Sentence is rephrased for clarity.]

Pronoun Shift

Be careful not to shift the point of view from one person to another when you use pronouns.

Pronoun shift: *I* love going to the beach early in the morning because *you* can see the dolphins jumping in the waves.

Correct: *I* love going to the beach early in the morning because *I* can see the dolphins jumping in the waves.

Pronoun shift: Most *students* realize that college has changed a lot since *your* parents' time.

Correct: Most *students* realize that college has changed a lot since *their* parents' time.

Pronoun shift: *One* often has to take on large debts before *you* graduate nowadays.

Correct: *You* often have to take on large debts before *you* graduate nowadays.

Correct: *One* often has to take on large debts before *one* graduates nowadays.

Problem-solving Practice 8

Correct the following sentences for errors in pronoun agreement, pronoun case, pronoun reference, and pronoun shift. Cross out the incorrect words and insert correct ones. You may need to change a verb form to agree with a new pronoun.

1. A law that is not enforced loses their validity.

2. Because he has taken the recommended steps, John has more confidence than her about passing the course.

3. A person who wants to do well in this sport must consider how much time they are willing to spend practicing.

4. Angie, Bill, and him are eager to see the new play.

5. Although a man may be born in poverty, you can set your own course in America.

6. Please put your briefcase next to the bookcase and be careful not to tip it over.

7. Our impression of an essay's introduction is as important as one's impression of the essay's conclusion.

8. Whom will be the best administrator for the company?

9. Everyone on the *Titanic* was certain they were going to have a peaceful cruise.

10. If a parent is too permissive, some people believe you will raise an irresponsible child.

SOLVING ADVERB AND ADJECTIVE PROBLEMS

adv/ adj

Adverb and Adjective Usage

To decide whether to use the adjective or the adverb form of a word, ask yourself the following questions:

- Does the word answer the question *which, what kind of,* or *how many* about a noun or pronoun? If it does, use an adjective.

- Does the word answer the question *how, when,* or *where* about a verb, an adjective, or an adverb? If it does, use an adverb.

Many adverbs end in *-ly.* For example, *badly, beautifully, poorly, really,* and *surely,* are adverbs. The corresponding adjectives are *bad, beautiful, poor, real,* and *sure.*

> **Incorrect:** I feel *real* happy today.

> **Correct:** I feel *really* happy today.
> [The adverb form is needed because it modifies the adjective *happy.*]

Incorrect: My computer screen is not lit *bright* enough.

Correct: My computer screen is not lit *brightly* enough.
[The adverb form is needed because it modifies the verb *lit*.]

The words *good* and *bad* are adjectives; they modify nouns and pronouns. The words *well* and *badly* are adverbs, although *well* can also be used as an adjective.

Incorrect: My friend Erica plays the piano good.

Correct: My friend Erica *plays* the piano *well*.
[The adverb form is needed because it modifies the verb *plays*.]

Incorrect: She feels well about her courses this term.

Correct: She *feels good* about her courses this term.
[Adjectives are used after state of being verbs.]

But also correct: I *feel well* today, thank you.
[*Well* is used as an adjective meaning "healthy."]

Double Negatives

A *negative* word changes the meaning of a sentence. Don't use two or more negatives in the same sentence. Negative adverbs include *barely, hardly, never, not,* and *scarcely*. The most common negative adjective is *no*. These words should not be used with negative nouns (for example, *none, nothing*) or with words that are contractions for a verb plus *not* (for example, *can't, couldn't, didn't, don't, hadn't, hasn't, haven't, won't, wouldn't*).

Double negative: I *don't* have *no* time for sports this week.

Corrected: I *don't* have *any* time for sports this week.
[To keep the negative *don't,* change the negative *no* to the positive *any*.]

Corrected: I have *no* time for sports this week.
[To keep the negative *no,* drop the negative *don't*.]

Double negative: We *couldn't* see *nothing* on the stage.

Correct: We *couldn't* see *anything* on the stage.
[To keep the negative *couldn't,* change the negative *nothing* to the positive *anything.*]

Correct: We *could* see *nothing* on the stage.
[To keep the negative *nothing,* change the negative *couldn't* to the positive *could.*]

Faulty Comparison

Comparative Forms

With adjectives of one syllable, use the ending *-er* to show a comparison of two items. With adjectives of two syllables that end in *-y,* change the *y* to *i* and add *-er.*

Incorrect: This book is *more light* than that one.

Correct: This book is *lighter* than that one.

Incorrect: This was the *more happy* of the two films.

Correct: This was the *happier* of the two films.

Superlative Forms

Use the ending *-est* to show a comparison of three or more items.

Incorrect: She is the *wealthier* of the three cousins.

Correct: She is the *wealthiest* of the three cousins.

Incorrect: This is one of the *greater* efforts of filmmaking we've ever seen.

Correct: This is one of the *greatest* efforts of filmmaking we've ever seen.

With some adjectives of two or more syllables, do not change the ending but use instead *more* or *less* to compare two items and *most* or *least* to compare three or more.

Incorrect: Professor Griswold is *cheerfuler* than Professor Stanton.

Correct: Professor Griswold is *more cheerful* than Professor Stanton.

Incorrect: Of the four possibilities, this one is the *less precise* instrument for measuring.

Correct: Of the four possibilities, this one is the *least precise* instrument for measuring.

Most adverbs also take *more* or *less* for comparing two items and *most* or *least* for comparing three or more items.

>**Incorrect:** This jar will open *most easily* than that one.

>**Correct:** This jar will open *more easily* than that one.

>**Incorrect:** Of the five men, Bart is the *less happily* married.

>**Correct:** Of the five men, Bart is the *least happily* married.

The adjectives *good* and *bad,* and the adverbs *well* and *badly* change their forms completely when they are used to compare:

	Comparative	**Superlative**
good, well	better	best
bad, badly	worse	worst

Problem-solving Practice 9

Complete the following sentences by writing the comparative or superlative form of the adjective or adverb in the blank.

1. Many people enjoy films that are _____ (long) than the usual ones.

2. Length, of course, does not make a boring film _____ (enjoyable).

3. Still, audiences often expect a long film to provide a _____ (rich) experience than a short one.

4. One of the _____ (long) films was *The Human Condition,* which lasted nine hours and twenty-nine minutes.

5. Robert moves _____ (quick) than his opponent.

6. Many people find that grammar is _____ (interesting) than bungee jumping.

7. Antonio did _____ (good, well) in the class because he worked hard.

8. Your comments about your physical health lead me to believe you haven't been feeling _____ (good, well).

9. This is the _____ (extreme) case of chickenpox I've ever encountered.

10. Ionna said that her blind date last week was the _____ (bad) experience of her life.

◆ ◆ ◆

SOLVING MODIFIER PROBLEMS

A **modifier** is a word or group of words that describes another word or group of words in a sentence.

Dangling Modifiers

Dangling modifiers most often appear at the beginning of a sentence; they lack a clear, logical relationship with other words in the sentence. Dangling modifiers can be corrected by adding proper subjects to the main clauses or by clarifying the wording of the sentence.

Incorrect: *While drying her hair,* the clock radio suddenly began blasting.

Correct: *While Jenna was drying her hair,* the clock radio suddenly began blasting.
[A subject and helping verb have been added.]

Incorrect: *As a teenager,* school became boring and homework a drag.

Correct: *As a teenager,* Peter found school boring and homework a drag.
[A subject has been added and the sentence reworded.]

Misplaced Modifiers

Misplaced modifiers result from the failure to place a word or phrase near enough to the word it describes. Reposition words or phrases for clarity.

Incorrect: She wanted an apartment with space enough for two children *with plenty of light.*
[The phrase "with plenty of light" does not make sense as a description of the two children; it belongs next to the word *apartment.*]

Correct: She wanted an apartment *with plenty of light* and space enough for two children.

Incorrect: Several customers sent the lamb stew back to the chef, *which was too salty.*

Correct: Several customers sent the lamb stew, *which was too salty,* back to the chef.

Problem-solving Practice 10

Circle any dangling or misplaced modifiers in the following sentences. Use arrows to reposition the modifiers. If necessary, reword phrases.

1. Susan gave Ted a poster for his room in the dormitory that looked like a spring landscape.

2. After buying three tickets, on the way home it became apparent that they would need four.

3. Julio had to drive his old pick-up truck to get to the party on time without a spare tire.

4. Learning how to use a home computer, a surprising number of tasks suddenly became easier.

5. Checked three times by the examiners, his answers nevertheless proved all correct.

6. While using the hair dryer, the doorbell was inaudible.

7. The people usually vote for a candidate they see on television with charm and poise.

8. Sally gave the names of three dentists to Tom's cousin listed in the phone directory.

9. In V formation, we watched the jets flying overhead.

10. Eating an ice cream cone, the truck almost collided with the boy.

◆ ◆ ◆

SOLVING PUNCTUATION PROBLEMS

Commas

Use a comma to separate two complete thoughts connected by a coordinating conjunction (any of the FANBOYS: *for, and, nor, but, or, yet, so*). Place the comma before the conjunction.

I like to study with the radio on, *but* this music makes me nervous.

You can turn left at the next light, *or* you can follow the main highway for three blocks.

Use a comma after introductory words, phrases, and clauses.

Yes, this segment of the soap opera is certainly absorbing.
[Introductory word is set off.]

Taking her baby along, Phyllis joined Shane on a business trip to Orlando.
[Introductory phrase is set off.]

When the results came back positive, the patient was advised to return to the doctor.
[Introductory clause is set off.]

Use a comma before and after nonrestrictive words, phrases, and clauses. Nonrestrictive words, phrases, and clauses are not essential to the meaning of the sentence.

Her husband, Bill, will sail to Bermuda this summer.
[Bill is not essential; it renames the word *husband*. If *Bill* was restrictive—essential to the meaning of the sentence—then no commas would be used, and the sentence would mean "her husband Bill" as opposed to "her husband Fred" or "her husband James." That is, *Bill* would be one of her three husbands.]

Electronic mail, *which sends messages instantaneously,* is beginning to replace "snail mail," as some call the postal service.

Philip Johnson, *who designed some of America's most interesting buildings,* failed the New York State licensing examination.

Samuel Taylor Coleridge, *a Romantic poet of the nineteenth century,* was a heavy user of opium.

Do not use commas to set off restrictive words, phrases, or clauses. Restrictive words, phrases, and clauses are essential to the meaning of the sentence. Do not use a comma with clauses beginning with *that*. The word *that* always introduces an essential clause.

Incorrect: The novel, *Beloved,* earned Toni Morrison the Pulitzer Prize.
[The name of the novel is essential to the meaning of the sentence.]

Correct: The novel *Beloved* earned Toni Morrison the Pulitzer Prize.

Incorrect: Students, *receiving A grades,* may skip the second course.
[Without the phrase "receiving A grades," the sentence has a different meaning.]

Correct: Students *who receive A grades* may skip the second course.

Incorrect: The essay, *that won the prize,* was about illiteracy.
[Without the clause "that won the prize," the sentence does not specify which essay was about illiteracy.]

Correct: The essay *that won the prize* was about illiteracy.

Use a comma after each element in a series except the last one.

Books, records, and *magazines* lay on the table.

The company preferred *sales managers who were cordial with employees, knew the business,* and *demonstrated loyalty to the organization.*

Use a comma between adjectives that modify the same noun. If you can put *and* between the adjectives, separate the adjectives with commas.

Incorrect: The Lakers had an *intimidating overpowering* defense.
[You can mentally insert *and* between *intimidating* and *overpowering.*]

Correct: The Lakers had an *intimidating, overpowering* defense.

Incorrect: The class enjoyed the *enchanting imaginative subtle* performance.
[You can mentally insert *and* between *enchanting,* and *imaginative,* and *subtle.*]

Correct: The class enjoyed the *enchanting, imaginative, subtle* performance.

Incorrect: He spread a *navy, blue, beach* towel on the sand.
[You cannot insert *and* between *navy, blue,* and *beach.*]

Correct: He spread a *navy blue beach* towel on the sand.

Use a comma to set off interrupters from the rest of the sentence. Use one comma if the interrupter appears at the beginning or at the end of the sentence; use two commas if the interrupter appears in the middle of the sentence.

However, the check will not be honored at this bank.

Some new cars have too much fiberglass, *for example.*

She knew, *by the way,* that the television didn't work.

Use a comma (or commas) to set off a noun of direct address from the rest of the sentence.

Barbara, will you please give me some advice.

I hope, *Dr. Jones,* to see you soon.

Use a comma with direct quotations. Before quoting a whole statement, put a comma after the introductory words.

He said, "This is the road to Seattle."

The catalog stated, "This course includes intermediate algebra."

Do not use commas with short quoted phrases that fit smoothly into the rest of the sentence.

Incorrect: Trevor called his brother a, "universal genius."

Correct: Trevor called his brother a "universal genius."

Incorrect: Shakespeare called music the, "food of love."

Correct: Shakespeare called music the "food of love."

At the end of quoted material, put the comma *inside* the quotation marks.

"After dinner, let's play Scrabble," Sue suggested.

Put a comma inside the question marks and after words like *he said* and *she asked* if a quoted sentence is interrupted.

"Don't leave any questions blank," the instructor said, "even if you have to guess at the answer."

Use commas with dates and place names.

Jackie Robinson was born on January 31, 1919, in Cairo, Georgia.

The address is 1600 Broadway, New York, New York 10019.
[Do not use a comma to separate the state from the ZIP code.]

Problem-solving Practice 11

Correct the following sentences by inserting missing commas and crossing out unnecessary ones.

1. We toured China Japan the Philippines and Bali.

2. The counselor was prepared for the quarrelsome rebellious student.

3. The antiques dealer looked longingly at the fine, old chair.

4. Nevertheless he washed his car every Saturday.

5. Alfred Kinsey who was a pioneer in sex research was known in high school as a boy who never had a girlfriend.

6. My only sister Karen will join us.

7. "You know Steve that the rest of us agree with you."

8. "Let's meet in the cafeteria for lunch" Tamoy suggested.

9. "I admire your determination" the manager said "but there are some errors in the reports."

10. Leilani asked "Why should we wait for them to call us?"

11. She was born on Wednesday October 10 1968.

12. She adores the man who works at 10990 Wilshire Boulevard Los Angeles California 90024.

◆ ◆ ◆

Semicolons

Use a semicolon to separate two complete thoughts that are closely related and that are not linked by a coordinate conjunction (*for, and, nor, but, or, yet, so*).

Incorrect: The road was bumpy, it caused many blowouts and accidents.
Correct: The road was bumpy; it caused many blowouts and accidents.

Incorrect: We used to go surfing every Saturday afternoon then we would bake clams on the beach.
Correct: We used to go surfing every Saturday afternoon; then we would bake clams on the beach.

Use a semicolon to separate two complete thoughts linked by a conjunctive adverb (a word like *consequently, however, meanwhile, moreover, nevertheless, therefore.*) Put a comma after the conjunctive adverb.

Separate conference rooms are available for the two meetings; *however,* you may convene together afterward if you like.

We have sent you an application form; *meanwhile,* we will check your references.

Use semicolons in a series when the parts already have commas within them.

Incorrect: She had lived in Dallas, Texas, San Mateo, California, and Stamford, Connecticut.
Correct: She had lived in Dallas, Texas; San Mateo, California; and Stamford, Connecticut.

Incorrect: You will have to pass a reading test, given in multiple-choice format, a writing test, administered in the form of a one-hour essay, and a mathematics test, given on a computer.

Correct: You will have to pass a reading test, given in multiple-choice format; a writing test, administered in the form of a one-hour essay; and a mathematics test, given on a computer.

Problem-solving Practice 12

Correct the following sentences by inserting or deleting semicolons.

1. A medical checkup every few years may not seem necessary however, it could save your life.

2. Three special dates in Nicole's life are January 15, 1985, May 24, 1987, and October 10, 1991.

3. The course is too easy you should take a more advanced one.

4. After you lay the wooden pieces on the diagram; glue them together at the corners.

5. The police had not enforced the law against selling marijuana, therefore, the two men were surprised to be arrested.

◆ ◆ ◆

Colons

Use a colon to introduce a list.

She called out the following names: Roberta, Carl, Tracy, Juanita, Janice, and Lamont.

Open the bottle like this: press down on the lid, align the arrows, and turn the lid to the left.

Do not use a colon with *to be* verbs.

Incorrect: The book's shortcomings *are:* its unrealistic plot, its difficult style, and its improbable ending.

Correct: The book's shortcomings *are* its unrealistic plot, its difficult style, and its improbable ending.

Use a colon to introduce a direct quotation when the introductory words form a complete statement.

In the owner's manual, the section on maintenance clearly warns the consumer with these words: "The chemicals in this packet may be harmful if inhaled."

Use a colon to introduce a word, phrase, or clause that explains or summarizes the first part of the sentence.

Incorrect: Joan approached the interview with only one thought in mind, she intended to prove that she understood the job.

Correct: Joan approached the interview with only one thought in mind: she intended to prove that she understood the job.

Problem-solving Practice 13

Correct the following sentences by inserting the necessary colons.

1. In the spring of 1997, scientists made an important announcement a sheep had been successfully cloned.

2. Exciting breakthroughs raised speculations in the following areas of study biology, physics, philosophy, psychology, and law.

3. Some religious leaders have expressed disapproval of human cloning in the following ways calling for laws banning the cloning of human beings, preaching against human cloning, and expressing moral outrage in television interviews and debates.

4. Laws in the United States against cloning human beings will not prevent the practice for one chief reason U.S. laws do not control what scientists do in other countries.

5. There is one question people are asking each other everywhere who is the person you would most like to see cloned?

◆ ◆ ◆

.?!

End Punctuation

Use periods to end statements, requests, and indirect questions.

Incorrect: Would you please send me an application form?

Correct: Would you please send me an application form.
[This is a request, not a question.]

Incorrect: Sam asked whether the store was having a sale?

Correct: Sam asked whether the store was having a sale.
[This is an indirect question, not a direct one.]

Use question marks after direct questions.

Is this book overdue?

Why, if no one objects to the proposal, are we waiting until March to begin?

Use exclamation points after sentences or words that express excitement or strong feeling.

Watch out for that elephant!

Stop, thief!

Problem-Solving Practice 14

Place the correct end punctuation after these sentences.

1. The instructor asked whether the class had read the assignment

2. If you want help, why don't you ask one of us for it

3. Get out of that van It's going to explode

4. Would you please send me travel literature and maps of Florida

5. Will you be spending your vacation in Greece

◆ ◆ ◆

Apostrophes

Use an apostrophe in contractions—words in which letters have been left out.

The English language doesn't go back in history as far as Latin or Greek.
[*Doesn't* is a contraction of *does not*. An apostrophe replace the missing *o* in *not*.]

They're going to join us for dinner.
[They're is a contraction of they are. An apostrophe replaces the missing a in are.]

John reports that it's a nice day.
[It's is a contraction of it is. An apostrophe replaces the missing i in is. Do not use an apostrophe when its shows possession: The cat licked its paw. In this case its is not a contraction of it is.]

Use apostrophes with nouns to indicate possession. Add *'s* to singular nouns, whether or not they end in *s*.

This is Martin's jacket.

He received half a day's pay.

The waitress's hours are long.

Add only an apostrophe to plural nouns that end in *s*.

All students' grades are posted in the office.

The secretaries' luncheon was held at the Biltmore Hotel.

Add *'s* to plural nouns that do not end in *s*, such as *men, women, children*.

This is the men's restroom.

The children's lockers are just down the hall.

Do not add apostrophes to possessive pronouns: *its, mine, his, hers, ours, yours, theirs, whose*.

Incorrect: The new car in the parking lot is her's.

Correct: The new car in the parking lot is hers.

Incorrect: The rabbit returned to it's burrow.

Correct: The rabbit returned to its burrow.

Problem-solving Practice 15

Circle the correct form in parentheses.

1. According to most (expert's, experts') opinions, Old English, or Anglo-Saxon, (did'nt, didn't) exist in the time of the ancient Greeks.

2. Old English, in any case, (could'nt, couldn't) really be called English as we speak it.

3. Many influences altered the way English was spoken over the centuries, but English (has'nt, hasn't) lost (its, it's) basic structure.

4. After the Norman Conquest in A.D. 1066, the biggest change in English came from the French (aristocrats', aristocrat's,) speech.

5. Consequently, most languages (can't, cann't) compete with English for richness of vocabulary.

6. Even (childrens', children's) books contain a wide variety of words.

7. People in (Shakespeares', Shakespeare's) time probably (wouldnt, would'nt, wouldn't) have believed how widespread their language would become.

◆ ◆ ◆

Quotation Marks

Use quotation marks to set off someone's exact words.

> **Incorrect:** He said please pass the butter.

> **Correct:** He said, "Please pass the butter."

Do not use quotation marks if the person's words are quoted indirectly—if the person's *exact* words are not used.

> **Incorrect:** Susan reported that "she was feeling much better this morning."

> **Correct:** Susan reported that she was feeling much better this morning.

Use quotation marks for titles of essays, articles, short poems, short stories, songs, chapter titles, and episodes of television programs.

> Felippe said that "Sonny's Blues" by James Baldwin was one of the best short stories he had ever read.

> They danced cheek to cheek to the music of "Unchained Melody."

Do not put quotation marks around the title of your own essay, either on the first page of your paper or on the title page.

Problem-solving Practice 16

Insert quotation marks where necessary in the following sentences. Some sentences require commas with quotation marks.

1. How many times have you read the short story The Shawl, by Cynthia Ozick?

2. Taylor replied You have the same opinion I do.

3. The chapter is entitled Getting to Know Your Pet Tarantula.

4. Did Naima say that she wanted to return to the park today?

5. I just listened to an old recording of Smoke Gets in Your Eyes.

6. You may do aerobics the doctor said only if you wear this knee brace.

7. The essay A Case of Mistaken Identities: The Human Body describes Rafael Campo's self-discoveries as a medical student.

◆ ◆ ◆

Italics

ital

Italicize the titles of books, plays, movies, works of art, complete record albums, television programs (not the titles of separate episodes), magazines, newspapers, periodicals, and electronic publications such as tapes, disks, computer programs, CD ROMs, and online databases. Italics is shown by underlining when an italics font is not available.

The novel *For Whom the Bell Tolls* was written by Ernest Hemingway.

Every Sunday, they sit in a sunny café and read *The New York Times*.

Janika was disappointed to discover that the *Mona Lisa* is behind glass.

When you have time, try to access the *Los Angeles Times Online*.

Problem-solving Practice 17

Correct each sentence by underlining the words to be italicized.

1. Vincent van Gogh's painting Starry Night took my breath away.

2. Every time Victor goes to the dentist's office, he catches up on his reading of People magazine.

3. Have you read the book Always Running, by Luis Rodriguez?

4. She watched so many episodes of Saturday Night Live that she felt she had seen them all.

5. The Readers' Guide to Periodical Literature can help you find articles for your research paper.

◆ ◆ ◆

Hyphens

Use a hyphen to connect a compound adjective that appears before a noun. (A compound adjective is two or more descriptive words used as one word.)

This is a *well-constructed* house.

Refer to these *up-to-date* reports.

The *thirteen-year-old* girl was excited to be in the house alone.

Unless the dictionary indicates that the compound adjective is always hyphenated, do not use a hyphen when the words appear after a form of the verb *to be*.

This house is *well constructed.*

These reports are up-to-date.
[Dictionary shows that *up-to-date* is always hyphenated.]

The girl was thirteen years old.

Do not use a hyphen if one of the words used to describe the noun ends in *-ly*. The *-ly* usually indicates an adverb rather than an adjective.

Incorrect: The *neatly-made* bed was proof of his domestic skills.

Correct: The *neatly made* bed was proof of his domestic skills.

Incorrect: We walked into a *beautifully-decorated* office.

Correct: We walked into a *beautifully decorated* office.

Use a hyphen in the following compound nouns and words with prefixes. Check your dictionary when you are not sure how to punctuate a compound noun. Some compounds are closed (makeup), some are open (cross section), and some use hyphens (mass-produced).

My *sister-in-law* will arrive on Tuesday.

Your *self-confidence* will soar upon completion of the course.

Use a hyphen to divide a word at the end of a line. Divide words only on sylla-ble breaks. Never divide a one-syllable word. Check a dictionary if you are not sure of a word's syllable breaks.

Incorrect: The instructor began the class with a discussion of the m-any obvious hallmarks of success.

Correct: The instructor began the class with a discussion of the many ob-vious hallmarks of success.

Incorrect: She wondered why the bus was late when it never had been la-te before.

Correct: She wondered why the bus was late when it never had been late before.

Dashes

Use a dash to show a sudden break in thought.

Incorrect: I was sure I saw him wait here he comes!

Correct: I was sure I saw him—wait, here he comes!

Incorrect: That's not what she asked you to do, it's the complete opposite.

Correct: That's not what she asked you to do—it's the complete opposite.

Use dashes to set off information that is less important than the rest of the sentence but too important to enclose in parentheses.

Certain dishes—none of them very complicated or exotic—have made the restaurant quite popular.

Edgar's latest tutor—the one with the small gold earring and the spiked hair—is about to give up on him.

Use a dash before a statement that is a summary or an explanation of the first part of the sentence.

She had everything she needed for the trip—her new boyfriend and the plane tickets.

Motivation, intelligence, perseverance—these are the ingredients for a successful career.

( )

Parentheses

Use parentheses to set off comments that are less important than the rest of the sentence or that provide additional information, such as phone numbers and dates.

> Heather's date of birth (June 14, 1980) had been lovingly embroidered on a pillow by her grandmother.

> Please call me (576-3471) if you have any additional questions about this worthy candidate.

> Remember to clean out your locker by the end of this week. (Items left in lockers will be disposed of on March 15.)

Periods go inside the closing parenthesis if a complete sentence is enclosed in the parentheses.

> **Incorrect:** Remember to bring your own Coleman lanterns. (The campsite has no extras available).

> **Correct:** Remember to bring your own Coleman lanterns. (The campsite has no extras available.)

Periods go outside the closing parenthesis if you have enclosed less than a complete sentence in parentheses.

> **Incorrect:** Please enclose the materials we discussed earlier (résumé and reference letters.)

> **Correct:** Please enclose the materials we discussed earlier (résumé and reference letters).

Question marks and exclamation points go inside the closing parenthesis if they belong with the material in parentheses.

> **Incorrect:** Twentieth-century writer Richard Wright (died 1960)? Was greatly influenced by Nathaniel Hawthorne.

> **Correct:** Twentieth-century writer Richard Wright (died 1960?) was greatly influenced by Nathaniel Hawthorne.

Question marks and exclamation points go outside the closing parenthesis if they go with the rest of the sentence.

> **Incorrect:** Can you believe she asked me for money (ten dollars?)

> **Correct:** Can you believe she asked me for money (ten dollars)?

Commas go outside the closing parenthesis.

> **Incorrect:** When you arrive, (aim for twelve noon,) we'll eat lunch.

> **Correct:** When you arrive (aim for twelve noon), we'll eat lunch.

Problem-solving Practice 18

Correct the following sentences by inserting hyphens, dashes, and parentheses where appropriate.

1. The dealer placed the old fashioned china piece on top of the cupboard a place that she felt would be safe from juvenile fingers.

2. The coach surprised them by saying, "It's not how you play the game it's whether we beat our rival!"

3. The gentleman at the post office carefully printed his address 435 South Maple in beautiful handwriting in the middle of the envelope.

4. My mother in law will visit us for two weeks can you come to meet her?

5. He chose three roses were they tea roses? and placed them in tissue.

6. The instructor remarked that Paul had submitted a well organized essay.

7. These running shoes Nike, Adidas, Brooks are available in many different sizes.

◆ ◆ ◆

Brackets

[ ]

Use brackets to enclose explanatory comments within a direct quotation.

The commentator reported, "He [the President] adamantly denies all charges and vows to fight them."

Use brackets with the word *sic* to indicate a grammatical or spelling error that was made by the speaker in a direct quotation. This way your reader will know that the person you are quoting, and not you, made the mistake.

Al wrote, "I'm not use [sic] to missing a day of work—I'm very conscientious."

Ellipsis Points

• • •

Use **ellipsis points**—three periods with a space before and after each period—to indicate that words have been omitted from quoted material.

> Latisha wrote the following in describing her mother: "The first film about American history she ever saw was . . . *Gone with the Wind*."
> [The writer has omitted the words *the well-known movie classic.*]

If you omit words at the end of a quoted sentence, or if you omit a sentence ending within a quoted passage, use four periods instead of three. The fourth period indicates the ending of a sentence.

> Janet says, "I usually like films about history and biography. One I didn't like was . . . *Birth of a Nation. . . .*"
> [Some of Janet's words within the sentence and at the end of the sentence have been omitted.]

Use ellipsis marks to show a thought that is interrupted or incomplete.

> Cuong works extremely hard in the class; his brother, on the other hand . . . well, that's a different story.

SOLVING MECHANICS PROBLEMS

cap

Mechanics refers to correct use of capitalization, abbreviation, numbers, and overall manuscript format.

Capitalization

Capitalize the first word of every sentence.

> The tape is missing.

Capitalize the first word of every quoted sentence. If what is quoted is not a complete sentence, do not capitalize the first word.

> Kyle's coworker replied, "You can take your lunch break whenever you like."

> The narrator describes Enrico as "tall, dark, and ruggedly handsome."

Capitalize all proper nouns: names of people, places, and products.

> After Chihiro Gonsho sent in her name and address on the back of a Cheerios box top, she won a trip to Paris, France, to view the Eiffel Tower.

Capitalize adjectives formed from proper nouns.

> Natalie has a strange but endearing habit of dipping French fries into Russian dressing.

Capitalize days of the week, months, and holidays. Do not capitalize the seasons: spring, summer, fall, or winter.

The first day of spring, March 21, falls on a Tuesday this year.

Capitalize all main words in the titles of short stories, poems, novels, articles, chapters, speeches, plays, films, songs, works of art, and television shows. Do not capitalize small or insignificant words such as *a, an,* and *the,* or prepositions and conjunctions unless they begin or end the title.

Sandra Cisneros wrote a wonderful book called *The House on Mango Street.*

Capitalize the specific names of companies, organizations, religions, schools, colleges, and courses. Do not capitalize these general words if they stand alone.

The Ford Motor Company hired Vikram to speak about the company to local colleges and high schools.

Francesca transferred from History 101 to a mathematics class.

Capitalize titles when they are used along with a person's name. Do not capitalize titles used after a person's name.

She told the group that Vice-President Johnson would submit the proposal.

Give the note to Vincent Ramirez, president of the company.

Capitalize the directions *north, south, east,* and *west* when these words refer to particular sections of the country or of a region but not when they simply refer to a direction.

This new company manager hails from the South.

Maria decided to drive west.

Problem-solving Practice 19

Capitalize any words in the following sentences that need capitalizing.

1. The chapter entitled "raising hamsters for fun and profit" drew many laughs from the audience.

2. The sing family, newly arrived in new york from canada, had never celebrated presidents' day before.

3. Attending the meeting were president Boscone, vice-president Wilson, and Jonas Slovadnich, the secretary of the sloan center for genetic research.

4. Shonte entered the house, opened the refrigerator, took out wonder bread, kraft mayonnaise and bumble bee tuna, and made herself a sandwich.

5. Last summer we flew on a Wednesday to the grand canyon in arizona.

◆ ◆ ◆

Abbreviations

abr

Abbreviate standard titles when they come immediately before or after names.

Ms. Susan Winters and Mr. Eduardo Lopez will officiate.

Silvana Olea, M.D., will perform the operation.

Use time-related abbreviations: A.M., P.M., A.D., B.C. (A.M. and P.M. often appear in small capital letters, like this.)

Many people look forward to millennium festivities to occur at 12 A.M. of the year 2000 A.D.

Abbreviate the names of well-known organizations, schools, and groups if you have first introduced the full name for the reader.

Jovan had worked for the Central Intelligence Agency for three years, and he considered himself a CIA asset.

Numbers

num

Use numerals rather than words for dates, page numbers, street numbers, telephone numbers, measurements, and hours of the day or night when used with A.M. or P.M.

At 2 A.M. on October 4, 1997, Celene completed page 290 of her great American novel.

Use numerals rather than words for numbers of three or more words.

After stacking 349 tangerines on his stomach, Fenton decided to call the *Guinness Book of Records*.

Use numerals rather than words if a sentence contains several numbers, even if some or all of the numbers are small.

Incorrect: The manager told Jerome to order thirty-five reams of paper, forty-eight felt-tip pens, two new computer mousepads, and fifty-five legal pads.

Correct: The manager told Jerome to order 35 reams of paper, 48 felt-tip pens, 2 new computer mousepads, and 55 legal pads.

Use a word rather than a numeral if a sentence begins with a number. This rule applies regardless of the size of the number.

Incorrect: 453 excited participants and 325 well-wishers crowded the hall.

Correct: Four hundred fifty-three excited participants and 325 well-wishers crowded the hall.

Problem-solving Practice 20

Circle any numbers used incorrectly in the following sentences. Write the correct form in the space to the left.

1. _____ 15 senators addressed the convention and asked those in attendance to vote before five P.M.

2. _____ We test-drove three Hondas, two Accords, and four Fords—I never want to see another car dealership as long as I live.

3. _____ She told the class to turn to page twenty nine and begin to read the essay.

4. _____ Johann resides at twenty four Blanche Street, and he has 2 cats.

5. _____ She is hoping to be tall, at least five feet, eight inches.

◆ ◆ ◆

Manuscript Format

ms

Always check with your instructor concerning preferred manuscript format. If your instructor has no special requirements, follow these guidelines:

• For handwritten essays, use smooth-edged, lined, white notebook paper and write with blue or black ink only, using appropriate margins.

• For typewritten or word-processed essays, use good quality 8½-by-11-inch, unlined, white paper. Use a normal, legible font (12-point type if possible), double-space all text, use approximately one-inch margins on the top, bottom, and sides of your paper, and be sure to detach side guide strips if your paper has them.

For all essays, whether typed or handwritten, indent for paragraphs and write on one side of the paper only. Make sure that your essay has your name, date, class, and the instructor's name in the upper right-hand corner. Unless your instructor has specified a title page, center your title near the top of the first page above the text of your essay. Finally, proofread your paper carefully for any errors. If you need to make one or two last-minute insertions, deletions, or corrections, make them neatly in black or blue ink.

SOLVING SPELLING PROBLEMS

Spelling Rules

Even though there are exceptions to almost every spelling rule, the following guidelines can help you improve your spelling.

Rule 1: *i* before *e,* except after *c,* or when the combination sounds like *a* in *neighbor* and *weigh.*

ach*ie*ve, fr*ie*nd, f*ie*nd, p*ie*ce, conc*ei*ted, dec*ei*ve, *ei*ght, v*ei*n, w*ei*ght

Exceptions: financ*ie*r, soc*ie*ty, spec*ie*s, *ei*ther, l*ei*sure, n*ei*ther, s*ei*ze, w*ei*rd

Rule 2: Words that end in *e* keep the *e* if the new ending starts with a consonant.

arrange + ment = arrangement;   hope + ful = hopeful;   nine + ty = ninety

Rule 3: Words that end in *e* drop the *e* if the new ending starts with a vowel.

give + ing = giving; have + ing = having; guide + ance = guidance

Exceptions: manageable, serviceable

Rule 4: Double the consonants for words that end in a single consonant after a single vowel and have the accent on the last syllable.

begin = beginning; commit = committing; occur = occurring; control = controlling

Words Frequently Misspelled

The following one hundred frequently used words are often misspelled by writers. Mastering this list may substantially improve your spelling.

ONE HUNDRED FREQUENTLY MISSPELLED WORDS

academically	exhibition	privilege
accessible	familiarize	procedure
accidentally	forfeit	prove
accommodation	fulfill	pursue
accompaniment	fundamentally	quietly
acknowledge	incidentally	receive
acquaintance	independent	recommendation
adequately	indispensable	reference
adolescent	inevitable	rehearsal
advantageous	initiative	relieve
apparent	institution	remittance
attendance	interference	resources
behavior	license	responsibility
beneficial	maintenance	seize
calculation	manageable	separation
catastrophe	miniature	significance
changeable	misspelled	statistics
comparative	necessity	succeed
competition	noticeable	suppress
conscientious	nuisance	surroundings
consciousness	obedience	symbolic
controlling	occasionally	temperature
deceitful	occurrence	tendency
descendant	opportunity	tolerance
desirable	outrageous	tomorrow
devise	pamphlet	tragedy
dilemma	perceive	transparent
discrimination	permanent	universal
dissatisfied	permissible	unnecessary
efficiency	persistent	variation
emphasize	phenomenon	vehicle
endeavor	physician	yield
enthusiastically	playwright	
environment	politician	

Using the Wrong Word

The following *list* contains words that are often confused with each other because they look or sound alike. To use this list effectively, compare the words in the left and right columns, as well as their definitions. Then select the word that best meets your needs.

CHOOSING THE RIGHT WORD

accept = (verb) to receive

except = (preposition) excluding

advice = (noun) suggestion

advise = (verb) to recommend or suggest

affect = (verb) to influence

effect = (noun) result or outcome

already = (adverb) previously

all ready (adverb) completely ready

brake = (noun) device for stopping

break = (verb) to shatter

conscience = (noun) moral sense

conscious = (adjective) awake, aware

coarse = (adjective) rough, not refined

course = (noun) series of studies; a path

lead = (noun) a heavy metal

lead = (verb) to go first (past tense is *led*)

loose = (adjective) not tight, free

lose = (verb) to suffer loss

past = (noun) an earlier time; (preposition) having already occurred; beyond

passed = (verb) approved, proceeded ahead of

personal = (adjective) private

personnel = (noun) employees

principal = (noun) head of a school; (adjective) important

principle = (noun) a rule or law

quiet = (adjective) still, silent

quite = (adverb) completely, wholly

sight = (noun) ability to see

site = (noun) location   **cite** = (verb) to give an example or quote an authority

there = (adverb) place

their = (pronoun) belonging to them

they're = (contraction) they are

through = (preposition) inside

thorough = (adjective) complete

threw = (verb) past tense of *throw*

two = (adjective) a number

to = (preposition) toward; (infinitive verb form) *to run*

too = (adverb) in addition, very

whose = (pronoun) belonging to who

who's = (contraction) who is

Glossary

abstract subject A subject possessing no physical properties but still existing as an idea, concept, or principle.

academic research Exploration of sources completed formally and according to an accepted format for a collegiate audience. Such research requires the acknowledgment of sources.

active reading Reading in which the reader remains engaged with the text, constantly questioning and responding to the material.

ad hominem A logical fallacy that refers to an attack on specific people associated with an issue; from the Latin phrase meaning "to the man."

analyze To break each idea in a text down into separate parts in order to consider each part individually.

annotate To mark up, highlight, or take notes in a text.

antonyms Words with opposing meanings.

argument A writing strategy that involves persuading an audience to agree with the writer on a controversial issue.

audience The people who read a writer's words on paper or on a computer screen.

autobiographical Having to do with people, places, or events connected to the writer's own life.

begging the question A logical fallacy in which the writer repeats a claim rather than offering any real proof to support it.

beliefs Ideas that are held as true for each individual but can't be proved to others.

body paragraphs Paragraphs that form the middle of the essay and develop the writer's thesis through the use of details, examples, and evidence.

brackets ([ ]) Punctuation marks that permit a writer to insert additional information within a direct quote.

brainstorming A group prewriting activity in which participants call out ideas and comments on a subject while one person records them.

branching A prewriting technique in which the writer takes a subject and breaks it into three or four main areas or subdivisions, using a subject "tree" with a main trunk for the subject and separate branches for major ideas.

cause/effect A writing strategy that explores why something happens or inquires into the results or consequences of an occurrence.

cause/effect map A prewriting sheet designed for cause/effect essay planning.

chronological order An arrangement of material based on the time order in which events occur.

circular definition A statement that renames the subject to be defined rather than offering a meaningful explanation.

citing sources (also referred to as **documentation**) The writer's indication in an accepted format that he or she has used the words, ideas, or information from a source or sources.

claim An assertion that forms the thesis statement for an essay using argument as a writing strategy.

classification A writing strategy that brings several separate items together under the same category so that distinguishing characteristics can be closely examined.

clustering A prewriting technique for randomly discovering information in a visual rather than a linear way.

comparison A writing strategy that explores the similarities or likenesses between two subjects.

composing process The various stages involved in taking an idea from its beginning to its final written presentation to a reading audience. The composing process includes discovering, drafting, revising, and polishing.

conclusion The closing paragraph or paragraphs at the end of an essay emphasizing the author's thesis, offering closure, and tying the contents of the essay together.

concrete subject A subject possessing physical properties.

connotative meaning The particular emotional associations of a word in the reader's mind.

context The grasp of a word's meaning that results from careful reading of the words, phrases, and sentences directly before and after the word in question.

contrast A writing strategy that explores the differences between two subjects.

controlling idea The writer's opinion about the subject or limitation placed on the subject. Each thesis statement within an essay needs a controlling idea just as each topic sentence in a paragraph does.

coordination Two independent clauses are joined with a comma followed by a coordinating conjunction.

critical thinking The kind of thinking college students engage in when they examine a reading. Critical thinking involves analysis, summary, and evaluation of a text.

cue words (also called **transitions**) Words or phrases that allow readers to anticipate what is to come in the essay and to move smoothly from one idea to the next.

current evidence Support material from sources that have shared information within the last few years.

definition A statement of the exact nature of a subject, establishing boundaries for what the subject is and is not.

denotative meaning The standard dictionary definition of a word, conveying information in the reader's mind rather than emotional associations.

description A writing strategy that depicts an observable subject with vivid sensory detail.

dialogue Words or sentences spoken by people and set off from the rest of the text by quotation marks or indentation.

direct quote (see **dialogue**) The exact words of a source without omissions, changes, or additions and set off from the rest of the text by quotation marks or indentation.

direct quotes Passages from a text copied word for word.

directives Instructive words, usually verbs, that tell what is expected of a student in a timed writing.

discovering (also called **prewriting**) The first stage of the composing process, which involves exploring and gathering ideas and information, and selecting and grouping this material.

division A writing strategy that breaks the subject down into smaller parts and analyzes these parts in relation to the whole.

documentation (see **citing sources**)

draft A rough sketch or early version of an essay.

drafting The second stage of the composing process. The writer gets thoughts on paper in the form of sequenced sentences, paragraphs, and sections.

ellipsis points (. . .) Punctuation marks that permit a writer to signal the reader that words have been omitted in a direct quote.

emotional appeals A writer's calls for help from an audience based on persuasive and often emotionally laden word choice.

equivocation A logical fallacy in which the writer uses vague or unclear words to mislead the reader.

essay A writing comprised of a number of paragraphs that develop and support a single idea, impression, or point.

ethical appeals A writer's calls for the reader's support of the writer's opinion or thesis based on the audience's sense of fairness or moral values.

evaluate To judge the ideas in and work of a text.

evaluation portfolio A collection of writing limited to a writer's best writing samples and compiled for the primary purpose of assessment.

evidence Support material for an essay. Evidence may consist of facts, statistics, expert testimony, examples, personal interviews, firsthand experience, or observations.

exemplification A writing strategy in which illustrations are used to develop the main idea.

extended definition Statements describing the exact nature of a subject and involving many sentences, paragraphs, or an entire essay.

facts Data that are regarded as true rather than controversial.

false dilemma A logical fallacy in which the writer presents only two sides of a complex issue; also referred to as the "either/or fallacy."

final draft The draft of an essay that is shared with the reading audience as a finished piece of writing.

first person A writer's point of view that utilizes the words *I, me, my,* or *us, we, our, ours.*

flashback An interruption in the forward chronological movement of a narrative that returns to some prior time in the sequence of events.

focus A writer's choice of subject and the main point being made about that subject.

follow-up questions Questions that spontaneously arise in an interviewer's mind as a result of the interview subject's answers to an original, pre-determined set of questions.

formal outline A list of the main points and subpoints in an essay presented according to certain rules for numbering, lettering, and general format.

freewriting Writing on a given topic that proceeds nonstop for a fixed length of time.

future tense A verb tense used to describe actions that have not yet occurred.

hasty generalization A logical fallacy in which the writer jumps to a conclusion without considering all evidence.

immediate connections Those connections that have occurred recently and that are fairly obvious.

implied topic sentence A topic sentence that only hints at the main idea of a paragraph.

impossibilities Proposals not feasible in the real world and which should be avoided as subjects for argumentative essays.

indexes to periodicals Lists of articles organized by subject and author and available online and in local and college libraries. (The writer can also find indexes to books by subject and author.)

informal outline A rough list of the main points the writer wants to develop in an essay.

introduction The beginning part of an essay that approaches the subject and captures the interest of the audience.

journal writing Written responses to readings, events, or specific questions in a notebook or binder.

journalist's questions A prewriting technique in which the writer asks a set of standard questions about a subject: *Who? What? When? Where? How? Why?*

listing A prewriting technique in which the writer makes a random list of everything related to a subject.

logical appeals A writer's calls for help based on the audience's sound reasoning and good common sense.

logical fallacies Errors or flaws in reasoning or logical thinking.

logical order An arrangement of material that proceeds in a rational order dictated by the subject. Logical order might be cause and effect or comparison/contrast, for instance.

main point The most important idea in a reading, essay, or any other written work.

manuscript format The layout of a final piece of writing with title, margins, and page numbers. A specific manuscript format may be specified by the instructor.

material The content of a piece of writing, including details, facts, and all supporting evidence.

metaphor A direct comparison of one thing with another.

microfilm A film on which printed sources are copied in a much smaller size for easier storage.

narration A writing strategy that involves recounting an event or series of events, usually in chronological order, with close attention to specific details related to the place and people connected to the event.

obituary A description of a deceased person's life and accomplishments, usually published in a newspaper.

objective Having to do with facts rather than feelings or impressions about a subject.

off-topic A situation that occurs when a writer's supporting details no longer clearly relate to the thesis of the essay or the topic sentence of the paragraph.

opinions Issues of public concern about which a person feels strongly.

oversimplification Attributing only one cause or one effect to a situation.

paragraph Several sentences that together develop one thought or main point.

parallel sentence structures Similar sentence structures that are repeated for dramatic effect.

paraphrase A piece of information taken from a source and then put in the writer's own words.

passive voice A voice in writing in which the subject does not perform any action but is acted upon by an outside agent.

past tense A verb tense used to describe actions that have already occurred.

peer editing (also called **peer response**) Sharing a draft with another class member or members in order to get feedback on the draft.

personal interview A prearranged meeting with a person in which particular questions are asked in order to gather information for a writing assignment.

plagiarism The act of stealing someone's words, ideas, or facts without crediting the source.

plan of development In some thesis statements, a group of words that breaks the subject into separate parts.

planning file A file on computer or in a notebook, in which a writer records and saves plans for a particular essay or writing assignment.

point of view The writer's attitude about the subject under consideration.

points The ideas to be discussed equally for each of the two subjects in a comparison/contrast essay.

polishing The fourth and last stage of the composing process. The writer refines language for effect, proofreads for correctness, and checks for correct manuscript format.

portfolio A collection of writing in a folder, notebook, or binder.

post hoc fallacy A false assumption that just because one event precedes another, the first event caused the second event to happen. From the Latin phrase *post hoc, ergo propter hoc,* which means "after this, therefore because of this."

preface An introduction or statement that briefly reveals the plan or purpose of a longer work.

preferences Personal likes and dislikes shaped not by reason but by background and emotions.

preliminary draft The first draft of an essay.

premise A specific piece of evidence, often used to begin an argumentative essay.

present tense A verb tense used to describe actions that are currently occurring.

preview To examine the chapter headings, background information on the author, title, length, and complexity of the text.

prewriting (see **discovering**)

private writing Writing that is for the writer's eyes only and not meant to be shared with a reading audience. Examples of private writing include journals, diaries, and personal notes.

process A writing strategy that explains how to do something or how something works.

process portfolio A collection of writing that may include essays, essay drafts, in-class writings, journal writings, and possibly poems and short stories.

proofread To read over and make corrections before presenting a piece of writing to its intended audience.

public writing Writing meant to be read by a specific audience. Examples of public writing include college essays, memos, reports, business letters, and resumes.

purpose A writer's primary goal in writing, whether it is to express, inform, or persuade the reader.

range The extent of the subject or the boundaries placed on the subject.

reading log A type of journal in which the writer sets up two columns on each page: the left column contains important direct quotes from the text, along with their page numbers; the right column contains writer's personal reactions to these quotes.

recursive Capable of being returned to and repeated, as in the case of all the stages of the composing process.

reliable evidence Support material that comes from qualified sources.

remote connections Those connections that are not obvious or that might have come about quite some time ago.

research To delve into a subject further by going beyond what the writer already knows to explore various sources.

responding An important and recurring part of the composing process; involves reacting to and interacting with a writer's draft either as a shared or as an individual activity.

résumé A written summary that lists information and vital statistics that a prospective employer needs to know about a job applicant; organized with headings for different categories of information.

revising The third stage of the composing process. The writer reflects on a draft and re-sees it to examine the effectiveness of the whole paper in terms of the ideas presented and the ordering of those ideas.

scratch outline A brief, quickly written outline of main points; can be useful in preparing for a timed writing.

second person A writer's point of view that utilizes the words *you, your,* and *yours.*

sensory detail Specific fine points related to the senses.

simile A direct comparison of one thing with another using *like* or *as.*

simple definition A brief statement describing the exact nature of a subject in one or two sentences.

spatial order An arrangement of material proceeding left to right, top to bottom, front to back, and so forth.

specific language Words or groups of words that paint a strong, clear, precise picture for the reader.

stereotypes Preconceived notions that place someone or something into a group.

structure A writer's arrangement of the material to support the main point clearly and completely.

style The way a writer puts words together to form sentences and then groups of sentences to form longer passages; the grammatical "correctness" of a piece of writing; the proper appearance of a finished piece of writing as far as acceptable format.

subject The topic on which the writer focuses.

subjective Stressing feelings and impressions rather than factual information about a subject.

subordination A complex sentence is formed by joining two independent clauses with a subordinating conjunction that makes one clause dependent on the other.

summary A statement of the main points of a text, written in the writer's own words.

synonyms Words with similar meaning.

thesaurus A book that contains an alphabetical list of words along with their synomyms and antonyms.

thesis A statement, usually a sentence, that contains the main point, idea, or opinion the writer wants to convey about a subject along with his or her attitude toward the subject.

third person A writer's point of view that utilizes the words *he, him, his,* or *she, her, hers,* or *they, their, theirs..*

tone The writer's attitude and whether or not this attitude is appropriate for the subject and audience.

topic sentence The sentence that states the overall idea or point the writer is trying to make in a paragraph.

truisms Statements that, while true, are overly obvious or general.

types Kinds or groups.

unabridged dictionary A book that contains thousands of alphabetically listed words along with their part of speech, definition, origin, and history of usage.

unifying principle A basis for breaking down and sorting a subject in a division/classification essay development.

voice The writer's personality and the way this personality is communicated in a piece of writing.

working draft A draft that is in progress.

Credits

Klass, Perri. From "Ambition" by Perri Klass. Copyright © 1990 by Perri Klass. First published in *Self* magazine. Reprinted by permission of the author.

Lee, Chang-Rae. From "Mute in an English-Only World" by Chang-Rae Lee, *New York Times,* April 18, 1996. Copyright © 1996 by The New York Times Co. Reprinted by permission.

Mech, L. David. From "Where Can The Wolves Survive?" by L. David Mech as appeared in *National Geographic* magazine, October 1977. Reprinted by permission of the author.

Morrison, Toni. From "A Slow Walk of Trees" by Toni Morrison, originally published in *The New York Times,* July 4, 1976. Copyright © 1976 by Toni Morrison. Reprinted by permission of International Creative Management, Inc.

Mulvaney, Kieran. "Rainforests of the Sea" by Kieran Mulvaney, originally published in *BBC Wildlife,* August 1997. Reprinted by permission of the author and BBC Wildlife Magazine.

Naylor, Gloria. "The Meanings of a Word," originally titled "Mommy, What Does Nigger Mean? A Question of Language" by Gloria Naylor from *The New York Times Magazine,* Feb. 20, 1986. Copyright 1986 by Gloria Naylor. Reprinted by permission of Sterling Lord Literistic, Inc.

Nizer, Louis. From "How About Low-Cost Drugs for Addicts?" by Louis Nizer, *New York Times,* June 8, 1996, Op-Ed. Copyright © 1996 by the New York Times Co. Reprinted by permission.

Orwell, George. "A Hanging" from *Shooting an Elephant and Other Essays* by George Orwell, copyright 1950 by Sonia Brownell Orwell and renewed 1978 by Sonia Pitt-Rivers, reprinted by permission of Harcourt Brace & Company. Copyright © 1931 George Orwell. Reprinted by permission of Mark Hamilton as the Literary Executor of the Estate of the Late Sonia Brownell Orwell and Martin Secker & Warburg Ltd.

Russell, Bertrand. "What I Have Lived For" from *Autobiography of Bertrand Russell* by Bertrand Russell, 1967. Reprinted by permission of Routledge Ltd. and Bertrand Russell Peace Foundation.

Ryan, Michael. From "Who's Taking Care of the Children?" by Michael Ryan. First published in *Parade.* Copyright © 1997 by Michael Ryan. Reprinted by permission of his agent, Jack Scovil, SCG, Inc.

Sims, Shari Miller. From "Violent Reactions" by Shari Miller Sims. First published in *Self,* March 1989. Courtesy Self. Copyright 1989.

Smith, Kimberly. "How to Produce a Trashy TV Talk Show: The Four Secret Ingredients" by Kimberly Smith. Reprinted by permission of the author.

Suina, Joseph H. From "And Then I Went to School" by Joseph H. Suina in *Linguistic and Cultural Influences on Learning Mathematics* edited by Rodney Cocking and Jose Mestre. Reprinted by permission of Lawrence Erlbaum Associates, Inc.

Swanson, Craig. "The Turning Point" by Craig Swanson. Reprinted by permission of the author.

Tannen, Deborah. From "Teachers' Classroom Strategies Should Recognize that Men and Women Use Language Differently" by Deborah Tannen. Copyright © 1991 Deborah Tannen. Reprinted by permission.

Thio, Alex. From *Sociology: A Brief Introduction* by Alex Thio. Copyright © 1991 HarperCollins College Publishers. Reprinted by permission of Addison-Wesley Educational Publishers, Inc.

Thomas, Dylan. "Do Not Go Gentle Into That Good Night" by Dylan Thomas from *The Poems of Dylan Thomas.* Copyright © 1952 by Dylan Thomas. Reprinted by permission of New Directions Publishing Corp. and David Higham Associates Limited.

Trebay, Guy. From "Gravity's Rainbow" by Guy Trebay, first published in *The Village Voice,* October 8, 1996. Copyright © 1996 by Guy Trebay. Reprinted by permission of the author.

Tuman, Joseph S. From "Hate Speech on Campus" by Joseph S. Tuman as appeared in *Inside,* San Francisco State University. Reprinted by permission of the author.

Updike, John. From "A & P" in *Pigeon Feathers and Other Stories* by John Updike. Copyright © 1961 by John Updike. Reprinted by permission of Alfred A. Knopf, Inc.

Watson, Larry. Excerpted from *Montana 1948* by Larry Watson (Minneapolis: Milkweed Editions, 1993, pp. 35–36, 59). Copyright © 1993 by Larry Watson. Reprinted with permission from Milkweed Editions.

Webster's. Excerpted with permission of Macmillan USA, a Simon & Schuster Macmillan Company, from *Webster's New World™ College Dictionary, Third Edition, Updated.* Copyright © 1997, 1996, 1994, 1991, 1988 by Simon & Schuster, Inc.

Williams, Bryan and Sharon Knight. From *Healthy for Life: Wellness and the Art of Living,* by B. K. Williams and S. M. Knight. Copyright © 1994 Brooks/Cole Publishing Company, Pacific Grove, CA 93950, a division of International Thomson Publishing Inc. By permission of the publisher.

Yuhfill, Ji-Yeon Mary. "Let's Tell the Story of All America's Cultures" by Ji-Yeon Mary Yuhfill. Reprinted with permission from *The Philadelphia Inquirer,* June 30, 1991.

Zevin, Dan. From "Roommatism" by Dan Zevin from *Rolling Stone,* October 20, 1994. By Straight Arrow Publishers Company, L.P. 1994. All Rights Reserved. Reprinted by Permission.

Index

STUDENT VOICES IN THIS BOOK

Each student text illustrates the stage or strategy under consideration in the chapter.

[Please see the next page for a list of professional readings.]

These occur in every chapter and expose student writers to a range of professional authors and genres, including traditional as well as journalistic essays and excerpts from novels, short stories, interviews, and poems.

[Please see previous page for a list of readings by student writers.]